Liberalism
and the
Good

*This volume is part of a series
of publications resulting from the
Bicentennial celebration
of Georgetown University
(1789–1989).
The conference
on which it draws was
sponsored and supported by
Georgetown University's
Bicentennial Office.*

GEORGETOWN
1789
LEARNING
FAITH
FREEDOM
1989

Bicentennial

Liberalism and the Good

Edited by
R. Bruce Douglass,
Gerald M. Mara, and
Henry S. Richardson

ROUTLEDGE • New York and London

Published in 1990 by

Routledge
An imprint of Routledge, Chapman and Hall, Inc.
29 West 35 Street
New York, NY 10001

Published in Great Britain by

Routledge
11 New Fetter Lane
London EC4P 4EE

Library of Congress Cataloging in Publication Data
Liberalism and the good / edited by R. Bruce Douglass, Gerald M. Mara, and Henry
  S. Richardson.
      p.   cm.
  Includes bibliographical references.
  ISBN 0-415-90242-8 : ISBN 0-415-90243-6 (pbk.) :
  1. Liberalism. 2. Political ethics. I. Douglass, R. Bruce.
II. Mara, Gerald M. III. Richardson, Henry S.
JC571.L5365 1990
320.5′1—dc20   89-29623

British Library Cataloguing in Publication Data
Liberalism and the good.
  1. Political ideologies: Liberalism
  I. Douglass, R. Bruce II. Mara, Gerald M. III. Richard, Henry S.
  320.51

ISBN 0-415-90242-8
ISBN 0-415-90243-6 pbk

Contents

Acknowledgments

This volume is the fruit of a conference held at Georgetown University under the joint auspices of the Departments of Government and Philosophy and the Graduate School. The conference was held on the main campus of the university in Washington, D.C., November 3–5, 1988, as a part of the celebration of the Georgetown Bicentennial. All of the papers presented here were prepared in their initial form for discussion at the conference, where they were presented by their authors.

The conference itself was, we feel, in important respects a model for how discussions of this sort should proceed. The papers were available, to participants and authors alike, before the event, so that the time given over to their actual presentation could be cut to a minimum and a premium placed on the give and take of discussion. What resulted was an unusually stimulating series of conversations. Credit for this result goes entirely to the participants, especially the authors, who took the responsibilities of participation seriously and enthusiastically. With few exceptions, those who had written papers were present— and active—for the entire two and one-half days, continually interrogating and challenging one another in constructive ways. More broadly, moreover, it quickly became evident that the "audience" as a whole had arrived prepared to engage in conversation, and the resulting questions were such that the sessions repeatedly turned into many-sided, ongoing collaborations rather than individual displays. In general, the contributions made by individual participants in this regard are too numerous to mention, but we would like to acknowledge, with special appreciation, the questions and comments of William Galston, presently a member of the faculty of the University of Maryland in College Park.

The conference was funded entirely by Georgetown sources, and we want to acknowledge in this regard our debt to Deans Richard Schwartz and Royden Davis, S.J., of the Graduate School and the College of Arts and Sciences, respectively, as well as John Bailey and Terry Pinkard, who chair the Departments of Government and Philosophy. The Rev. Charles Currie, S.J., director of the bicentennial celebration, was also very generous in his encouragement and support.

The administration of the conference itself could not possibly have been done effectively without the able support of Ms. Nora Kelly, then of the Graduate Dean's Office, as well as David Boyer and June Creasman. Valuable logistical support was also provided by a number of Georgetown graduate and undergraduate students—notably, Alfred Alonso, Daniel Carpenter, William Gould, Dinnhe Hua, and, especially, Pamela Kaleugher.

The final version of this book owes a great deal to the careful criticism of Routledge's anonymous reader. And we are very grateful to Jay Wilson, Karen Sullivan, and the rest of the Routledge staff, who have seen this project through to completion with grace, good humor, and admirable professionalism. We have found them accommodating to a fault and a source of many helpful criticisms and suggestions.

R. Bruce Douglass
Henry S. Richardson
Gerald M. Mara
Washington, D.C.
September 1989

Liberalism
and the
Good

1

The Problem of
Liberalism and the Good

Henry S. Richardson

Section 1 What is Liberalism For?

As a normative theory about the justification and ideals of political institutions—which is how we are thinking of it here—liberalism is imperiled by
its successes. To the extent that liberalism has triumphed against feudalism,
aristocracy, intolerance, and repression, it has lost the original historical opponents that served, by making concrete what it was that liberalism was *against,* to
help one infer what liberalism was *for.* Liberalism has stood, in part, for equality;
but if equality as an ideal can no longer mean an end to aristocratic privilege and
feudal homage, then the question, "equality of what?" is forced to the fore.[1]
Similarly, if the call for toleration can no longer merely mean an end to Test
Oaths and other forms of state-enforced religious uniformity, the question of its
further concrete content cannot be evaded. And where the banner of liberty no
longer is needed to rally citizens in defense of basic rights of association and
movement, then the question of its proper use is open to debate.[2] Indeed, on all
fronts, liberalism can be seen as having unleashed social forces that undercut it.
Joseph Schumpeter's characterization of capitalism might be taken to apply
equally to liberalism:

> [It] creates a critical frame of mind which, after having destroyed the moral
> authority of so many other institutions, in the end turns against its own; the
> bourgeois finds to his amazement that the rationalist attitude does not stop at
> the credentials of kings and popes but goes on to attack private property and
> the whole scheme of bourgeois values.[3]

While mainly focusing more on the general value of toleration and the traditional
liberties of speech and association than on anything specifically capitalist or

I am grateful to Peter de Marneffe and to my co-editors for many helpful comments on earlier
drafts of this essay.

bourgeois, the essays in this volume will ask whether, in fact, the kind of "rationalist" justification typical of liberalism can limit itself—can find a way of stopping at some values taken as fundamental—or rather is doomed to erode its own basis of legitimacy.

This question can be asked in a practical, institutional way or more abstractly and philosophically. That is, attention could be directed to what Rawls has called the question of "stability"—whether liberal institutions can generate and maintain their own support—or rather to the conceptual coherence and theoretical grounding of the principles that define a liberal polity.[4] As befits a collection of essays mainly directed to exploring constructive ways to get beyond recent polemics between liberals and their communitarian critics, most of our contributors focus more on the conceptual obstacles to imagining a coherent liberalism than on the practical difficulties of realizing one. This introductory essay will do the same, addressing itself mainly to the dilemmas that apparently arise when liberal theorists attempt to explain how their commitment to toleration can avoid logically undercutting the grounds on which their justification of liberalism rests or, conversely, how those grounds can avoid displacing their concrete commitment to toleration.[5]

I have two aims in this introductory essay. The first is to survey the conceptual terrain of these apparent dilemmas, developing distinctions helpful in locating each of our contributors' positions therein. Along the way, I will discuss relevant portions of the background literature. Since John Rawls's theory of justice looms so large in the background, and since so many of our contributors discuss it, its contours will frequently be noticed. To be sure, none of our contributors is restricted simply to the common horizon to be scanned in this introductory essay. Although each offers a valuable perspective on the core problems of liberalism and the good, each also presents a distinctive insight into other related difficulties and explores regions of the central problem that I will be unable to treat. Nonetheless, each also does bring a perspective to bear on the central problem generated by that strand of liberalism that would promote toleration for a wide range of commitments and ways of life—a toleration given minimal institutional force by certain traditional liberties of expression, association, and worship. My second aim in this introductory essay is to argue that the terrain of the good *must* be explored by the liberal; that, indeed, liberals (like their opponents)[6] must grapple with the difficulties of defending a conception of the good under conditions of pluralism.

To show that the liberal must take a stand in favor of some good, however political and non-metaphysical, however procedural or higher-order it may be, I will begin in the next section by setting out the dilemma of liberal toleration more fully. In Section 3, I will examine what it means to claim that a conception of the good is metaphysically grounded, and will argue that requiring a *general* metaphysical basis for a political theory is unnecessary and misguided, in part because of what I will call "the depth of pluralism." This notion, and the nature of the contemporary plurality of seemingly irreconcilable conceptions of the good, will be examined in Section 4, where various theoretical strategies for coping with pluralism will be canvassed. To assess different versions of these strategies, we will also need to have in mind the different ways in which the notion of a "conception of the good" may be understood. I set out important variations of this idea, central to our study, in Section 5. In Section 6 I examine the role within liberal theory for the idea of neutrality among conceptions of the good, arguing that while it may have an important place, its function is not to address the central dilemma of toleration. Alternative liberal stances of detachment from conceptions of the good, more promising for this purpose, are assessed in Section 7. Finally, Section 8 takes up the possibility that liberals can lay to rest worries about the coherence of toleration more straightforwardly by articulating a conception of the good that expresses what they stand for in terms that are comprehensive enough to be compelling, yet vague enough to allow room for substantial variation and disagreement as to details.

Section 2   Beyond Sophistication:
The Dilemma of Liberal Toleration

Michael Sandel has recently contrasted "naive" and "sophisticated" styles of political argument. A naive view holds that the justice of laws depends largely upon the moral goodness or badness of the conduct it regulates. A sophisticated view holds that the justice of laws depends not upon this but upon considerations less specific to the context, having to do with the balance between individual liberty and the claims of the democratic majority. Sandel shows in effective detail how the "sophisticated" tendencies of recent U.S. Supreme Court decisions have distorted the presentation of some substantive concerns and crippled others. For instance, he documents how advocates of homosexual rights, attempting to meet the constraints of sophistication, have cast their arguments largely in terms of the rights of individuals to "choose" whatever life-style they desire, thereby foregoing the potentially stronger claims about the substantive goods realized in a loving, long-term relationship between two persons of whatever sex.[7] In thus defending what is true about the naive view—the inescapability in politics of a discussion oriented by context-specific substantive goods—without exactly suggesting a return to naiveté, Sandel is urging us to go beyond "sophistication."

Everyone should agree with that broad recommendation, for both the naive and the sophisticated views are hopelessly oversimplified. The justice—and more generally the moral acceptability—of laws depends not just upon the goodness or badness of the conduct regulated nor solely upon an abstractly defended balance between individual and majority rights, but upon both. The challenge for any political theory worth considering is to go "beyond sophistication" by finding a coherent way to combine the grain of truth in naiveté with what is indispensable in sophistication. In this volume, the focus is on whether liberals can achieve this—that is, whether they can progress beyond the sophomoric relativism of some without returning to a pre-liberal dogmatism devoid of recognition of human rights or individual liberties.

This task is a delicate one for liberal theory. Toleration is realized in particular freedoms of expression, liberties of action, and rights of participation that are kept invariant, within certain limits, with respect to the content of the views being expressed or furthered. Instituting these freedoms, liberties, or rights will always offend against some who hold that some of the views tolerated—in favor of a woman's right to choose an abortion, say, or against public religious displays— are evil. In a society as diverse as the United States, to borrow the language of Senator Helms's proposed restriction on the National Endowment for the Arts, it will be hard to avoid measures that "denigrate the objects or beliefs of the adherents of a particular religion or non-religion."[8] Importantly, some of those offended will hold normative political views that (expressly or implicitly) condemn liberal toleration.

To be sure, few liberals would put forward toleration as an absolute. That there must be some boundaries to a commitment to toleration is shown, on the practical level, by the impossibility of tolerating the militantly intolerant.[9] In addition, the liberal will also undoubtedly want to recognize and to justify certain other concrete limits upon toleration. I have in mind not flag-burning, specifically, but rather the more general point made above that toleration is realized in a range of concrete rights and liberties. As the American constitutional jurisprudence of libel and of the separation of church and state makes plain, there are many difficult political choices to be made at the boundaries of these freedoms. Even if a maximum of liberty were well-defined in each of these cases, few liberals would hold out for it.

Nonetheless, a liberal theory clearly claims to start from normative assumptions that rule out giving full political sway to the conceptions of the good of its illiberal citizens. Accordingly, an apparent dilemma arises.[10] On the one hand, if these assumptions are really so strong, then how is it that they could fail to give rise to their own account of the highest good, or moral perfection, that would in the end swamp toleration by requiring adherence to a "liberal" ideal? On the other hand, if the liberal refuses to own up to such strong normative assumptions, and instead rests on a skeptical rejection of "absolutes," then on what reasonable grounds are illiberal conceptions of the good held to be false? Since the self-defeating nature of such a skeptical stance is now well known, most of the essays here concentrate on the first horn of the dilemma.[11]

This dilemma may be illustrated by reference to a familiar tension in the political philosophy of John Stuart Mill. Mill held that once he had identified happiness as the highest good, the utilitarian standard followed as a fairly straight-forward consequence; but he also claimed that a scheme of liberty allowing wide scope for toleration followed from his quite complicated notion of that in which happiness consists. Interpreters have long struggled with how to reconcile these two aspects of Mill's view, for it seems that the utilitarian standard threatens to squeeze out the liberty by requiring that one act to maximize the happiness of all.[12] This tension in Mill's theory illustrates the first horn's general challenge for the liberal: how to articulate normative premises powerful enough to rein in the expression of illiberality without thereby implying a conception of the good that will, in the end, drastically narrow the scope of toleration.

This apparent "dilemma of liberal toleration" can also be concretely illustrated by the stances of two institutions toward the good. Threatened more by the second, skeptical horn was the American Civil Liberties Union when its members split over whether its lawyers should support the right of Nazis to march in Skokie, Illinois. If the ACLU were truly committed to a basic set of beliefs about the value of liberty, could these really be consistent with tolerating Nazis? How is doing so not to fall into a self-defeating relativism? Courting more the first, perfectionist horn of the dilemma is the Roman Catholic church, as interpreted by John Langan in Chapter 6. Arguing here that the church can accommodate itself to a considerable degree to liberal principles, Langan is nonetheless quite sensitive to the concern this horn of the dilemma poses. He quotes official church pronouncements to the effect that there is a right to freedom of expression, but that it is conditioned upon remaining "within the limits laid down by the moral order and the common good." The question is whether these limits imply that this commitment to freedom is as illusory as Henry Ford's commitment to choice ("any color you like, so long as it's black").

For liberal theory to respond adequately to the dilemma of toleration, it must meet three subordinate challenges. First, the liberal's way out of the dilemma will presumably depend either upon drawing some distinction between types of normative premises or upon some limitation to the confidence with which these premises are to be held. This central conceptual task we may call the challenge of *articulating limits*. The liberal theorist may sympathize with the following lines from President Bush's Inaugural Address: "In crucial things—unity; in important things—diversity; in all things, generosity." It must be admitted, however, that with respect to delimiting the bounds of toleration this statement is quite inarticulate. The distinction between the crucial and the important is not only opaque but also, more importantly, dependent upon an underlying, unarticulated gradation of value. To articulate how they can take a normative stand, yet leave room for toleration, liberal theorists must articulate limits that are more explicit than this.

A conceptual distinction that defines a way between the horns of the dilemma of liberal toleration will not well serve liberal theory unless it also succeeds in meeting two further challenges. The first of these has already been touched upon. Since toleration is necessarily realized in a set of more concrete rights, in order to remain genuinely committed to liberal toleration a theory must be able to generate some of them. These will presumably have to include some of the constitutional principles and political policies with which liberalism has traditionally been associated, such as principles of freedom of association and speech. This is the challenge of *arriving at liberal policy prescriptions* from liberal starting points—a necessity emphasized in Chapter 3 by Brian Barry. Finally, liberals must show that the limits they articulate do not imply that appealing to the very normative premises on which they purport to ground their political arguments is illicit.[13] This is the challenge of *avoiding a self-defeating specification of limits*. For instance, a middle way that proposes that political argument may proceed only from those principles or values that can be accepted by all reasonable persons will be useless to liberals unless the premises upon which they propose to rely can be accepted by all reasonable persons.

According to a once-dominant point of view, all attempts to evade the dilemma's perfectionist horn by defining some middle way must fail, for there is no way to support fundamental normative premises without leaning upon a comprehensive and metaphysically grounded conception of the human good, which in turn will sharply limit the scope allowed to liberal toleration. If this is correct, then those political theorists who persist in their attempts to champion liberal toleration are doomed to fall into a self-defeating skepticism. A natural first step, therefore, in considering whether liberal theory can answer the challenges set for it is to consider the validity of this purported link between political theory and metaphysical teleology.

Section 3   Metaphysics and Politics

Kenneth Schmitz's essay, "Is Liberalism Good Enough?" does us the invaluable service of reminding us what an unrestrainedly metaphysical politics would look like. In the boldness and sweep of his synthesis of strands of criticism initiated by Hegel, C. B. MacPherson, and others, Schmitz's criticism reaches a more general metaphysical plane than does that of Michael Sandel, for instance.[14] Sandel confines himself to posing problems for liberalism involving the nature and identity of the *human* individual. On Schmitz's view, by contrast, a genuine metaphysics of the human individual is inseparable from a conception of individuals of all kinds. Thus, Schmitz focuses his praise not on Aristotle's conception of the human good, but on his treatment of the *tode ti,* the "this somewhat" of the *Metaphysics*. Schmitz is concerned to emphasize that on the Aristotelian view, individuals are not self-sufficient entities, but must be viewed in terms of what they have in common with other individuals; but again, the notion of "self-sufficiency" Schmitz invokes is not the specifically practical or ethico-political sort developed in *Nicomachean Ethics* I.7 and X.7 and in the *Politics* (*autarkeia*), but rather a sort that applies to all substances. It is the *kath' auto*—the *per se* or "in itself"—of *Metaphysics* Z.4, which characterizes the essential relations between any substance (*sc.* any living substance, animal or plant) and its attributes.[15] Because of the generality and depth of his concern with the nature of individuals,

Schmitz sees the decisive blow to the Aristotelian world view in the reprise—with the sixteenth century corpuscular theory—of a search for the atoms of matter.

Another reason that it is very valuable to have such a vivid expression of a fully metaphysical approach on the table is that many of the other positions taken by our contributors are defined by their reactions against this one. Perhaps the most extreme rejection of a metaphysical approach is one that follows the logical positivists in declaring metaphysics a domain beyond discursive verification to which truth and falsity do not apply and about which no assertions may meaningfully be made. Against this criticism, Schmitz could persuasively protest that positivism is itself a discredited metaphysical view.[16] More compelling are a series of other *prima facie* problems with relying upon such a general metaphysical conception to ground political conclusions that cannot be generated from specifically moral or political premises whose metaphysical commitments, if any, are less general.

First, even if we could establish certain "commonalities" grounded in the order of being, do normative principles really follow from them? Schmitz is skittish on this issue, speaking less committally of an obligation such as that of honoring one's parents "arising" from what one essentially shares with them. More significant, however, than the general problem posed by the purported "fallacy" of moving from "is" to "ought" are the case-by-case questions that arise. In what way does the obligation to honor one's parents "arise" from anything about what one has in common with them? What follows about the concrete content that this obligation is supposed to have? And so on.

Second, even if metaphysical claims are not without truth-values and are in principle subject to rational justification, it is no easy matter to ascertain the truth of one. As William Connolly points out in Chapter 4, there is no guarantee either that the metaphysics that we need to complete our politics is true or that the essences that it posits are available for our inspection.[17] If the downfall of teleology was the resurgence of physical atomism, will it take a metaphysical incorporation of the lessons of quantum physics to reverse things? Query whether a metaphysics that arose from the new unified field theories would prove helpful to the sort of political theory that the communitarian imagines.

Finally, there are too many metaphysical views, and the contest among them can be seen to exacerbate, rather than alleviate, the political problem posed by the clash of irreconcilable conceptions of the good. While it may be tempting to generalize over variations to make it seem as if there were only two metaphysical options—the bad liberal one and the good communitarian one—in fact this hardly does justice to the importantly different metaphysical views available within (and outside) each camp. Hegel's mode of philosophizing made us familiar with the idea of an historical succession of dominant metaphysical views. We are apt to retain this idea without Hegel's further notion that this history exhibits the inexorable progress toward Absolute Spirit. Accordingly, reliance on metaphysics can threaten to introduce a further layer of historicism or conceptual relativism beyond that which already looms in more straightforward political arguments.

For all these reasons, it might be wise to develop one's political theory independently of a general metaphysics. This is not to say that one's political principles will not rule out any metaphysical views, or that one's approach will be compatible with every possible metaphysical position.[18] Rather, the idea would be not to use reliance on metaphysical claims as a primary means of furthering one's argument. This approach is more easily taken by those, such as Amy Gutmann and Dennis Thompson in Chapter 7, who rest no weight on claims about the nature of persons, relying instead on specifically moral claims about the values of democratic citizenship, rational deliberation, and civility. William Sullivan, in seeking to revive the conception of community of T. H. Green's "social liberalism"—like Rawls, who develops the social contract tradition in terms of an ideal conception of the person as reasonable and rational—will have more explaining to do to show how these conceptions can be defended on specifically political grounds that are independent of a general metaphysics. Such explanation, however, can be given.[19]

Section 4   The Facts of Pluralism

While the plurality of metaphysical views heightens the theorist's predicament, the "pluralism" with which we are primarily concerned involves conceptions of the good. In speaking of "facts" of pluralism, I obviously have in mind some form of social description.

To be clear, I must set aside some other meanings of "pluralism" that are not what I intend. "Pluralism" is sometimes used as the name of a normative doctrine, for instance one founded on Mill's claim that individual diversity is an intrinsic good.[20] Alternatively, a politically pregnant relativism, such as one denying the existence or availability of the sort of metaphysically grounded teleology described in the last section is also sometimes called "pluralism" on account of its purported consequences. I have in mind, rather, a more simply factual set of claims about some modern societies, claims which neither follow logically from relativism or from the value of individuality nor imply either of these.

Among "the facts of pluralism," then, I mean first of all to rank a fact that obtains in most contemporary societies, namely that individuals affirm different, incompatible conceptions of the good.[21] This basic social fact is related to a complex of others that increase its political significance in many societies. First, these conflicting conceptions of the good typically give rise to some of the most intractable political disputes. Second, the conflicting conceptions of the good often appear to be incommensurable with one another, in that they mark out radically different ways of giving reasons or describing value. Accordingly, third, there typically is no obvious or publicly accepted way to adjudicate reasonably among these conflicting views. (This is not simply a matter of being unable to arrange different Values—Liberty, Equality, Community, etc.—in a hierarchical order. Rather, the plurality of conceptions of the good is linked to a plurality of ethical and political theories, many of which will put forward their own competing and incompatible ways of interpreting these capital-letter abstractions and arranging them into hierarchies.) Finally, the multiplicity of metaphysical conceptions noted in the last section will conspire to deepen the basic pluralism, generating further competing conceptions of the good and generally exacerbating the apparent incommensurability among them.

On both ends of the theoretical spectrum there will be views that are not much impressed by the *facts* of pluralism. On the one hand, a nonliberal objectivism might both retain confidence in its conception of the human good and refuse to make concessions to the pluralism that exists. If pluralism exists contingently, it is to be overcome. As Connolly notes in reference to Charles Taylor, below, there is always the possibility of an Augustinian combination of faith and hope.[22] Thus Alasdair MacIntyre suggests that we must wait for a new St. Benedict;[23] and Sandel, in quite another tone, writes that if we follow the liberal in simply accepting that we are stuck in conditions of pluralism, we will "forget . . . the possibility that when politics goes well, we can know a good in common that we cannot know alone."[24] Objectivist perfectionists of a less democratic persuasion might not let the existence of even a necessary pluralism shape the content of their ideal. On the other end of the spectrum, as noted above, there are liberal versions of objectivism (such as Mill's and Kateb's) that would pursue pluralism as an ideal if it did not exist in fact.

Even if pluralism will not disappear, it is possible that it may be kept within bounds or overcome to some limited extent. Consider the Augustinian model for the remark in President Bush's Inaugural Address: "In necessary things, unity; in doubtful things, liberty; in all things, charity."[25] Can we divide the doubtful from the necessary (or the necessary though doubtful from the merely doubtful)? Suggestions about how to do so differ importantly as to their treatment of political principles and their grounds (whatever these may be). People might reasonably agree, or might come to agree upon due reflection, about one or the other, neither or both. Accordingly, we can define four possible configurations of the facts of pluralism. (See Figure 1.1.)

At one pole is (a) full agreement on both political principles and the grounds for justifying them. Although this may seem out of reach, at least one of our contributors asserts its possibility in a qualified way. At the other pole is (b) pluralism—that is, disagreement—both about political principles and about the sorts of propositions that might count as grounds for justifying political principles. This possibility of a thoroughgoing disagreement is presumably what is generally meant by a clash of "incommensurable" conceptions of the good. This thorough disagreement nonetheless allows for a limited kind of agreement about what is

Figure 1.1   Four Configurations of the Facts of Pluralism

Is there agreement on the grounds
for political principles?

		yes	no
Is there agreement on political principles?	yes	(a) full agreement	(d) overlapping consensus
	no	(c) constrained *modus vivendi*	(b) bare *modus vivendi*

to be done, which we might call a bare *modus vivendi*. In these circumstances, there is a practical accommodation expressed in terms of principles not necessarily regarded as true or even reasonable by anyone, for reasons that are not shared.

In between these two poles are two intermediate possibilities. The first is (c), a (partial) agreement on grounds that neither implies nor automatically produces an agreement on political principles. This condition holds out the possibility of what we might call a constrained *modus vivendi*, which is like a bare *modus vivendi* except that the practical accommodation is constrained by an agreement on some general normative premises. An example of this is Charles Larmore's interpretation of neutrality as grounded on mutual respect and as requiring one to abstract from, or set aside, premises that are disputed.[26] The only premises allowed to enter political debate are ones that all reasonable people can agree upon. Since other beliefs—which might imply contrary conclusions—are suppressed, the principles justified from this core may not end up being regarded by any individual as good or right. Still, they have at least some support from the constraining common commitment to mutual respect. The contrasting intermediate possibility is that there is (d) *bona fide* normative agreement on political principles, but not on the grounds that justify them. This is the condition described by Rawls's newly influential idea of an "overlapping consensus."[27] Here the idea is that citizens agree upon principles of justice (for example), while the premises to which they appeal in order to ground these principles are quite disparate. What makes an overlapping consensus truly moral, and more than a mere *modus vivendi* (of either variety), is that those who agree are not required to suppress any of their justifying beliefs, even though they do not agree with others about them. The principles that are the object of the overlapping consensus are regarded as theorems derivable from a number of different axiom systems (or supportable in terms of different sets of data).

As thus abstractly characterized, the distinctions among these four possibilities can be elusive. John Langan's essay helps make them concrete by surveying the Catholic church's responses to varyingly pluralistic conditions. Directly contradicting the claims of Brian Barry's chapter, Langan argues that in some social circumstances, at least, the Catholic church can reach a morally grounded accommodation with liberalism. In reflecting upon the various ways in which the Catholic church has incorporated liberal principles in the different national settings with which it must cope, ranging from Eastern European Marxist totalitarianisms and Latin American military dictatorships to Western pluralist democracies, Langan notes how its responses span the range of possibilities from complete, unfettered agreement (in some Catholic countries) through overlapping consensus and constrained *modus vivendi* and on to a bare *modus vivendi*. Most intriguing is the possibility that in favorable circumstances a core Catholic conception of the good might be detached from what are sometimes thought to be Catholicism's illiberal consequences and instead shown to support liberalism as a theorem. As a practical matter, were such an overlapping consensus between the Church and liberalism to exist in some circumstances, it would have to be explained more fully why the Church's conception of the good seems to allow a retreat to a *modus vivendi* with liberalism in other circumstances. To evaluate the conceptual possibility of this kind of overlapping consensus, we need to understand better what is meant by a "conception of the good."

Section 5   Conception of the Good, What?

Numerous specifications of what it is to have a conception of the good are possible and are themselves contested, a point of sometimes bitter disagreements between liberals and their opponents. If "conception of the good" is glossed by the liberal in terms of what is "good for" the individual whose conception it is, the liberal will be accused of accepting an egoistic individualism. If "the good" can include what is good impersonally, though no one experience it, some liberals will doubt its political or moral relevance.[28] Because of the contested character of this notion, any proposed definition would be problematic. It is better to approach this matter more indirectly, by indicating dimensions along which the notion of a conception of the good might be differently specified. There are at least four significant dimensions of variation, which we might label, respectively, the metaphysical depth, critical structure, scope, and detail of a conception of the good.

The *metaphysical depth* of a conception of the good has to do with the extent to which it leans on the sort of general metaphysical conception described in Section 3. It will depend upon how intimately the conception of the good is related to general conceptions of individuals, (personal) identity through time, human nature, the place of man in the world, and so on. While some conceptions of the good will make their home in such metaphysics, others will avoid this sort of dependence. In Section 3 I offered reasons why a political theory should avoid the extremes of metaphysical depth. Whether a liberal can succeed in doing so depends in part on whether there can be a coherent and compelling conception of the (political) good that is less deep. An interesting and central test case of this claim is provided by Rawls's theory.

In *Liberalism and the Limits of Justice,* Sandel influentially argued that although Rawls meant to avoid metaphysical entanglement, his ideal choice situation, the "original position" [OP] would lose its justificatory force if it were not seen as reflecting a deeper underlying metaphysics of the person. Sandel's strategy was to use the OP as a refracting lens that can be reversed, generating its implicit metaphysical assumptions from the principles of justice that Rawls defends.[29] This reading of the role of the OP as an argumentative fulcrum is suggested by some of Rawls's language in *A Theory of Justice*. In addition, the idea that what is needed to do the theoretical work in defense of the principles of justice is a conception of the person was encouraged by Rawls's subsequent Dewey Lectures.[30] In response to Sandel, however, Rawls has emphasized that he never meant to be endorsing a conception of the person that was metaphysically deep.[31] Rather, the aspects of moral personality that he brings forward are each defended and interpreted on the basis of a specifically political ideal of social cooperation.[32] This means that Rawls is building his theory of justice on a political conception of the good; and Rawls has been increasingly willing to admit that there is a sense of "conception of the good" according to which this is true.[33] Despite the historically influential presumption in favor of depth, I submit that Rawls's strategy represents a consistent—and attractive—way of developing a conception of the good for the purposes of political theory. As I have noted, it represents a broad strategy of minimizing metaphysical depth to which Sullivan is also drawn.

The question that at once arises for a political conception of the good that eschews reliance on metaphysical depth is how it can attain the kind of distance from common political views and institutions that is necessary in order to be critical of them.[34] The general answer is: by the way in which its conception of the good is internally ordered. I will call this aspect of a conception of the good its degree of critical structure.

The *critical structure* of any conception of the good is its ordering—hierarchical, procedural, or otherwise—in a way that allows for criticism of some of its elements on the basis of others. In particular, on most views, it will allow for the criticism of some of an individual's desires, commitments or ends on the basis of others of them.[35] It is easiest to explain this notion in terms of examples. An extreme of a lack of critical structure is what might be called a "present-aim" theory of the good: something is good just in case it satisfies a current desire. On such a view, there is obviously minimal room for criticizing the desires that give the content to this theory of the good. A theory of self-interest, or rational prudence, which takes account of future aims allows for somewhat more critical purchase, but not much more. At the more critical end, two important examples are the Kantian and Aristotelian theories, today represented respectively by Rawls and (here) Nussbaum. Since Nussbaum's theory will be described in Section 8, let me here build on my previous partial characterization of Rawls's view by sketching the critical structure of his political conception of the good.

The critical structure of the Rawlsian conception of the good reflects the fact that within it the relatively unstructured and "thin" conceptions of the good represented by rational prudence are subordinated and "framed" by what Rawls calls the conception of the "right." Whereas Rawls's usage in *A Theory of Justice* had limited the term "good" to its more unstructured varieties, his more recent writings have recognized that the structured ideals of right can also sensibly be called conceptions of the good.[36] Accordingly, we may array the structure of the Rawlsian conception of the good in terms of an interpretive hierarchy of decreasing abstraction (N.B.: not a hierarchy of justificatory priority). Most abstract is the ideal of social cooperation among free and equal persons. These notions in turn get interpreted and together represented in the OP. Since the principles of justice therefore reflect these ideals, they represent the next layer in this conception of the good. Finally, these principles delimit the permissible elaboration of individuals' self-interest and, in a well-ordered society, bring this initially unstructured layer into congruence with the ideals of justice by structuring them.[37]

"But if the basis of criticism is limited to what can be found internal to our desires and aims, our ends and our considered judgments about justice," it will be objected, "then this criticism will be pale indeed!"[38] In response to this objection, two points need to be made. First, one must ask, "limited" compared to what genuinely available and effective mode of criticism? Second, must a theory be able to criticize everything at once, or can it effectively pick a limited range of topics on which to focus its critical energies? This second question points us toward the third dimension of a conception of the good, its scope.

The *scope* of a conception of the good has to do with the range of subject matters to which it applies. As adumbrated above, a person's conception of the good might be limited in the scope of its application to assessing his or her own actions and life. Alternatively, he or she might also apply it—in perhaps specialized and differing ways—in judging the well-being of others or the impersonal value of states of affairs. Whether these different fields of application are to be sharply marked off from one another will, again, be a matter of dispute between liberals and some of their opponents. Some communitarians, for instance, will want to attack the separation between public and private that may be seen to underlie this topical restriction,[39] while some liberals will insist on the importance of a constitutional enforcement of this boundary.[40]

Rawls's strategy for attaining critical distance hinges largely upon his developing a conception of the good whose scope is limited. Its central notions are specially interpreted for the purpose of coping with the problem of the justice of the "basic structure" of society.[41] While a conception of the good developed for the purposes of this limited topic may or may not be metaphysically deep, it is by definition not comprehensive. Although principles developed on the basis of our considered judgments about justice can never wholly transcend their context, Rawls's aim is to rely upon ones that are relatively independent from the causal taint of any particular basic structure.[42]

Among our contributors, Sullivan is most attracted to the idea of limiting the scope of a public conception of the good to the political.[43] Spurning metaphysical grounding, he instead argues for broadening the sort of conception of the good that can be developed for political purposes in public discussion. In Sullivan's view, the political can be seen to include more than Rawls seems to allow. Urging a return to something more like the "social liberalism" of such figures as T. H. Green, Sullivan suggests that liberalism will have more success in forging a reasonable agreement about the good—and hence in overcoming the facts of pluralism—if it abandons its recent exclusive focus on individualistic rights and returns to the more robust conceptions of the good that a social liberalism allows. He documents how the rhetoric of abstract rights can frustrate the attempt to reach reasonable agreement on issues such as abortion and affirmative action, and argues that to build a viable account of the common good one must recognize the importance of social institutions in constituting citizens' conceptions of the good. The limitation of scope to political conceptions can perhaps explain how this robust notion of the common good will avoid succumbing to the core dilemma of liberal toleration, for on Sullivan's view there will remain a series of more comprehensive and more metaphysical views of the good that will require toleration and will join the liberal (if at all) only as members of an overlapping consensus. If it is limited in scope to the political, the common conception of the good will not have the pretensions of ruling the entire domain of human action. Whether such a reasonable political consensus can be forged, of course, remains to be seen. There can be no hope for one, Sullivan urges, until we recognize that there is an indispensable place for the "collective interpretation of ends."

This idea of interpretation brings us back to the final dimension of variation in the notion of a conception of the good, namely the degree of *detail* that we imagine one to have. Detailed interpretation can be incorporated into even the most objectivist theory of the good. For example, consider that even Aquinas, who developed a considerably detailed natural-law theory grounded in a conception of the highest good, nonetheless thought that there remained a vital need for specification (*determinatio*) of the law on even more detailed matters that remain properly subject to legislation by civil authorities.[44] Similarly, the nonmetaphysical Thomist John Finnis, for whom a pervasive appeal to the "self-evidence" of certain abstractly defined goods replaces a grounding in the order of being, nonetheless lays great stress on the need for specifying them.[45] On almost any view, goods will need to be interpreted and specified; what varies is whether this is taken to be a task of theory rather than being left to individual preference or conscience to settle or to social practices of discussion and adjudication to work out. Either way, a fully articulated conception of the good can be considered at various levels of abstraction—as I have already illustrated with respect to Rawls's theory. For this reason, as I will explain in Section 8, the dimension of detail can help a liberal theory meet the challenge of articulation, providing a way to overcome incommensurable clashes among conceptions of the good without collapsing into relativism.

Section 6   Liberal Neutrality

Now that we have examined the notion of a conception of the good, we are in a position to assess one tempting response to the dilemma of liberal toleration, the idea that liberal theory must remain neutral among conceptions of the good. In its most sophisticated moments, the liberal theory of recent decades has given the impression that a commitment to neutrality is definitive of liberalism.[46] The idea of neutrality is taken by many to be the liberal's way of articulating a political conception that (a) avoids a commitment to a comprehensive conception of human flourishing while (b) also avoiding falling into a thorough skepticism. Although Rawls has recently written that "the term 'neutrality' is unfortunate [and] some of its connotations are highly misleading,"[47] and although even the two theorists, Ronald Dworkin and Bruce Ackerman, who did the most to inject the term into the debate now express some regret at having done so,[48] this idea is not so easily set aside. The reason for this is that the dilemma of liberal toleration requires an answer: if a revisionist liberalism is going to admit its commitment to a more substantive conception of the good, it still needs to explain how this conception will avoid squeezing out toleration. The idea of neutrality seems to provide a handy way of doing so.

In focusing on neutrality as a possible part of the liberal theorist's answer to the dilemma of toleration, I thereby set aside some other meanings of "neutrality."[49] For instance, "neutrality" might be used to characterize the "disenchanted" world, the cosmos shorn of a *telos,* that many nonliberals as well as liberals now see.[50] By contrast, I will use the term solely to characterize the stance of liberal theory towards (some subset of) conceptions of the good. Here, the appropriate metaphor is not the cosmic one of disenchantment, but the social one of disengagement. Regarded as governing political dialogue, this sort of neutrality can be understood as keeping certain issues "off the agenda," meaning, as Gutmann and Thompson explain, that "they are to be regarded as settled by a society's written or unwritten constitution."[51] In the public arena, neutrality can be understood in terms of "principles of preclusion" or "gag rules" backed up by constitutional rights.[52]

From the perspective of liberal theory itself, this sort of neutrality is a virtue of an impartial arbiter or umpire, suggesting a condition of fair suspense among alternatives.[53] It is the neutrality of the liberal theory's grounds or premises that matters, here, not a causal neutrality of the effects (actual or intended) of liberal policies.[54] The latter is an outcome widely recognized to be impossible.[55] Whereas causal neutrality is a feature of regimes or policies, neutrality of grounds is a feature of justifications, and in particular of the premises employed in political justifications.

As Brian Barry persuasively argues here, a defense of liberal neutrality that is itself fundamentally neutral is also impossible. While Barry is sympathetic to the idea that a liberal neutrality among conceptions of the good can be seen as fair arbitration, he argues that this notion will be attractive only to those who have already accepted what he calls "liberal attitudes." Including the ideas that social institutions "have to be justified on a basis that starts from a premise of the fundamental equality of all human beings," that all institutions should be held up to critical scrutiny, and that "religious dogma" must be challenged, these "attitudes" are obviously not entirely neutral among conceptions of the good, and might themselves be taken to sketch a distinctively liberal one. Barry endorses the recent arguments of Joseph Raz[56] and Alasdair MacIntyre[57] to the effect that liberal neutrality cannot be neutrally defended, and extends them by noting the difficulties that arise because of (what I have called) the depth and structure of the competing conceptions of the good at large in society. If everyone took their good to hinge entirely on their own pleasure, then defending neutrality would be easier. In fact, however, people are attached to conceptions of the good that have a structure and depth—partly due to religious and political beliefs—that typically introduce irreducibly other-regarding elements.[58] And while Barry finds the notion of a fundamentally neutral defense of liberal neutrality implausible, he is not sanguine about the alternative possibility that liberalism might be acceptable as a theorem in overlapping consensus.[59]

Barry's argument, which is persuasive, indicates that any liberal commitment to neutrality of grounds will have to be carefully delimited to present even a coherent possibility. One way to bound neutrality is to exclude some marginal conceptions of the good from consideration, as being in some way "beyond the pale."[60] One might also distinguish different levels of a political theory, and invoke neutrality to characterize only one of them. For instance, one might want to distinguish, for these purposes, among the justifications of the constitutional essentials of a regime, of legislation, and of applications of law to particular individuals.[61]

Bruce Ackerman's line of distinction is a somewhat more abstract version of this institutionally realized separation of levels. Well aware of the difficulties of offering a neutral defense of neutrality—and of the conceptual incoherence of a total neutrality of grounds—Ackerman distinguishes two different contexts of political justification. First-order normative political discussion concerns the justification of power differentials. It is this discussion that must be constrained by neutrality. A higher order discussion treats the way in which the first-order discussion ought to be structured.

The interpretation of first-order neutrality that Ackerman first developed in *Social Justice and the Liberal State*[62] presupposed an idealized hypothetical dialogue among citizens who aimed to justify political policies to each other. While this conversation might begin with egoistic statements of wants, its goal is to arrive at political principles justified to each person. In the pervasive struggle for power, persons are viewed as being required to give reasons for their enjoyment of superior positions. This activity of reason-giving is, on Ackerman's liberal view, subject to the following neutrality constraint: No reason is a good reason if it requires the power holder to assert: (a) that his conception of the good is better than that asserted by any of his fellow citizens, or (b) that, regardless of his conception of the good, he is intrinsically superior to one or more of his fellow citizens. Neutrality is thus invoked by Ackerman as a constraint on conversations of a certain type. Note, too, that he defines neutrality of grounds by banning an explicit claim to superiority, rather than by reference to any more implicit way of begging the question of superiority.[63]

As Ackerman emphasizes in his essay for this volume, neutrality as a conversational constraint differs markedly from other sorts of neutrality that one might conceive. In particular, it does not constrain the kinds of higher order grounds one might have for setting the conversation up in the way that he does. In his book, Ackerman develops four sorts of ground for imposing the neutrality constraint on justifications of power: skepticism or uncertainty about the good (pp. 11, 365ff.), the positive instrumental value of experimentation in ways of living (p. 11), the intrinsic good of "autonomous deliberation" (pp. 11, 367f.), and the importance of avoiding the repression threatened by sectarianism (pp. 361-5). His later writings have also explored another good fostered by neutral dialogue, that of mutual intelligibility, as expressed in "the pragmatic imperative to talk to strangers as well as to soul-mates."[64]

While there is much that is attractive and sensible in Ackerman's approach, note that the role it assigns to the neutrality constraint makes clear it is not by itself an answer the dilemma of liberal toleration set out in Section 2. That dilemma hinged upon the strength and nature of the liberal theorist's normative premises. To assess the implications of Ackerman's in this respect, we would need to hear more both about the content of the premises he would rely upon and about how he would structure their contribution to his theory. On the latter question, it seems that Ackerman may have shifted away from imagining something like an overlapping consensus (see his book, p. 8) and towards a constrained *modus vivendi* organized around a single good.

What may be particularly troubling about neutrality as a way of interpreting or implementing either of these justificatory ideals is that in seeking a fair suspense among competing conceptions it both muzzles them and yields principles that will in practice inevitably favor the pursuit of some of them over the pursuit of others. This conjunction invariably raises the question whether it makes sense, in constructing the edifice of political theory, to ask citizens to check their deepest convictions at the door. Stephen Holmes discusses a case that dramatizes this worry, that of the historic Lincoln-Douglas debates, which occurred at a time when the U.S. House of Representatives had literally silenced legislative discussion of the question of slavery:

> The unionist Douglas asserted that national unity was compatible with a diversity of laws and customs concerning slavery. The nation was not based upon moral consensus about black slavery: northerners thought it evil, while southerners thought it good. The Constitution was nevertheless able to unify the country by abstracting from this underlying normative dissonance. . . .
> But tongue-tying neutrality on this issue was unacceptable. Especially in the final debates, Lincoln repeatedly maneuvered his opponent into an either/or situation.[65]

The moral stakes of this debate parallel those of the abortion debate today. The question, again, is how an attempt to "*abstract* from what is in dispute" (to use Larmore's phrase) can possibly yield an acceptable justificatory stance.[66]

While it is possible that the "second-order" conception of the good may enable neutral liberals to explain why silencing their opponents is fair, this is a heavy burden to bear. Liberal toleration might prove easier to defend if it did not require such a drastic narrowing of the public debate. One possibility, as we have seen, is simply to encourage a dialogue about the common good limited in scope to the political, as Sullivan suggests.[67] Another is to develop an alternative way of distancing the liberal's core conception of the good from the multiplicity of conceptions competing in the polity as large—a way that does not wholly exclude an appeal to them in constructing a political justification.

Section 7   Liberal Alternatives
to Neutral Dialogue

In this section, I will canvass several important liberal alternatives to neutrality that our contributors put forward, each of which nonetheless shares Ackerman's focus on the conditions for an ideal political dialogue. They are alternatives *to* neutrality in that they each seek to explain how liberalism, with admittedly its core theory of the good, can consistently foster a genuine toleration of comprehensive conceptions of the good that clash with it. They are *alternatives* to neutrality in that, by letting comprehensive conceptions into the debate more fully, they give up the idea that liberal theory can "abstract" from a disputed issue simply by taking no stand on it.

While Gutmann and Thompson avoid metaphysical entanglement in presenting their own theory in "Moral Conflict and Political Consensus," they affirm the need for comprehensiveness in public debates. As they explain, their proposal rejects a limitation of scope to the political in two ways: "by permitting, under certain conditions, disagreement on aspects of the basic structure itself," they aim at "*less*" than does Rawls's ideal of overlapping consensus; by continuing "to seek agreement on substantive moral principles—even comprehensive ones" they aim at "*more*." Society must actively encourage an unconstrained conversation in which no issues are banned from the agenda. Instead of absolutely barring the entry of comprehensive views into political discussion, their "principles of preclusion" allow them entry so long as they count as moral positions and are either susceptible to empirical confirmation or at least not "radically implausible." And Gutmann and Thompson place much more reliance on what they call "*principles of accommodation,* which govern the conduct of the moral disagreement on issues that should reach the political agenda." Here, the guiding idea is the value of mutual respect, which they interpret as an attitude that reflects the discussants' mutually positive appraisal of each other's deliberative virtues. To exhibit mutual respect, they argue, citizens must be willing to try to understand an opponent's position *as* a moral point of view, to remain open-minded about it, and to minimize their rejection of it. By the last, they mean that individuals must try to come to terms with as much of their antagonists' comprehensive conceptions of the good as they can, rather than simply prescinding from those elements of them about which they disagree. Thus, whereas Larmore suggests building a constrained *modus vivendi* around the value of mutual respect,[68] Gutmann and Thompson aspire for something much more like full agreement.

Despite obvious differences with Gutmann and Thompson, William Connolly's proposal of a "militant liberalism" nonetheless stands as a comparable alternative to neutrality—at least if it is fair to take Connolly as making any proposals at all that he would not wish subsequently to "unsettle." Drawing on Nietzsche and Foucault, Connolly resists the programs of constructive theory. Like Gutmann and Thompson, however, Connolly is highly suspicious of solving the problems of liberalism by putting some questions outside the bounds of the "political," and like them he rejects the authority of a transcendent ideal of objectivity. While the charge to unsettle prejudices and institutions is not directly an ideal for dialogue, it obviously will have strong implications about the shape of public discussion. By unsettling their own prejudices, militant liberals can remain open to the views of others. Yet since Connolly shows few signs of expecting (or even desiring) a reasonable consensus, his ideal resembles a *modus vivendi* constrained by an overriding commitment to averting "cruelties." Since Connolly defines his view as an *Aufhebung* of the liberal individualism of Hobbes and Locke and the liberal individuality of Emerson and Kateb, it may be able to meet the challenge of generating a specifically liberal content; however, one wonders how that content, once generated, could remain stable in the face of a relentless unsettlement.

Section 8   Interpretive Judgment and the Liberal Good

Whereas the proposals treated in the last section are developed as interpersonal ideals for dialogue, the two remaining views look at another face of dialectic, the reflective judgment of someone informed by a reasoned debate with others. For neutrality, the natural imagery is adjudicative. The liberal theory strives for the virtues of an impartial judge and, as in the Anglo-American adversary system, steps back from the fairly structured fray. The alternatives to neutrality I have just canvassed depart from neutrality, placing more of their trust in the active and unsupervised virtues of the participants. By contrast, the model appropriate for the final pair of proposals is that of a less detached—and more Continental—judge.

In neutrality's adjudicative imagery, liberal theory serves as an impartial court of final (political) appeal. This relatively detached mode of settling political disputes between proponents of conflicting and incommensurable conceptions of the good may seem forced on us under conditions of pluralism. In particular, the need for an appeal to a higher authority will appear inescapable if the competing creeds are understood as ranged around the capital-letter Values alluded to in Section 4: big abstractions such as Freedom or Equality or Salvation. When Values clash, it might seem that the only recourse is to appeal to something deeper or more ultimate that commensurates them. The utilitarian idea of the general happiness can seem to provide the liberal such an ultimate good that maintains at least a semblance of neutrality.[69]

If we admit the possibility of considerable detail in a conception of the good, however, it then becomes undeniable that values such as freedom, equality, and salvation—let alone happiness—both require and are capable of multiple alternative specifications.[70] If we also recognize that conceptions of the good can be structured in terms of values initially recognized as vague or indeterminate, this opens up a two-part strategy for rational reconciliation of conflicts among conceptions of the good. The first step is to argue that there is an abstract core conception on which people reasonably agree, though they disagree about details. The second step is to fashion a reasonable compromise specification of the core that extends the range of relatively detailed agreement. This combination of detail and structure thus allows for a strategy of rational *rapprochement* of differing conceptions of the good that (with luck) ratchets back and forth between establishing the vague sketch and showing how a fuller interpretation of this sketch harmonizes the details. This would be one possible description of the way Rawls hopes his theory could become the subject of a shared reflective equilibrium: first, by appealing to a vague ideal of social cooperation, which is then specified so as to yield determinate principles of justice, and finally adjusted and corrected in light of the fit with more detailed considered judgments about the justice of political institutions.

The strategy is not to "abstract" *away from* (to prescind from) points of disagreement, but to "abstract" *toward* a common core and then try to work out the details anew. What would make the latter a truly distinct proposal would be an effort to show that each of the initially clashing conceptions of the good differently specifies or particularizes the constructed (or discovered) common ground. Resolution of conflict between incommensurable conceptions of the good becomes possible on the basis of an appeal not to a "higher" impartial authority— not to abstract first principles of theory from which practical policies may be deduced—but rather to a given specification's superior ability to accommodate the detailed concerns addressed by each vague value.

To represent these interpretive possibilities, the metaphor (if not the reality) of first-personal reflective judgment seems particularly apt. When a single person's values conflict with each other, it makes little sense to suggest that she come to terms with this conflict by bracketing, or excluding from her internal dialogue, the claims of the contending values. Instead, she must try to come to some sort of reflective resolution, taking everything into account. The model of first-personal political judgment carries this sort of idea, which contrasts sharply with neutrality, to the level of society.

In contemporary political theory, the model of first-personal judgment is being pursued along at least three distinct avenues. The first is Socratic, emphasizing critical self-examination. While the specifically Socratic legacy played a small role in Rawls's explication of reflective equilibrium,[71] it is being more fully worked out by others, notably in Stephen Salkever's essay. The second is Aristotelian, emphasizing the irreducible role of the trained perception of the person of practical wisdom. Nussbaum mines this vein, explaining how the discerning perception of particulars will introduce individual variations into judgments nonetheless informed by a core conception of human flourishing.[72] A third is Kantian, represented, for instance, by Rawls's "constructivism" and Scanlon's "contractualism."[73]

For a political theory of reflective judgment, a crucial question is where theorists are to look for the detailed content that will provide the stuff of their interpretations. Salkever's answer is to turn to actual liberal institutions, to see in detail how these specify and implement the key liberal virtues of ironic self-detachment and reflective questioning. Salkever's development of the Socratic ideal of self-examination nicely combines the themes of reflective first- personal judgment and ironic self-detachment. This way of introducing a kind of distance between individuals and their views avoids arbitrarily begging the question against liberalism's communitarian opponents, who would object to achieving this distancing via a Kantian detachment from contingency and particularity.[74] Salkever takes care to locate the attitude of irony in flourishing liberal institutions and practices of education and adjudication in the United States, thus giving it a firm grounding in the particulars of history. In addition, this Socratic attitude has a definite dialectical component, working with the particular material offered by the interlocutor, or by oneself when one is of two minds. The very fact that the paradigm exponent of this attitude was Socrates tends to defuse somewhat the charge that it begs the question in favor of liberal toleration of a modern sort. In terms of the challenge of consistency, it seems that irony may not be so corrosive as to undercut itself. A more serious challenge for Salkever's position is that of generating appropriate content. Is the likelihood that ironic and detached dialogue will reach liberal conclusions dependent on the historical and institutional context? Or is there a more intrinsic connection between irony and liberal toleration, of the sort that one can discern in Ackerman's neutrality constraint?[75]

Salkever's development of the political role of judgment is tinged by his suspicion of the pretensions of "theory"—a suspicion he shares with Connolly. Salkever is especially critical of theories according to which the details fall out deductively from a few abstract first principles. Not all theories, however, claim a deductive governance of practice. As a number of our contributors point out, for instance, Rawls's recent "hermeneutic turn" exemplifies the way in which a fully elaborated constructive liberal theory can avoid being *a priori* and deductive ("Cartesian") in its justification.[76] Less well noticed is the fact that Rawls does not imagine a deductive application of his theory to practice, but rather a "four-stage sequence" involving a constitutional assembly, a legislature, and courts in which a full range of learning from practice could occur.[77] Another nondeductivist theory that works from within human practices and beliefs is Martha Nussbaum's—a theory into which is built, as I have noted, an essential role for reflective judgment and discernment.

Nussbaum does us the great service of setting out a richly structured conception of the good. Although she does not intend it to provide for an unqualified defense of liberalism, it is nonetheless compatible with many of the liberal's central tenets. Whereas Salkever looks to particular social institutions as a crucial source of content, Nussbaum develops her theory of the good with a more universal (though not transcendent) ambition that is at once more characteristically liberal and more truly Aristotelian. Faulting Rawls's Kantian conception of the person for failing to give due weight to human neediness and the way the exercise of basic moral powers is dependent upon social support, and criticizing his recent, more explicitly "hermeneutic" stance for its inability to speak to urgent international problems, Nussbaum looks to "the constitutive circumstances of the human being (or: the shape of the human form of life)."[78] These constitute the first level of her Aristotelian theory of the good; a list of "basic human functional capabilities" is the second.

In claiming to establish by reference to these a universally valid conception of the good—too richly detailed and structured to summarize briefly here—Nussbaum's essay in this volume exemplifies the strategy sketched above for combining the dimensions of detail and of structure. She argues that the Aristotelian conception of the good that she puts forward on an objective basis is "thick," but "vague."[79] It is "thick" in dealing comprehensively with the full range of human ends, but it remains vague enough to leave individuals substantial freedom to decide how to fill in the sketch of human flourishing (it is quite detailed for a theory, but still just a sketch for living). This degree of freedom in particularizing, of "plural specification," she implies, is all the liberal should really care about securing. On this view, the challenge of articulating limits is met by distinguishing between levels of abstraction: in the outline sketch—unity; in the details—diversity.

Nussbaum asserts that although this theory is genuinely Aristotelian in the structured conception of human flourishing that it builds up, it nonetheless is not metaphysical in "the sense that worries liberals"—the sense I elaborated in Section 3. "That is," she argues, "it is not a theory that is arrived at in detachment from the actual self-understandings and evaluations of human beings in society; nor is it a theory peculiar to a single metaphysical or religious tradition." Especially given the contrasting way that Schmitz appropriates Aristotle in his article, this claim may excite a struggle over the legacy of the Philosopher. The question of whose interpretation of Aristotle's theory of the human good is truer to his texts lies outside the purview of this volume.[80] And in any case, we should not let the question of fidelity to Aristotle distract us from the very real attractions of Nussbaum's approach.

The greatest of these virtues is that Nussbaum comes closest to providing what, by all indications, a liberal theory (like any other) sorely needs, namely an adequately elaborated conception of the good. Whether Nussbaum's "thick, vague" theory can resolve the dilemma of liberal toleration will depend largely on the answers to two questions: First, while its vagueness leaves room for individual diversity, can it go beyond merely permitting toleration, and affirmatively require or protect the liberties that implement toleration? Second, can a conception of the good of as much differentiation and structure as Nussbaum lays out really be defended without positively relying upon any metaphysical claims of the sort that the liberal would (or should) find threatening?

The tremendous variety and subtlety of our contributors' constructive responses to the dilemma of liberal toleration should not obscure the fact that they all recognize, in one way or another, that liberals must take some stand on the good—must say what they are *for*. The provocative essays in this volume explore some of the pitfalls liberals must avoid in attempting to do so, and put forward a fruitful variety of distinct and innovative ways in which tolerant liberals might develop their conception of the good coherently and forcefully. In closing, I should note that these strategies are of interest not only to liberals but to every political theorist. Although nonliberal theorists may not face anything exactly like the dilemma of toleration that forces these strategies upon them with a logical necessity, a sane respect for the facts of pluralism will require them to provide a parallel explanation of how they can be confident in the truth or reasonableness of their conception of the good despite the depth and pervasiveness of disagreement about these matters.

Notes

1. Equality is given preeminence by Ronald Dworkin, "Liberalism," in his *A Matter of Principle* [*MP*] (Harvard University Press, 1985), Ch. 8; originally published in Stuart Hampshire, ed., *Public and Private Morality* (Cambridge University Press, 1978); and "Why Liberals Should Care about Equality," in *MP*, Ch. 9; originally published in *The New York Review of Books*, February 3, 1983. The latter essay, in particular, makes explicit that any commitment to neutrality or toleration should be seen as deriving from the ultimate principle of equal concern and respect. Cf. Amartya Sen, "Equality of What?" in *The Tanner Lectures on Human Values*, vol. 1 (University of Utah Press and Cambridge University Press, 1980); reprinted in his *Choice, Welfare, and Measurement* (Cambridge, Mass.: MIT Press, 1982).

2. Unfortunately, all of these questions must be phrased in the conditional, for there are many nations that are still dominated by aristocratic privilege and plagued by the equivalent of feudalism, that demand a religious or quasi-religious uniformity, and that fail to allow their citizens basic liberties of association and movement.

3. Schumpeter is quoted in Robert Heilbroner, "The Triumph of Capitalism," *The New Yorker*, Jan. 23, 1989, p. 101. On the liberal "demand for a justification of the social world," see Jeremy Waldron, "The Theoretical Foundations of Liberalism," *Philosophical Quarterly* 37 (1987): 127–150.

4. The notion of "stability" is defined in John Rawls, *A Theory of Justice* (Cambridge, Mass.: Harvard University Press, 1971) [*TJ*], pp. 6, 496–504, and addressed throughout Part III of that work. On Rawls's view, while the relative stability of a set of principles is one element in its justification, it is one that is nonetheless distinguishable from the more abstract argument for the principles of justice offered in Part I of *TJ*. To elaborate his argument that a liberal society could be stable, Rawls has recently introduced the notion of an "overlapping consensus" (to be explained below). See "The Idea of an Overlapping Consensus," *Oxford Journal of Legal Studies* 7 (1987): 1–25 [*IOC*]; and "The Domain of the Political and Overlapping Consensus," *New York University Law Review* 64 (1989): 233–255 [*DPOC*], §7.

5. For an exploration of the parallel issues that arise with regard to stability, see, e.g., Thomas A. Spragens, Jr., "Reconstructing Liberal Theory: Reason and Liberal Culture," in Alfonso J. Damico, ed., *Liberals on Liberalism* (Totowa: Rowman & Littlefield, 1986), 34–53.

6. As is recognized by, e.g., Kenneth Schmitz, "Is Liberalism Good Enough?" (See Chapter 5, this volume.)

7. Michael Sandel, "Moral Argument and Liberal Toleration: Abortion and Homosexuality," *California Law Review* 77 (1989): 521–538.

8. Quoted in *New York Times*, July 27, 1989, p. 1.

9. See the carefully qualified discussion of this point by Rawls in *TJ*, *§35*.

10. Although I think that this dilemma can be overcome, I will for brevity often omit the word "apparent."

11. Although largely discredited in philosophical circles as being self-defeating, a defense of liberalism in terms of a blanket normative skepticism is still quite popular. Cf., e.g., Arthur M. Schlesinger, Jr., "The Opening of the American Mind," *New York Times Book Review*, July 23, 1989.

12. The tensions between Mill's *Utilitarianism* and his *On Liberty* are well known. For a recent and discerning reconciliationist reading, see Fred R. Berger, *Happiness, Justice, and Freedom: The Moral and Political Philosophy of John Stuart Mill* (Berkeley: University of California Press, 1984).

13. Again, I am focusing on questions of conceptual coherence, rather than stability: see Spragens, Jr., "Reconstructuring Liberal Theory."

14. G.F.W. Hegel, *The Philosophy of Right*, tr. T.M. Knox (Oxford: Oxford University Press,

1967); C.B. MacPherson, *The Political Theory of Possessive Individualism* (Oxford: Oxford University Press, 1962); Michael Sandel, *Liberalism and the Limits of Justice* (Cambridge: Cambridge University Press, 1982) [*LLJ*].

15. Since Aristotle held that some types of animals have essentially in common that they are monadic or solitary, and man partakes of both solitary and gregarious features (*Historia Animalium* I.1, 487b33–488a7), it is not clear how his general ontology by itself can suffice to yield a communitarian result.

16. Cf. Schmitz, "Is Liberalism Good Enough?" (See Chapter 5, this volume, note 2.)

17. William E. Connolly, "Identity and Difference in Liberalism." (See Chapter 4, this volume.)

18. Cf. John Rawls, "Justice as Fairness: Political not Metaphysical," *Philosophy and Public Affairs* 14 (1985): 223–251, n. 22.

19. Sandel's effort, in *LLJ*, to pin such a conception of the self on Rawls is effectively rebutted by *PNM*. On Sandel's argument, see further below, Section 5.

20. For Mill on the value of diversity, see *On Liberty*, Ch. 3, par. 1. This also would be one way to label the theory of individuality developed by George Kateb, and discussed by William Connolly in Chapter 4.

21. I take the phrase, "the facts of pluralism," from Rawls, and in addition his basic way of filling them out (I abstract a little from Rawls's focus on political justice). See esp. *IOC*, p. 6.

22. Connolly, "Identity and Difference in Liberalism." (See Chapter 4, this volume). In "The Logical Structure of *Sittlichkeit:* A Reading of Hegel's *Philosophy of Right*," *Idealistic Studies* 18 (1989): 62–78, I reinforce the contrast between the wishfulness of Taylor's appropriation of Hegel and the inexorable depth of the essential synthesis of liberal rights, individuals' conceptions of the good, and the community posited by Hegel himself.

23. Alasdair MacIntyre, *After Virtue*, 2nd ed. (Notre Dame: University of Notre Dame Press, 1984), p. 263.

24. Sandel, *LLJ*, p. 183.

25. *In necessiis, unitas; in dubiis, libertas; in omniis, caritas.* The translation is that of the motto of Richard Baxter, a seventeenth-century Puritan dissenter.

26. Charles Larmore, *Patterns of Moral Complexity* (Cambridge: Cambridge University Press, 1987), 51ff. See also Terry Pinkard, *Democratic Liberalism and Social Union* (Philadelphia: Temple University Press, 1987). Pinkard illuminatingly canvasses a number of "strategies for pluralism" more concretely delineated than the ones set out in the text, and vigorously argues that pluralism can be seen as constrained by a regulative commitment to the value of autonomy that is hospitable both to liberalism and to the common good.

27. Cf. Rawls, *IOC*.

28. See, e.g., Will Kymlicka, "Rawls on Teleology and Deontology," *Philosophy and Public Affairs* 17 (1988): 173–190, p. 181.

29. Sandel, *LLJ*, p. 47.

30. John Rawls, "Kantian Constructivism in Moral Theory: The Dewey Lectures 1980," *Journal of Philosophy* 77 (1980): 515–572. Norman Daniels's elaboration of Rawls's justificatory ideals in "Reflective Equilibrium and Archimedean Points," *Canadian Journal of Philosophy* 10 (1980): 83–103 interestingly imports a presumption in favor of depth.

31. Rawls, *PNM*. Bruce Ackerman, "Neutralities," (See Chapter 2, this volume) credits Sandel with derailing the Dewey Lectures' "neo-Kantian foundationalism." To the contrary, I find nothing foundationalist in the Dewey Lectures, and nothing in *PNM* that is inconsistent with them.

32. Thus, Rawls's insistence that the conception of the person on which he relies is "Political Not Metaphysical" also carries with it an attenuation of the sense in which it is a conception of the person at all, as opposed to simply being an element in a political conception. Richard Rorty praises what he takes to be the pragmatic turn that this essay of Rawls's represents in "The Priority of Democracy to Philosophy," in *The Virginia Statute of Religious Freedom: Two Hundred Years After*, ed. Robert Vaughan (Madison: University of Wisconsin Press, 1988). Rorty's position is vigorously attacked on

this point by Richard J. Bernstein, "One Step Forward, Two Steps Backward: Richard Rorty on Liberal Democracy and Philosophy," *Political Theory* 15 (1987): 538–563, esp. pp. 553, 557. Rorty responds, arguing that "nitty-gritty advantages and disadvantages" are far more important in political justification than the metaphysics of the self, in "Thugs and Theorists," *Political Theory* 15 (1987): 564–580, n. 20.

33. See especially John Rawls, "Priority of Right and Ideas of the Good," [*PRIG*] *Philosophy and Public Affairs* 17 (1988): 251–276, which elaborates "five ideas of the good found in" his theory of justice; and *DPOC*, p. 244, which claims that "the values of the political are very great values indeed and hence not easily overridden."

34. This question is raised in this volume by Stephen Salkever, "Lopp'd and Bound." (See Chapter 9, this volume); and by Connolly, "Identity and Difference in Liberalism." (See Chapter 4, this volume.)

35. Even to apply to a conception of goodness so strongly objectivist that individuals' desires, incentives, and aims are seen as irrelevant, this formulation of the notion of orderliness obviously would have to be revised. A significant degree of orderliness of the sort defined implies something like what Christine M. Korsgaard has called "rationalism" about the good, in "Aristotle and Kant on the Source of Value," *Ethics* 96 (1986): 486–505.

36. See above, no. 33.

37. Cf. Rawls, *TJ*, §86, and *PRIG*, pp. 270–271. That a liberal conception of the good can attain this degree of structure should suffice to put to rest a long-standing criticism, namely that liberalism is, at bottom, predicated upon an uncritical egoism.

38. Cf. Salkever, "Lopp'd and Bound," Connolly, "Identity and Difference in Liberalism." (See Chapters 9 and 4, this volume.)

39. See Sandel, *LLJ*, p. 182.

40. See the essays in Jon Elster and Rune Slagstad, eds., *Constitutionalism and Democracy* (Cambridge: Cambridge University Press, 1988).

41. On Rawls's scope limitation to the "basic structure," see *TJ*, §2, "The Basic Structure as Subject," in *Values and Morals*, Alvin Goldman and Jaegwon Kim, eds. (Dordrecht: Reidel, 1978), and *PNM*, p. 224.

42. This is the limited application of Rawls's notion of an "Archimedean point": see *TJ*, pp. 260–263, 520.

43. William Sullivan, "Bringing the Good Back In." (See Chapter 8, this volume.)

44. Thomas Aquinas, *Summa Theologica* I–II, Q. 95, Art. 2. In the terminology of Martha Nussbaum's note 95 in "Aristotelian Social Democracy." (See Chapter 10, this volume.) This is "local specification" rather than "plural specification."

45. John Finnis, *Natural Law and Natural Rights* (Oxford: Clarendon Press, 1980), pp. 34, 51. Ironically, despite Finnis's emphasis on the need for specification, his own efforts at it are singularly unpersuasive, perhaps because he tends to identify specification with brute choice by those in authority (289).

46. For recent definitions of liberalism in terms of the idea of neutrality, see—in addition to Larmore, *Patterns*, p. 42—D.A. Lloyd Thomas, *In Defense of Liberalism* (Oxford: Basil Blackwell, 1988), p. 1.

47. Rawls, *PRIG*, p. 260.

48. See the opening of Bruce Ackerman, "Neutralities." (See Chapter 2, this volume.) Dworkin's doubts already began to be apparent in "Why Should Liberals Care about Equality?"

49. Compare the meanings of "neutrality" distinguished by William Galston, "Liberalism and Public Morality," in Damico, ed., *Liberals on Liberalism*.

50. Salkever seems sometimes to use "neutrality" in this way to label the alternative to metaphysical teleology. Note that if the *telos* were as Mill says it is, it would be compatible with (some form of) liberalism.

51. Amy Gutmann and Dennis Thompson, "Moral Conflict and Political Consensus." (See Chapter 7, this volume.)

52. Ibid. As I will explain in the next section, Gutmann and Thompson emphasize that principles of preclusion have played too great a role in recent liberal theory. The term "gag rule" comes from Stephen Holmes, "Gag Rules or the Politics of Omission," in Elster and Slagstad, eds., *Constitutionalism and Democracy.* In *IOC,* p. 14 n. 22, Rawls adopts the idea of keeping certain issues off the agenda as a way of explaining the significance of constitutional rights.

53. For an argument in favor of the cogency of proceeding with practical reasoning while remaining in suspense about certain value conflicts, see Isaac Levi, *Hard Choices: Decision Making under Unresolved Conflict* (Cambridge: Cambridge University Press, 1986), esp. Chaps. 1, 2.

54. This terminology is adapted from unpublished lectures by Michael Sandel. See also the similar distinction between "neutrality of outcome" and "neutrality of procedure" developed by Larmore, *Patterns,* 43f.; and elaborated by Rawls in *PRIG,* pp. 260–263.

55. This obvious fact of the impossibility of a causal neutrality was noted by, for example, Brian Barry, *Political Argument* (N.Y.: Humanities Press, 1965), pp. 74–79. See also Rawls, *PRIG,* p. 262. Both focus on the inevitability of differential effects on adherence to the various conceptions of the good. Differential effects on the achievement and pursuit of goods variously conceived are equally inevitable and obvious.

56. Joseph Raz, *The Morality of Freedom* (Oxford: Oxford University Press, 1986), Ch. 5.

57. Alasdair MacIntyre, *Whose Justice? Which Rationality?* (Notre Dame: University of Notre Dame Press, 1988), p. 345.

58. That is, it introduces (to put it flatly) what Dworkin has called "external preferences," as Barry notes in Chapter 3, this volume. Dworkin has since implicitly conceded that the exclusion of "external preferences" relies on too narrow a notion of harm (or benefit): see his "Liberal Community," *California Law Review* 77 (1989): 479–504, Section II.

59. Since Barry uses the Roman Catholic church as a prime example of what would resist joining such a consensus, much of the force of this part of his argument depends partly on whether Langan's case is convincing.

60. Cf. Gutmann and Thompson's preclusion of views that fail to count as moral points of view because they are not universalizable (see Chapter 7, this volume); and Larmore's declaration that his "liberal defense of liberal neutrality" is not meant to apply to those "fanatics and would-be martyrs" who are willing to compromise civil peace in the pursuit of their conceptions of the good (60), nor to possible conceptions of the good that are not actually disputed in society (67).

61. This particular division of levels follows Rawls, *TJ,* §31. Peter de Marneffe has persuasively argued in a stimulating unpublished paper that neutrality of the grounds of constitutional essentials does not generally imply neutrality of grounds at the legislative level, nor on the judicial level in constitutional cases.

62. Bruce Ackerman, *Social Justice and the Liberal State* (New Haven: Yale University Press, 1980).

63. Deep questions arise concerning what it is to "beg the question" against an opponent. Neutrality of grounds, in general, will forbid appeal to premises that in some way beg the question against any of the relevant class of conceptions of the good. To beg the question, in the relevant sense, must a premise *state* or *mean* that some conception of the good is inferior or false, or is it enough that the premise *implies* this? And if implication is enough, implication by virtue of what other background premises? Similar questions lurk in the notion of what putting forward a reason "requires" one to assert.

64. Bruce Ackerman, "Why Dialogue," *Journal of Philosophy* 86 (1989): 5–22, p. 22.

65. Holmes, "Gag Rules," p. 39; cf. pp. 31–35. This question of the context of preclusion is crucial. Excluding certain premises from Ackerman's hypothetical dialogues or from Rawls's original position is a very different matter than excluding certain issues from discussion by a legislature; and just as a legislature is not the whole of a polity, so Ackerman's dialogues and Rawls's original position are not the whole of their respective political theories.

66. Larmore, *Patterns,* p. 50. To be sure, it is often possible to justify a stand on one issue while

abstracting from disagreements about other issues; but as Raz notes (pp. 122–124), the fact that the central political conflicts that are troubling us are between proponents of conflicting comprehensive conceptions of the good means that if we abstract from *these* disagreements, the positions on no issue will be left undisturbed.

67. See Section 5, above.

68. Larmore, *Patterns*, pp. 53f., 61.

69. The paradigmatic liberal statements of the need for an appeal to general utility as a unique highest authority are John Stuart Mill, *A System of Logic, Ratiocinative and Inductive* (London: Longmans, Green & Co., 1911), Bk. VI, Ch. 12, §7; and Henry Sidgwick, *The Methods of Ethics,* 7th ed. (London: MacMillan, 1907; reprinted Indianapolis: Hackett, 1981), p. 406. I discuss the latter in "Commensurability as a Prerequisite of Rational Choice: An Examination of Sidgwick's Position," forthcoming.

70. See the end of Section 5, above.

71. Rawls, *TJ,* pp. 48–49: "The notion of reflective equilibrium . . . is . . . characteristic of the study of principles which govern actions shaped by self-examination. Moral philosophy is Socratic."

72. See, in addition to Nussbaum's essay here, her "Discernment of Perception," in John Cleary, ed. *Proceedings of the Boston Area Colloquium in Ancient Philosophy,* vol. 1 (Lanham, Md.: University Press of America, 1986); reprinted in revised form in her *Love's Knowledge: Essays on Philosophy and Literature* (Oxford: Oxford University Press, in press).

73. Cf. Rawls, Dewey Lectures, esp. the third lecture, "Construction and Objectivity." Also T.M. Scanlon, "Contractualism and Utilitarianism," in Amartya Sen and Bernard Williams, eds., *Utilitarianism and Beyond* (Cambridge: Cambridge University Press, 1982); and "Levels of Moral Thinking," in Douglas Seanor and N. Fotion, eds., *Hare and Critics* (Oxford: Clarendon Press, 1988). More directly linked to Kant's *Critique of Judgment* is another Kantian strand stemming from Hannah Arendt's work on the place of judgment in politics. See Hannah Arendt, *Lectures on Kant's Political Philosophy,* ed. Ronald Beiner (Chicago: University of Chicago Press, 1982); Ronald Beiner, *Political Judgment* (Chicago: University of Chicago Press, 1983); and the assessment of these by Seyla Benhabib, "Judgment and the Moral Foundations of Politics in Arendt's Thought," *Political Theory* 16 (1988): 29–52.

74. This Kantian route is proposed by Thomas Nagel in "Moral Conflict and Political Legitimacy," *Philosophy and Public Affairs* 16 (1987): 215–240.

75. For reasons to doubt that an intrinsic connection exists between liberal toleration and Socratic irony, see Gerald M. Mara, "Socrates and Liberal Toleration," *Political Theory* 16 (1988): 468–495, esp. 489f.

76. Salkever himself recognizes this shift in Rawls: see also Sullivan, "Bringing the Good Back In," (Chapters 8 and 9, this volume) and Ackerman, "Neutralities," (Chapter 2, this volume). Although §§9 and 87 of *TJ* already implied that Rawls was no kind of foundationalist, Rawls's more explicit casting of his theory as interpreting and systemizing the "fundamental intuitive ideas" of the western liberal tradition came in *PNM*.

77. Rawls, *TJ,* §31.

78. Nussbaum, "Aristotelian Social Democracy." (See Chapter 10, this volume.) Nussbaum also criticizes the "thin theory of the good" presented in *TJ*: the so-called "primary goods." In this introductory essay, I have ignored this level of Rawls's theory, concentrating instead on the conception of the good that, as he increasingly admits, is expressed by the ethical interpretation of the original position.

79. See also Salkever, "Lopp'd and Bound," (Chapter 9, this volume) and William Galston, *Justice and the Human Good* (Chicago: University of Chicago Press, 1980), p. 56.

80. Nussbaum's interpretive claims are partially defended in her notes. They are set out more fully in a trio of papers she summarizes briefly at the outset of her essay. Schmitz, too, cites three of his own articles to bolster his interpretation of Aristotle.

2

Neutralities

Bruce Ackerman

Perhaps I made a mistake, some time ago, in helping popularize the notion that something called Neutrality was at the heart of contemporary liberalism. But perhaps not. Doubtless other labels—say, Impartiality—would have been equally provocative, bringing (somewhat different) clouds of confusion to the storm-center of debate. Anyway, what's done is done; all I can do now is try my best to clarify the confusion.

After reading more than my fair share of critical commentary, one thing is very clear: Neutrality can mean a lot of very different things. Indeed, I frequently find myself agreeing completely with the critic's triumphant critique: if *this* is what Neutrality means, let's just stop talking about the whole idea and move on to other, more promising, subjects for conversation! Hence, much of this chapter is an effort to distinguish four different kinds of Neutrality, and explain why at least three-and-a-half of the critiques launched in their direction seem to me right on target. At the same time, I hope to convince you that none of these valid criticisms so much as touch the ideal of Neutrality that lies at the core of the project described in *Social Justice in the Liberal State*.[1] Of course, even after we have put Neutrality in its place, there will be lots to be said against it—and for it. But at least the conversation will be on target.

Let's begin by getting a couple of things straight. First, whatever else it may be, Neutrality is not a way of transcending value; it *is* a value, which can only be defended by locating its relationship to other values. Second, neither Neutrality, nor any other single concept, can possibly do all the work required of a plausible political theory. To understand the point of Neutrality, then, it is best to approach our subject indirectly—sketching the larger whole of which the ideal of Neutrality is a part. This will allow me, I hope, to reach an accommodation with some (though hardly all) of Neutrality's critics. As I have suggested, many of their points are right on target; rather than serving as objections to a proper understanding of the value of neutrality, they serve to caution liberals—and not only liberals—against a number of wrong turns on the path toward a critical perspective on political life.

The Model of the Power Struggle

Any plausible political theory comes in (at least) two parts. The first presents a diagnosis of the basic problems of political life; the second offers a solution to these problems—which may, of course, include reasons for believing that no satisfactory solution is possible. For me, Neutrality is part of this second part. Since no solution can make any sense apart from the problem it is intended to solve, it is best to defer all talk of Neutrality for a while so as to focus on the problem.

The problem, quite simply, is the struggle for power. Short of death, none of us can escape. Even the hermit must have the power to exclude intruders who wish to transform his desert into Disneyland. Not that the struggle for power is all there is to life. To the contrary, that is why finding a reasonable solution to the problem is so important: the more we can control the struggle by processes and principles we find reasonable, the more we can use our time and energy for other purposes. But no mortal can imagine that she can put the problem of power completely to one side so that the focus may be entirely on "better things."

The Building Blocks of Power

This leads immediately to the first great challenge for theory: how to diagnose the struggle for power? There are two basic ways: micro and macro. The micro-theorist takes a real world case—desegregation in Yonkers, acid rain over the Northeast—and explores the complex way concrete structures of power and authority structure its debate and resolution. While this kind of work is particularly trendy right now—with all the Geertzian talk of "thick description" hovering[2]—it has in fact been a mainstay of modern political science, as well as anthropology, for a long time. Long enough for its limitations, as well as its genuine merits, to be understood.

The problem, quite simply, is that the case student is at the mercy of his cases. He is at his best studying the power struggles that break out on the surface of social life. While these phenomena are surely important, it is no less important to recognize the other face of power—the power that keeps issues off the agenda, the structures that demoralize protest before the issue has been fairly joined.[3] It is my concern with the political control of these kinds of power that has convinced me that micro-theory can never be enough; that we must constantly cultivate a double vision, supplementing the microscope of case study with the telescope of macro-theory. I am concerned, in short, with the building blocks of power, and how they may be reshaped in a more just society. But what *are* the building blocks?

This, transparently, is a deep question; while there are some famous historical answers, I won't try to review them here. It will be more productive to sketch my own approach to the subject for, among other things, it deeply colors my response to a number of popular critiques of Neutrality. Join with me, then, in a series of reflections on a simple idea: power is the capacity to get things done in the world. Thus, to define the basic building blocks of power, we must reflect—in a suitably generalizing way—on a single question: what does *any* actor need in order to get *anything* done in the world?

Well, to begin with the basics, every actor needs a body. Without a body, he is quite literally nowhere—at least so far as this world is concerned—and hence cannot participate in the worldly power struggles I am interested in modeling. Obvious enough, but the obvious will become increasingly important to political theory in the next few generations. With the notable exception of Plato, even our most provocative thinkers took the human body pretty much as they found it—as if it were part of a natural order whose genetic constitution was beyond self-conscious human control. The philosophical task, instead, was to define the social implications of the fact that different bodies were born with different genetic abilities, weaknesses.

But no longer. Normal men and women are already beginning to take for granted the power to go into a doctor's office and determine the genetic constitution of the next generation. An analysis of the building blocks of power, then, must begin with this decision. Who should be empowered to make these genetic decisions that so profoundly shape the power struggle that lies ahead? What principles should regulate this decision?

My point here is not to answer these questions,[4] but to insist that an adequate model recognize the struggle over genetic power as a basic element in the larger power analysis. While this aspect of the problem will bulk increasingly large in the next era of human relations, it obviously does not exhaust the kinds of power struggle with which we are already familiar. So let us move onward in the same spirit we have begun: nothing fancy, sticking to the obvious. Ready?

Just having a body isn't enough to act effectively in the world as we know it. Before a human actor stands any chance at success, he or she must be socialized into a repertoire of symbols and behaviors—a culture, in short. This basic point provokes a second kind of power struggle, in which people use power to shape the kind of culture to which others have access. This struggle is most obvious in the educational process in which adults compete with one another to socialize children into different languages, ideals, behaviors, each would-be "educator" seeking the power to impose very drastic sanctions on those children who stray from the culturally approved path; but, of course, the power to control one another's access to cultural resources continues to be exercised—in both subtle and not-so-subtle ways—throughout our lives.

Genes, Culture. The outcome of each generation's struggle over these two variables determines the native talents and cultivated abilities that the next generation brings to its struggle for power. It is not enough, however, to describe each individual's power position by evaluating his genetic and cultural endowment. To see the need for a third variable, the following primitive observation should suffice: even if a person were endowed with a marvelous range of talents and provided with an extraordinarily rich education, he would be completely powerless if others denied him the right to occupy a place in the *material world*. When that happens, the individual—however well endowed in the G and C dimensions—is dead.

This simple point suggests that we must, at the very least, enrich our model by introducing a third basic dimension, which specifies the extent of each individual's control over material things. This dimension notoriously marks a variable, not a constant. I may only control the dirt on which I stand or half the planet; and we will be struggling endlessly over how much each of us should control. For the moment, though, I am not trying to describe the particular ways in which this struggle is mediated in one or another society. Instead, I am concerned only with the primitive point that no model of the power struggle could plausibly be considered complete without recognizing this material dimension as no less fundamental than the struggle over genetic and cultural resources.

Genes, Culture, Material Resources. Our power strugglers are coming to be modeled along a rather complicated set of dimensions. But not complicated enough. While our M variable serves to mark the material things each of us controls in one way or another, it must be enriched by another analytic dimension which describes the different ways this control may be exercised. To what extent can I exercise exclusive control over M, to what extent do I control it together with one or another group? To what extent can I/we trade our M to others? To what extent is M inalienable? If there is a system of exchange, is it competitive or monopolistic? Answers to such questions specify a *transactional framework;*[5] and it is only after we have located an actor's G,C,M within such a T-framework that we can begin to have a pretty good idea of his *basic power position,* as I shall call it.

This conceptual matrix is basic in at least two senses. First, it provides a set of categories that is, in principle, capable of describing any *particular act* of power, however trivial or grand it may be. Thus, you are able to read this essay because (a) I have been endowed with a set of genes that allowed me to write it; (b) I have been socialized into a culture which allowed me to develop my native talents in the authorial way; (c) I have sufficient power over the material world to enable me to control the word processor in front of me; (d) I am linked to you by a complex set of market institutions that allows me to communicate with you via the book trade, and prevents others from stealing the book. Second, the matrix can simultaneously serve to define the basic terms for analyzing the problem of distributive justice: How is one or another political-legal system resolving the ongoing struggle over G,C,M, and T? How should these struggles be resolved?

A First Critique:
Neutrality and Invisibility

This last question marks the transition from the statement of the problem to the effort at defining its legitimate solution. And it is here, be it recalled, that my concept of Neutrality will enter.

I have already said enough, though, to define an objection to many exercises in political theory with which I have a great deal of sympathy—and which critics often have in mind in denying the claims of one or another theory to "neutrality." This critical exercise involves unmasking a theory's claim to neutrality by revealing its failure to confront, let alone resolve, one or another dimension of the power problem. Thus, it is easy to find standard "liberal" tracts[6] that seem more inspired by Botticelli's *Birth of Venus* than any other source. Rather than seriously confronting the uses of power involved in determining each person's endowment of genes, culture, and material property, they talk about people as if they were born as adults, though endowed rather differently from Botticelli's Venus. Instead, they are presented as if they were adult owners of private property, already equipped with genes and education, and concerned merely to gain the power to contract their way to self-fulfillment. With so much of the power problem assumed away, no wonder this kind of "liberalism" easily degenerates into bourgeois apologia: rather than asking hard questions about the way in which our society distributes and rewards talent, education, property, the only power problems that seem worth talking about are those involving the design of a liberal market system. After defending (one or another) theory of market freedom, they then condemn as un-Neutral any attempt to protest against the underlying distribution of property, culture, genes presupposed by the theorist's idealized "free market." Such a use of the rhetoric of Neutrality only serves to keep crucial questions off the agenda of serious debate.

I entirely accept this criticism so long, of course, as it is consistently applied to all exercises in political theory, and not only liberal ones. Thus, it won't do for a critic to explore the "hidden" sources of power presupposed by a market system and then turn a blind eye to the coercive powers exercised by parents, educators, and bureaucrats in alternative systems. Any credible theory of justice— liberal or otherwise— must confront the struggle for power in *all* its basic dimensions; or else it is nothing other than an apologia, giving the exercise of certain forms of power the priceless advantage of invisibility. This allows those who are powerful, along whatever power dimensions ignored by the theory, to pretend that their advantages were an unalterable part of "human nature," which it is pointless even to expose to the question of justice.

The critique of this kind of apologetic is an unending task for political theory.

A Second Critique:
The Science of Power?

But power analysis must not only aim for comprehensiveness; it must also be realistic. We must try as best we can to see the dynamics of power without the rose-colored glasses of the moralist. Thus, in defining each of the four basic power variables, I have not tried to identify the kinds of power an actor must have in order to accomplish *good* in the world. I have asked myself to identify the kinds of power an individual requires to accomplish *anything at all* in the world as we know it—good, bad, or indifferent. For example, in seeking to persuade you that each individual's cultural endowment deserved treatment as a diagnostic building block, I have not tried to argue that the acquisition of a suitable symbolic repertoire is essential to the cultivation of the Good Life (though I think this is true as well). Instead, it was enough to emphasize that, given the centrality of symbol-manipulation in the social world as we know it, no human being can plausibly achieve *any* objective without gaining *some* kind of competence along this dimension.[7]

Not that my basic power matrix does not itself raise its own kind of deep philosophical questions. Most importantly, I do not claim that [G,C,M,T] represents the only plausible macro-way of defining the basic terms of the power problem, though it should not be too quickly supposed that disagreements on other levels of argument carry over to this level as well. Consider, for example, the "old-fashioned" Marxist belief that only one thing is really important to the power struggle—who owns the means of production. This view, I think, can be readily expressed within my basic framework: what the Marxist is saying is that the T-structure of property rights determines the outcome over power struggles in all four domains. This may be right or wrong (I think it is obviously wrong), but it is not clear to me that the Marxist wants or needs to challenge the basic [G,C,M,T] framework to find out.

But perhaps other explanatory enterprises do raise such fundamental challenges. For example, consider the diagnostics of contemporary feminism. Within my framework, the nerve of the feminist indictment is that human beings who are genetically endowed with an X-chromosome are coercively socialized into a cultural repertoire that encourages their passive subordination to Y-chromosome types; this kind of cultural indoctrination is allowed, in turn, to shape the terms of competition over the control and transfer of material resources in pervasive ways. To the extent that this single-sentence summary captures the feminist critique of power relations, [G,C,M,T] once again represents common diagnostic ground; and one which, as I shall suggest, permits the powerful elaboration of a liberal feminist critique of the status quo. It is possible, however, that some feminists are trying to say more than this; they are proposing a power diagnostic that insists that *sexuality is a term that is no less fundamental in the analysis of power than genes or culture*.

If this is the claim, I can hardly give it the serious treatment it deserves in the short space of a single essay. For the present, it will have to be enough to emphasize that it raises very different questions from those involved in establishing that women are coercively socialized into a culture of subordination. Instead, what is required is an inquiry into the conceptual structure of the particular theories of sexual power under discussion. Does the particular S-theory deploy concepts which are irreducible to theories about [G,C,M,T]? If so, does this point to particular inadequacies in existing theories of [G,C,M,T] or does it suggest that any such four-variable theory cannot give sexual power its explanatory due?

In inviting such questions, I have at least succeeded in laying bare yet another level of presupposition, which exposes the possibility of a second kind of Neutrality critique. In calling for a comparison of my power diagnostic with possible rivals in terms of their "explanatory power," I obviously believe that competing efforts at explanation can be meaningfully evaluated *in terms of their truth*. But does this presupposition make sense?

However different Michael Oakeshott may be from Michel Foucault, their partisans can join together in condemning the very idea of a social science as perhaps *the* illusion of the age, empowering a new class of technocratic shamans to work their will on the rest of us. While this is not the place to explore the foundations (dare I even use the word?) of the Michael/Michel critiques, I should emphasize that, unlike the others addressed in this chapter, I am fundamentally unsympathetic to them. Not that I long for the glory days of the Vienna Circle: surely the relationship between fact and value is far more complex, in both the physical and social sciences, than Carnap imagined. Nonetheless, it hardly follows that there should be no differences at all between the way we try to establish the validity of empirical and normative propositions; and that the effort to do social science is indistinguishable from the sheer exercise of power. If this idea—in either its neo-Burkean obscurantist, or postmodernist trendy, version—carries the field, it will indeed mean the death of the liberal project as I understand it. Are we really willing to abandon as an illusion the idea that men and women might, after an insightful analysis of their relative power positions, use this knowledge to build a world that is more (or less) just than the one they inherited from their predecessors?

Not, mind you, that I want to minimize the dangers of technocratic tyranny which do arise from the use of social science as a tool for social improvement. We are all familiar with the evils that have been perpetuated in the name of social science in this century. Thus, once we strip away the foundational pretention of their critique, there is much to be learned from both neoconservative and postmodernist efforts to expose the extent to which scientism, like any -ism, can be used to cover the perpetration of heinous crimes against humanity.

On the other hand, there is the other hand: the relatively primitive stage of social science is constantly being used to excuse the passive acceptance of injustice—let's study the problem forever while I continue to enjoy my privileged position in the power struggle! Thus, even if we reject the corrosive skepticism of Oakeshott or Foucault, there remains a great challenge for practical statesmanship: how to steer a sensible path between blind interventionism and callous acceptance of the status quo. The practical challenge is to develop a discriminating liberal activism that is alive to the weakness of social science and the dangers of bureaucratic tyranny, but does not allow these very real problems to defeat the hope for realistic and ongoing reform of illegitimate power structures. Easier said than done; and there is nothing neutral in the mix of common sense and analytic ability required for the modern art of liberal statesmanship.[8] While statesman and citizen alike cannot afford to turn their backs on the best social science of their time, they can't afford to give it an uncritical embrace either—not only because the "best" have been corrupted by the promise of money and power, but also because the "best" we have is far from the truth.

The Liberal Solution?

The Place of Dialogue

So much for diagnostics: Even the most incisive power analysis can do us no good without some notion of how we might use it to build a better world. How is this process of political construction to occur?

My answer is through dialogue, in which each of us must be prepared in principle to justify our basic power position to others when they challenge its legitimacy. The basic idea is this: If I can't explain to others why it is right for me to have the power that I have, I shouldn't have it. The limits of our dialogue should mark the limits of my power.

Now the defense of this simple proposition is a multifaceted affair.[9] The facet most relevant here is the way dialogism challenges familiar canards about liberalism and human nature. Whatever its failings may be, dialogic liberalism does not rely on an image of humans as asocial creatures who gain a sense of themselves and their rights in isolation from one another, and view politics as merely a way of safeguarding their "natural rights." Dialogue is, first and foremost, the name of a *social* process of interpersonal interaction. We cannot know the rights we have until we figure out what we can say to one another about our basic power position.

Nor need dialogic liberalism rest on the neo-Kantian foundations that Rawls sought to construct before Sandel's critique cut him short.[10] The case for dialogue in no way depends on the priority of some mysteriously noumenal self unencumbered by its worldly projects and commitments. To the contrary, like it or not, we find ourselves very much encumbered by a struggle for power with every other member of the human race. The question is how we are to respond to this very serious encumbrance: Are we prepared to talk with our fellow humans about the best way to regulate the power struggle or should we try to silence their questions with the use of overwhelming force? (Is there a third way?)

Placing Neutrality in Dialogic Theory

It is within this dialogic framework, and only within this framework, that I mean to defend the ideal of Neutrality. On my understanding, the ideal requires liberal citizens to refrain from making two basic conversational moves as they talk to one another about the basic terms that should regulate their ongoing power struggle. In justifying any particular proposal for regulating each individual's access to [G,C,M,T], no liberal citizen may either assert that: (1) her own ideal of the good life is worthy of special endorsement by the political community as superior to the ideals affirmed by others or (2) she is worthy of special community endorsement as intrinsically superior to fellow citizens on grounds that are independent of the particular ideals that she affirms. A political conversation constrained in these ways is Neutral in two senses—it refuses to express a principled public preference either between citizens or between their ideals of the good.

Upon first inspection, this kind of Neutrality may seem entirely negative. It operates as a *conversational filter,* requiring citizens to eliminate many of the things they might otherwise say to one another to justify their basic power position. To put the point in a simple picture (see Figure 2.1), let A stand for all the things the citizenry might want to say in justification of one or another particular solution to the power problem; what N does is to require citizens to screen their conversational repertoire so as to limit it to those remarks that fall within the N space.

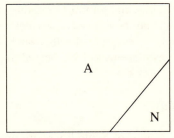

But this simple picture need not be understood in a purely negative spirit. We may think of the liberal's conversational filter as a kind of cultural tool by which citizens may carve out a discursive public space which has been self-consciously structured so as to express certain fundamental normative commitments. Just as a sculptor eliminates many bits of marble that might have been used for expressive purposes, but which are inconsistent with the meaning he wishes to convey, so too the citizenry of a liberal state eliminate certain parts of their expressive repertoire so as to focus their collective energies upon the discursive possibilities that remain: Can they manage to construct a political culture that imposes a meaningful order on the power struggle, without offending the Neutrality constraints?

There are four interesting answers here. The first is a simple no. In terms of our picture, the N-set is empty: no discursive elements remain once the un-Neutral commentaries are chipped away. The second is at the other extreme: A very large number of justifying reasons remain with the N-set, so large that it is possible to find a Neutral reason for any proposed regulation of the power struggle. These two diagnoses represent two familiar critiques of Liberal Neutrality—on the one hand, the ideal may be said to be "bankrupt," in that there is no such thing as a Neutral reason (N-set empty); on the other hand, the ideal may be denounced as an "empty formalism," in that almost any reason can pass the test of Neutrality (N-set [almost] as large as A-set). The other two answers are more promising: One is Uniqueness—here the exercise of conversational constraint reveals that there is one, and only one, discursive element that remains in the N-set that is capable of imposing a dialogic discipline on the struggle for power. The other answer I will call Incisiveness—several different reasons can be articulated within the constraints of Neutrality, which lead to different solutions to the power problem. Under this scenario, no regime is uniquely selected by the method of Neutral dialogue; nonetheless, the number of legitimate dialogic solutions is not so large as to permit any and all regimes to pose as plausible approximations of one or another version of the liberal ideal, hence the dialogic method is sufficiently incisive to identify many possible regimes as positively illegitimate.

Now a principle purpose of my book about *The Liberal State* is to convince you that a commitment to Neutrality leads neither to intellectual bankruptcy nor empty formalism, but to an incisive form of liberal political culture, capable of providing direction for the ongoing reform of existing systems of domination.[11] My aim here, however, cannot be to resolve any doubts you undoubtedly have on this score. It is simply to suggest why this kind of dialogic Neutrality is immune from two critiques it seems to have helped to provoke.

A Third Critique:
Consequentialist Neutrality?

Probably the common critique of Neutrality seems unable to escape the consequentialist orthodoxies of the preceding generation. It seems to imagine that Neutrality is a criterion like Utility, which seeks to judge political decisions by evaluating the outcomes they produce. Suppose, for example, that the political community were assessing the relative merits of two rival proposals to regulate the power struggle over material possessions. One group of citizens propose a political principle that guarantees each person, upon maturity, an equal material endowment with which to start off adult life (the rule of initial equality); the second proposes to leave each citizen's initial material endowment up to the unfettered control of his parents (the rule of parental discretion). How should the political community make its choice?

On this critical (mis)interpretation, the Neutralist proceeds to evaluate the proposal in basically the same manner as the Utilitarian. Thus, just as the latter would seek to determine whether the rule of initial equality or parental discretion would maximize overall utility, so too the Neutralist wants to know which rule produces greater Neutrality.

So understood, Neutrality seems a conceptual nonstarter. Whatever one may say about the utilitarian's inquiry, it makes no sense at all to ask whether the rule of parental discretion is "more neutral" in its consequences than the rule of initial equality. When one rule is compared to the other, it may be perfectly possible to predict, say, that the rule of parental discretion will leave poor orphans worse off than will the rule of initial equality; and vice versa. But it doesn't seem to make any sense to ask which rule has "more neutral" consequences: if you think it good to make poor orphans better off, then choose initial equality; if you think it better to improve the lot of rich parents and their offspring, choose parental discretion. But it is nonsense to assert that one or another of these rules has a neutral impact.[12]

Nor are matters much improved if, in order to make Neutrality more meaningful within a consequentialist framework, we treat it as a (rather inept) synonym for something else. For example, Joseph Raz has suggested that the Neutralist might be understood as insisting that a proposed decision rule has a *proportionate* impact upon those it seeks to regulate—before going on to enumerate the many analytic weaknesses of such a proportionality test.[13]

Lest there be any mistake about it, I agree with Raz's critique.[14] I part company only when it comes to the consequences of repudiating this consequentialist interpretation of Neutrality. Raz's repudiation is part of a ground-clearing operation that prepares the way for a new kind of consequentialism—one that would involve the state, to my mind, making all sorts of intolerant public pronouncements about the nature of "human flourishing."

In contrast, my response is to deny that Neutrality is a way of directly assessing consequences. The key here is to recognize that consequences do not speak for themselves. Only people talk. Moreover, in a dialogic theory, it is the way they talk that determines the legitimacy of their political decisions. Of course, in talking to one another in defense of competing substantive rules, people may well want to appeal to the desirable consequences to justify the public adoption of one or another rule. But it is the way they try to bring these consequences into their justificatory conversation that determines whether their appeal to consequences offends Neutrality. In particular, can the protagonists appeal to consequences in ways that do not violate the conversational constraints imposed by Neutrality? To pursue our hypothetical problem about inheritance, suppose the advocate of the rule of initial equality sought to persuade his fellow citizens to support the rule by arguing that "orphans ought to be benefited because they are intrinsically superior to children of rich parents." This way of appealing to consequences would offend Neutrality since it asserts the intrinsic superiority of one group of citizens (orphans) over another (children of rich parents). Similarly, the advocates of the rule of parental discretion would violate Neutrality by arguing that the polity should commit itself to a reverse ordering of public values. The question is whether either side can appeal to consequences in a way that justifies their proposal in a way that satisfies the Neutrality constraints.

Perhaps one side may succeed here; perhaps both; perhaps neither. I have argued elsewhere that constrained liberal conversation only allows the principled defense of a prima facie right to initial equality in the inheritance of material assets.[15] My aim here, however, is not to review the range of legitimate liberal argument on one or another issue, but to explain why a perfectly valid refutation of outcome-oriented Neutrality simply misses the mark when aimed at the liberal enterprise of constructing a Neutral political culture. It is perfectly okay, of course, for a consequentialist to disagree with my emphasis on Neutral dialogue; but then he is attacking the dialogic foundations of the theory, not its conception of Neutrality.

A Fourth Critique:
The Biases of a Partial Neutrality

While the consequentialist argument against Neutrality was valid in its own terms, it proceeded on a basic misunderstanding of the dialogic foundations of a dialogic theory of liberal legitimacy. Not so, a final critique. To the contrary, it contains an important insight into a recurrent abuse of dialogic methods by liberals, especially when these liberals have been trained as American lawyers. While I believe that a cultural anthropologist would find that this professional group has learned to constrain their repertoire of argument by use of constraints that resemble the Neutrality principle, he or she would also isolate other features of American legal discourse that are far less conducive to the systematic effort to regulate the struggle for power through liberal dialogue. The particular pathology I want to emphasize here has its source in the characteristically piecemeal way that American lawyers approach a problem: while they are happy to discuss one or another concrete case or rule, they exhibit acute discomfort if they are obliged to discuss a matter as "large" as the Law of Contract or Torts, let alone such a vast question as the way legal doctrine, considered as a whole, shapes the basic transactional framework of the modern mixed economy. And yet, as we have seen, even this question only succeeds in focusing upon one fundamental aspect of the power struggle, and is not remotely complete without a comparable analysis of the power systems that control the distribution of genetic, cultural, and material resources in our society.

In remarking upon the particularistic bent of American lawyers, I do not deny the many virtues of this no-nonsense demand that we get down to particular cases if we are ultimately to accomplish something of value. Nonetheless, when they talk of "neutral principles," their particularism continually gets them into trouble. Rather than asking whether *the entire system* of power relations approximates the conclusions that could be reached through Neutral dialogue, these lawyers inquire into the "neutrality" of one or another doctrine or practice as if it could be assessed intelligently without considering its relationship to the larger system.[16]

Consider the workplace. A "neutralist" of the particularist kind I have in mind would seek to assess the legitimacy of power relationships by asking whether a firm treated blacks or women in the same way it treated white males. Such a limited view, however, simply ignores the ways in which women and blacks had been subjected to illegitimate domination at previous stages in their struggle for power. For example, I take it to be pretty obvious that women, as a group, have been the victims of pervasive forms of cultural domination. They have been socialized into a very narrow range of cultural ideals, and have confronted a broad range of coercive sanctions if they departed from socially approved models during their formative years. Since this kind of socialization cannot be justified in a Neutral dialogue, it is hardly neutral of the particularist to ignore the way it continues to shape life in the workplace. Such blindness only allows the beneficiaries of an un-Neutral advantage at an early stage in life to insulate their power from critique at later stages of life. If this is Neutrality, the less of it the better!

This, alas, has been the verdict of many black and feminist activists who have encountered neutralism principally in its legal particularist guise.[17] But there is a big price to be paid for this misdiagnosis. Rather than calling upon American law to reject particularism so to better live up to its claim of Neutrality, many have rejected Neutrality while remaining remarkably uncritical in their acceptance of particularism. This has been especially true of those who have allied themselves with the so-called Critical Legal Studies Movement, which has used the word "positivist" to condemn social scientific efforts to trace systemwide consequences of illiberal stereotyping in the educational system and the maldistribution of wealth in the economic system. In terms of our power diagnostic, the challenge is to understand the complex ways in which injustice in the distribution of [G,C,M] can be plausibly rectified in designing the rules for regulating [T], the transactional structure within which adults form and reform their institutional and contractual relationships within which they engage in their working lives.

Analytically, the situation is comparable to the one economists call the "problem of second best." As Lipsey and Lancaster have shown,[18] once an economy is afflicted with monopolies and other market imperfections, even those sectors that are reasonably close to the competitive ideal may no longer escape systemic critique. Similarly here: even a transactional system which would be reasonably close to liberal ideals may well require substantial modification given the way it serves to perpetuate underlying injustices in the [G,C,M] subsystems. Of course, over time, it is better to respond to these injustices by acting directly on the underlying subsystem. In the case of women, this means that we must deepen our polity's commitment to liberal education—an education which aims to provide each child with the cultural materials that will allow her, over time, to move beyond the effort by her parents and other primary educators to monopolize her moral vision, an education which allows her to shape her self-understanding without accepting the compulsions of traditionalist blinders.[19] But it will be a long time before this will be accomplished. Until that time it will be necessary to confront the liberal perplexities of "second-best" policy—how to rectify underlying injustice in [G,C,M] while retaining a T-system that allows a substantial degree of freedom for all to pursue their ideals in association with like-minded others?

While I have presented some tentative suggestions elsewhere,[20] I am not at all satisfied with them. The only thing that is clear is that the search for practical second-best accommodations is unlikely to be advanced unless liberals move beyond particularism and recognize that the aim is to regulate *the entire power system* in a way that can be defended as a plausible approximation of the outcomes that could be reached by citizens seeking to construct a Neutral political culture.

Conclusion

This has been a search for common ground. Even more than many of my critics, I accept the need for a comprehensive analysis of the power struggle, and a resolute effort to root the dialogic assessment of particular institutions in a larger framework that takes systemic injustice into account (Critiques One and Four). I also agree that it is silly to think that there is any such thing as a Neutral outcome (Critique Three) and that it is dangerous to put too much faith—or too little—in our scientific capacity to understand the power struggle in which we are engaged (the modest half of Critique Two).

Four critiques, leading to more clarity about the aims and hopes of liberal dialogue? But surely there are many more questions, many more answers and no final solutions.

Notes

1. Bruce Ackerman, *Social Justice in the Liberal State* (New Haven: Yale University Press, 1980).

2. C. Geertz, *The Interpretation of Cultures* (New York: 1973).

3. See, P. Bachrach and M. Baratz, "Two Faces of Power," *American Political Science Review* 56 (1962): 947–52.

4. See Ackerman, *Social Justice in the Liberal State*, Chap. 4.

5. For a useful elaboration of this idea, see J. Coleman, *Markets, Morals and the Law*, Chap. 2 (Cambridge: 1988).

6. The most influential works of this kind written recently are by Robert Nozick, *Anarchy, State, and Utopia* (New York: 1974) and David Gauthier, *Morality by Agreement* (Oxford: 1986). Perhaps the word "libertarian" better describes these books' intention than does the word "liberal." Whatever one calls them, the crucial point is to see that, even before we begin to inspect the character of their proposed solutions to the problem of power, we should reject these books on the basis of their painfully inadequate model of power.

7. From this angle, there might seem to be a certain family resemblance between these basic power variables and Rawls's idea of primary social goods: goods which it would be rational for his ignorant contractors to value even though they are ignorant as to their more particular moral ideals and objectives. But appearances here are misleading. I'm interested in the realities of power; he is interested in a "thin" conception of the good, which can be used as the foundation of an appropriately liberal theory of justice. It is true, of course, that once I have developed a satisfactory model of the power struggle, I shall then use it to define a normative problem: How are all of us power strugglers going to resolve our struggle on reasonable terms? But I think there are many advantages in keeping the model of the power struggle as free as possible of the morally controversial elements of the kind that Rawls helps himself to in formulating his "thin" theory, especially the one to be found in his Dewey Lectures, "Kantian Constructivism in Moral Theory," *Journal of Philosophy* 77 (1980): 515–72.

8. For more on this aspect of the matter, see my *Reconstructing American Law* (Cambridge, MA: 1984); and my "Constitutional Politics/Constitutional Law," *Yale Law Journal* 99 (1989): 453.

9. See my "Why Dialogue?" *Journal of Philosophy* 86 (1989): 5–22.

10. M. Sandel, *Liberalism and the Limits of Justice* (Cambridge: 1982). For Rawls's rejoinder, which, in my mind, inaugurated a sharp change in the direction of his thought, see "Justice as Fairness: Political not Metaphysical," 14 (1985): 223–51.

11. Note here that I am only claiming incisiveness, not uniqueness.

12. In the language of economics, one may say that the "opportunity cost" of adopting one rule is precisely the consequences foregone by failing to adopt the other.

13. J. Raz, *The Morality of Freedom* (Oxford: 1986), p. 112, where he presents two conceptions of Neutrality, both consequentialist in character, and then proceeds, at pp. 117–24, to show why these are conceptually impossible.

14. See Ackerman, *Social Justice in the Liberal State*, pp. 49–53.

15. See ibid., Chap. 7.

16. For a classic statement of this kind of particularistic Neutrality, see H. Wechsler, "Toward Neutral Principles of Constitutional Law," *Harvard Law Review* 73 (1959): 1–35.

17. This seems to be at the root of Catherine MacKinnon's unceasing denunciation of liberalism and neutrality, see, e.g., her *Feminism Unmodified* (Cambridge MA: 1987), Chap. 2, though it may be that she is also making the far more fundamental objection to the model of power that I outlined earlier. So far as a critique of particularist Neutrality on the matter of race relations is concerned, nothing I have read recently manages to equal Charles Black's great essay on "The Lawfulness of the Segregation Decisions," *Yale Law Journal* 69 (1960): 421–30.

18. R.G. Lipsey and K. Lancaster, "The General Theory of the Second Best," *Rev. of Econ. Studies* 24 (1956): 11–32.

19. See Ackerman, *Social Justice in the Liberal State*, Chap. 5.

20. See ibid., Part 3.

3

How Not to Defend
Liberal Institutions

Brian Barry

Introduction

My object in this chapter is to ask how liberal institutions, liberal laws, and liberal policies can be justified. In particular, I want to ask what arguments are available to persuade people who are not liberals—people who do not have a liberal outlook on life—that they ought nevertheless to subscribe to liberal institutions. I will examine four such arguments, three traditional and one recent, and conclude that they are either limited in scope or dependent on dubious factual premises. The implications to be drawn is the rather depressing one that the only people who can be relied on to defend liberal institutions are liberals.

Let me explain briefly, before I go any further, what I mean by liberal institutions. I believe that there are three features that defined liberal states as they emerged in the seventeenth and eighteenth centuries. These were: religious toleration, freedom of the press, and the abolition of servile civil status. Modern liberal institutions may be seen as extensions of each of these elements in the historic core. Thus, the principle of religious toleration has been generalized to the "harm principle": the principle that people should be free to act as they wish provided they do not harm others. Freedom of the press has been generalized to cover freedom of expression of all kinds. And the principle that there should be no servile civil status has been generalized to a concept of equal citizenship rights due to everyone without regard to social class, race, or gender. There are, of course, many disputes about the formulation of these generalizations of the venerable liberal institutions. But nothing I have to say will turn on the precise way in which such disputes are resolved.

The other expression that I have used is 'a liberal outlook,' and I want now to

I am grateful for comments to participants in the conference, members of the Carlyle Club, the audience at the annual public lecture sponsored by the Centre for Criminology and the Social and Philosophical Study of Law at the University of Edinburgh, Peter Jones, and Albert Weale. Also, special thanks to the *British Journal of Political Science* where this essay first appeared.

explain what I mean by that. Again, I suggest that we should approach the question historically. Liberalism is par excellence the doctrine of the Enlightenment, and by liberal ideas I intend to refer to the attitudes characteristic of the Enlightenment. There is no definitive list, but I shall again suggest three ideas that it would be hard to exclude. First is the belief that inequalities are a social artifact, and therefore have to be justified on a basis that starts from a premise of the fundamental equality of all human beings. Second is the belief that every doctrine should be open to critical scrutiny and that no view should be held unless it has in fact withstood critical scrutiny. And third is the belief that no religious dogma can reasonably be held with certainty.

It so happens that I agree with these ideas, but it is no part of my purpose here to defend them. (In any case John Stuart Mill seems to me to have done a good enough job already.) What I am concerned with is, rather, the logical relations between these liberal ideas and support for liberal institutions. First, I will show (what is not very difficult) that the possession of liberal ideas is a sufficient condition for supporting liberal institutions. Then I address the central problem of this chapter: how far the possession of liberal ideas is a necessary condition of support for liberal institutions.

From Liberal Ideas to
Liberal Institutions

If liberal attitudes had been defined in terms of support for liberal institutions, it would be a logical necessity that people with liberal attitudes support liberal institutions. As it is, however, the two have been defined independently. There is, nevertheless, a strong connection between them in that, given some reasonable assumptions about the way in which the world works, liberal attitudes should give rise to support for liberal institutions. Let us take in turn the key features of liberal institutions outlined at the beginning of the paper, and see how each may be derived from elements on the list of liberal attitudes just presented.

We begin, then, with religious toleration. If all claims to religious truth (including dogmatic atheism) deserve a skeptical reception, it is surely a plausible implication that no religious faith should ever be put in a position that enables it to coerce people into adhering to it or be granted a monopoly of schooling. What about the modern extension of religious toleration to the idea of a "private sphere" within which people should be free from state-imposed constraints? The connection with liberal attitudes is less immediately apparent here, but it can still be traced. For if religious beliefs are too doubtful to provide a solid basis for the persecution of deviant religions, they are by the same token too doubtful to underpin the suppression of behavior which constitutes no threat to the public but is condemned as sinful by the tenets of some religion.

This would be conclusive if everybody who claimed that an act of a certain kind was immoral though harmless to the community was explicit in grounding the claim upon the authority of some religion. However, we find people in contemporary societies who are prepared to say that, for example, homosexual acts between consenting adults are wrong, even though they are not willing to invoke any tenet of religion to back up their claim. What are we to make of this? I think that here (though only here) Alasdair MacIntyre's diagnosis of the modern predicament is valid.[1] That is to say, the moral condemnation of acts that are not harmful to others makes sense only against a background of religious belief. Take that away and words like "wrong" and "immoral" in such contexts become literally unintelligible. It is clear that the things subject to this kind of free-floating condemnation are precisely the same as those condemned on religious grounds. The phenomenon is one of a sort of religious hangover. From a liberal point of view, we may surely conclude that, if religiously based condemnation of harmless acts is inadequate to ground their legal suppression, then condemnation of harmless acts that does not rest on any intelligible basis at all is even less adequate.

Freedom of the press, and, by extension, freedom of expression in general would seem to follow pretty straightforwardly from the premium that the liberal outlook places on critical thinking. For although it could hardly be said that the absence of prohibitions is a sufficient condition for a society of free thinkers, we may at the same time say that it is hard to see how critical attitudes could be fostered by the suppression of ideas. Finally, the opposition to servile civil status, and by extension to other legal inequalities such as the legal disabilities of women, can be plausibly seen as the working out of the implications of the premise of fundamental equality.

A point which is worth drawing attention to here, since it will be of crucial importance later in the chapter, is that support for liberal institutions by no means exhausts the policy implications of the liberal outlook. (This confirms their logical independence, as I have defined them.) Even in what I described as their modern extended form, these liberal institutions are quite limited in their scope, in that they are concerned exclusively with civil rights. But the liberal vision of the good life points toward a more active role for the state. As the "new liberals" pointed out,[2] the spirit of critical thinking and the practice of autonomous decision-making favored by the liberal outlook can be fostered by positive state action. Formal rights embodied in liberal institutions have material conditions for their enjoyment. What is especially relevant here is that the kind of critical inquiring spirit valued by liberals will be aided by such things as subsidizing the dissemination of the results of social scientific research that challenges existing prejudices and stereotypes, and by underwriting the costs of publishing books and the costs of producing plays that present new ways of looking at things. Above all, an educational system designed to foster a liberal outlook will be one that encourages independent thinking and in particular works to undercut religious dogmatism by promoting the active questioning of all religious beliefs.

Liberalism for Nonliberals:
Traditional Arguments

I shall take it that a liberal outlook has been established to be a sufficient condition of support for liberal institutions. The question now to be raised is, how far is it a necessary condition? To answer this question we must ask whether there are valid arguments that can be addressed to nonliberals to show them that they too have good reason to support liberal institutions. Let us begin by looking at three arguments that have been put forward in the past. These are: the argument from *social peace,* the argument from *prudence,* and the argument from *inefficacy.*

The argument from social peace runs as follows. Suppose we have a society which is roughly equally divided between the followers of two sects, denominations, or religions, each of which is officially committed to using state power to compel universal adherence to its tenets. Then it can be said (and frequently was in the seventeenth and eighteenth centuries) that the only chance of achieving social peace is for both sides to abandon their demands and instead settle for a general policy of religious tolerance. This argument is, obviously, perfectly sound as far as it goes. But it must be observed that its force presupposes that those addressed by it attribute a high value to social peace and are thus at any rate to that extent already secularized.

The argument from prudence avoids this problem by suggesting that under some conditions a concern for the ability to practice one's own religion should lead to agreement on a policy of toleration. Thus, suppose again that rival religious groups are evenly balanced within a society. Then it can be said to each group: if you fight, you may win and be able (at whatever cost) to impose your beliefs on all the members of the society. But it is equally possible that if you fight you may lose and have an alien set of beliefs imposed on you. In this situation, religious toleration presents itself as a maximum strategy for both sides, not giving either the outcome that it wants most but guaranteeing it against the outcome that it wants least.

This argument has the advantage over the first of making religious claims self-limiting. But it has in common with the first the feature that its cogency depends upon there actually being a balance of forces within the society. It thus brings no comfort to unpopular minorities, especially powerless ones. Since it is of the essence of liberal laws and policies that they should protect minorities, it is clear that these arguments cannot be said to provide general support for them.

The argument from inefficacy breaks out of these limitations. Rather, it seeks to show that persecution is pointless because it fails to achieve the ends of the persecutors. The argument, which was like the others commonly made in the seventeenth and eighteenth centuries, ran along the following lines.[3] What matters is religious belief, not religious practice. But belief cannot be coerced. Therefore religious persecution is pointless, because it cannot achieve its justifying end.

The argument depends on the following assumptions, all of which are questionable: (1) the sole purpose of coercion is the salvation of the person coerced; (2) salvation is a matter of inner belief rather than outward observance; and (3) coercion cannot produce alterations in inner belief. The first premise is the most vulnerable. The persecutor may be less concerned with converting existing heretics than with preventing them from gaining new adherents from the ranks of the currently orthodox, and for this purpose it may well be sufficient to prohibit all outward manifestations of the heretical belief. Even more importantly, the persecutor may well consider that, in the great scheme of things, saving the souls of the present generation of adults is of trivial significance compared with what is at stake in saving the souls of their descendants. And here the historical record is extremely clear. Most of the contemporary adherents of Islam are the descendants of people who originally adopted it at the point of a sword, but the quality of their faith today is no less for that. The same goes for many Protestant and Catholic areas in Europe. The effectiveness of coercion in producing genuine belief over the course of a few generations is beyond question.

I pass more briefly over assumptions (2) and (3), simply observing in connection with (2) that, whatever may be the case with Christianity, some other religions appear to attach primary importance to the carrying out of prescribed rituals rather than to the state of mind of the person carrying them out. And as far as (3) is concerned, it is by no means evident that beliefs cannot be changed by coercion. If outward conformity is obtained by coercion, the machinery of cognitive dissonance reduction comes into play to create a pressure toward bringing belief into line with performance.

When we shift from beliefs to actions, this third argument becomes even weaker. Suppose we accepted that coercion is inefficacious in inducing belief. It is a good deal less implausible to think that it must be inefficacious in suppressing what is deemed to be wrong behavior. If you believe that, say, homosexual acts are wrong, prohibiting them by law will, it seems reasonable to suggest, at any rate reduce their incidence.

A version of (3) could be maintained independently of any facts about human psychology by stipulating th ᐧ God does not assign any value to religious beliefs acquired under duress. This would rule out coercion justified entirely by its beneficial effects on those concerned. But it would not rule out coercion motivated by the other ends mentioned above. And in any case it has to be observed that the relevant view of the Deity is one that is far from universal among religious believers. Moreover, this variant is no more successful in relation to actions than is the argument from inefficacy. For even those who take the view that true beliefs brought about under duress are of no value may well think that right acts brought about by duress, while no doubt less valuable than right acts chosen freely, are still not without value. Those who believe some kind of act to be wrong will normally think it better if such acts do not occur, even if the motive for refraining from them is fear of punishment.

Let me make it clear that I have no wish to disparage the significance of these three arguments. They were unquestionably crucial in the development of liberal states. The beginnings of liberal institutions antedate the prevalence of liberal attitudes, and it was precisely pragmatic arguments of the kind outlined here that led to support for such practices as religious toleration. Nevertheless, such pragmatic arguments are valid only under quite restrictive conditions and even then limited in the range of activities they cover.

It is true that we move away from pragmatism with the variant of the third argument that ascribes value only to freely chosen beliefs and actions. But this is in itself a viewpoint characteristic of liberal individualism and is by no means standard among religious believers. What we are looking for, it should be recalled, is an argument that can be addressed to nonliberals to induce them to support liberal institutions while retaining intact their nonliberal attitudes. This requirement is not met by showing that converting people with nonliberal religious ideas to liberal religious ideas would result in their supporting liberal institutions. The pragmatic arguments do meet the requirement, but with severe limits. We are still, therefore, left seeking an argument of general applicability that is (a) addressed to nonliberals and (b) not designed to operate by changing their basic nonliberal outlook.

Liberalism for Nonliberals: Neutrality

Can the problem tackled unsuccessfully by the traditional arguments still nevertheless be solved? In recent years several political philosophers have taken up the challenge, and proposed a principle that is claimed to generate support for liberal institutions without invoking liberal premises. This is the principle of neutrality: the principle that states should, as a matter of justice, be neutral between different ideas of the good. What is meant by this is that in their laws and public policies states should avoid doing anything to favor one idea of the good over others. "Idea of the good" is here something of a term of art, including such things as religious beliefs, moral convictions, or judgments of value, such as the superiority of poetry to pushpin.

The names most prominently associated with the principle of neutrality are those of Bruce Ackerman, Ronald Dworkin, and John Rawls.[4] It is hardly surprising that the first two are professors of law who cut their teeth on the decisions of the Warren Court, while the closeness of Rawls's thought to American constitutional jurisprudence has often been noticed. For the best way of looking at the principle of neutrality is to see it as a generalization of the line of postwar Supreme Court cases that interpreted with increasing stringency the constitutional requirement that Congress shall make no law establishing a religion.

What is the rationale of the principle of neutrality? It might be defended on pragmatic grounds similar to those canvassed in the previous section. But even if such an argument were successful as far as it went, it would go no further than the pragmatic arguments in favor of liberal institutions themselves. What we are seeking is an ethical justification of the principle of neutrality. Does one exist?

There is indeed an argument, and it is one that claims to derive neutrality from a consideration of the demands of distributive justice. The argument runs as follows. We imagine a society as made up of a set of individuals each of whom has an ordered set of wants, derived from biological needs, conceptions of the good, and so on. The society at the same time disposes of various resources, a resource being defined as something whose deployment is a means to the satisfaction of wants. These resources include money (a means to the satisfaction of whatever wants lend themselves to satisfaction through the market); legal rights, such as the right of free expression and the right to worship the god of one's choice (as President Eisenhower once felicitously put it); and opportunities, such as the opportunity to enter Harvard Law School. We then pose the problem of justice as that of allocating these resources among the claimants. And the answer we give is that a prima facie just distribution is an equal one. Our three theorists have somewhat different answers to the question of what justifies a departure from equality. We need not follow them into these ramifications, however. For there is one point on which they all agree, and that is the negative point that what *cannot* count as a good reason for allocating a smaller share of resources to one person than he would otherwise be entitled to is that he would use these resources to pursue unworthy ends. This is the principle of neutrality, the principle that public policy should not be based on an evaluation of people's conceptions of the good. If we go on to assert "the priority of the right over the good," so that considerations of justice trump all others, we can conclude that the principle of neutrality should be the organizing principle of every society.

Now it is no part of my object to deny (though others have done so) that the principle of neutrality can be operationalized. Nor do I wish to deny that when the principle of neutrality is operationalized it leads to the endorsement of liberal policy prescriptions. If we follow up Rawls's hint that we are looking for the maximum equal liberty, it is hard to see how we could do other than support equal rights of worship and of expression, with no restrictions on what people can do in practicing their religion or expressing themselves provided they do not harm others—"harm" being interpreted pretty robustly here so as to exclude shocked sensibilities from its scope. Equal citizenship rights also follow straightforwardly from neutrality, at any rate when it is combined with the egalitarian premise common to Ackerman, Dworkin, and Rawls.

So far so good. Have we then succeeded in deriving liberal policy prescriptions without relying on liberal attitudes? What might lead us to think so is that we have called upon something called a principle of neutrality. If the principle of neutrality were itself neutral between different belief systems and conceptions of the good, we would be home and dry. But this is not so. The principle of neutrality does indeed put them all on the same footing, but to accept that this is how things ought to be organized it is necessary to have an outlook that is, in broad terms, liberal.

The simplest way of illustrating this point is to take Ronald Dworkin's idea that what he calls "external preferences" should not be counted in the calculus of wants operated to determine public policies. What this means can be explained as follows. Suppose I have certain wants derived from my sexual orientation. These are unproblematic, and should go into the calculus. But suppose I also have a preference that you should be frustrated in satisfying wants derived from your sexual orientation, because it conflicts with my theory of the good. This is an "external" preference and should not be counted because there is no reason why my preference for your not being able to pursue your conception of the good should lead to your having a less than equal opportunity to pursue it. This would be to impose an unfair burden on you. The case just given is referred to as "the present argument" in the following quotation:

> It is often said that [the] liberal thesis [that the government has no right to enforce popular morality by law] is inconsistent with utilitarianism, because if the preferences of the majority that homosexuality should be repressed, for example, are sufficiently strong, utilitarianism must give way to their wishes. But the preference against homosexuality is an external preference and the present argument provides a general reason why utilitarians should not count external preferences of any form. If utilitarianism is suitably reconstituted so as to count only personal preferences, then the liberal thesis is a consequence, not an enemy of that theory.[5]

To see what is wrong with this let us ask the following simple question: Under what conditions could Dworkin's proposed formulation have any application? It would have none in a society of utilitarians, because in such a society the problem of what Dworkin calls "moralistic preferences" could not arise in the first place. For there could be no "popular morality" that held things to be wrong for any reason other than they were contrary to the maximization of utility, since, by definition, everyone would apply the utilitarian principle in determining what was wrong.

Now consider a society whose common morality was based upon some set of beliefs antithetical to utilitarianism, for example, a society in which people took their morality from the priests or mullahs. Obviously the members of such a society would have no time for utilitarian criteria in any shape or form. So once again Dworkin's reformulated utilitarianism would hold no interest for them.

The only use I can see for Dworkin's proposal is that it might be construed as advice to the utilitarians in a society many of whose members were not utilitarians. On this interpretation, it would tell them how to factor in the preferences of these nonutilitarians when applying the utilitarian calculus in order to decide what they thought public policy should be. And if in such a society the utilitarians controlled the government, public policy would then be founded upon Dworkin's version of utilitarianism. However, although Dworkin's proposal would have application in such a context, a problem still remains. For the moral beliefs of the nonutilitarians would then be treated in a way that they would regard as a travesty. It could therefore scarcely be put forward as a way of dealing in a generally acceptable fashion with differing "conceptions of the good."

What I mean by saying that the nonutilitarians could not accept Dworkin's proposal is that to do so they would have to abandon their own conception of the status of their moral convictions. They could never agree that these convictions should be discounted as "external preferences" because they would regard "preference" as a wholly inappropriate category in which to put them.

Once concede that it is merely a matter of whose preference gets satisfied and it is indeed hard to deny that someone who wants to have his "external preferences" to count is being greedy. But of course someone who really believes that homosexual acts are sinful and wicked will disclaim any notion that they should be prohibited to please him. Rather, he will say that if it is a matter of pleasing anyone it is a matter of pleasing God. But really, he will add, pleasing is not what it's all about. Homosexual acts are wrong and that is why the law should prohibit them.

It is not essential to the argument from neutrality that one should follow Dworkin's crass suggestion that moral convictions ought to be treated as mere "preferences" and then rejected as a basis for public policy on the ground that they are an inappropriate kind of preference. John Rawls has proposed an alternative approach that leaves moral convictions to be regarded as falling into the category of beliefs rather than that of preferences, but suggests that they should be held in a special way that precludes their being translated into public policy.

According to Rawls, we should seek in a contemporary pluralistic society to base public policy on uncontroversial beliefs. All conceptions of the good (in which Rawls includes religious doctrines) are, Rawls says, inherently controversial. Therefore neutrality between different conceptions of the good must be the watchword of such a society.[6] On this view, people with illiberal beliefs— about the wickedness of homosexuality, for example—can continue to hold them without challenge. But they must hold these beliefs in a special way: as private opinions that they do not seek to impose on anybody else through the machinery of the state.

There is no doubt that some people do in fact adopt the position recommended by Rawls. John F. Kennedy, to give a prominent example, undertook when running for the presidency not to allow himself in exercising the office to be influenced by the teachings of the Roman Catholic Church on public issues. But the point to be made about this phenomenon is essentially the same as that already made in the context of Dworkin's idea that people should not ask to have their "external preferences" put into the calculus of public policy. This point is simply that any understanding of the Church's teachings that treats them as matters of personal opinion is profoundly at odds with the claims that the Church itself makes for its teachings. Exactly the same can be said of those who derive their notions of right and wrong directly from an authoritative book such as the Bible rather than from an authoritative organization such as the Roman Catholic Church. Either way, for someone to be prepared to say "Homosexuality is wrong but that's just my private opinion" he or she must already have swallowed a large dose of liberalism.

What such a person is saying is that wrongful acts fall into two categories. There are those that are wrong because they injure others. These are legitimate objects of prohibition, though the principle of *de minimis non curat lex* may imply that in some cases they should not actually be prohibited. Then there are those that are wrong because they are condemned by some authoritative religious book or body. Some of these acts will also be wrong because they injure people (for example, murder). Others, however, will be wrong only in the second way, and these are not legitimate objects of prohibition. Of course, even if one believed that a wrongful but harmless kind of act could legitimately be prohibited, one might still be against actually prohibiting it for practical reasons.[7] But on the view we are now discussing prohibition is ruled out in principle, so that the practical issues do not even come into play.

We should observe that this second sense of "wrong," which has no potential implications for law or public policy, is a very weak one. Operationally, saying that something is wrong in the second (and not also in the first) sense would seem to commit one to little more than refraining from the act oneself. This is plainly to withdraw what are usually the major implications of saying something is wrong. When I said that the position presupposes that the person holding it has already swallowed a large dose of liberalism, what I had in mind was this: it is hard to see how anyone could hold it except on the basis of a skeptical attitude toward the religious teachings which provided the basis for the belief in the wrongness of certain nonharmful acts.

If I am right about this, we have to abandon as illusory the hope that people might be left undisturbed in their dogmatic slumbers while somehow being cajoled into accepting liberal policy prescriptions. Dogmatism must give way to skepticism before the appropriately attenuated concept of wrongness can become attractive. I would, indeed, speculate (through the truth of this speculation is inessential to my overall argument) that the position advocated by Rawls, and many other liberals, finds few adherents. From a psychological point of view I suspect that it is radically unstable, and tends to function as a half-way house between the thought that homosexual acts (say) are wrong in the old-fashioned sense and the thought that they are not wrong at all. Thus if we take the proportion of the population that, according to British or American surveys, would like to see homosexual acts prohibited, and make a guess about the proportion that thinks there is nothing wrong with homosexuality, it looks as if people who believe it is wrong but should not be prohibited must be very thin on the ground. To put it bluntly, I wonder how many of the philosophers who espouse the Dworkinian or Rawlsian position personally believe that there are kinds of acts that are wrong in spite of not being harmful. My guess is that the doctrine is usually offered for general consumption by people who have no use for it themselves.

Should Liberals Embrace Neutrality?

The conclusion at which I arrive is, then, that a liberal outlook is not only a sufficient condition for supporting liberal institutions but is also (except in circumstances where the arguments discussed in Section 2 apply) a necessary condition. Or, more precisely, this is the conclusion that must be held until we find some better argument than that from justice for the principle of neutrality—and I find it hard to believe that any such argument is waiting to be discovered.

What I have suggested is that there is no way in which nonliberals can be sold the principle of neutrality without first injecting a large dose of liberalism into their outlook. But I now want to add that, unattractive as the principle of neutrality must be to nonliberals, it is not necessarily very attractive even to liberals. For although a liberal outlook does support liberal institutions, it goes beyond them, as I suggested in Section 2. And the destination to which it goes is not neutrality.

This point can be brought home by examining the reasons given by Ackerman for espousing the principle of neutrality. One is that "you might think that you can only learn anything true about the good when you are free to experiment in life without some authoritative teacher intervening whenever he thinks you're going wrong. And if you think this, Neutrality seems made to order." Another is that "you may adopt a conception of the good that gives a central place to autonomous deliberation and deny that it is possible to *force* someone to be good. On this view, the intrusion of non-Neutral argument into power talk will seem self-defeating at best—since it threatens to divert people from the true means of cultivating a truly good life."[8] The ideas that Ackerman outlines here clearly correspond to my description of liberal attitudes. But the confidence with which he asserts that they naturally lead to support for neutrality seems misplaced. In fact, Ackerman's arguments would seem to underwrite support for liberal policy prescriptions but not for the principle of neutrality. For the liberal conception of the good, which is what Ackerman is in effect building on, can be promoted by the state in the kinds of ways mentioned in Section 2. If we want to prevent intervention by authoritative teachers, we shall do better to insist that parents should not be allowed to send their children to schools that teach some inherently dubious doctrine as unquestionable truth than to allow them to do so on the ground that we have (for purposes of public policy) no idea whether such indoctrination is a good thing or not. Similarly, autonomy is not likely to be fostered by a society which treats the ideal of human good that gives a heavy weight to autonomy as just one ideal among many and no better than any others. The bogey of forcing people to be good can be laid to rest once we bear in mind that enforcing the criminal law is only a tiny part (albeit an important one) of what a modern state does, and that much of its activity is facilitative rather than repressive.

I think that there is nevertheless a line of argument that can be addressed to liberals. As we have seen, the problem with neutrality is that it asks people with moral convictions to treat them as external preferences or matters of personal opinion. This goes as much for those with liberal beliefs as for those with nonliberal ones. It can, however, be suggested that liberals suffer substantially less than nonliberals from the truncation exercised on their beliefs by the operation of the principle of neutrality. For although liberals believe, of course, that it is better if people are more rather than less capable of making up their own minds and steering their own course through life, it is only in really extreme cases that they have a sense that departure from their standards is actually wrong, as against simply being unfortunate. A liberal will tend to regard the denial of autonomy as actually wrong only in cases where it is so gross that it can reasonably be regarded (at any rate from the liberal point of view) as constituting harm. Nonliberals, by contrast, characteristically do think that a variety of practices that would be protected by the principle of neutrality are wrong, typically on the basis of some religious authority. If we take the view that being prevented from prohibiting what you believe to be wrong is a more severe restriction than being prevented from promoting what you believe to be good, we can conclude that the principle of neutrality bears more harshly on nonliberals than on liberals.

Another way of approaching the same conclusion is to observe that neutrality underwrites the liberal policy prescriptions outlined in Section 1, and that these are congruent with liberal attitudes. Nonliberals, however, will tend to find that the liberal policy prescriptions, at any rate as extended from the classical core to include the notion of a "private sphere," run counter to the policies that they would favor. Thus, we once again arrive at the point that neutrality suits liberals better than it suits nonliberals.

It has to be said that nothing immediately follows from this. But it does lend some support for the idea that liberals could afford to be generous and pull back from the implementation of the full liberal program, adopting instead the principle of neutrality. In doing so they would perhaps be lending some credence to the gibe that a liberal is someone who is not prepared to take his own side in an argument. But it could be suggested that this kind of forbearance—in effect applying liberal skepticism to liberal beliefs—redounds to their credit.

It has to be observed, however, that this line of reasoning does nothing to advance the cause of neutrality as a general solution for conflicts among rival conceptions of the good. It would be nice if the liberal could say, "There you are. We adopt neutrality when in power. So you should reciprocate by adopting it when *you* are in power." But this is liable not to cut much ice with a nonliberal. Nor, I suggest, is there any good reason why it should.

It is a familiar idea that to be consistent a society committed to liberal policy prescriptions should tolerate Nazi or Communist propaganda. But this has no implication that a Nazi or Communist regime should allow liberal propaganda. Liberalism is true to itself by opening the public sphere to Nazis and Communists. But Naziism and Communism (at any rate as understood in the Soviet Union until now) would be false to themselves by failing to control the flow of information so as to ensure that only "correct" ideas are disseminated.

This provides an analogy (though I emphasize that it is no more than that) for the point to be made about neutrality. If we apply liberal skepticism to liberal beliefs we get neutrality. But there is no similar pressure from considerations of internal consistency to get a dogmatist to apply liberal skepticism to his beliefs. A dogmatist is consistent all the way down by holding his beliefs dogmatically.

I have presented an argument that can be addressed to people with a liberal outlook to press them toward neutrality. I have, however, been careful not to endorse the argument myself. I shall conclude this essay by offering two reasons for doubting that liberals should embrace neutrality.

The first reason for questioning the argument is that it relies on the implicit assumption that liberal beliefs are on all fours with dogmatic beliefs. But we must ask if this kind of self-depreciating stance is warranted. A dogmatist, for the purposes of this discussion, is not simply someone who adheres to a dogma, but someone who adheres to it dogmatically. This means that he wishes the young to be brought up in it without any opportunity to question it, and wishes to shield it from public debate. Inasfar as his dogma condemns certain types of action, he considers it legitimate to use the state to attempt to suppress them, even if they would be immune under liberal policy prescriptions.

A liberal, by contrast, has no objection to anyone holding a dogma, so long as it is not held dogmatically—that is to say, so long as it has to take its chances in competition with other ideas. Again, liberals want to open up more opportunities for people to express themselves rather than prevent them from doing things that pose no harm to the public. It seems reasonable to suggest on the basis of these contrasts that departures from neutrality in a liberal direction have a different status from departures in a nonliberal direction. It is not simply a matter of saying, "This kind of thing is all right when I do it but not when you do it" because the "kind of thing" involved is actually different in its nature.

The second reason for doubting that liberals should abandon liberalism for neutrality is that the defense of liberal institutions requires those with a liberal outlook to go on the offensive and promote liberalism actively. If I am right in this chapter, there is little chance of selling neutrality to nonliberals, which means that nonliberals will continue to hold views about the proper role of state action that run counter to liberal policy prescriptions. Even if he has no wish to promote liberal attitudes as an end in itself, anyone attached to the liberal institutions sketched in Section 2 is going to have to recognize that their prospects of survival depend on there being in the population a large proportion of people with a liberal outlook.

The optimistic hope of the Enlightenment was that the cessation of persecution and censorship would over time lead to the triumph of liberal attitudes. We know now that things do not work like that. These purely negative conditions leave the outcome to the play of social forces that are not necessarily favorable to liberal values. The rise of fascism within societies with liberal institutions showed the vulnerability of those institutions in the most dramatic way possible. Currently the retreat from liberalism is far less dramatic but the evidence is there for all to see. The churches that have made the biggest concessions to liberalism are losing ground while those that strain credulity the most gain the most adherents. (The international success of the Mormons is the most remarkable exemplification of this rule.) The popular press in Britain (and wherever else Rupert Murdoch has penetrated) reinforces and makes respectable the more atavistic impulses of its readers. The idea is gaining ground that schools should teach what parents want taught. And so on.

Under these conditions, I do not think that liberals can afford the luxury of unilateral disarmament. Very likely we are headed for a new Dark Age, and nothing philosophers of a liberal persuasion can do will prevent it. But given the choice between trying to persuade nonliberals to accept the principle of neutrality and trying to discredit their beliefs, I think that the second is clearly the better strategy.

Notes

1. "What I have suggested to be the case by and large about our own culture [is] that in moral argument the apparent assertion of principles functions as a mask for expressions of personal preference." Alasdair MacIntyre, *After Virtue* (Notre Dame, Ind.: University of Notre Dame Press, 1981), p. 18.

2. See Michael Freeden, *The New Liberalism* (Oxford: Clarendon Press, 1978).

3. See Preston King, *Toleration* (London: Allen and Unwin, 1976), esp. p. 101. The most familiar version of this argument among Anglophones is John Locke's "Letter Concerning Toleration" in J. W. Gough, ed., *The Second Treatise of Civil Government* (Oxford: Blackwell, 1946), pp. 123–65, but what should be emphasized, and is made clear by King, is how widespread within Europe arguments of this kind were.

4. Bruce A. Ackerman, *Social Justice in the Liberal State* (New Haven: Yale University Press, 1980), p. 11; Ronald Dworkin, "Liberalism," in Stuart Hampshire, ed., *Public and Private Morality* (Cambridge: Cambridge University Press, 1978), pp. 113–43, reprinted in Ronald Dworkin *A Matter of Principle* (Cambridge, Mass.: Harvard University Press, 1985), pp. 181–204; and John Rawls, *A Theory of Justice* (Cambridge, Mass.: Harvard University Press, 1971).

5. Ronald Dworkin, "Reverse Discrimination," in *Taking Rights Seriously* (Cambridge, Mass.: Harvard University Press, 1977), pp. 223–39, quotation from p. 236.

6. "Briefly, the idea is that in a constitutional democracy public conceptions of justice should be, so far as possible, independent of controversial philosophical and religious doctrines." John Rawls, "Justice as Fairness: Political not Metaphysical," *Philosophy and Public Affairs* 14 (1985): 223–51, quotation from p. 223.

7. Since, *ex hypothesi*, these would be "victimless crimes" their enforcement would be a greater threat to liberty than other forms of law enforcement, since it would require collecting information about consensual transactions. Corruption of the police and opportunities for organized crime tend to

arise from the prohibition of harmless acts. And, to the extent that members of the society do not see anything wrong in harmless acts, the law is liable to fall into disrepute. Another point often made is that the pursuit of victimless crimes diverts police effort from more important crimes. But this in effect presupposes that preventing harm is what matters, so it is essentially a variant on the view considered in the text.

8. Ackerman, *Social Justice*, p. 11 (italics in original).

4

Identity and Difference in Liberalism

William E. Connolly

The Paradox of Difference

My identity is what I am rather than what I choose, want, or consent to. It is the dense self from which choosing, wanting, and consenting proceed. Without that density, these acts could not occur; with it they are said to be mine. Our identity, in a similar way, is what we are and the basis from which we proceed.

An identity is established in relation to a series of differences. These differences are essential to its being. If they did not coexist as differences it would not exist in its clarity and solidity. Entrenched in this indispensable relation is a second set of tendencies, themselves in need of exploration, to congeal established identities into fixed forms, thought and lived as if their structure expressed the true order of things. When these pressures prevail, the maintenance of one identity (or field of identities) involves the conversion of some differences into otherness, into evil—or one of its numerous surrogates. Identity requires difference to be, and it often converts difference into otherness to secure its self-certainty.

Identity is thus a slippery, insecure experience, dependent on its ability to define difference and vulnerable to the tendency of entities it would so define to counter, resist, overturn or subvert definitions applied to them. Identity stands in a complex, political relation to differences it seeks to fix. Its complexity is intimated by variations in the degree to which differences from self-identity are treated as complementary-identities, contending identities, negative identities or non-identities, variations in the extent to which the voice of difference is heard as that to which one should remain engaged or as a symptom of sickness, inferiority or evil, variations in the degree to which self-choice or cultural determination are attributed to alter-identities, variations in the degree to which one's own claim to identity is blocked by the power of opposing claimants or they are blocked by one's own power, etc. The sensualist, the slut, the homosexual, the transvestite, the child abuser, and madness may merely suggest a few of these multifarious gradations at the level of the individual; the foreign, the terrorist organization, the dark continent, and the barbarian may do so at the level of culture.

Such complexities already suggest political dimensions in these relations. The bearer of difference may be one open to your appreciation or worthy of your tolerance or an other whose claim to identity you strive to invert or a being who fails to enclose some of its own dispositions into its positive identity while you insist upon treating them as central to its negative identity or a mode of being which internalizes as its own the negative identity imposed upon it by others or an impoverished mode of existence you refuse to recognize as an identity or an anonymous mode of life which resists the drive to secure a public identity in pursuit of a certain freedom, etc. Power plays a prominent role in this play of definition, counter-definition, and non-definition.

What if the human is not predesigned to coalesce smoothly with any single, coherent set of identities, if life without the drive to identity is an impossibility while the claim to a natural or true identity is always an exaggeration? And what if there are powerful drives, overdetermined by the very inertia of language, psychic instabilities in the human mode of being, and social pressures to secure consensus for collective action, to fix the truth of identity by grounding it in the commands of a god or the dictates of nature or the requirements of reason or a free consensus or a discovered truth?

If and when this combination occurs then a powerful identity will strive to constitute a range of differences as *intrinsically* evil, irrational, abnormal, mad, sick, primitive, monstrous, dangerous or anarchical. As other. It does so to secure itself as intrinsically good, coherent, complete, rational, etc., and to protect itself from the other which would unravel its own certainty and capacity for collective mobilization if it established its legitimacy. This constellation of constructed others now becomes essential to the truth of the powerful identity and a threat to it. The threat is posed not merely through *actions* the other might take to injure or defeat the true identity but through the very visibility of its mode of *being* as other.

If there is no natural or true identity, power is always inscribed in the relation an exclusive identity bears to the differences it constitutes. *If* there is always discrepancy between the identities a society makes available and that which exceeds, resists or denies them then the claim to a true identity is plagued by the persistent shadow of the other it constitutes. These "ifs" are big and contestable ifs. Big in their implications and contestable in their standing. Anyone who thinks within their orbit should periodically reconsider the strictness with which they apply and the status endowed upon them. So, too, should anyone who forsakes them in pursuit of more harmonious, teleological conceptions of identity and difference.

The paradox of difference has several dimensions or formulations. One is that if there is no true identity the attempt to establish one as if it were true involves power, while if there is a true identity susceptible to realization the attempt to pluralize and politicize identities mitigates against achievement of the highest good. If we are not in a position to establish either of these claims with confidence, the double relation of interdependence and strife between identity and difference converts the theoretical problem of knowledge into a practical paradox of practice. For the practice which secures identity in its truth may involve repression of otherness while that which problematizes established identities may foreclose the recognition of a true one.

I will not deal with this issue extensively or directly here. Rather, I will deal with it indirectly by considering the paradox of difference as it emerges within a philosophy which *projects* an answer to this ontological "if." A projection is offered because thinking cannot proceed here without invoking, implicitly or explicitly, consciously or unconsciously, a social ontology in the very language selected by it. It is treated as a projection because I cannot now discern a way to prove or demonstrate its truth without invoking it again as part of the proof. I am selected by this particular projection because . . . well, at least partly because the history of teleological theories reveals them to be beset by severe internal difficulties; partly because the relative lack of presence of this alternative in contemporary America currently gives too fixed and secure a status to contending projections which exercise hegemony over discourse; partly because the introduction of this alternative perspective into contemporary reflection helps to politicize the ontological dimension of academic political discourse. No affirmative theory can proceed without invoking an ontological dimension; many political theories today conceal their own while occasionally drawing attention to the way opposing theories invoke them.[1]

This projection opposes teleological theories that ground identity in a higher purpose in being and transcendental philosophies which treat reason or the normal individual or reciprocal rules of discourse as media sufficient to establish a true identity. It does not deny that it too invokes such presuppositions; rather, it seeks to problematize those presuppositions even as they are made.

Now the paradoxical element in the relation of identity to difference is that we need personal and collective identities to be, while the multiple drives to stamp truth upon the identities stamped upon us functions to convert difference into otherness and otherness into scapegoats created and maintained to secure the appearance of a true identity. To have a true identity is to be false to difference while to be true to difference is to sacrifice the drive to a true identity.

Thus, for instance, madness as unreason or (in a more contemporary vein) severe abnormality or instability is doubly entangled with the identity of the rational agent and the normal individual: it helps to constitute practical reason and normality by providing a set of abnormal conducts and "vehement passions" against which each is defined; but it also threatens them by embodying characteristics which would destabilize the normal if they were to proliferate. Madness and its corollaries stand in a double relation to normality: they constitute it and they threaten it, and the threat is the most serious if the constituted normality is construed to be intrinsically true rather than, say, an entrenched identity consonant with a particular set of institutional limits, possibilities, and imperatives.

The double relation of identity to difference fosters discursive concealment of the most difficult political issues residing in these relations. I will summarize the spiral of concealments in this way. First, as one's doubts about the ontological credibility of teleological and transcendental philosophies become acute, the suspicion grows that while no social life could be without bestowing privilege upon a particular constellation of identities, most historically established systems of identity veil the element of arbitrary conquest in the differences they create and negate. But, then, once this doubt has impressed itself upon thought, a reactive impulse emerges to dissolve the new ethical paradoxes freshly created by this admission. For how, it is asked, is the impression of violence in the formation of identity to be grounded if there is no transcendental basis for discriminating between violence and realization? This new anxiety refuels the quest to endow some identities with transcendental privilege. The first impulse to expose and respond to violence in the relation of identity to difference now often gives way to a renewed attempt to vindicate an ethic in which the identity affirmed (the good) is seen to be unambiguous, inclusive, and free from dirt.

Thought moves to and fro here. Thinkers accuse each other in one respect to excuse themselves in another. And recognition of the ugly moment in the refusal of transcendance fosters a cover-up of the ugly element in its affirmation. And vice versa. You might call this the politics of transcendental ugliness.

Such a tendency is discernible in recent responses by Anglo-American theorists to thinkers who refuse to dissolve the paradox of difference in a transcendental solution. Critics treat the quest by Nietzsche, Heidegger, and Foucault to expose paradoxes in the relation of identity to difference as expressions of incoherence or self-contradiction or amoralism in their thought. One set of ethical concerns (to expose a paradox and confront the violence within it) is countered by a moral charge against the carriers of the message, namely, that they are unable to formulate an ethical stance which is free of violence or self-contradiction or incoherence.

Critics translate the code of paradox into the charge of incoherence and easily enough convict opponents of the sin they have defined. They then slouch back down on familiar ontological scaffolding, forgetting that they stand upon it and that they have not shown this particular support to be true. Must one always ride the turtle he came in on?

Hobbes, Madness, and
Onto-theology

Hobbes responded in one way to this issue when he thought about madness in relation to the individual who could be rational, steady, stable, calculable, and self-contained enough to serve as the building stone of a stable order. His thought in this regard is revelatory because he does not assume, as some contemporary liberals do who are indebted to him, that there is a social form in which the claims of individuality will mesh smoothly with the dictates of a well-ordered civil society. He refuses to bury the political paradox of difference beneath complacent rhetorics of individuality, plurality, dialogue, tolerance or harmonization; and this refusal, in turn, draws him toward a transcendental politics many contemporary liberals would hesitate to endorse.

Hobbes deploys the category of madness simultaneously to characterize behavior which deviates dangerously from his norm of personhood, to identify those whose conduct falls outside the confines of protections the sovereign offers persons abiding by their obligations, to warn individuals from falling prey to a madness which haunts the interior life of human beings, and to advise the sovereign to dispose of those who become too mad to be governed by other means. His conception of madness expresses the severity of strife in his theory between the dictates of order and the claims of individuality, and this severity would become even more intensified in late-modern societies where the demands of regularity, calculability, self-containment, and social coordination are more extensive than they were in Hobbes's day.

"The secret thoughts of a man," says Hobbes, "run over all things, holy, profane, clean, obscene, grave and light, without shame or blame."[2] The ghost of madness roams around the interior of the self, though only a few selves become overtaken by madness as a condition. It is "want of discretion that makes the difference." Sometimes this difference, construed by Hobbes as "extraordinary and extravagant passion," is caused by "the evil constitution of the organs"; other times by the "vehemence or long continuation of . . . pride, . . . self-conceit, or great dejection of mind."[3]

> In sum, all passions that produce strange and unusual behavior, are called by the general name of madness. But of the several kinds of madness, he that would take pains, might enroll a legion. And if the excesses be madness, there is no doubt but the passions themselves, when they tend to evil, are degrees of the same.[4]

It is the duty of all subjects to practice self-restraint so that unruly, lustful, unguided, and vehement passions do not render them so unsteady that they fall into madness and "utterly lose themselves." For if the self is lost, if it becomes overtaken by "vehement passions," it becomes a danger to be disposed of in whatever way the sovereign deems appropriate for protection of the order.

We can hear these several messages inside the Hobbesian rhetoric of rationality and madness as he presents his fourth "precept of nature":

> That every man render himself useful unto others: which that we may rightly understand, we must remember that there is in men a diversity of dispositions to enter into society, arising from the diversity of their affections, not unlike

that which is found in stones brought together in the building, by reason of the diversity of their manner and figure. For as a stone, which in regard of its sharp and angular form takes up more room from other stones than it fills up itself, neither because of the hardness of its matter cannot well be pressed together, or easily cut, and would hinder the building from being fitly compacted, is cast away, as not fit for use; so a man, for the harshness of his disposition in retaining superfluities for himself, . . . being incorrigible by reason of the stubbornness of his affections, is commonly said to be useless and troublesome unto others. . . . Whence it follows (which we were to show) that it is a precept of nature, that every man accommodate himself to others. But he who breaks this law may be called *useless* and troublesome.[5]

It is imprudent to be called useless or troublesome in a Hobbesian world, and this is partly because he loads both the burdens of difference and the responsibilities for "complaisance" onto the self (the stones) rather than construing these clashes to flow from frictions between the dictates of an order and unexpected modes of difference engendered within it. This latter perspective is suggested by Willie Bosket, a long-term ward of the state and delinquent whose vicious attacks of abstract revenge against his wardens has confounded attempts to explain and subdue him. He said, "I am what the system created, but never expected, . . ." refusing thereby to treat himself either as a passive effect or as a defective stone which contains the source of its defectiveness in itself.[6]

Every theory (and every society) must develop strategies for dealing with differences engendered by the identities it enables. It is not this necessity which calls for questioning now, nor, in the first instance, the particular strategy Hobbes himself culls from the western storehouse of possibilities. What calls for questioning is, first, the range of imagined alternatives from which particular selections are made, and, second, the terms of justification which set and delimit these possibilities.

Hobbes answers these questions in a way which locates him within a philosophical tradition his theory is sometimes thought to escape. He concentrates on one possibility within that tradition: he treats a significant range of differences as otherness (for example, as madness, drunkenness, atheism, obscenity, and sinfulness) which falls below an identity known to be coherent and true in itself; he then warns those susceptible to the pull of otherness to guard themselves from it or to reform themselves if they have already fallen into it *or else* to find themselves conquered or excluded by a power which represents the "dictates" of reason. The pull of the first two demands is bound up with the "or else" clause accompanying them; it, in turn, is justified by a minimalist theology binding the dictates of reason to the commands of an otherwise unknowable God who makes a portion of his Will for humanity discernible through laws of nature "he hath given them."

These latter gestures place Hobbes within the onto-theological tradition of the West. To vindicate the conception of madness as a lapse from the true identity, rather than a tragic discrepancy between the dictates of a type of order and certain types of self-formation engendered within it, he moves to the transcendental plane. The sustenance he draws from this source enables him to treat madness as a nullity which deviates from both the rational order and the dictates of true identity together. Hobbes gives primacy to the rationalist/containment strand within onto-theology while vociferously opposing its teleological/attunement strand.

I borrow the awkward term "onto-theology" from Heidegger, though I do not use it exactly as he does. By it I mean a tradition of thought which demands or presupposes an ultimate answer to the question of being, an answer which includes an ethical principle humans are either commanded authoritatively to follow or internally predisposed to recognize once distorting influences have been lifted from their souls. "Being, since the beginning of western thought has been interpreted as the ground in which every being as such is grounded."[7] The ground might be the will of God revealed in scripture or in a founding act or in the dictates of reason "given" by God or it might be a *telos* inscribed in the soul or nature or the body or history or language or the community or the principle of subjectivity. The ground must be treated as knowable, either by God or humanity, either now, in the past or in the future; and the human link to this ground can be one of faith, intuition or knowledge. Such theories are grounded by appeal to a higher command (a law, a will) or an internal predisposition (an intrinsic purpose or potentiality), and they function to provide ontological reassurance to those who draw upon them.

Of course every constructive theory is teleological in some senses of this protean word. It endorses some ends, purposes or goals over others and offers considerations in their defense. A theory is teleological in the more elevated sense I have in mind, though, if it insists that the ends it endorses express a higher direction in being itself and that the closer a self and a "polity" approach to that direction the more true, harmonious, and inclusive they will be in their inner being and outer relations to each other. A constructive, purposive theory might identify resistances, conflicts, disturbances in the very ideal of self, discourse or statehood it commends while a constructive, teleological theory points to a way of being in which these frictions are minimized without significant repression because the structure of order has become attuned to a higher directionality (a ground) in being itself.

Some modern pragmatist, utilitarian, and Marxist theories repeal the onto-theological demand for transcendental or teleological reassurance and then refill the vacancy created with assumptions about the predisposition of the world itself to mastery by human communities organized in the most propitious way. They replace obedience to the will of God with an implicit premise of the responsiveness of the world itself to human use and organization. I consider these latter perspectives to be a continuation of onto-theology by other means: They compensate for the loss of transcendental reassurance by loading secular thought with a faith that the world itself is predisposed to be mastered in support of the ends and identities they favor, and then they forget the element of faith operating in their doctrines.

They shift faith from God to the world, trusting that it is *plastic* enough to respond to the drive for mastery without reacting back with a vengeance borne from its indifference to their ends and the diversity of forces and energies flowing through it. And then they pretend that the withdrawal of faith from God is the elimination of faith altogether. They thus secularize the "oblivion of difference" which, in Heidegger's text, is a defining mark of onto-theology.

The demand for a final authority to which one bows or for a world predisposed to human mastery does not have to emerge as the singular demand of an insistent thinker or set of actors. It is already inscribed in the cultural terms of discourse which carry us along in the late-modern age. If the western tradition of onto-theology is inscribed in established conceptions and assumptions, we might expect a theory which explicitly eschews "metaphysical" and "ontological" reflection to be a particularly effective vehicle for its transmission. When John Rawls says, for example, that "in a constitutional democracy the public conception of justice should be, so far as possible, independent of controversial philosophical and religious doctrines,"[8] he does not escape the onto-theological tradition; he adopts a position within it that defuses its internal controversies. He looks "to our public political culture itself, . . . as the shared fund of implicitly recognized basic ideas and principles" without entertaining the thought that denial and danger might be lodged within those commonalities.[9]

The later Rawls draws liberalism away from its proclivity (in the academy especially, but not only there) to locate a principle or ground in the universal human subject or the dictates of reason; he draws it toward a liberal hermeneutic in which each of the elements in liberal culture is reinforced and refined by defining it with respect to the others with which it is implicated. This hermeneutic strategy represents an advance over the liberal foundationalism by which Rawls himself was once tempted, and the dialectic by which Rawls has arrived at this juncture can be instructive to a range of rights theorists, rational choice theorists, and economic individualists who have not yet arrived here. But, I want to say, this sojourn of Rawlsian thought is not the consummation of liberalism: it prepares liberalism to engage the debate between those who think a benign hermeneutic can continue to revolve within the established parameters of traditional liberal assumptions, demands, and faiths and those who think that this shift prepares Rawlsian theory for its next set of debates. For genealogy, deconstruction, intertextualism, etc., define themselves not just against the structuralist version of rationalism; they also define themselves equally against the transcendental reassurances operative in the dominant forms of hermeneutics. By saving his theory from one set of criticisms Rawls opens it to another set of debates.

Individualism and Individuality

Liberal individualism and liberal individuality are not equivalent. They converge in giving the individual moral primacy over the interests of the collectivity.

But individual*ism* postulates a model of the normal or rational individual against which the conduct and interior of each actual self is to be appraised. This standard of the "stiff, steadfast, individual," as Nietzsche would characterize it, provides the ground for a theory of rights, justice, responsibility, freedom, obligation, and legitimate interests.

The doctrine of the steadfast individual (the autonomous agent, the self-conscious subject, the self-interested agent, the normal individual) easily becomes—seen from the standpoint projected here—a doctrine of normalization through individualization. Its tendency is to reduce the political to the juridical: to condense most issues of politics into juridical categories of rights, justice, obligation, and responsibility and to treat the remainder instrumentally as contests by which individuals and aggregations compete within juridical rules to advance their "interests" and/or "principles" by rational means. Politics gets bifurcated into a dualism of principle and instrumentality, with one group of individualists (for example, rights theorists, theorists of justice) celebrating the former and the other group (utilitarians, pragmatists) insisting upon the incorrigibility of the latter. Neither faction comes to terms very robustly with the constructed character of *both* the virtuous self and the self-interested self or with complementarities which link them together, even though one of the early progenitors of individualism, Thomas Hobbes, emphasized exactly this point with respect to the self-interested self and a progenitor of the virtuous self, Jean-Jacques Rousseau, paid considerable attention to it with respect to the virtuous self.

For these very reasons—the presentation of a single model of the generic individual, the minimalization of the contingent, constructed character of virtuous and self-interested individuals, and the reduction of politics to the juridical—theories of liberal individualism discount the *politics* of identity and difference.

A theory of the normal individual does not establish its parameters of normality by specific argumentation as much as it does by omissions in its generic characterization of the individual. Certainly, once a general characterization of the rational agent as bearer of rights, virtues, and interests is presented, the presenter is now free to contest a whole series of actual demands of normality imposed upon concrete selves but yet not required by the generic definition of the self. But this is not how such theories proceed. Rather, they insinuate a dense set of standards, conventions, and expectations into the identity of the normal self *by failing to identify or contest a constellation of normal/abnormal dualities already inscribed in the world they idealize*. One can discern this tendency through retrospective exemplification and by comparing the rhetorical structures of liberal texts defending the generic individual with that of critical texts interrogating the density of the normal individual.[10] We will merely offer one exemplification here.

In the 1950s in the United States, a topic of debate was whether "homosexuality" (a medical term for a sexual disposition) was a moral fault—the then conservative view—or a personal sickness—the then liberal view. Neither party discerned how both sides presupposed "it" to be a defect in the self of one type or the other nor how the joint constitution of this disposition as a defect of one sort or the other protected the self-certainty of heterosexual identity. And this example could be replicated along a whole range of issues concerning the normal self. The normal mode of discourse governing individualist theory does not support a problematization of established standards of normal individuality; it does not pose disturbing questions about the dense construction in actuality of the normal individual and its abnormalities.

The politicization of abnormality is difficult in any event because of institutional silences and constraints which typically envelope the formation of normal identities. The theory of individualism exacerbates these difficulties through its mode of theorization. It is pulled, by its minimalist understanding of how politics enters into the constitution of identity and difference, toward tacit endorsement of the politics of normal individualization.

A theory of liberal *individuality* is another kettle of fish. It gives primacy to the individual while qualifying or problematizing the hegemony of the normal individual. Here the individual's non-identity with its normal or official self constitutes a sign of its individuality. Individuality, indeed, consists in the appreciation of a range of conduct which is distinctive, stretches the boundaries of identity officially given to the normal self, reveals artifice in established standards of normality by superseding or breaking them, and brings new issues into public life by exposing through its resistance, eccentricity, refusal or excessiveness a series of contestable restraints built into fixed conventions.

George Kateb has done much, certainly the most in contemporary America, to clarify and advance this perspective. His version of the theory is inspired by Emerson, salted by Nietzsche. He celebrates "democratic individuality," insisting, against Nietzsche, that the unsettled character of democratic politics and the insistence upon institutional respect for the self which tends to accompany the exercise of citizenship together provide an institutional context in which any self might express its individuality. Democracy "unsettles everything for everyone, and thus liberates democratic individuality."[11]

Kateb strives to elicit from the lived experience of individuality both a public appreciation of diversity and an enhanced appreciation of the value of existence itself beyond its encapsulation in any particular network of identities, conventions, norms, and exclusions. One who expresses individuality and appreciates its expression in others tends, first, to say no to further encroachments by the state into new areas of life; second, to accept responsibility for oneself and one's life-projects; and, third, to "acquire a new relation to all experience, which may be called either a philosophical or poetical relation to reality."[12]

This last formulation speaks to an appreciation of existence as such—gained through the experience of individuality and ratified by its best poets. It emerges less as an argument in favor of individuality and more as a solicitation of the moment of individuality in each self, less as a proof that we owe allegiance to existence as such and more as a revelation of the attachment to existence already implicit in the appreciation of individuality. It is Wim Wenders's "Wings of Desire" transcribed into prose.

In this way Kateb signals a Nietzschean (and Emersonian) refusal to ground ethics in reason alone, asserting that if there is not already an attachment to existence flowing from the self to its own life and overflowing into the care for other lives, no rational ground of ethics will ever generate ethical conduct. Foucault's formulation of this thesis is that "care of the self" is an essential preliminary to care for other selves, and care for others emerges from an abundance cultivated by the self. Lawrence Taylor, the talented and controversial linebacker for the New York Giants, expressed one side of this thesis while responding in his own way to a reporter interrogating about his lack of concern for teammates and fans adversely affected by his drug habit:

"A friend of mine recently asked about my driving habits. I told him I don't wear seat belts because if I ever get in a crash at the speed I go, I wouldn't survive anyway. . . . But I also told him what I tell anyone else who asks: If I don't care what happens to me now, can I really think about what might happen to others?"[13]

Care for the self precedes and often precipitates—through affirmations it spawns reflecting and exceeding the requirements of self-care—care for others. If one lacks care for oneself one will surely lack the abundance from which care for difference might emerge.

Kateb has placed himself on a plane of reflection which invites co-respondence with a contemporary mode of thought he would like to dismiss. The link between Katebian individuality and Foucault on power and freedom is forged by Nietzsche, to whom both are significantly indebted.

While Kateb emphasizes the roots of his philosophy in the American transcendentalists—Emerson, Whitman, and Thoreau—there is one element in Nietzsche's articulation of individuality and the resistances to it particularly pertinent for contemporary experience. This is the first point at which my solicitation of liberal individuality—its paradoxes and possibilities—diverges from Kateb's.

Consider three assertions. First, Nietzsche is the philosopher who exposes the roots of resentment in theism and secularism and who seeks to elicit a nontheistic reverence for life to combat the subterranean politics of resentment. Second, liberalism as a contemporary philosophy of rights and justice which has become an object of resentment in contemporary politics. Third, most paradigmatic defenses of liberalism today refuse to ask whether its doctrine embodies and contributes to the resentment it receives.

A reconstitution of liberal individuality might begin, then, by ascertaining whether there is something in individual*ist* liberalism which expresses resentment and something in it which tends to elicit resentment from many who receive its messages. Such an analysis, indebted to Nietzsche, may help to reveal traps liberal individuality must avoid and directions its supporters might consider.

That contemporary liberalism is an object of resentment seems undeniable. This is so especially at those points where its welfarism and its individualism intersect: for these determine how freedom and responsibility are to be distributed among the various constituencies of the welfare state. Since the 1960s, many liberal-welfare programs established to rectify injustice have been received by a variety of constituencies as the imposition of new injustices upon them. Programs in busing, aid to dependent children, affirmative action hiring, ecology, criminal parole and rehabilitation, and gun control laws often encounter virulent opposition, indicating that they touch the identities of the opponents even more than their interests. Juridical doctrines and judgments in support of civil liberties and civil rights encounter similar reactions.[14]

Of course these responses have several sources, but one of them is particularly pertinent here. Many of those asked to bear immediate economic and psychic costs of ameliorative programs already resent some of the conditions of their own existence. But this resentment is not typically emphasized in the rhetoric or programs of liberalism: the resentment is accentuated by liberal programs and subdued in its rhetoric.

Think of white, working-class males. They are subjected to a variety of disciplines and burdens that limit their prospects for life, but liberal programs devised since the 1960s tend to treat them as responsible for their own achievements and failures. And they are then told by liberals that many women and minorities are treated unjustly if they do not rise to or above working-class levels of attainment.

Liberal representatives inadvertently manipulate the rhetoric of self-responsibility and justice in ways which assault the identity of this constituency. By insisting that one constellation of professional and corporate males has earned its position while women and minorities are victimized by discrimination, liberals implicitly say that only one group *deserves* to be stuck in the crummy jobs available to it: white, working-class males. The liberal glorification of self-responsibility, juridical justice, and welfare together thus accentuates the resentment of those whose identity is most immediately threatened by its ameliorative programs.

But why is this resentment often so virulent and volatile? Does liberalism today simply encounter a resentment it does not itself harbor? Or does a culture in which liberal individualism is prominent help to dig a well of resentment which then flows into the culture in which it participates? I believe that any effort to reconstitute liberalism must explore this latter possibility. And Nietzsche provides clues from which such an exploration might be launched.

From a Nietzschean perspective, the self constituted as a unified, self-responsible, free agent contains resentment within its very formation. The basic idea behind this formation is that for every evil there must be a responsible agent who deserves to be punished for it and for every quotient of evil in the world there must be a corollary quotient of assignable responsibility. No evil without responsibility. No responsibility without reward or punishment according to level of desert. No suffering without injustice and no injustice unless there is a juridical recipe for removing it in life or afterlife. Life is organized around the principles of individual responsibility governing a baseball game.

When a liberal hears these equivalencies questioned he tends to think immediately that all freedom, responsibility, and justice must disappear if these ideals are dragged through the mud. If the purity of these principles is sullied, everything else good and admirable will be soiled too. Perhaps. But the ethical brilliance of these categorical imperatives may blind adherents to injuries and cruelties residing within them. To explore dangers and cruelties which may reside within these categories it may be helpful to illuminate them from a different angle, to lower the source of illumination so that the shadows they throw become more discernible.

At the root of this demand for equivalence between evil and responsibility is the demand that the world contain agency in the last instance. Seen from this angle, these categories themselves represent a modernized version of the traditional Christian demand that there be a responsible agent or purpose for all suffering in the world, that human finitude and suffering be redeemed by an agency of responsibility. What Nietzsche has called the slave revolt in morality—the formation and consolidation of a subject and guilt-centered morality—is not merely the invention of a God by enslaved beings who want to hold the masters responsible for their fate. Certainly the invention of this God involves an act of "imaginary revenge" against those whose initial powerlessness makes actual revenge untenable. Certainly the habitual practice of this revenge eventually becomes consolidated into the creative demand that everyone acquire the honesty, meekness, industriousness, virtue "we" are already compelled to assume. Certainly there is the transformation of weakness into merit, so that what the slave must be becomes the standard against which every difference is measured as a deviation to be punished, reformed, or converted, by man or by God.

But the early, intense transfiguration of overt resentment into the demand to convert or conquer the other for its own good symbolizes a more pervasive set of dispositions rooted in the human condition.[15] Only the presence of such a voice somewhere in anyone and everyone could explain the successful extension of slave morality to the internal life of masters. Humans tend to resent the transiency, suffering, and uncertainty of transcendental reassurance or redemption which marks the human condition. We suffer from the problem of our meaning and we demand that meaning be given to our suffering. After the idea of a purpose in existence residing in nature or God loses its self-confidence the insistence that we are rational, responsible agents comes into its own. For if these previous sources of responsibility are dead some new agency must be created. We give meaning to suffering, then, by holding ourselves responsible for it. "Quite so my sheep," we say to each other, "someone must be to blame for it (suffering); but you are this someone, you alone are to blame for it."[16] God cannot be to blame, or he would be responsible for evil; and no evil god could be trusted to grant salvation. That means that only one set of agents remain. "Quite so my sheep."

The modern, normal individual—though it is certainly not exhausted by this reading—can be seen to redirect resentment against the human condition into the self, first, by holding the rational, self-interested, free, and principled individual morally responsible for anything that diverges from the identity it endorses and, second, by treating that in oneself and other selves which falls below the threshold of responsibility as in need of conquest or conversion, punishment or love. The modern individual, in short, contains resentment against the burdens of its own identity, and this comes out most clearly in its resentment against that which deviates significantly from it. For the latter deviations, if they proliferate, make the self-identical self appear to be a sucker for accepting the disciplines and restraints required to maintain its artificial identity. Only if they are false can it see itself as true. Resentment against the injuries to oneself flowing from the standard of self-responsibility become translated into rancor against those below one who one construes to escape its dictates. And the definition of those others as irresponsible escapees becomes entangled in one's own identity as a self-responsible agent.

The authoritarian personality is thus not merely a personality type which threatens liberal tolerance. It is that and also an internal product of a liberal demand for normal individuality in itself and others. Anyone who seeks to verify this statement can do so by picking ten liberals at random: the odds are high that four of them will display the characteristics of this personality type in relations with radicals and conservatives; this number will grow to five or six whenever the purity of liberal conceptions of selfhood, responsibility, freedom, and individuality is challenged from a left-Nietzschean perspective.

No liberal philosopher has ever proven that the human animal is predesigned to correspond to the shape assumed by the modern, normal, individual, and thus none has proven that this formation can be forged and maintained through each generation without imposing cruelty upon those who adjust to its dictates as well as to those who are unable or unwilling (can we ever sort out these proportions with confidence?) to do so. These are modes of categorical insistence from which liberal individualism begins. Seen from the perspective of those who deny this faith in the telos of the normal individual—seen even from the perspective of those who endorse subjectivity as an ambiguous achievement while refusing to endorse the fiction that it corresponds to what we naturally are—the pretense that humans are predesigned to be responsible agents casts a veil of ignorance over elements of cruelty and revenge in the formation of this identity and its differences. The most direct sign that liberal individualism disables itself from discerning cruelty in its own constructs emerges from the fact that the most startling exposés of new disciplines and containments of individuality in late-modern society have come not from this corner but from the work of Michel Foucault, a left-Nietzschean working outside the philosophical fold of liberal individualism.

My first disagreement with Kateb, then, is a matter of emphasis. I place greater emphasis on the element of resentment already residing in the identity of the normal individual. Liberal individualism thus becomes a more ambiguous ally of liberal individuality than Kateb has acknowledged.

And this along three dimensions. First, its concentration on the normal individual renders it less sympathetic to the claims of diversity, encouraging it to enclose the space for diversity within a closely defined band of standards of abnormality such as irrationality, irresponsibility, immorality, delinquency, and perversity. Second, its insistence on the standard of normal individuality helps to foment a generalized resentment tending to disable its normal and abnormal bearers alike from affirming an ethic which appreciates, as Nietzsche would say, "the rich ambiguity of existence." Third, its juridical conception of politics tends to downplay the degree of politics, militance, and struggle required to establish space for individuality in a liberal society.

A philosophy of individuality and nontheistic reverence for existence needs to identify ways and means to wage a battle against existential resentment and to elicit respect for the diversity of existence while doing so.

I agree with Kateb, Emerson, Nietzsche, and Foucault that no ethic of individuality (or anything else) will be grounded securely in rational proof, partly because such attempts are always contestable and partly because even a successful proof would not guarantee the production of motives to obey its edicts. But this does not mean that a political ethic is merely a matter of "choice" either—the only alternative the rationalist tends to recognize. Rather, such an ethic is solicited from or inspired in us, first, by coming to terms with the element of resentment in the way extant moralities convert difference into otherness and, second, by enabling the implicit attachment to existence to find greater expression. Nontheistic reverence for existence redraws the line between secularism and religion by refusing either to eliminate the reverence historically associated with the first or to link the moment of reverence in its ethic to the transcendental or telelogical demand historically associated with the second. It has reverence for life because life is never exhausted by any particular identity imposed upon it. Its reverence is sustained through its nontheism and its refusal of transcendentalism.

Nietzsche's texts draw attention away from the centrality of nontheistic reverence in his thought, first, by presenting it typically in the context of celebrating Greek nobility or castigating Christian culture and, second, by expressing this mood within the ambiance of an antidemocratic ethic. But these formulations can also point beyond those particular Nietzschean convictions for thinkers who seek to enter into a relation of antagonistic indebtedness to Nietzsche, for thinkers who seek to construct a new liberal politics upon a Nietzschean reverence for life without transcendence, for thinkers who seek an ethic which expresses reverence for the diversity of existence coupled to appreciation of the impossibility of embodying everything admirable in any single way of life.

The relevant spirit can be discerned in Nietzsche's attack on the early Christian church:

> To shatter the strong, to infect great hopes, to cast suspicion on the enjoyment
> of beauty, to break down everything autonomous, manly, victorious, domina-
> ting, all the instincts natural to the highest and best turned-out type of mankind,
> and bend it over into uncertainty, distress of conscience, and self-destruction—
> to reverse every bit of love of earth and things earthly and control of earth into
> hatred of things earthly and of the earth: *this* was the self assumed task of the
> church.[17]

If we shift the focus away from the apparent misogynism and aristocraticism
in this passage, the attempt to elicit reverence for the world because it is not
governed by a transcendental law or purpose becomes apparent. This reverence
is not established directly; it is solicited through exposés of extant identities and
moralities which contain or suppress it. And, given Nietzsche's reading of the
human condition (that is, the incompleteness of the human animal without social
form, his understanding of the density of language, the quest for closure of
identities, and the absence of a sufficient principle of harmonization of difference
in being), these struggles will always be necessary because there are so many
pressures in the human condition to fix conventional identities in truth and to
reduce difference to falsity and evil.

To endorse *this* Nietzschean perspective is not to adopt the particular antagonists Nietzsche selects at the end of the nineteenth century. It is, rather, to insist
that a political ethic appropriate to a reconstituted liberalism requires this mode
of defense and elaboration, that neither liberal individuality nor a reconstitution
of liberal politics can gain assent without invoking such a human ground.

Reasoned argument about specific rules and standards appropriate to liberal
individuality and its political virtues must invoke and presuppose this nonrational
(but not irrational) basis if they are to advance.[18]

I realize that these comments are cryptic and preliminary. But I want now to
turn to a consideration of Kateb's politics, treating them as exemplary of the
doctrine of liberal individuality today.

While Kateb advances a compelling ethic of individuality, the dilemmas and
paradoxes within it cannot be engaged until that ethic is translated into a political
theory. To put the point starkly: *theorists of liberal individuality offer an ethic of
individuality in lieu of a political theory of individuality,* in lieu of a theory which
confronts disjunctions between limitations to diversity intrinsic to a specific order
and the demand for diversity which flows from an ethic of individuality. Once
the outlines of such a theory are elucidated one must either establish the desired
harmony by making questionable teleological assumptions or confront a tragic
element residing within the institutionalization of individuality itself. Engagement
with the institutional limits to individuality can be evaded either by succumbing
to the teleological temptation or by restricting oneself to an *ethic* of individuality
situated in a generically defined culture of liberal democracy.

Kateb pursues the second strategy. It finds expression mostly in silences with
respect to the structural limits of a late-modern, capitalist, liberal society. To the

extent the state leaves the individual alone, Kateb inclines to believe, to that extent individuality will flourish. And if we do not demand too much from the state, particularly in the area of economic life, it can afford to leave us pretty much alone. So, while democratic politics is a necessary precondition of individuality, a too active and organized democratic agenda will suffocate it. The individual's political involvement, therefore, should be limited, confined, episodic. Kateb quotes Whitman's advice to "always vote," but to limit oneself severely with respect to other modes of political involvement:

> Disengage yourself from parties. They have been useful, and to some extent remain so, but the floating, uncommitted electors, farmers, clerks, mechanics, the masters of parties—watching aloof, inclining victory this side or that side— such are the ones most needed, present and future.[19]

Notice the assumptions of early nineteenth-century America forming the silent background of this sentiment. "Floating, uncommitted electors," etc., rather than role bearers whose conditions of daily existence enmesh them in corporate and bureaucratic structures imposing refined schedules and norms upon them; a self-subsistent state rather than one entangled in a global structure of interdependencies and conflicts which it is pressed to convert into disciplines for its most vulnerable constituencies; a domestic politics of "parties" from which the individual can be "disengaged" and "aloof" without becoming an object of power struggles over norms, regulations, penalties, and incentives governing the details of life.

Kateb modestly qualifies this portrait of the American past in his political orientation to the present, suggesting that "a *modern equivalent* would perhaps be the *episodic* citizenship of loosely and *temporarily* associated individuals who seek to protest and end *great atrocities;* or seek to protest and end violations of the Constitution, with special attention to defending the Bill of Rights and to warning against executive and bureaucratic *lawlessness* and overreaching."[20] That is, he reasserts the early American idealization of self-reliance by reabsorbing contemporary politics into its juridical dimension and by treating political engagement as normally secondary to the pursuit of individuality.

But the past ain't what it used to be. What's more, it probably never was. We do not reside today in a world where individuality could flourish by leaving state, corporate, and associational institutions of normalization to their own devices except when they overlap clear constitutional boundaries or commit glaring atrocities. The atrocities which glare most brightly today are undergirded by everyday politics. Constitutional boundaries must be creatively redefined and enlarged through political pressure speaking to new circumstances.

The proliferation of drug tests, the extension of corporate codes into new corners of everyday life, credit tests, the increasing numbers of people subjected to security tests along with the enlarged number of criteria invoked in them, the bureaucratic definitions and regulations of safe, healthy, normal sexuality, the introduction of home detention for convicted felons which allows definitions of illegality to be extended indefinitely, the computerization of individual files enabling a variety of authorities and semi-authorities to record the life history of each individual for multifarious uses, the militarization of welfare and scholarships, the refiguration of deviations construed in the nineteenth century as sins or moral faults into psychological defects of the self in need of correction and therapy, and most pervasively, the individual's vague sense that each of his actions today *might* form part of a record which *might* be used for or against one in the future—these signify a *regularized* politics of normalization through observational judgment and anticipatory self-policing.

Individuality secures space to be through resistance and opposition to these bureaucratic pressures. Gay rights movements; feminism; minority politics; emergent movements to attack the institutionalization of homelessness; efforts on behalf of the elderly in nursing homes; prisoners' rights; embryonic drives to resist the universalization of drug tests and other closures in codes of employee conduct; institutional demands by those afflicted with terminal illness; periodic dissidence among young men and women in military, intelligence, and security agencies; localized pressures to rollback corporate and state disciplines forged under the star of efficiency, productivity, and normality; antimilitarist movements to create alliances with dissidents in second and third world regions—these protests and movements, however ineffective they may be on occasion, simultaneously signify a broadening and deepening of institutional investments in the life of the self and a corollary politics of resistances, disinvestments, and subversion on behalf of individuality.

The apolitics of individuality is too easily squeezed to death by this intensification of institutional investments. In a highly structured state episodic, juridical politics of dissent against extreme atrocities lapses into a nonpolitics of nihilistic consent—the most ominous form nihilism assumes today—to the everyday extension of discipline and normalization.

The minimalist politics of individuality is thus not merely a benign view that does not go far enough. It is an anachronism which misreads paradigmatic threats to individuality in late-modern society. These threats reside in the normal operation of a political economy of productivity within a society of increasing surveillance and normalization. They are lodged in the state, civil society, and in some of the interior dispositions among individuals participating in these arenas. Their accumulation requires a politics in which established definitions of normality and rationality are contested along a variety of dimensions in multifarious ways.

Certainly there are costs to individuality to be borne by the politicization of individuality. But these costs can hardly be avoided anymore. The pathos of distance which individuality prizes can no longer be located in some fictive marginal social space or sanctuary or "sphere" of privacy generally exempt from political intrusion. These have become political spaces rather than "geographical" or "spherical" or "social" or "interior" places. In late-modern society the pathos of distance means the politicization of distance.

A mere *ethic* of individuality evades an encounter with the Foucaultian world of discipline and normalization not through the social ontology it endorses—for here the two are remarkably close, but through the temporal reference it fixes. It eludes the encounter through an ethic of individuality floating in the clouds of a nineteenth-century ideal.

The finely grained arrangements of self-regulation operative today must be countered by more sustained, organized, multifrontal counter-pressures, pressures which interrogate established definitions and intrusions of necessity, truth, normality, utility, and goodness while they identify and strive to reconstitute larger institutional imperatives which drive the politics of normalization. A politics of counter-knowledges and counter-organization supports counter-individualization. For a proliferation of deviations, defects, discrepancies, abnormalities, perversities, and sicknesses is not equivalent to the flowering of diversity: these are the regular means by which individuality is crushed and deformed under the star of the normal individual.

There is always conflict as well as interdependency between the claims of individuality and the dictates of identity in a particular order. A political theory which admires the first set of claims will support constitutional ways to install legal protections for those claims consonant with the order in which it resides. But it will also develop more political protections for those claims which express the paradox of difference in a particular setting, countering and contesting tendencies to naturalize the identities enabled in a particular society, exposing and testing limitations imposed by the structural characteristics of a particular social type and exposing the double pressures to conformity and naturalization which emerge when a closed set of identities is reinforced by the structural characteristics of the order in which they reside. The advocates of individuality will strive to identify from an alien perspective a range of disciplines and intrusions which are made to appear natural or necessary or consensual or rational or normal in established political discourse, subjecting some to political tests while holding others up for critical scrutiny. They will acknowledge that a set of commonalities must exist for individuality to be, but they will also insist that each set of commonalities deserves contestation and politicization to counter closures and categorical imperatives invested in it.

When the paradox of difference is confronted in the context of late-modern society, it turns out that an ethic of individuality requires a multifarious politicization of difference to sustain itself.

Communitarianism Liberalism

Liberal individualism evades the paradox of difference first by insinuating particular dictates of order into the identity of the normal individual and then by naturalizing the identity it has solidified. Liberal individuality softens the paradox by treating an ethic of individuality as if it were a political theory of individuality. There is a third scholarly version which completes the contemporary circle of evasions. Communitarian liberalism corrects defects in the first two positions by reminding us how a set of identities is defined and enabled within the context of institutionalized commonalities. It then naturalizes this insight by insisting that there must be a way of life, either now, in the past or in a possible future where established identities are harmonized into a unified whole.

Its strategy with respect to difference is this: the paradox of difference must be dissolved into a common good which enables every form of otherness to reform itself until it fits into the frame of a rational community and enables the community to perfect its terms of inclusion so that excluded constituencies can find a home within it. Communitarianism fosters normalization through the nonpolitics of gentle assimilation.

"Communitarian liberalism" will seem like a category mistake to some. But most contemporary communitarian (or civic republican) theories are variants of liberalism for the following reasons. First, they provide space for rights and individuality within the context of the commonalities they admire. Second, they emphasize the juridical and communal sides of politics over its role in disturbing and unsettling established routines. Third, they want identities and commonalities endorsed to be brought to a peak of self-consciousness and rational legitimacy unimagined in traditional theories of community. Fourth, they hesitate to interrogate structures and priorities in the established political economy. Fifth, they maintain a corollary commitment to incremental change by democratic means over transformation by revolutionary or authoritarian means.

The communal strategy typically begins by trying to show how implicit pre-understandings in contemporary life point toward a coherent set of standards which justify a more inclusive and fulfilling good. We are already implicated in the circle of commitments it articulates and perfects, and our mutual rights, duties, and aspirations will be harmonized more effectively as we are brought to greater self-consciousness of their preconditions and implications.

But the question arises: What justifies the exclusions, penalties, restrictions, incentives needed to sustain this common good among those who might otherwise deviated from it? What if some would significantly shift priorities within the sanctified circle of implications if they had the power to do so? What if commonly established assumptions about the capacity for realization of the embodied self in a higher community encounter persistent resistances in many selves against these forms of self-organization? What if the circle of discourse in which these commonalities are articulated closes out other possibilities which would disturb, unsettle, fragment, ambiguate, politicize the achieved sense of unity if they were to find expression? When such questions are pursued persistently the hermeneutic circle of mutual self-validation among interdependent components of the culture must have recourse to a supplement; it must appeal to a supplementary authority which redeems or perfects the common good when some subset of deviants resist the assimilation it makes available.

The most reflective communitarians endorse such a supplement explicitly, at least when faced by objections which require either that they do so or that they ambiguate more radically the good they endorse. Charles Taylor is exemplary here. In a recent exchange, while insisting that he rejects strong teleological assumptions represented in Hegelian theory, he affirmed the presence of a supplemental principle of teleology in his political ontology.

> For what is meant by a "teleological philosophy"? If we mean some inescapable design at work inexorably in history, à la Hegel, then I am of course not committed to it. But if we mean by this expression that there is a distinction between distorted and authentic self-understanding, and that the latter can in a sense be said to follow from a direction in being, I do indeed espouse such a view. And that makes a big part of my "ontology" of the human person. . . . It does not seem to me to be in worse shape than its obvious rival, certainly not than the Nietzschean notion of truth as imposition.[21]

A "direction in being"; Taylor proceeds from a rhetoric of self-realization within community through a rhetoric of communal realization by harmonization of the diverse parts of an ongoing culture culminating to progressive attunement to a higher direction in being. The latter supplement is a requirement of his theory. But to say that "we" need such a supplement to ground community, or, more strongly, that others who explicitly reject the ideal of community nonetheless presuppose a facsimile of this supplement in their own thinking, or, most strongly, that such a supplement is even an inescapable component of social thought as such, is still not to show that a supplemental direction (and a being who provides it) actually exists and is available to "us."

Taylor argues effectively that such a supplement is needed if the communal ideal is to succeed, but he then reveals its possibility, not through particular arguments but by insinuating into his texts tropes which presuppose its availability. Taylor's Augustinianism emerges in this dimension of his texts. We are called upon to believe first so that we can come to know. "Lord," says Augustine, "my faith calls upon you, that faith . . . which you have breathed into me. . . ."[22] And Taylor breathes faith in the truth of this ontological supplement into the rhetoric which governs his characterizations.

I do not mean to protest against this dimension of Taylor's work as such. For no affirmative theory of politics can avoid some such strategy of supplementation. I do mean to call attention to it, to contest the directionality of this particular supplementation, and to note how it does not call attention to its central role in communitarian texts.

Part of the problem is that Taylor not only breathes this supplement into the narrative and rhetorical structure of his texts, the realization of his community requires that most members of the realized community become attuned to the supplement approximately as he construes it, and it requires that they then treat this attunement not as an implication of thought at one moment to be questioned or cancelled at another moment, but as a condition of thought as such which co-responds to an essence of being, to, "in a sense," a higher direction in being.

But can't "we" take this step of faith with him? After all, it seems a small step, once the initial web of common preunderstandings governing our culture has been articulated. And the return seems so great: the paradox of difference becomes dissolved into a project of assimilation where those who now fall outside the range of communal identifications are drawn into the folds of a higher, more rational, more inclusive community. Is it not time at last to be reasonable?

The step must be resisted by those who doubt the faith that sustains it. The gentle rhetoric of articulation, realization, community, purpose, attunement, fulfillment, integration, harmonization, and articulation reinscribes the common life significantly, obligating people and institutions to reform and consolidate themselves in ways which might be arbitrary, cruel, destructive, and dangerous *if* those numerous gaps between life world and faith are not supplemented by a higher direction in being. Taylor's rhetoric of communal harmony must be ambiguated and contested by those who have not had its faith breathed into his or her soul, particularly by those who express nontheistic reverence for the rich ambiguity of existence rather than theistic reverence for a higher direction in being. We thus return to the "if" from which we have never actually departed.

The rhetoric of community places too many possible disciplines outside its critical purview, revealing in its persistent folding of experience into its specific modality that the supplement it invokes does not require such a small step after all. It must constantly be tested and contested by those whose hermeneutic draws supplemental sustenance from another ontology, one in which there is no higher direction in being, in which the fit between human designs and the material drawn into those designs is always partial, incomplete, and likely to contain an element of subjugation and imposition, in which the possibilities of individuality and reverence for existence are enhanced when we refuse to pretend that God retains enough life to give supplemental direction to late-modern life.

There is a certain asymmetry in the debate between communitarians and post-Nietzschean thinkers which deserves elaboration. Taylor says, "It [the assumption of a direction in being] does not seem to me to be in worse shape than its obvious rivals, certainly not the Nietzschean notion of truth as imposition."[23]

Leaving aside the need to amplify and modify the suggestion that truth is *simply* imposition for Nietzsche, the Tayloresque presumption of a direction in being to which we strive to become attuned must attain significantly better standing than the alternative projections of its opponents if the ideal of community is to be approximated in life. The Nietzschean position requires only that an active minority of the population advance it in thought and action and that the culture in general come to see this stance too as one worthy of their respect as a competitor and worthy therefore of agonistic engagement with it as an alternative response to the mysteries of existence. For a range of existing settlements becomes politicized if a significant element of the populace credibly and insistently refuses to treat them as natural, thoroughly rational, reflective of a dialogic consensus or grounded in a higher direction and if another cluster of participants evinces agonistic respect for this orientation even while opposing it. But the communitarian ontology must receive a more consensual and secure endorsement than this picture of agonistic engagement allows. It must triumph over the perspective of its opponents (and not merely its left-Nietzschean opponents) for its ideal of community to be realized. A stalemate in ontological politics is exactly what it must overcome to enact its ideal of communality.

This epistemic asymmetry leads one to suspect that there may be a protective power in being after all. It protects us from the imposition of unambiguous community on the sophomoric (and populist) grounds that, hey, my lack of faith in its ontological preconditions are at least as sound as your faith in them.

The Politics of Paradox

I have contended that liberal individualism, liberal individuality, and liberal communitarianism generate complementary strategies to evade the paradox of difference. How, then, might it be engaged? My response is to acknowledge it and to convert it into a politics of the paradoxical, into a conception of the political as the medium through which the interdependent antinomies of identity and difference can be expressed and contested. This orientation is offered (again) not as a definitive *solution* to the paradox of difference, but as a way through which to contest affinities and closures shared by dominant responses to this issue.

This perspective on politics endorses dimensions from each of the theories criticized here. From the individual*ist* and the communitarian it draws the understanding that any way of life that enables people to act collectively must embody a set of norms and commonalities which are given variable degrees of primacy in the common life. From the communitarian it draws appreciation of the hermeneutic character of ethical and political discourse, whereby debate and argumentation proceed from preconceptions and convictions which already have a presence in the life of the self and the society. From the theory of liberal individuality it draws the understanding that the claims of individuality often clash with the claims of conventionality, order, and normality, emphasizing more than theorists of individuality tend to that both sets of claims enter into the interior of the self as well as into public arenas of discursive engagement. From the Nietzschean legacy it draws nontheistic reverence for the ambiguity of existence and the idea (the iffy idea) that every identity is a contingent artifice which encounters resistances and recalcitrance to these formative pressures. In each of these instances, though, it politicizes elements which the single-minded bearers of these insights tend to treat in unpolitical ways.

It may be pertinent to note how, according to the perspective advanced here, each of the other traditions represses an essential ingredient of politics. Kateb, Taylor, and Nietzsche provide excellent exemplifications. The first seeks to insulate the individual from political intrusions, endorsing minimalism in politics in the name of individuality. The second thematizes politics as a gathering together of disparate forces into a shared purpose realized in common, deflating the corollary idea of politics as perpetual contestation of established commonalities so that injuries and injustices within them will not become too thoroughly naturalized, rationalized or grounded in a higher direction in being. The third projects an overman who engages the ambiguity of existence largely outside the reach of politics.[24]

On the model of liberalism projected here, the politicization of identities and commonalities is intrinsic to the ideal itself: the good life is one in which creative tension is generated between the claims of individuality and commonality, the claims of identity and that in the self which resists those claims, the drive to transcendence and that which is repressed by any particular claim to transcendence, the imperatives of the present and the claims of the future, the existing field of discourse and latent possibilities residing in its partially repressed history. From this perspective juridical politics, minimalist politics, and communitarian politics emerge as complementary ideals of apolitical politics; each deflates one or more of the dimensions needed to keep the politicization of difference alive.

What, then, is the paradox of politics and how does it relate to the politicization of identity? Since I use the word in its dictionary senses and not in any technical sense, it can be given a variety of formulations. Here is one. A politics of the common good is essential both to sustain a particular set of identities worthy of admiration and to enable the collectivity to act self-consciously in support of justice and the public interest as they emerge in the common life. But this politics of public rationality presents an essentially ambiguous face. The very success in defining and acting upon commonalities tends to naturalize them, to treat them as unambiguous goods lodged in nature or consent or reason or the universal character of the normal individual or ideal dialogue or a higher direction in being. If humans are not predesigned, and if they therefore do not fit neatly into any particular social form, then any set of enabling commonalities is likely to contain corollary injuries, cruelties, subjugations, concealments, and restrictions worthy of opposition and contestation. Each set of identities will generate differences which themselves need to find a political voice.

Another way to pose the paradox is this. The human animal is essentially incomplete without social form; and a common language, institutional setting, traditions, and political forum for enunciating public purposes provide the indispensable means through which human beings acquire the identity and commonalities essential to life. But every form of social completion and enablement also contains subjugations and cruelties within it. Politics, then, is the medium through which these ambiguities can be engaged and confronted, shifted and stretched. It is simultaneously a medium through which common purposes are crystallized and the consummate means by which their transcription into musical harmonies is exposed, contested, disturbed, and unsettled. A society that enables politics as this ambiguous medium is a good society because it enables the paradox of difference to find expression in public life.

This perspective is, of course, a liberalism, an alternative, militant liberalism which enters into indebtedness and debate with other liberalisms and nonliberalisms contending for presence in late-modern life. It is a liberalism in its refusal of the options between revolutionary overthrow and the idealization of traditional culture, in its appreciation of the claims of individuality, in its attentiveness to rights and constitutional protections, in its extension of these concerns to forces which extend the dialectic of discipline and reactive disaffection into new corners of life, in its skepticism about any definitive resolution of the paradoxical relationship between identity and difference, in its radicalization of liberal battles against the singular hegemony of teleological and transcendental theories, in the ironic distance it insinuates into the identities it lives and modifies, in the ironic dimension in its politicization of difference in a world in which identity is essential to life, in its insistence on questioning fixed unities even while admiring some more than others.

It is not the best liberalism which could be dreamt, only the best which could be lived if we are incomplete without social form in a world not predesigned to mesh smoothly with any particular formation of personal and collective identity.

Notes

1. I treat it as a "projection" but not as one for which no *comparative* defense can be given. Perhaps the best defense is one which proceeds at the level of a critical history of both lived ontologies and formally developed ones. Hans Blumenberg, *The Legitimacy of The Modern Age,* trans. by Robert Wallace (Cambridge: MIT Press, 1983), is exemplary here. It traces the history of teleological/transcendental philosophies, the internal difficulties they have encountered, and the obstacles a new version of such a philosophy will have to overcome. Michel Foucault, *The Order of Things* (London: Tavistock Publications, 1970), provides an exemplary account as well, reaching its peak in the account of "Man and His Doubles," indicating how the modern episteme presuppose assumptions about finitude which are incapable of grounding themselves. My own effort at this level for political theory is *Political Theory and Modernity* (New York and London: Basil Blackwell, 1988).

2. Hobbes, *Leviathan,* edited by Michael Oakeshott (New York: Collier Books, 1962), Part I, ch. 8, p. 61.

3. *Leviathan,* Part I, ch. 8, p. 63.

4. Ibid.

5. Thomas Hobbes, *Man and Citizen,* edited by Bernard Gert (New York: Doubleday and Co., 1972), ch. 9, p. 141. Another version of this law, now the fifth law of nature, appears in *Leviathan,* Part I, ch. 15, p. 119. Once human beings have *become* self-interested beings with a moral face, *then* Hobbes strives to create some room for them to exercise individual freedom within an absolutist order. But it is the first step that needs more attention in readings of Hobbes, partly through attention to his discussion of madness. Hobbes, on my reading, treats the self-interested self as a construction valued to a considerable degree because it is a solid bulwark of order. The individual is not prior to order or consistently a limit to it: it is partly an effect of order and a bearer of it. Contemporary individualism might be seen to be closer to those who give primacy to order than usually thought when these themes are developed.

6. Quoted in an op-editorial, "Bosket's Law: Trouble Sets You Free," *New York Times,* April 21, 1989.

7. Martin Heidegger, *Identity and Difference,* translated by Joan Stambaugh (New York: Harper and Row, 1969), p. 32.

8. John Rawls, "Justice as Fairness: Political not Metaphysical," *Philosophy and Public Affairs* (Summer 1985), p. 1. I participate in the onto-theological tradition in one way but not in two others. For this essay invokes a social ontology as it engages alternative theories of liberalism. But it problematizes its own projections at this level and it refuses to endorse one of those perspectives which either treats being as if it were designed *for us* in some fundamental way or treats the world as if it were a standing reserve thoroughly susceptible to mastery *by us*. It refuses the transcendental reassurances associated with onto-theology.

9. Ibid., p. 4.

10. Michael Shapiro examines the rhetorical strategies of some contemporaries in a way which is relevant to this issue. See "Politicizing Ulysses: Rationalistic, Critical and Genealogical Commentaries," in *Political Theory* (February 1989), pp. 9–31, and *The Politics of Representation* (Madison: University of Wisconsin Press, 1988), especially chapter 1.

11. George Kateb, "Democratic Individuality and the Claims of Politics," *Political Theory* (August 1984), p. 335.

12. Ibid., p. 343.

13. *New York Times,* August 30, 1988, p. 30.

14. This portion of the argument is developed more extensively in William Connolly's *Politics and Ambiguity* (Madison: University of Wisconsin Press, 1988), especially chapters 2 and 5.

15. The sources of closure and naturalization in identity are multiple and overdetermined as Nietzsche represents them. That is why it is so difficult and important to confront and contest these pressures. His treatment of language as a dense medium which condenses and consolidates values of the herd; of the limited capacity for consciousness and the extensive demands for social regularization which combine to drive many commonalities to the level of the tacit, the implicit, the unconscious and the habitual; of the disturbance sown when a lived identity is exposed to be conventional or artificial; of the limited capacity within each social order to tolerate diversity of identities— all of these themes must be considered when evaluating the quest to open up those themes and norms which have become closed. Nietzsche insists, first, that the sources of closure are powerful and, second, that no closed set of commonalities reflects a higher direction in being.

16. Friedrich Nietzsche, *On the Genealogy of Morals,* trans. Walter Kaufmann (New York: Vintage Books, 1969), p. 127.

17. Friedrich Nietzsche, *Beyond Good and Evil,* translated by Marianne Cowan (South Bend: Gateway Editions, 1955), pp. 70–71.

18. George Kateb's essay, "Thinking About Human Extinction," *Raritan* (Fall 1986), pp. 1–29, brings out this dimension of Nietzsche superbly. Nietzsche's own version of individuality is brilliantly elaborated in Werner Hamacher, "Disgregation of the Will: Nietzsche on the Individual and Individuality," ed. Harold Bloom, *Friedrich Nietzsche* (New York: Chelsea House, 1987), pp. 162–212.

19. George Kateb, "Democratic Individuality and the Claims of Politics," *Political Theory* (August 1984), p. 355.

20. Ibid., p. 356.

21. Charles Taylor, "Connolly, Foucault and Truth," *Political Theory* (August 1985), p. 385. A more extensive comparison of Taylor to Foucault within the territory of language can be found in Connolly, "Where the Word Breaks Off," *Politics and Ambiguity* (Madison, University of Wisconsin Press, 1987), ch X.

22. Jean-Jacques Rousseau, *The Confessions* (New York: Doubleday, 1960), p. 43.

24. Charles Taylor, "Connolly, Foucault and Truth," p. 385.

25. I am aware that Nietzsche does not always or consistently prove to be apolitical. But the overman, as presented in *Thus Spoke Zarathustra*, trans. Walter Kaufmann (New York: Penguin Books, 1954), seems to me to provide a highly apolitical presentation. I further suggest that any other references to the overman, especially in the unpublished texts, might be referred to this foundational text for clarification and contextualization.

5

Is Liberalism Good Enough?

Kenneth L. Schmitz

> And so begins a chat (*sermo*), not about other men's homes and estates, nor whether Lepos dances well or ill; but we discuss matters which concern us more, and of which it is harmful to be in ignorance—whether wealth or virtue makes men happy, whether self-interest or uprightness (*usus rectumne*) leads us to friendship, what is the nature of the good and what is its highest form.
>
> Horace, *Satires* II, vi. 70–76

A free market will undoubtedly offer several varieties of goods for sale, including a variety of theories of the good. As we enter the bazaar we can expect to be offered the very best theory of the very best good; nor should we be surprised to find the trademark "Liberal" stamped upon it, and perhaps the logo: "Produced by the Forces of Liberalism." And yet, it seems prudent to look over a few other wares, some older perhaps, some even newer, even some that seem bizarre. The wary customer may be excused if he or she does not by impulse (subliminal or otherwise) take up the most popular brand, but looks about a little. For the advertisements, however insistent, may not be finally persuasive. Indeed, one of them may even claim that the liberal theory is so good that it can't be classified as a mere theory of the good, much in the same way that for a time General Electric claimed to produce "Progress" instead of light bulbs. It may claim that liberalism rises above the fray, stands indifferent to the competing theories of the good and does not abandon its neutrality even when it referees the inevitable competition that arises. So that the good life is best lived without the encumbrance of a theory of the good. Well and good; but the prospective buyer must still test both claims: (1) that liberalism has the best theory of the good, and (2) that it doesn't need one.

It is still wise to ask whether liberalism is the best we can do. It is no secret that liberalism promotes the individual; that headline won't sell newspapers. It is said, too, by older voices, that it neglects the common good. My discontent is lodged, however, in its central affirmation, and how liberalism understands the very individual whose interest it strives to promote. What is unsatisfactory about liberalism is neither the central importance it attaches to the individual, nor its pursuit of the individual's good. What is at issue is the nature of the individual's good. What is good for the individual, however, is relative to what he or she is and how he or she is understood. And it is just here, it seems to me, that liberalism fails its clients, because—or so it seems to me again—liberalism does not give full value to the individual. My thesis, then, is that liberal liberty is reductionist.

For there is a richer, fuller understanding of the individual available in the long tradition cf so-called Western thought. I go back to Aristotle for the beginning of its career; but I do not mean that we should rest there. For not only has the notion of the individual changed since the citizen of the Greek *polis* has passed into history, but the reality itself has changed. What it is to be an individual has greatly changed, and liberalism has striven to take account of that. By using the words "good enough" in the title, I mean to indicate that I do not reject liberalism outright—whole and entire. Rather, my subordinate thesis is that its account of the massive change we call "modernization" is only partial; and that liberal liberty is reductionist because classical modern liberalism has expressed only the moment of *difference* in that change, even though it has often expressed that aspect with clarity and verve. But the same Aristotle also tells us that change combines novelty with permanence, unites alteration with identity, and bridges discontinuity with continuity. Now, in expressing only what had changed, liberalism caught what was different between old and new, but (so far as it was possible) discarded the old in favor of the exclusive value of the new. Heir to the Renaissance and companion of the Enlightenment, it proclaimed a radical new beginning. Its ahistorical stance is not incidental to it, nor is its antitraditional voice accidental.[1]

It is hardly possible to retain a focus upon such a broad front as "Liberalism," since there are many different versions, even among classical modern proponents. And so, it is fair to ask: Whose ox is being gored and which fields are being left unploughed? Moreover, the approach taken will determine in part what is to be considered an essential feature of liberalism and what is not. My own philosophical—indeed, I admit it, metaphysical[2]—analysis casts its net rather broadly, so that important features of liberalism tend to merge with the more general movement of thought associated with the Enlightenment and its antecedents. Yet, despite the variety, there is need to address the question in broad terms. Of course, it does not make the discussion easier that the apostle of change itself has changed: liberalism has not stood still. Indeed, somehow even against its spirit, we can speak now of a liberal "tradition," for it has continued to develop an understanding of the individual on the basis of its early modern beginnings and within that particular horizon. Recent versions of liberalism have displayed imagination and ingenuity in meeting new and stressful circumstances. This is no small achievement. For in the sphere of politics, our century has shown an alarming proclivity toward illiberal regimes, and in economics it has exhibited an insensitivity to minimal government, low taxation, and minuscule national indebtedness. In response to current conditions, some contemporary theorists supply the liberal individual with a social conscience rather different from the one supplied by Adam Smith. He rested conscience upon the implacable cycle that was to bring about general prosperity as even-handedly against an unwary or unlucky merchant as against the laboring poor, whereas they place it within the context of democratic social policy.[3]

In a variety of versions, liberalism continues to thrive in moral theory, political discourse, and the law; while in economic policy it offers a range of advice from sophisticated free-market capitalism to redistributive social democracy.[4] The accents of public debate also show how deeply liberal values are embedded in our democratic *mores*.[5] This is not surprising if, as I have indicated and will argue further, liberalism offers a plausible interpretation of the complex of forces that has shaped the modern individual, even though its interpretation is but a partial and deficient expression of that complex. One need not endorse a metaphysics of the Zeitgeist in order to recognize that a prevailing wind does billow forth today, so that shouting into it may seem as pointless as a mere puff of contrary air. Or, to change the image, to look for something better than liberalism pits one against a main current in modern Western life in whose flow the social, political, and economic values of conventional wisdom find their buoyancy. And yet, if the liberal understanding of the individual arises out of profound and interconnected changes in science, technology and economics; in society, culture and politics; in philosophy, religion and art—the general features of liberalism may be brought into higher relief and sharper profile by a consideration of those interconnected changes. I neither can nor wish to document all of these changes, any more than I can address all versions of liberalism at once and in detail. But I do need to sketch points that are salient for my story of the individual, and salient, I hope, in reality too.

The Search for "Elementary Particles"

We know that the science of mechanics, and the industrial technology that eventually drew power from it, did much to shape early modern thought and practice. The mechanistic mode of analysis swept other spheres of thought and life along with it in the aura and with the impetus of its brilliant successes. Of course, science and technology were not exclusive agents of change. It seems, rather, that they were bearers and indicators of a deeper movement, which had its immediate antecedents in a broader trend. That drift included a theoretical shift during the late Middle Ages to nominalism in logic and metaphysics, and to empiricism in natural philosophy. Now, modern science and technology drew upon a conception of unity that was shaped by those antecedents and that put its stamp upon what was to become the liberal understanding of individuality.

Against the background of nominalism,[6] and in the spheres of physics, astronomy and various technologies, sixteenth-century mechanics launched scientific enquiry and technique upon a search for ultimate and elementary particles—at first called *minima*, corpuscules, and more rarely, atoms.[7] It is a search that continues to this day, though it is presently yielding pride of place among some theorists to more holistic approaches. According to its own terms, the search for absolutely ultimate and simple particles has been in vain; and yet its "vanity" has produced the most remarkable, and mostly beneficial, results. My present interest, however, is not directly in its contributions to scientific knowledge and technical application, but in its indirect influence. For mechanism helped to shape and to confirm the underlying conceptions of social interaction and to curtail the scope of rationality by defining rigor in terms of precision. Two features of this bias stand out: the twin demands for *self-sufficiency* and for *separateness*. The mathematization of scientific enquiry in its early modern phase led to a triumph of the ancient definition of geometrical points of space as "parts outside of parts." It is a victory that instrumental versions of rationality still cling to and that brings with it tendencies to social fragmentation. The search for elementary particles of matter lent support and gave expression to an analytic habit of mind that jealously guarded the principle of differentiation and the self-sufficiency of each particular idea or sensation. Among the intellectualists, Descartes pressed for clear ideas absolutely distinct from one another, Hobbes defined elementary bodies as concrete points in space, and among empiricists, Hume insisted upon the self-enclosed and discrete completeness of each impression. Among the transcendentalists, Kant posited the discreteness of data in the sensory manifold.

Now, a certain kind of unity requires separateness and the consequent externality of relationships. For the nature of the unity of anything determines the character of the relations into which the real or ideal unit (that is, the particle or idea) can enter. The status of an ultimate and elementary particle in mechanism is that it possesses a self-sufficiency which it retains even after it has entered into relations with other elementary particles. For that reason, its relations must remain external to it. In sum, then, the ultimate nature of the differential unity proposed by nominalism and pursued by mechanism consists in its *incomplexity*. For the ultimate nature of such differential units resides in their lack of parts. The ultimate units were ultimate precisely because they were simple in the sense of being the last possible point of analysis. To be one was to be simple, and to be ultimate was to be absolutely one—indivisible and irreducible. All relationships had to fall "outside" of them, therefore, taking the form of attachments to and detachments from a distinct and separate elemental unit.

Translated into the order of freedom, ultimate unity took the form of the discrete movement of the individual will. Moreover, voluntarism, often associated with nominalism, promoted the primacy of the will in the human individual. None celebrated the new sense of freedom more felicitously, however, than the eclectic Platonist, Pico della Mirandola. His *Oration on the Dignity of Man* places that dignity in the lack of a given nature in the human being, who possesses instead the open power of free choice. In more lapidary terms, Descartes espoused a minimal conception of human liberty as the absolute indifference to any and every alternative, an indifference extensive with the infinitude of the individual human will.[8] More generally, the notion of *conatus*, as the spontaneous striving of the individual human appetite (whether passional or rational), runs through the thought of philosophers from Hobbes to Leibniz to Hume and beyond. The conception of natural right is often cast along these lines at this time. Hobbes's dramatic formulas are well known, such as: that in the natural condition of mankind, "every man has a right to everything; even to another's body."[9] And Spinoza understood by natural right: "that every natural thing has by nature as much right as it has power to exist and operate."[10] Even Leibniz, who repudiated the extended separateness of the fundamental units, still understood each self-enclosed monad to be driven by its own wholly internal appetition.[11] Locke takes volition to be a simple rather than a complex idea.[12] And for Hume, a passion is "an original existence," moving the individual prior to rational deliberation, and therefore able to be countered only by another original impulse.[13] Insofar as conatus takes the form of will proper, we may speak of it as the power to choose, but in the broad sense it is appetite, passion, desire, sentiment or choice. What holds for all variant positions is that the individual human will or conatus is the impetus moving us prior to all else and the ground of all value. Even Kant, who speaks of obligation, means by it self-obligation, the principle of moral autonomy: the relation of the pure self-legislating reason to itself. All other relations must remain external to such a self-will. It follows, then, that everything other than the self is converted into the status of alternatives for choice and potential objects of possession. All else, in the broadest sense, then, becomes potential property. In sum, will, passion, appetite, desire, sentiment, and choice are but various ways of naming and understanding the striving for self-assertion and appropriation of others that, according to liberalism, is the conative element—passional and/or rational—at the moving core of each individual human being.

There is, however, a more basic feature of the archetypal mechanistic science of early modern times that takes us more deeply still into the liberal character of freedom. Modern science was, and still remains, a science of motion. Motion is understood as displacement, and rest is merely the temporary absence of motion; or, in entropy, it is the permanent unavailability for further movement. With the abandonment of final causes in seventeenth-century science, rest was emptied of one of the meanings it had once possessed, namely, that of the fulfillment of the individual through the attainment of its purpose. To the extent that social and political thought were in part influenced by mechanics, and in part themselves expressive of a deeper thrust that was concomitant with mechanics—to that extent the liberty possessed by the individual will becomes not simply the power to choose, the ancient *liberum arbitrium*. The nature of choice itself had changed. Or rather, the character of liberal liberty is not simply the power to choose: it is equally, even primarily, the power to *unchoose*. For what has primacy in this general view of the self is not that it is free to complete itself by choosing a good already somehow prescribed for it or inscribed in it, but rather that it achieves its own highest good by retaining the power not only to choose but also to relinquish that choice and to take up another. For, in retaining *that* power, it retains in the currency of freedom the very mobility that is of supreme import and interest in the science of nature. The foundation and force of liberalism lies in the simplicity of the individual's power to move—the impulse to change one's mind and one's place and, where possible, the world. In this motility lies its exaltation of the freedom of the individual.[14]

The Primacy of the Subject

So far, then, I have argued that liberalism is the socioeconomic, moral, and political interpretation of those features by which the modern individual differs from the past. Moreover, in the process that formed the modern individual, liberalism has given pre-eminence to a conception of unity as simplicity and of freedom as mobility. There is no doubt that liberal ideas have won for themselves an impressive authority, in part at least through their promotion of tolerance and defense of civil peace. In guarding the difference, however, liberalism has created the mythology of a discredited preliberal past as part of its antitraditional weaponry; and, in catching at the moment of difference, discreteness, and fragmentation that is an operative force in the formation of the modern individual, liberalism has assumed the shape of the distinctions and dichotomies that emerged four centuries ago in Europe. They arose in many fields, but let me remind you of them by telling of their emergence in modern philosophy. Philosophers sometimes trouble their neighbors by raising doubts over what seems indubitable. In so doing, they may articulate a sense of unease wider than their own. But philosophers also live in society, and they sometimes reinforce its certainties. It is likely, too, that those who are or become influential are those who formulate what the society intuits to be the fundamental nature of things.

Consider modern *epistemology*, which is receiving rather rough treatment from deconstructionists these days. According to it, the human subject proclaims itself to be the first and overriding principle. It certifies itself in virtue of its rationality or its experience, and variously according to the criteria of rationalism, empiricism, or transcendentalism. The powerful certainty of self-consciousness purchases for the subject a self-conviction that construes everything else as set over against it: in a word, as *ob-ject*. The canons of objectivity are the protocols by which the subject dominates its objects. On the basis of this certainty (which not even the skeptical Hume denied), various philosophers devised various mental shapes and methods to account for the way in which the object could be represented to the subject—could be brought to the bar of Reason (Spinoza), or into the vivid associations of the senses and passions (some empiricists), or led before the tribunal of the understanding (Kant). What prevails in these positions is the operative primacy of the subject.[15]

It is not surprising, then, that in the *ontology* of the modern period the human subjectivity, so dominant in epistemology, should put its imprint upon the very shape of things perceived, rendering them into objects admitted to "real" status only insofar as they are able to meet the conditions of subjectivity understood as the primary principle. To the scientists of the time, busy as they were discovering the secrets of nature, it may well have seemed (as Hegel is reported to have said) that the very world was being created before their wondering eyes. But it is also true that the world that was being discovered agreed wonderfully with the emerging dichotomies.

The principal aim of modern *technology* was enthusiastically proclaimed by seventeenth-century philosophers: it was to gain control over nature for human ends. With industrial technology, control easily took the form of active domination of nature which was approached as a passive field for human exploitation. The dichotomy of active manipulator and passive material fitted easily into the reigning parent dichotomy of subject and object. Obviously, it makes a considerable difference in the approach to nature whether a technologue sees himself as a dominant self who sets the agenda according to subjective human wants or as a human being who is situated in a less dominant position and is associated with nature in a more companionable way.

Finally, the very scope and nature of *rationality* came to be determined by the subjective pre-eminence that is inveterate in the parent dichotomy. The unequal status of subject and object can be seen in the double role enjoyed by the subject. On the surface it seems to be an equal and correlative partner in the relation between subject and object; but a deeper look discloses that it colors the whole relationship. That is, the subject functions in both a partial and an integral way: it is a party to the relation but it also lends to things its *own* shape and takes their utility for itself to be *their* significance. In admitting them as objects it validates them according to its demands for mathematical precision, systematic order, and verifiable evidence. In this way, the very limits of acceptable rational discourse come to be drawn closely about what is deemed to fall within the horizon of the individual human subject. Under such limitations it was all but inevitable that everything deemed to be in any way transcendent or mysterious (the matters of religion) should fall outside the pale of "rational" discourse. And this exile was prelude to such matters losing their place in the public discourse. The political disestablishment of any particular church or religion (justifiable on grounds of the freedom of conscience implicit in biblical religions) became the separation of church and state. But that *political* separation was preceded by the *epistemological* eviction of religion from "intellectually respectable" conversation. Reduced to mere opinion or belief, it was to be left wherever other private things are kept.

As we turn to *social thought,* I am aware that the logic of implication does not rule over events, which lend their own weight to the way ideas come to rest in the domain of social actuality. Nevertheless, ideas do offer a pathway along which events may take shape, especially if the ideas represent, express, interpret, or facilitate possibilities already imminent in the situation. At the beginning of the modern period the parent dichotomy of subject and object was rooted in (and gave further credence to) a growing sense of the inadequacy of the established institutions and the received traditions of the late medieval and early modern period—their perceived inability to cope with the unprecedented and burgeoning energies of individual agents. For the latter became increasingly independent of, and in many instances alienated from or hostile to, established authority.[16] Now, the parent distinction between subject and object gave canonical expression to that distance, and gave added weight to what I have called the differential. That differential at once gives distance to the social, cultural, and political "space" between the subject and its objects; but it also opens up a distance between the subject and other subjects. The negative fallout of that distance expresses itself in isolation, fragmentation, and alienation. On the positive side, however, it permits the subject to preserve its own individual freedom, to assert its primacy over objects, and to maintain its inviolability in the face of other subjects. The modern insistence upon individual rights is on its way.

In the classical versions of this view, self-interest (enlightened or not) has prior claim to legitimacy, even though it may require negotiation and qualification to settle rival claims and arrive at a guarded civility.[17] This strategy recognizes the indifferent equality of a plurality of dominant selves, and—out of a prudent fear—negotiates rival claims by contract, by appeal to the maximization of happiness, or more recently by procedural rules. The liberal strategy has as its primary aim to safeguard and promote—not happiness or virtue so much—as the liberty of the differential individual.[18]

Nevertheless, in the classical versions, self-love need not be invariably ungenerous or selfish. On the contrary, the self can extend itself to encompass concern for others. British (notably Scottish) philosophers and moralists placed emphasis upon the softer, gentler passions, while novelists (in eighteenth-century England, France, and Germany) paid tribute to the more tender sentiments.[19] Certainly, the promotion of tolerance in politics and of moderation in social mores marks one of classical liberalism's proudest moments, though it is offset by neglect of the poor, rapacity of unregulated competition, and excess of civil litigation. No doubt, the general spirit of tolerance was shaped at least in part by the pervasive distinction of subject and object mentioned earlier. For within that distinction the built-in primacy of the subject gained for the self a certain privilege in the way in which benevolence was understood. The continuum of loves divided into subjective interest and objective concern and, according to the parent dichotomy, this meant that love divided into egoism and altruism. The very language betrays the double role of self mentioned earlier. Moreover, the primacy of self gives rise to a "hermeneutics of suspicion" that purports to uncover self-love even in the seemingly purest altruistic motive.

In any event, altruistic or not, the high value placed by liberalism upon the individual self is, in my view, continuous with and a distortion of a more general hallmark of so-called Western culture. Christianity and biblical religion generally, so important in the formation of that culture, proclaim the spiritual equality and worth of each person. As well, however, the worth of the individual also has remote origins among the ancient Greeks. For it finds among them an early echo in the honor paid to self-subsistence and in the striving for self-sufficiency and even autonomy (*kath'auto,* cf. *ens per se*). In attempting to recover what, it seems to me, is a more adequate and timely sense of the worth of the individual and the inherent equality of individuals, it is with the Greeks that I begin—and particularly with Aristotle.

The Complex, Constitutive Individual

Now, Aristotle's individual is a complex affair.[20] He calls it "this somewhat" (*tode ti,* cf. *hoc aliquid*), "this something of a certain kind." The two factors, 'this' and 'what', are distinct in thought and speech, but they are not separate in reality. For the primary realities of Aristotle's world—and of ours as well, I must add—are composite but not composed. They are really complex, but they are not put together out of independent and separate entities. One never meets a this that is not also a what, nor a what that is not in reality a this. The 'this' captures the *singularity* of each real and individual thing, while the 'somewhat' indicates what it shares with other things, and which I call its *commonality*. By the latter term I do not mean merely the abstract character which comprises its species and genus, but all of the constituent principles that it shares with other things. To Aristotle, the 'somewhat' (*ti*) stood in the first instance for the essence or substance of the thing (*ousia,* cf. *substantia, natura*). By calling the 'what' (*ti*) 'commonality', however, I mean to extend it so as to include the cultural and social constituents that make up our changing individuality. Without attributing the extension to Aristotle himself or minimizing the difference between his problematic and mine, we can nonetheless recognize that for him no individual could be complete without the relationships brought about by life in the *polis*.

To be sure, Aristotle acknowledges the necessity of tradition for building up the skills of artisans and by implication for social life as a whole. Undoubtedly, however, we give more weight today than he did to the role played by time and history in the constitution of the individual. With the disruption between past and present introduced by historical consciousness and with the emphasis upon the differential that is thought to separate us from the past, we have become aware of the situatedness of the individual in time in general and within a particular cultural and social space-time context. This need not mean, however, that an individual is so radically immersed in the situation that all individuality is lost. The singularity secures its uniqueness. For the singularity and commonality that constitute the *integrity* of the individual do not relate as part to part but as whole to whole. That is, the individual is through and through singular, but also in regard to many of the commonalities he or she is fully and entirely them. The individual is not of French culture or German-speaking or an American citizen with only a part of himself or herself, but is such commonalities whole and entire. So, too, is he or she entirely singular.

Aristotle's complex individual, and the constitutive individual here developed on the basis of it, differ from the primary sense of individuality entertained by the ancient atomists and the late medieval nominalists. As I have already mentioned, the original, primary, and paradigmatic sense of unity was for them the absolutely simple. The unit was a single particular point, irreducible and solitary, radically incomplex.[21] Aristotle's individual, on the other hand, far from being isolated in ultimate self-closure, receives its very constitution—for good and for ill—from and through its causes and in its ongoing relatedness to others. The real and shared presence of others is constitutive of the individual through its commonalities.[22]

I have avoided calling the commonalities 'conditions', because an inflationary use of the latter term would treat the commonalities as though they were external to an alleged 'core'.[23] It is not easy to find a suitable name for the primacy of the individual self that can be applied commonly to the varieties of liberalism, and yet such a core is part of liberal understanding. The core is, or would be, a free self: an *elector* self in the root sense of the Latin term. For, as far as possible, and in some sense prior to other individuals and society, it would select the terms under which it relates to them; let us say, then, in shorthand: a *selective* self. It is in some sense a law unto itself: hence we might call it an *autonomous* self, since even Kant's law-obligated moral ego is self-governed. Again it is in some sense a *pre-institutional* self, since the institutions to which it subscribes are in principle its own product and derive their legitimacy in some way from its consent.[24] It is in some sense an *independent* self, since it holds itself in reserve and apart.[25] In contrast, the constitutive individual, whose integrity consists of its singularity and its commonality, has no separate core. It is singular with a singularity that is not something independent, related to its conditions by external relations. The singularity, even as the commonality, is an inseparable though distinguishable factor in the constitution of the individual. Once again, these complex constitutive individuals are primary realities; in their own order—the primary order of reality, if Aristotle is right—they are not products, not mere juxtapositions of ultimate, independent, separate components. Rather, such components—taken in themselves and in isolation from their context—are abstractions from concrete, complex, composite (but not composed) individuals.

Nor would I call the commonalities 'properties'. John Locke gave to the term 'property' a wide meaning, to include life, liberty, and estates, and within that, we may suppose convictions, ideas, and free speech.[26] Now, these are among the constituents that enter into the formation of the modern individual, along with other traits, physical, psychological, and spiritual, such as genetic endowment, familial custom, educational formation, social circumstances, and moral ideals. But the way we name things usually indicates the focus of our interest, the ordering of our values, and where our heart or our desires are. Here the two different names demonstrate the contrast between the selective self and the constitutive individual. For to use the term 'commonalities' rather than 'properties' is to reverse the flow of individual and social life.[27] Now, the term 'commonality' looks to the community as an integral part of what it means to be an individual. It names those constituents within the individual by which he or she is released from and enabled to transcend the singularity which is equally constitutive. The term 'property', on the other hand, looks back toward privacy and ownership (*proprium*), and to the exclusivity of the radically selective self. It follows in that view that all of its relationships must fall outside of the individual as special forms of possession. Indeed, in at least one version, the given talents and inherited advantages are alienable by the society, as though they are so much property.[28] My quarrel with liberalism, then, is that, try as it may, and however much complexity it admits, it holds that complexity at arm's length.[29] If it did not, it would have to revise its understanding of the individual and with that it would have to revise what it means by freedom and by choice.

The constitutive individual, on the other hand, is not a selective self, fortifying itself by preference or by guarded civility; nor does it hide behind an adroit management of masks (*personae*). It is a composite unity of singularity and commonality that from its inception is already underway, continually undertaking and undergoing its own constitution—not by election merely, but by participation. I cannot separate out my genetic endowment or my enculturation from me: I do not have them as property. I *am* them; they do not belong to me, they are not mine, they are *me*. This identification does not entail the loss of my identity through submergence in the community, because I am not simply my participation in commonalities; I am also and equally my singularity.

Equality is not only an affair *among* individuals; it is also an ontological parity *within* each individual. This intrinsic, constitutive equality is, in its origins, not only a moral demand. Rather, the moral sanction is grounded in and rises out of an ontological necessity: there can be no *what* without a *this,* no commonality without singularity, and conversely. The equality of integrity constitutive of each individual grounds the moral sanction, on the one hand, against irresponsible singular behavior and, on the other, against repressive collective conformity. From equality within the individual there arises equality among individuals, and that equality sanctions the just freedom of the individual. That is why it is *not* good or just that one be forced against his or her will to die for the people. On the contrary, in the scales of justice, each individual person is equal in right to the whole people and to the entire apparatus of the state. The "hard" choice is not one which forcibly sacrifices the one for the many, but that which refuses to consider such an option.[30]

Commonalities that Bind

Of course, nowadays few are likely to deny the influence of the social milieu upon the individual.[31] It is agreed upon on all sides: no man is an island, Robinson Crusoe notwithstanding. The issue is not the social fact, but how we are to understand it, what implications it might hold, and why we understand it variously. For liberals, it seems to me, the social milieu must remain a set of conditions, the complex property of the selective self. If, on the other hand, we accept 'commonality' as an initial interpretation of the social milieu, we arrive at a different understanding. Many commonalities are accidental, of course, and even dispensable; nor do all have moral implications, though some do. Nor are all commonalities benign. But in any event, an important number of them are not simply detachable; at least some are not simply preferences to be dealt with in whatever way I choose or on the basis of agreed upon conventions. Some commonalities set up a claim upon me prior to any election on my part; I have not elected them. To be sure, I can, and perhaps may, choose to ignore the claim. But some commonalities give a certain disposition to my life and person and constitute a certain directive for me. I am not entirely free, nor ever am. I am provided with norms prior to my choice, norms that are not simply given and neutral facts, but that come to me already bearing the weight and inclination (*pondus*) of some value and some good.

Commonalities do not so much reside in me as I in them, since I live with them and in them. That I am a male is not simply a fact, nor did it arise by my preference. Nevertheless, it orients me in the social world in definite ways. It would be silly to give moral value to such a status, even though we must admit that in the past, social authority was often denied to women on that basis, and that our own society is not without bias in this and other ways. Such a commonality, without having moral value in itself, nonetheless plays a part in determining the way in which the individual enters into social and moral relationships. Sometimes such a commonality will give rise to moral responsibilities, including those of fatherhood. Consider another commonality, that binds me to two individuals as their son, and which binds me to them in certain ways by a bond that lies prior to my choice. It would be silly again to give moral value to the mere fact of the bond itself, but from it there arises a certain norm that is directive of my conduct toward them: honor thy parents. Or yet again, I am called to acknowledge teachers from whom I have received a cultural and intellectual formation, and friends who cooperated in the formation of my character. Such commonalities present themselves as dispositive, even directive, even sometimes as normative. They are often prior to any choice on my part, nor is my acknowledgment of them and response to them what for the first time endows them with value. They are not simply benevolences. Liberalism neutralizes such givens, puts them out of play, and then may reappropriate them selectively and by election.

Once again, I do not mean that the influences which we receive through our participation in society and which I have called 'commonalities' are uniformly benign; neither we nor our societies are that perfect. Nothing I have said should lead to complacency. To the contrary, our involvement in such processes and relations from the beginning of our formation as individuals should urge us to increased constructive efforts to improve our social as well as our natural environment. I am not pleading for sentimentality and warm feelings, nor for benevolence or altruism, however desirable that may be. I am not directing my argument primarily toward the will or the feelings, but above all toward the understanding. I am arguing that the ground of certain directives is built into and inseparable from our own formation and character. Liberalism can certainly countenance and even recommend benevolent feelings, for not all liberals envisage a rival power struggle that results at best in guarded civility and more likely in disciplined greed. Nor am I urging that the commonalities be treated as common assets to be handed over to the collectivity. The generosity at work in the constitution of the individual lies in the very nature of things, and much of it at a depth prior to the choices of individuals. It is the very dynamic of the natural and social world. The constitutive participation of the individual does not depend in the first instance upon good-feeling, but rather upon the processes by, in, and through which the individual is constituted. The civic friendship that Aristotle thought inseparable from a healthy society is based not simply upon good intentions—though it can hardly flourish without them—but upon the fact of our individual as well as of our social and political constitutions. For, in the end and from the beginning, our individuality is situated in what is neither wholly mine nor wholly yours, but ours. We are none of us self-made, and we owe "debts" that by the nature of time we often cannot directly pay, but are called upon to repay to society and to others than those to whom we are directly indebted.

In liberalism the question of the good seems to be an affair of barter between selective selves on the basis of a negotiated justice; but in fact the human good does not involve humans alone. Among the commonalities that make up the individual are those in which each of us is involved in and with the world of nature. Now, not only is liberalism deficient in acknowledging the contribution of others to the constitution of the individual; it has in the past reinforced the exploitative bent that has been so pronounced an animus in industrial technology from its beginning. While the liberal may negotiate a compromise with other selective selves, nevertheless, in putting the selective self first, it is disposed to approach nature as something to be mastered and put to uses dictated by our preferences. Today's liberal can no longer put his trust in a "hidden hand" that is supposed to rectify imbalance, the happy coincidence of individual wills each pursuing its own interest, apparent or real, and unwittingly to the overall benefit. For just as we, so too has he discovered that the hidden hand is ours. It is no judicious and impartial judge: it is us.

No doubt the power we have accumulated is awesome. For the most part it has been to our real benefit, but lately nature has been showing signs of exhaustion and worse. Now, the putative "law of market forces" puts no brake upon the limitless exploitation of nature to the satisfaction of our wants, real or artificially simulated. To the contrary, advocates still seek solutions through ever-increasing productivity. Eventually, even our politicians will have to stop crying: jobs, jobs, and more jobs! and salesmen stop beckoning: buy, buy, consume still more! It may be demurred that the liberal can always take matters in hand and negotiate the best ways in which to resolve ecological issues such as we face today and are likely to face for years to come. However, his clear-headed but prudent fear may prove too late to be timely, and may be too indecisive in the face of the plethora of individual wants. In retaining the primacy of the selective individual self, he will be tempted to set the limits of choice too wide.

There is need, instead, of a renewed solidarity with nature that liberalism is unlikely to provide. If, on the other hand, we are indeed constitutive individuals, then that solidarity is already there, often unrecognized, but nonetheless working in us and in our dealings with nature. Is not nature telling us something about the good when we treat it well and also when, in our thoughtless pursuit of goods, we treat it ill? That frantic pursuit throws a dark light upon the profile of the good. It is as though we have been treating nature like the dummy hand at bridge, only to realize lately (if not too late) that it has begun to play its own hand and is beginning to deal us some rather unwelcome cards—in the disvalues of pollution, exhaustion of resources, and similar evils. For they in actual fact are commonalities, too. Along with the stimulus of a salutary fear, constitutive individuals, conscious of themselves, may help to return Western attitudes toward the recognition of a deeper solidarity with the very constitution of the earth. On such a ground it would be possible to build our politics toward a renewed integrity.

Such a task does not call upon us to abandon civility; nor does it tolerate a totalitarian imposition of an arbitrary notion of the good. Our various commonalities are too diverse for that! And our freedom is too deeply rooted in the equality of integrity within each individual. Negotiation, discussion, and accountable judgment will still be needed. There will still be greedy, fraudulent, self-serving, and violent individuals, cynics and cheats as well. But the public discussion will not proceed on the basis of what is simply mine over and against what is simply yours, for many things are neither simply mine nor simply yours, but both mine and yours, or rather, ours. The public language will be less directed toward *my* rights than toward *our* possibilities. Instead of the primary language of litigation and private rights, the public language will have to include the recognition of our solidarity with others as well as with nature: with others on the basis of the equality of integrity, and with nature, because in our search for a reasonable individual and social good, we must build the good of nature into our concern *as it has already been built into us*. I do not think that liberalism has the resources with which to do this, since it does not have an adequate notion of the individual or its good. And yet, it needs one that it cannot have. Anyway, we, as individuals and in community, need it.

My strategy in this chapter has not been to ask what moral and social order I might prefer, and then to set out its conditions and presuppositions: that is a liberal strategy. I have tried, rather, to arrive at a more realistic understanding of the individual and to build up my moral and social expectations from there.

Notes

1. The call for new beginnings was, of course, quite general during this time, even among those who are not usually associated with liberalism. Thus, Descartes wrote in his *Discourse* (Part II): "Nevertheless, as far as the opinions which I had been receiving since my birth were concerned, I could not do better than *to reject them completely for once* in my lifetime, and to resume them afterwards or perhaps accept better ones in their place, when I had determined how they fitted into a rational scheme." *Discourse on Method and Meditations* (Indianapolis: Library of Liberal Arts, 1960), p. 12; emphasis added. Descartes protests that his revolution should remain within the sphere of ideas alone, but history has shown us that modes of thought may become institutionalized. The myths of the state of nature, made famous by early modern thought, may differ from one another, but they all agree in possessing a prehistorical character that is ahistorical and antitraditional. Moreover, this feature has been a propellent for social change, and it still remains in current versions of liberalism. Thus, John Rawls posits a hypothetical "original position" behind a "veil of ignorance." *A Theory of Justice* (Cambridge: Harvard, 1971), pp. 17ff and 136ff. And although Bruce Ackerman rejects all versions of the state of nature and of contractarianism, and although he permits us to bring the baggage of our opinions and our social conditioning on board his metaphorical "spaceship," and even later permits us to adjust the "perfect technology of justice" to meet real conditions, he stipulates that "no prior conversation has previously established the legitimacy of any claims to the manna [i.e., the primary goods] in dispute." Moreover, we are required to imagine ourselves "on a spaceship that comes upon a new world where the available manna has not, up to now, been claimed by anybody." *Social Justice in the Liberal State* (New Haven: Yale, 1980), p. 25.

2. It may be objected that I needlessly inject a "metaphysical" reading of the individual into a social context that can be better handled by games theory or social pragmatics. That can, of course, be matter for discussion, but I reject the positivist tactic of using "metaphysics" as a scare-word, or as a form of intellectual contempt. The question at issue is whether the individual is something like what I will set forth or not, and whether such an analysis is relevant to the problem at hand. It will not do, therefore, to arbitrarily put such an analysis out of play in social thought on the grounds that it is "metaphysics," or because Rawls or others did not intend a metaphysical reading, any more than a physician can dispense with diagnoses or an engineer with the physics of forces.

3. Cf. the oft-quoted passage from *The Wealth of Nations*, III, 4:

two different orders of people who had not the least intention to serve the public. . . . Neither of them had either knowledge or foresight of that great revolution which the folly of the one [the landed proprietors], and the industry of the other [the merchants and artificers], was gradually bringing about.

What was further urged by Adam Smith in the eighteenth century as *benevolence* toward the poor becomes in the twentieth a primary feature of *justice* as fairness toward the "least fortunate" or "least advantaged class." Rawls, op. cit., p. 98f.

4. John A. Hall, *Liberalism: Politics, Ideology and the Market* (Chapel Hill: North Carolina UP, 1987), pp. 35–62 *passim*, raises the issue of the connection between liberalism and capitalism. He is not alone in arguing that, despite their long-standing historical alliance, the connection is nonetheless contingent. The divergence of their central interests, he argues, puts them in potential conflict; for central to liberalism is the moral worth of the individual, whereas central to capitalism is the maximization of profit. He also notes the change in some versions of liberalism that has been brought

about by social democracy, which requires a strong social infrastructure and comprehensive safety net, in order to promote the moral worth of the individual. Thus, John Rawls insists upon the distribution of primary goods, including our inherited talents, in keeping with the needs of the least advantaged and in accordance with the principles of justice as fairness (op. cit., p. 101f., 179).

5. A MacIntyre, *Whose Justice? Which Rationality?* (Notre Dame UP, 1988), p. 392, writes:

> Liberalism, as I have understood it in this book, does of course appear in contemporary debates in a number of guises and in so doing is often successful in pre-empting the debate by reformulating quarrels and conflicts with liberalism, so that they appear to have become debates within liberalism, putting in question this or that particular set of attitudes or policies, *but not the fundamental tenets of liberalism with respect to individuals and the expression of their preferences.* So so-called conservatism and so-called radicalism in these contemporary debates within modern political systems are almost exclusively between conservative liberals, liberal liberals, and radical liberals. There is little place in such political systems for the criticism of the system itself, that is, for putting liberalism in question (emphasis added).

6. Commenting upon the relatively modern recognition of individual liberty as a conscious political ideal, Isaiah Berlin, in his essay "The Two Concepts of Liberty," commends "the valuable discussion . . . in Michel Villey, *Lecons d'histoire de la philosophie du droit,* who traces the embryo of the notion of subjective rights to Occam." *Four Essays on Liberty* (Oxford UP: 1969, 1986), p. 129, n.1.

7. For my own account of the shift to elementary analysis, see "Analysis by Principles and Analysis by Elements," in *Graceful Reason: Essays in Ancient and Medieval Philosophy Presented to Joseph Owens, CSSR,* ed. Lloyd P. Gerson (Toronto: Pontifical Institute of Mediaeval Studies, 1983), pp. 315–330.

8. For Pico, see *On the Dignity of Man,* etc., trans. Charles G. Wallis (Indianapolis: Bobbs-Merrill (Library of Liberal Arts), 1965); for Descartes, see the fourth meditation where he writes:

> (God) has given me a volition more ample than my understanding. For as the volition consists of just one body, (its subject being) apparently indivisible, it seems that its nature is such that nothing could be taken from it without destroying it.

Both Descartes and Pico find the amplitude of the individual human will, its infinitude in scope, to comprise the very image of God in the individual human being (ed. cit., p. 116).

9. *Leviathan* I, 14; also "the right of nature . . . is the liberty each man hath, to use his *own power, as he will himself,* for the preservation of his own nature" (emphasis added). Hobbes's use of the term 'will' properly speaking is to designate the last act or decision, whereas my emphasis is meant to draw attention to the primitive conatus that underlies the process of deliberation and will in Hobbes and others.

10. *A Political Treatise,* c. 2, secs. 3–5. Of course, each philosopher embedded the conatus in his own fuller thought, as Spinoza here identifies natural right with the power of God or Nature. See also *A Theologico-Political Treatise,* c. xvi:

> The power of nature is the power of God, which has sovereign right over all things; and, inasmuch as the power of nature is simply the aggregate of the powers of all her individual components, it follows that *every individual has sovereign right to do all that he can;* in other words, the rights of an individual extend to the *utmost limits of his power* as it has been conditioned. Now it is the sovereign law and right of nature that each individual should endeavour to preserve itself as it is, *without regard to anything but itself;* therefore this sovereign law and right belongs to every individual, namely, to exist and act according to its natural conditions. . . . As the wise man has sovereign right to do all that reason dictates, . . . so also the ignorant and foolish man has *sovereign right to do all that desire dictates* (emphasis added). *The Works of Spinoza,* trans. R.H.M. Elwes (New York: Dover, 1951), 2 vols., vol. 1, pp. 292 and 200 respectively.) See also *Ethics* I, Definitions I and VII.

11. *Monadology,* paras. 11–15. Cf. also his revival of the notion of *vis activa.*

12. *Essay Concerning Human Understanding,* II, 6.

13. *Treatise on Human Understanding*, II, iii, 3. See the discussion of passional motivation according to Hume, in MacIntyre, op. cit., pp. 300ff.

14. Ackerman (op. cit., pp. 198ff) asks whether the forty-year-old "Shifty" should be bound by contracts he made at twenty, and asserts that the advantage his own liberalism of neutral discourse about power relations has over contractarianism lies in its "courage to question the doubtful notion that a promise, once fairly made, must *always* be kept."

15. Obviously, I am critical of any elevation of the distinction between subject and object to a primary and privileged role such as it enjoys in liberalism. At the same time, however, I am reluctant to add my voice to the growing chorus of those hermeneutists, deconstructionists, and neo-Marxists who vent their disaffection with modern epistemology. It seems to me that many critics do not sufficiently relinquish the *effective and operative primacy* of the individual subject, but retain it instead in the form of an aggressive critical rationality.

16. In France it came to a head in the attack upon altar and throne. See Hegel, *Phenomenology*, c. vi. Cf. K.L. Schmitz, "Enlightenment Criticism and Embodiment of Values: The Hegelian Background to a Contemporary Problem," in *Indian Philosophical Annual 1985–86* (Madras: 1986), vol. 18, pp. 33–53.

17. Ackerman (op. cit., pp. 343–46) presents a current version of liberalism that seems neo-Hobbesian in tone. Rejecting both contractarianism and utilitarianism, he nevertheless finds the former superior to the latter on the score that "individuals have the *right* to put themselves first" (emphasis added). Still, the "true liberal," he writes, rejects the false individualism of Contract (with its hidden privileges and neglect of social influence) and also the false community of Utility ("brothers sharing in some mystical communion with the public good"). Instead the true liberal prefers (the word is mine) to base his position upon (1) the undefined and practically unlimited scope of individuals' subjective wants. In the beginning is the word, but the first words of the Ackerman dialogue are: "I want X!" "So do I!" The second assumption is (2) the scarcity of goods. I cannot help but observe that this is a scarcity by definition; that is, given the practically unlimited desires of individuals, an infinity of goods would not be enough. (3) The resultant conflict and struggle for power (Ackerman speaks of my rights against you, p. 347) needs containment. (4) A neutral dialogue is recommended which would consist of talk about power on the basis of "acceptable" reasons. The "neutrality" of the dialogue, however, remains suspect to me, and my suspicions are heightened by the demand for dialogic competence (p. 70), the obvious advantage of adult status (p. 110), the speculations about a world without moral significance, *sans* Creator, and in which we create "the only meanings we will ever know" (pp. 368–69), and the disposition made on several issues, including inter-generational conflict and the role of the family. Being invited to join such a "neutral" and "open" dialogue may turn out to be not unlike an invitation to a nudist camp, in which you are advised to divest yourself of your clothes only to arrive at the beach wearing considerably less than your hosts, who have retained what they regard as indispensable beach wear.

18. Brian Barry takes a stern view of these matters. He writes:

> Liberalism rests on a vision of life: a Faustian vision. It exalts self-expression, self-mastery and control over the environment, natural and social; the active pursuit of knowledge and the clash of ideas; the acceptance of personal responsibility for the decisions that shape one's life. For those who cannot take the freedom it provides alcohol, tranquilizers, wrestling on the television, astrology, psychoanalysis, and so on, endlessly, but it cannot by its nature provide certain kinds of psychological security. Like any creed it can be neither justified nor condemned in terms of anything beyond it. *The Liberal Theory of Justice: A Critical Examination of the Principal Doctrines in A Theory of Justice by John Rawls* (Oxford: Clarendon, 1973), p. 127.

The variety of contemporary interpretations of liberalism can be seen by reading the literature that has arisen around Rawls's book; compare, for example, Barry's study with those of M. Sandel, *Liberalism and the Limits of Justice* (Cambridge: 1982) and R.P. Wolff, *Understanding Rawls. A Reconstruction and Critique of A Theory of Justice* (Princeton: 1977).

19. See the discussion of the Scottish thinkers in MacIntyre, op. cit., esp. pp. 268ff. The novels I have in mind include Richardson's *Pamela*, Rousseau's *Emile*, and Schlegel's *Lucinde*.

20. For a more detailed development of my use of Aristotle, see: "Community: The Elusive Unity,"

Review of Metaphysics 37, no. 2 (Dec. 1983), pp. 245–64; "Metaphysics: Radical, Comprehensive, Determinate Discourse," ibid. 39, no. 4 (June 1986), pp. 675–94; and "Neither With Nor Without Foundations," ibid. 42, no. 1 (Sept. 1988), pp. 3–25.

21. The contemporary phenomenon of collectivism exhibits, it seems to me, the transference of the nominalist sense of unity (as incomplexity) from the individual members of society to society itself (writ with capital S). Leon Brunschvicg is reported to have commented upon the Nurnberg rallies:

> There is Durkheim's religion; the people worshipping themselves. The loss of effective identity on the part of the individuals is not surprising in such a conceptual scheme. If I am correct, then, collectivism is simply (i.e., conceptually, for things are never so simple in actual life) the contrary to liberal individualism, being founded upon the same notion of unity and identity. This may provide the conceptual basis for the recent drift of some liberal theorists towards a collectivist form of socialism under the pressure of the demands for equality and social justice. In opposition, the conservative liberal would hold on to the original identification of basic unity with the individual.

22. Isaiah Berlin (op. cit., p. 158) stresses the need of the individual for status (i.e., for acknowledgment by others). Hegel, too, has disclosed the necessary role of mutual recognition in the constitution of the self (*Phenomenology*, c. iv). No doubt, these commonalities are essential for human individuality, and I should want to include them in my own account; but I would also want to ensure that properly physical and metaphysical factors are operative in their own right and according to their modes.

23. In a recent version, even our inherited talents are assets external to the individual self. Discussing Rawls's proposals for the distribution of natural talents as common assets (see n. 1), Michael Sandel comments:

> No longer am I to be regarded as the *sole proprietor of my assets,* or privileged recipient of the advantages they bring. . . . I am not really the *owner* but merely the *guardian* or *repository* of the talents and capacities that *happen to reside* in me, and as such have no special moral claim on the fruits of their exercise. . . . By regarding the distribution of talents and *attributes* as a common asset rather than as *individual possessions,* Rawls obviates the need to "even out" endowments in order to remedy the arbitrariness of social and natural contingencies. . . . Although I am *entitled* to the benefits answering my legitimate expectations, I do not *deserve* them, for two reasons: first, given the assumption of common assets, I do not really *possess* the attributes that give rise to the benefits, or if I do possess them, it is only in the weak, accidental sense rather than the strong, constitutive sense, and this sense of possession is inadequate to establish desert in the strong pre-institutional sense (emphasis added, except for the last three instances). Op. cit., pp. 70–72.

24. Locke's solution to legitimacy (viz., that later generations have given their *tacit* consent merely by growing up in the society and accepting its benefits) is no longer persuasive to many liberals, so that the problem of legitimacy receives various and sometimes tortuous solutions.

25. *Apart:* Here again I stress the *disengaged* character of the liberal self and the externality of its relations as part to parts (as self to all others, all non-self). Ackerman is perhaps the most radical contextualist, for he insists upon the concrete individual's "interaction with society" (op. cit., p. 330). He further describes the individual as clothed with "the marks of our encounter with organized society." Still, he spurns any deeper grounding of the individual, because it would require "theological" (i.e., transcendent, and so unacceptable) arguments (p. 331). He rebukes the standing liberal traditions (Contract and Utility) for their appeal to "a hypothetical being who transcends the social situation in fundamental ways" (p. 332). It seems to me that Ackerman has here reached the conceptual limits of liberal individualism, and that in positivist fashion he shuts down the enquiry rather than move it toward an *a priori* self or to an overly situated and immersed self (cf. his critique of Utility, n. 16, and my remarks on collectivism, n. 21). Ackerman speaks freely of "our independent identities," despite his "contextualism." Here, it seems to me, lies the obscurity and ambivalence of liberalism, resident in the partial character of its account of modernity.

26. In respect to *conatus,* Locke places considerable qualification upon the acquisition of property.

It is to come about through labor and for use. Nevertheless, the individual's possession of property is central to his thought (see *Second Treatise on Government*, 5, 31–32).

27. For example, Sandel (op. cit., p. 64) puts Rawls's position thus: "as a person's values and ends are always *attributes and never constituents of the self,* so a sense of community is only an attribute and never a constituent of a well-ordered society. As the self is prior to the aims it affirms, so a well-ordered society, defined by justice, is prior to the aims—communitarian or otherwise—its members may profess" (emphasis added). The parallelism mentioned in n. 21 is explicit in this passage.

28. Cf. n. 4.

29. Sandel (op. cit., p. 64) writes:

> The assumptions of the original position (or Rawls) thus stand opposed in advance to any ("thick") conception of the good requiring a more or less expansive self-understanding, and in particular to the possibility of community in the constitutive sense. On Rawls' view, a sense of community describes a possible aim of antecedently individuated selves, not an ingredient or constituent of their identity as such. This guarantees its subordinate status.

There is much discussion of whether or in what sense Rawls is Kantian, and there are deontological as well as positivistic readings of his original position. But there can be no doubt of the essentially *pre-institutional* character of the Rawlsian self. I find some such priority of the self to be a constant feature of liberalism, whether "natural" or "postulational." See also n. 25.

30. Jacques Maritain brought the resources of personalism to this issue. See, among other writings, *The Person and the Common Good.* The situation between the individual and society is, of course, a quite different issue from "hard" choices between (inherently equal) individuals, as in health treatment and food aid; but such issues lie beyond the scope of the present essay.

31. Cf. n. 25.

6

Catholicism and Liberalism— 200 Years of Contest and Consensus

John Langan, S.J.

Seventeen eighty-nine is the date of the foundation of Georgetown University, a Catholic school in the then newly constituted United States of America, a school built on the traditions of the Society of Jesus and on the search for religious toleration in the colony and state of Maryland. It is also the date of signal events in the history of the country which has been both America's oldest ally and "the eldest daughter of the church." It is the year of the Stars and Stripes and of the tricoleur, a new order for the ages and the decisive revolution of the modern world.[1]

For Catholicism and for liberalism, 1789 is a year with an ambiguous legacy. For Catholicism in Europe, it raises the prospect of a society that affirms human freedom against the church and perhaps against Christianity and its God. For Catholicism in America, it opens up a prospect of free exercise and virtually unlimited expansion even in the midst of a largely hostile and suspicious population in its moment of victory. For liberalism in Europe, it raises questions about containing violence, anarchy, intolerance. For liberalism in America, it offers the opportunity to build government and order on a foundation of popular consent and constitutional guarantees of freedom. Given this difference in possibilities (deepened and intensified by the course of events from 1789 to 1800), it cannot be surprising that Roman Catholicism and liberalism both in Europe and America have been uneasy partners in the course of the last two centuries. One need only run over the names of John Carroll (the founder of this university, first archbishop of Baltimore, and active supporter of the revolt of the colonies)[2] and Joseph de Maistre, Pius IX and Camillo Cavour, Lord Acton and Cardinal Spellman, Woodrow Wilson and Francisco Franco, John Kennedy and Daniel Berrigan, John XXIII and Josef Mindszenty, John Courtney Murray and Josef Ratzinger to sense that liberalism and Catholicism have sometimes been mutually attractive, sometimes mutually repellent, both in Europe and in the United States.

It would be inappropriate in a volume which is primarily devoted to systematic issues to attempt to trace the complex history of the interrelations between Catholicism and liberalism over the last 200 years. But there are three doctrinal moments illustrating the convergence of and divergence between liberalism and Catholicism that should be highlighted and which can serve as guideposts for systematic reflection. I refer to them as doctrinal moments, although they do not involve matters of theological doctrine in the strict sense, because they are moments in which the church, and more specifically the papacy, appears as teacher on questions of social order and morality. The leaders of the church can also function as pastors, as priests, and (dare we say it) as political actors. Before we examine these doctrinal moments, we should remind ourselves that the church conceives of itself as having to meet demands and tests that are not always appropriate to political or legal theory. The three moments cover a span of 125 years and involve three quite different popes writing for different audiences in different political, cultural, and religious situations.

The Rejection of Liberalism by Catholicism: Pius IX (1864)

The first of the popes is Pius IX (1846–78), a pope whose central task was to confront the intellectual and political dominance of liberalism in Italy during the pan-European revolutionary fervor of 1848 and during the unification of Italy through the course of the next two decades, a process that he bitterly opposed even while good British liberals and Whigs like Gladstone and Palmerston backed it. It was under Pius IX's authority that the famous Syllabus of Errors was compiled in 1864. This is not a document that can stand by itself as a presentation of Catholic doctrine; rather, it is a listing, drawn from various Vatican documents, of positions that Catholics are not to hold. So each proposition is to be taken with a negation sign in front of it. Since some of the propositions are put forward in sweeping language or with specific justifying reasons, it requires only a little ingenuity to develop more acceptable versions of the condemned propositions. But the general impression that they conveyed to Pius's contemporaries was clearly a comprehensive rejection of the values of the liberal and progressive elements in European society, an impression that was confirmed six years later when the first Vatican Council defined the infallibility of the Pope's teaching *ex cathedra* on matters of faith and morals. Among the propositions condemned in the Syllabus are the following:

55. The church should be separated from the state and the state from the church.

56. Moral laws lack Divine sanction, and there is no need for human law to conform to the Natural Law or to receive obligatory force from God.

63. It is lawful to take away obedience from legitimate princes and even to rebel against them.

77. Similarly, it is not true that civil liberty for any religious sect whatever and the granting to all of full right to express any kind of opinion and thought whatever, openly and publicly, conduces to the easier corruption

of the morals and minds of peoples and the spread of the disease of indifferentism.

80.   The Roman Pontiff can and should reconcile himself and reach agreement with "progress," liberalism and recent departures in civil society.[3]

The condemnation of these and other propositions expressed Catholicism's desire in the mid-nineteenth century to retain its privileged position in Latin Europe and Latin America, where it wanted to deny the right of public worship to Protestant groups and to other religious traditions. For this and other reasons it is common to consider the Syllabus purely as an intolerant antiliberal document. Many of the condemned propositions, however, simply stated the government side of jurisdictional issues that had been contentious in European Christianity since the eleventh century. These disputes involved no necessary connection with liberalism: they were in fact often conducted by conservative or absolutist states anxious to assert dynastic or national control over an institution that was usually a significant center of wealth and influence in their societies and that often presented attractive possibilities for patronage and control to a manipulative government. In fact, when the Syllabus condemns propositions that would deny or restrict the liberty of the church it is defending ground that would also be protected by liberalism at least as liberalism is understood by liberals in the American tradition, although this defense is carried on from different premises. This is evident in the case of such propositions as the following:

39.   The secular government, since it is the original and source of all laws, is possessed of a type of law which can be circumscribed by no limits.

44.   The civil authority can intervene in matters which pertain to religion, morals, and spiritual discipline. Hence, it can decide concerning the instructions which the clergy of the Church issue, as part of their duty, for the regulation of consciences, and it can even reach decisions on the administration of the Divine Sacraments and the Dispositions necessary for their reception.

51.   Furthermore, the secular government has the right to depose bishops from the exercise of their pastoral ministry, and it is not bound to obey the Roman Pontiff in those things which concern the institution of bishops and bishoprics.[4]

On these and similar issues, Roman Catholicism would, in our own century, oppose totalitarian regimes, often with the sympathy and support of liberal governments.

In most Western countries liberal politicians and governments have had to work out a modus vivendi with established or culturally dominant churches. Catholicism, because of its international character and internal complexity and because it aimed at a greater degree of institutional autonomy than the Lutheran and Anglican churches, presented special difficulties in the working out of this modus vivendi. The modus vivendi is not likely to be conceived as the application of a single legal or constitutional principle such as the separation of church and state. The First Amendment to the U.S. Constitution in fact includes both a nonestablishment clause and a free exercise clause.[5] Only rarely do societies have the freedom which the United States had to determine a new basis for the relationships between church and state without provoking bitter civil strife and without negotiating involved compromises with existing interests and privileges.

A modus vivendi between church and state in a Western culture that is to be acceptable to liberals will have to include protections for freedom of conscience and of worship and for equal treatment of individuals in the social system, irrespective of their religious beliefs. It seems possible for societies to combine general acceptance of many liberal principles with a continuing religious establishment (Scandinavia, the United Kingdom). It is implausible to hold that establishment entails religious persecution; but it may well be reasonable to suspect that it is linked to religious discrimination of various sorts. There can also be cultural practices which fall short of the legal and financial reality of establishment but which express an acknowledgment of the dominant place of a particular religious group or tradition in the social and cultural life of the nation. Such an acknowledgment may be cherished or painful to different groups of citizens. In any event, there will be areas of social life that are objects of common concern both to the state and to churches. Among these are: education; the provision of health care; the solemnization of birth, marriage, and death; the conduct of worship in public places or in circumstances where there may be a threat to public order; the taxation of church property. In the controversies that arise in these areas, there are serious arguments both for public regulation of matters of public concern (such as the provision of elementary and secondary education) and for leaving room for individuals and groups to work matters out in a way that accords with their religiously shaped sense of the good. A great deal obviously depends on the size, vigor, and compatibility of the various religious groups. But disagreement in these areas should be no scandal in a liberal society which both affirms religious liberty and recognizes the different and conflicting accounts which the various religious groups offer of their social aspects. Here Catholicism and liberalism can and should find agreement in rejecting the efforts of statist, authoritarian, nationalistic, and totalitarian regimes to determine unilaterally the social dimensions of the exercise of religion or to exclude it altogether from the public space. At the same time, churches, even while they claim their own autonomy from the state, have to recognize not merely the right to liberty of other religions but also the autonomy of other spheres of society so that there are adequate economic, and cultural opportunities for those who are not affiliated with the dominant church group.

When the Syllabus of Errors is seen as addressing the issue of state control of religion and as affirming the freedom of the church, it turns out to be less antiliberal than most liberals had feared or than some conservatives had hoped. But there is little doubt that when the Syllabus is seen in the immediate context of Pius IX's struggles against European liberalism and Italian nationalism, its intentions and consequences are overwhelmingly antiliberal.

The Acceptance of Liberalism by Catholicism: John XXIII (1963)

A great deal changed in the hundred years that divided the Syllabus and the deliberations of the Second Vatican Council (1962–65). The collapse of the conservative monarchies of central, eastern, and southern Europe; their replacement in many cases by totalitarian regimes; the development of a great international conflict between liberal democratic regimes grouped around the North Atlantic and atheistic communist regimes in eastern Europe and Asia produced during the pontificate of Pius XII (1939–58) an effective alliance between Catholic leadership, both clerical and lay, and the liberal democracies of the West. Christian democracy, neo-Thomist philosophy (especially as interpreted by Jacques Maritain), and the social teaching of the church all came to include strong affirmations of many liberal institutions and values. Industrialization, internal and external migration, higher levels of education, and greater ease and speed of communication combined to create a situation in which older forms of social solidarity and social control lost their cohesiveness and in which liberal institutions seemed to be both the inescapable outcome of Western development and a welcome protection against Marxist hostility. Traditional rivalries between Christian confessions lost their intensity and militancy in the face of secularization. Even while secularization disappointed many of its early proponents, who had seen it as an unambiguous triumph of enlightenment over superstition, its steady growth, especially in western and northern Europe, forced the Christian churches and Catholicism in particular to reexamine basic aspects not merely of their relationship to the larger society but also of the ways in which they conceived and communicated the Christian message.

The crystallization of this change in Catholicism is to be found in the work of the Second Vatican Council and in the contemporary encyclical of John XXIII, *Pacem in terris* (1963). In *Gaudium et spes*, the pastoral constitution on the church in the modern world, the church presented itself as the spiritual complement of human society, capable of teaching and learning, of helping and being helped by the modern world. In *Dignitatis humanae*, the council gave a definitive and comprehensive acceptance to the value of religious freedom, both for individuals and for groups. This position is accompanied by an affirmation of the very limited competence of the government in religious matters:

> The protection and promotion of the inviolable rights of man are among the essential duties of government. Therefore government is to assume the safeguard of the religious freedom of all its citizens, in an effective manner, by just laws and by other appropriate means.[6]

However, it would clearly transgress the limits set to its power were it to presume to direct or inhibit acts that are religious. Moreover, government is to ensure that there is no religious discrimination among citizens.

The council's acceptance of religious freedom and of the open, nondiscriminatory form of society advocated by liberalism removed the last barrier to Catholicism's championing of the characteristically liberal and revolutionary doctrine of human rights. This was a position that the church had, in fact, already taken in supporting the Universal Declaration of Human Rights (1949) and in John XXIII's encyclical, *Pacem in terris,* issued in 1963. There human rights, derived from the nature of human beings as persons endowed with intelligence and free will, are affirmed to be "universal, inviolable, and inalienable."[7] The range of rights affirmed in this encyclical is broad and in many ways takes us beyond the pattern of social organization regarded as characteristically liberal. Thus it affirms:

> Every man has the right to life, to bodily integrity, and to the means which are necessary and suitable for the proper development of life. These means are primarily food, clothing, shelter, rest, medical care, and finally the necessary social services. Therefore a human being also has the right to security in cases of sickness, inability to work, widowhood, old age, unemployment, or in any other case in which he is deprived of the means of subsistence throughout no fault of his own.[8]

Satisfying these rights clearly requires a sophisticated welfare state, at least when we are dealing with advanced industrial societies. The encyclical also affirms in the economic sphere rights to free initiative, to work, to safe working conditions, to a fair wage, to ownership of private property, even of productive goods. In the spheres of intellectual and cultural life, it affirms rights to education, to free inquiry, to truthful information, to religious freedom, to freedom in the choice of a state of life, to free association. It also affirms rights to free movement and emigration, to participation in public life, and to juridical protection. Even though there are numerous specific differences between this listing of human rights and the classic political enumerations in the French Declaration of the Rights of Man (1789) and the U.S. Bill of Rights (1791), there is a strong family resemblance which makes it reasonable to think of *Pacem in terris* as proposing a set of human rights norms which require liberal institutions and practices as well as a welfare state. There are however, some important differences in the way in which rights are understood in *Pacem in terris* which take us away from characteristic liberal emphases. In the first place, rights are not treated as simply prior to duties or to natural law. John XXIII writes:

> For example, the right of every man is correlative with the duty to preserve it; his right to a decent standard of living, with the duty of living it becomingly; and his right to investigate the truth freely, with the duty of pursuing it ever more completely and profoundly.[9]

These correlative duties which fall upon the subjects of rights (which are distinct from the correlative duties falling on other persons to respect rights) are no more than what a Kantian would term duties of "imperfect obligation."[10] They may be vaguely put and may well be beyond the reach of legal enforcement. But they clearly presuppose a prior moral context in which human persons can understand both obligations and goods, a point that is either obscure or irrelevant in those liberal approaches that derive from Hobbes.[11] Agnosticism about good and about morality does not form part of the Catholic approach to theorizing about human rights.

This can also be seen in a second difference from the liberal mode of formulating human rights, namely, the inclusion (usually in adverbial form) of qualifications which ensure that rights guide activities to morally acceptable or successful outcomes. Thus the encyclical speaks of "the right to be informed truthfully about public events"[12] and "the right to honor God according to the dictates of an upright conscience."[13] It affirms "when there are just reasons for it, the right to emigrate to other countries and to take up residence there."[14] This qualification offers the attraction of attempting to ensure that rights are not misused or exercised in ways that conflict with moral norms and that they are not disruptive of social order, but it also opens up a series of challenges to rights and can weaken not merely their claim to absolute status (which many liberals would reluctantly concede) but even their prima facie urgency.[15] So, for instance, the qualification put on the right to freedom in expressing and communicating one's opinions "within the limits laid down by the moral order and the common good"[16] will strike most liberals, even those who are not "card-carrying members of the ACLU," as providing far too much room for restrictions on the exercise of this right, even if the restrictions are of a high-minded sort.

This brings us to the third difference in the Catholic approach to the affirmation and exercise of human rights, which is the insistence of a natural social context which includes as essential elements the state and the family, but which also includes in a more flexible and less clearly defined way "a great variety of intermediate groups and bodies" which enable people "to guarantee the dignity of the human person and safeguard a sufficient sphere of freedom and responsibility."[17] This encyclical, like all Catholic social thought of the last century, affirms the foundational role of the human family, "the first and essential cell of human society."[18] The human person is by nature a social being; since society requires authoritative direction to the common good, "every civilized community must have a ruling authority, and this authority, no less than society itself, has its source in nature, and has, consequently, God for its author."[19] The network of rights that human persons possess as an inherent aspect of their dignity as free and intelligent creatures is not to be understood as something that pertains to them in a pre-social state of nature but as an aspect of their shared life in a social and political community which is necessary for their fulfillment.

The appeal to human or natural rights can, however, in the Catholic tradition as well as in the liberal tradition, provide a point of leverage and criticism of the functioning of the actual political institutions of society, which are not to be simply equated with the naturally grounded and divinely established political authority mentioned in the text. John XXIII makes this point clear when he explicitly allows for a democratic determination of the form and limits of government.[20] This is a point on which there has been significant change within the Catholic tradition over the last hundred years. Leo XIII, for instance, in the encyclical *Immortale Dei* (1885), urges rulers to be mindful that God is the paramount ruler of the world and that they are to rule their subjects in a paternal spirit, for the common good. At the same time he admonishes subjects that they should be "convinced that their rulers hold authority from God" and should "feel that it is a matter of justice and duty to obey them."[21] Invoking Romans 13, he affirms: "To despise legitimate authority, in whomsoever vested, is unlawful, as a rebellion against the Divine Will; and whosoever resists that, rushes wilfully to destruction."[22] This should be contrasted with the position taken by Vatican II in *Gaudium et spes,* where the obligation to obey political authority is made conditional on its being exercised "within the limits of morality and on behalf of the dynamically conceived common good, according to a juridical order enjoying legal status."[23] At the same time the council affirms that "it is lawful for them [the people] to defend their own rights and those of their fellow citizens against any abuse of this authority, provided that in doing so they observe the limits imposed by natural law and the gospel."[24] This is probably as close as Catholic official teaching comes to an acceptance of the right of rebellion affirmed in liberal political thought.[25]

Catholic practice over the last twenty years has clearly moved in a liberal direction, with the church serving as an active critic and opponent of both authoritarian and totalitarian regimes and with its members being actively involved in both peaceful and violent protests against injustice and repression. Without accepting the individualism presupposed in most liberal and contractarian theories of the state, Catholicism has still been able to develop a practice that has strong affinities with liberalism as a political movement. The roots of this change lie in the church's affirmation of human rights and institutional pluralism and in its increasing acceptance of popular demands for economic justice (which can also be interpreted as demands for economic human rights.) The church has over the last twenty years shown itself increasingly ready to defend not merely its own rights and liberties and those of its members, but also the rights of those who are not members (for example, leftist political activists in Chile, black South Africans) and the rights of the people in general (in Brazil, Poland, the Philippines). This is an important indication of a universalized moral commitment and not of a mere change in political alliances or of a willingness to make compassionate responses in an emergency situation (as in rescuing some victims from the Holocaust).

If we look at the matter in more theoretical terms, we can see in the appropriation of human rights norms in contemporary Catholicism a sustained effort to integrate within the existing doctrinal and disciplinary structure of Catholicism a variety of norms that initially found expression as rights in the liberal and socialist traditions. These norms can be treated as "articles of peace" rather than as "articles of belief," to borrow a distinction made by John Courtney Murray in interpreting the First Amendment.[26] Insofar as these norms require modifications of the ideals and social goals that Catholicism aspired to in the long period from Constantine to Napoleon, they can be seen as encouraging either a progressive development of doctrine in social matters or a *resourcement* in which the church returns to patterns of organization and social aspiration which were appropriate to its early formative experiences as a minority group more concerned to survive hostility and contempt than to mold society. They clearly involve a departure from the Augustinian requirement that a just society worship the true God[27] though they may well be compatible with a modern form of the restricted scope of human law held by Thomas Aquinas.[28] The more prominent tendency in recent Catholic social teaching has been to link these norms very closely with the notion of human dignity[29] and to present the church as the preacher and protector of human dignity against forces in the world that diminish human dignity either by offering a reductive interpretation of the human person or by subordinating the human person to the state or the party.[30] This is an approach which promises a distinctive place in society for the church, but which also imposes a moral requirement on the church to uphold these same standards in its internal life.[31] Such an approach would be compatible with the strong agnostic tendencies present in liberalism and with a fairly sharp separation between the norms governing the larger society and the norms governing the community of faith, in which the limitations of agnosticism are overcome but in a way that limits what faith can say to the larger society. Entry into the community of faith depends on a voluntary commitment, a commitment which cannot be coerced and which cannot be given a full rational justification.

The Catholic version of human rights norms, while it is not without serious internal tensions, has been consistently reaffirmed by the magisterium or teaching authorities of the church and has produced a considerable body of practice which liberals find praiseworthy. But there is far from being a complete consensus between Catholic teaching and either the classic philosophical expositions of liberalism or the policy directions of most contemporary American or European liberals. Clashes are particularly apparent with regard to norms about the family. The Catholic position in recent public debates on divorce in Italy and in Ireland serves as a clear example of a long-standing tendency to prefer the goods aimed at by stable natural institutions to rights which are specifications of the autonomy of the individual in seeking the good as he or she conceives it.

Catholicism provides one pattern of what the effort to combine communitarian and liberal values might look like. In different societies there may be variations on these patterns depending on the strength and social imagination of various religious groups and community movements. The principal alternative form of combining communitarian and liberal values is more in the spirit of socialism. It would be a more egalitarian and less hierarchical, more secular and less religious, more futuristic and less traditional synthesis of communitarian and liberal values than Catholicism offers. The church in its own life as community, in its perennial affirmation of traditional sources of communitarian values, and in its more recent support of political movements with strong egalitarian and communitarian ideals such as Solidarity in Poland clearly endorses the inclusion of a wide range of communitarian values in the shaping of law and public policy for a pluralistic society. The concern of most Western liberals is that in such a synthesis the liberal values and practices expressed in human rights norms would be systematically subordinated.

The Criticism of Liberalism by
Catholicism: John Paul II (1987)

The third moment to be examined is the most recent and finds expression in the new encyclical of John Paul II on social concern, *Sollicitudo rei socialis,* which is dated at the end of December 1987 but which only became public in February 1988. This is an encyclical intended to celebrate the twentieth anniversary of *Populorum progressio,* an encyclical issued by Paul VI in 1967 and focusing on problems of international development. This purpose means that economic problems, particularly in the Third and Fourth Worlds, are the focus of papal concern in this document; less attention is paid to the issues that were fundamental for the formation of liberal political theory and for the response to the totalitarian challenges of the mid-twentieth century.

After reviewing some of the characteristics of the contemporary world situation, particularly those which stood in the way of the hopes expressed not merely in *Populorum progressio* but throughout the Third World, John Paul II examines the East-West conflict as this has taken shape since 1945. He sees this as an opposition which is geopolitical, political, ideological and ultimately military. He observes:

> In the West there exists a system which is historically inspired by the principles of the liberal capitalism which developed with industrialization during the last century. In the East there exists a system inspired by the Marxist collectivism which sprang from an interpretation of the condition of the proletarian classes made in the light of a particular reading of history. Each of the two ideologies, on the basis of two very different visions of man and of his freedom and social role, has proposed and still promotes, on the economic level, antithetical forms of the organization of labor and of the structures of ownership especially with regard to the so-called means of production.[32]

Three things are striking in this presentation of the great ideological conflict between liberal capitalism and Marxist collectivism. First, the stress on the disagreements on questions of economic organization rather than on metaphysical and anthropological issues. This is not controversial in itself, nor is it surprising given the focus and purpose of the encyclical. But it is not the preferred interpretive emphasis of most theological and political conservatives. Second, the stress on the historical context of these doctrines, which are not introduced as timeless competitors in an arena of world views, but as responses to particular historical stages. This stress accords better with Hegelian and Marxist and generally historicist ways of understanding the development of social and political theory than with the generally nonhistorical cast of both liberal and natural law theorizing. Third, the suggestion or hint that these ideologies and the conflict between them are passé, that they are not to be taken as responses to the most pressing contemporary needs.

This hint is made more explicit in the following section of the encyclical in which John Paul points to the way in which the conflict between East and West affects the developing world:

> The tension *between East and West* is not in itself an opposition between two different *levels* of development but rather between two *concepts* of the development of individuals and peoples, both concepts being imperfect and in need of radical correction. This opposition is transferred to the developing countries themselves, and these help to widen the gap already existing on the economic level between *North and South* and which results from the distance between the two *worlds:* the more developed one and the less developed one.

This is one of the reasons why the church's social doctrine adopts a critical attitude toward both liberal capitalism and Marxist collectivism. For from the point of view of development the question naturally arises: In what way and to what extent are the two systems capable of changes and revisions so as to favor or promote a true and integral development of individuals and peoples in modern society? In fact, these changes and revisions are urgent and essential for the cause of a development common to all.[33]

It is not my intention here to examine the correctness of the connections that John Paul II asserts between this ideological conflict and the difficulties of the Third World. I do want to suggest that at least in some cases conflicts in the Third World drew in the superpowers rather than vice versa (Biafra, South Africa, the Gulf War) and that the fundamental tasks of nation building and achieving a decent minimum of well-being for their citizens were bound to be very difficult for many Third World countries, no matter what policies the eastern and western blocs adopted. This is not to endorse the policies that they have adopted or to ignore the negative impact of many aspects of the East-West conflict on the South: rather, for our purposes we should direct our attention to the critical stance that the church adopts with regard to both the major ideological systems. Both are presented as in need of overhaul and updating.

While the church has in the period since 1945 come to recognize the necessity of appropriating the human rights norms of the liberal tradition, it has never been content with the outcomes produced by "unfettered capitalism" or with the motivations that it presupposes and endorses. Thus, it has supplemented its endorsement of the right to private property, a right that was affirmed by all the popes from Leo XIII (1891) onward, with an insistence that material creation is intended by God to meet the necessities of all persons so that "private property does not constitute for anyone an absolute and unconditioned right."[34] Furthermore, papal teaching has insisted on the need to regulate competition in the marketplace and to scrutinize the outcome of market transactions in moral terms. Paul VI put the challenge to liberalism thus: "Prices which are 'freely' set in the market can produce unfair results. One must recognize that it is the fundamental principle of liberalism, as the rule for commercial exchange, which is questioned here."[35] In reflecting on the process of industrialization, he denounces the system of "unchecked liberalism," which enshrines as its central tenets "profit as the key motive for economic progress, competition as the supreme law of economic life, and private ownership of the means of production as an absolute right that knows no limits and carries no corresponding social obligation."[36]

John Paul II then is not an innovator in criticizing economic liberalism. But he is an innovator when he turns around and denounces the suppression of the individual's right of economic initiative, "which is important not only for the individual but also for the common good."[37] He makes it clear that he does not favor a radical egalitarianism which would eliminate economic creativity. So, while John Paul II can rightly be seen as a critic of many aspects of capitalism, it would be a great mistake to count him among the defenders of the systems of bureaucratic socialism and state capitalism which are currently in crisis in so much of the world. Clearly, there are affinities between his position and those critics of both utilitarianism and free market institutions who call for regulation and redistribution in order to achieve distributive justice. These affinities come closer to the surface in *Economic Justice for All,* the pastoral letter of the U.S. Catholic bishops on the U.S. economy.[38] The Catholic approach as elaborated by both pope and bishops is to argue on a natural law basis for the right of everyone to a decent minimum rather than to establish principles of justice on a contractarian basis. The Catholic approach offers a critical assessment of the performance of both capitalist and socialist institutions, of both market and command economies; it also strongly insists on the need for active involvement and participation. It does not, however, seem to have the power or the vision to generate new kinds of institutions.

A regime that met the critical standards of economic justice proposed by recent Catholic social teaching would in all likelihood be a stable liberal regime. Satisfaction of the basic economic demands of the poor would protect a liberal constitutional regime from the popular disaffection or protests that have so often weakened such regimes in the developing world; at the same time the requirements of active participation and economic initiative would rule out regimes that are paternalistic or that entrust the management of the economy to centralized bureau-cracies. At the same time implementation of the decent minimum for all, given the imperfections of market systems and the incidence of personal and social disabilities, would require a fairly extensive apparatus of redistribution. For this and other reasons, it seems to me that those critics of *Sollicitudo rei socialis* who took some of the texts we have been examining as constituting an endorsement of "moral equivalence" between East and West were mistaken. There is, in my view, considerable convergence in practice between those forms of liberalism that endorse a welfare state and contemporary Catholic social teaching. There is even some convergence between that teaching and those libertarians who recog-nize the necessity of private provisions to meet basic needs and to anchor a social "safety net" (though there remain serious disagreements about both the adequacy of such provisions and about the confusion between rights and charity that is likely to affect such a way of meeting basic needs).

The insistence on society's meeting the basic needs of all is not, however, the only point that divides current Catholic social teaching and liberalism in the economic field. John Paul II, while deeply concerned about the problems of underdevelopment, which are indeed manifest and widely understood objects of concern around the world, is also a critic of what he calls "superdevelopment," which is, in his view, as unacceptable as underdevelopment "because like the former it is contrary to what is good and to true happiness."[39] Superdevelopment "consists in an excessive availability of every kind of material goods for the benefit of certain social groups."[40] It makes people slaves of possessions," and it is part of "the so-called civilization of 'consumption' or 'consumerism', which involves so much 'throwing-away' and 'waste'."[41] The pope relies on the contrast drawn by Gabriel Marcel and previously used by Paul VI between "being" and "having" and offers this moral assessment of superdevelopment: "The evil does not consist in 'having' as such, but in possessing without regard for the *quality* and the *ordered hierarchy* of the goods one has. *Quality* and *hierarchy* arise from the subordination of goods and their availability to man's 'being' and his true vocation."[42] John Paul II, like Paul VI before him, champions a notion of "authentic development" which "cannot consist only in the use, dominion over and discriminate possession of created things and the products of human industry, but rather in *subordinating* the possession, dominion, and use to man's divine likeness and to his vocation to immortality."[43]

This clearly brings us into territory where the economic pursuit of goods that can be produced and exchanged is to be subordinated to religious and moral goods. The presupposition of the papal view of development is that there is an intersubjectively valid hierarchy of goods which can serve as a measure for individual life-plans and for the priorities accorded to various goods within those life plans. At the same time there is a strong desire on the part of most proponents of Catholic social teaching not to allow such a subordination of the economic to the spiritual to be turned against the claims of the poor and the deprived to a necessary and just share in the goods of this world or to be used in support of a purely otherworldly conception of either Christian spirituality or the role of the church. There is also a strong desire not to adopt an anthropology or a reading of human nature which denies the centrality of bodily and social experience in the world to the formation and fulfillment of the human person. It is also clear that John Paul II's position here is formulated so as to support the idea of restraints on development for the sake of protecting the environment and ensuring a stable, long-term supply of the natural resources essential for human life. There may be possibilities of practical convergence between this relatively new emphasis in Catholic social teaching and movements that would urge care in the use of resources on prudential and humanistic grounds but that would be unwilling to endorse an explicit subordination to the spiritual and transcendent. At the same time this new emphasis is also a way of transmitting to a postindustrial world some traditional Christian values about poverty and simplicity of life. It also complements democratic beliefs about the lack of connection between the worth of human persons and the value of their possessions.

The conflict between John Paul II and economic liberalism on this notion of superdevelopment involves three points. The first is ethical and political and arises from the failure of large numbers of people to acknowledge the distinctions in the hierarchy and quality of goods which the pope proposes. (We should also note that there may well be many people who would agree with the pope on this matter but who would disagree on the implications of his distinctions for social policy). This lack of acknowledgment can be seen as either a deep theoretical problem or as an indication of moral obduracy, a hardening of the heart found in people who decline to recognize ethical principles that are in conflict with their interests and desires. Depending on which view is adopted, the task of the church is either to attempt to rethink the argument so as to make it more convincing at least to people who share some common premises with the Catholic approach, or to preach to the unconverted, offering them prophetic denunciations of current practices and persuasive depictions of spiritual values.

The Catholic argument has normally assumed that there is a clear hierarchy of values, an *ordo bonorum*, which can be appealed to in public policy debate.[44] If this hierarchy is not generally acknowledged in a comprehensive way, the church in a democratic society has to make much more of a piecemeal argument, combining its reliance on the hierarchy of goods with particular values that are acknowledged by other parties in the public debate—for example, the negative psychological effects of excessive consumption of various goods. This is in fact commonly done. One need not be a follower of St. Francis to have grave and well-founded doubts about the negative and inhumane character of the life-style of Howard Hughes or of Ivan Boesky. The life-styles of the rich and famous or not so famous may well contain significant irrational and pathological elements. I do not believe that liberals should think themselves compelled to give up the project of criticizing the desires and values of other persons.[45] Most of the social proposals that have been offered in Catholic social teaching have usually been commendable from a number of different standpoints. Doubts have been raised much more often about their attainability and about their compatibility with other important values than about their desirability when looked at in themselves.

The second point of dispute between Catholic teaching as John Paul II presents it and economic liberalism is essentially economic. One may grant that it is all well and good for the pope to encourage lower levels of consumption and greater generosity by the affluent. But if such a pattern becomes universal or even widespread in an affluent society such as the United States, what will be the effects on economic growth and on the prospects for exports from Third World countries? I am not an economist, and I cannot pretend to solve this as a problem of international trade. I should say that I do not regard it as an insuperable difficulty, but I do see it as pointing to the necessity for a more comprehensive set of adjustments and transfers than a mere lowering of standards of consumption by the affluent. In political practice, the battle may well turn out to be a battle over the level at which the rich are to be taxed. A less controversial approach to the problem lies in adopting policies that will encourage higher rates of saving and in efforts to channel investment in socially beneficial directions. This is likely to require a combination of intelligent government policy and private inventiveness.

The third point at issue is whether John Paul II and Catholic social teaching more generally show a proper awareness of the dynamic and transforming character of capitalism and the process of creative destruction that it normally brings with it.[46] The unstated assumption of much Catholic social teaching seems to be that we can move to a more equal distribution of income and of goods in a tranquil incrementalist fashion in which little damage is done to already established communities, institutions, and individual interests. Ideally, this may be so; and the normal course of argument in ethical and political theory inclines us to look with special favor on ideal possibilities and to search out a harmonious and stabilizing consensus. The religious imagination, when it is not in its apocalyptic mode, impels us in the same direction. But the experience of history should make us profoundly skeptical that real and profound changes in the opportunities open to people and in the burdens they are required to carry can be made without intense and sometimes violent social conflict. Whether confronted with the Marxist doctrine of class conflict or with liberal affirmations of the right of revolution, the Catholic response in recent times has usually (though not always) been to acknowledge the urgency of the problems and to insist on their peaceful resolution. I do not wish to challenge the normative value of this counsel, which is, after all, explicit in just war theory. But I want to suggest that attending only to such counsel, when it is combined with the affirmative and optimistic anthropology of *Gaudium et spes* and Vatican II generally, makes it easy for normative discourse to be pitched an octave or two above the ordinary rumble of conflicting social interests and for Catholic social teaching to be perceived either as moralistic nagging from above or as a utopianism of the center.[47]

Summary and Conclusions

The three moments in the development of Catholic social teaching that we have been examining illustrate three aspects of the church's complex and often uneasy relationship to liberalism. In the *Syllabus of Errors,* the church appeared as both adversary of liberalism and beneficiary of its commitment to limiting the competence and the power of the state. In *Pacem in terris* and the decrees of Vatican II, the church articulated its long and often painful experience of learning from liberalism and of appropriating in contemporary form such values as religious liberty, the autonomy of the world, pluralism in society and culture, the indispensability of human rights. At the same time, it attempted to interpret these values within its own understanding of the natural character of key social institutions such as the state and the family. It wanted to ensure that the rights affirmed by liberalism would be directed to the good as specified by the divinely created natural order. So in this moment the church functioned as both student and corrector of liberalism. In the third moment, in the encyclicals *Populorum progressio* of Paul VI and *Sollicitudo rei socialis* of John Paul II, the church acted primarily as a critic of the economic aspects of liberalism in the light of its conception of human fulfillment and as an advocate of fundamental changes in both liberalism and Marxism for the benefit of the needy in developing countries. At the same time the church, both in its teaching and its political practice, champions a form of society that encourages democratic participation, respect for human rights, nonviolent solutions to domestic and international conflicts, economic development, and private economic initiative. So even while it continues to criticize liberalism, especially in its economic manifestations, it does not wander too far from the liberal consensus of the West.

Nonetheless liberals, especially those who take the issues of political philosophy seriously, are likely to be dissatisfied and in some respects unconvinced about Catholicism's appropriation of liberal values. The relationship between Catholicism and liberalism is likely to remain tense and uneasy.

Let me briefly explore why this is bound to be so. The Catholic church has a continuing responsibility to be engaged with liberal societies and liberalism in four major ways. First, it is a participant in various liberal societies around the world through the institutions which it sponsors and exercises jurisdiction over, as well as through its members, who are both Catholics and citizens. Second, as an international institution, it is involved with various nonliberal societies, both secular (Marxist and non-Marxist) and religious, many of which are in more or less acute opposition to either particular liberal societies or to the whole body of social ideas and practices originating in the liberal West. These nonliberal societies are at various stages of economic and social development, though almost none of them (except a small number of oil-producing states) has anything like the wealth and resources of the liberal societies. Third, the church steps forward as a teacher about ethics and society on a universal level, addressing itself to both religious and nonreligious audiences.[48] This is the form of engagement with which we have been primarily concerned in this chapter. Fourth, the church is itself a social organization with its own status as an independent sovereign, its system of canon law and internal governance, and its own formal and informal patterns of practice and cultural assumptions. In its internal life, it is subject to comparison with liberal societies and is often evaluated by norms drawn from the practices and ideas dominant in these societies.

Even a brief reflection makes it clear that all of these ways in which Catholicism interacts with liberalism are complex. But we can attempt a broad overview. Thus, we can say that contemporary Catholicism appears as an active participant within liberal societies, even when it concentrates on an apparently antiliberal agenda of protecting its institutional interests, expanding the range of its influence, and criticizing the moral deficiencies of liberalism, especially with regard to economic justice and family values. For in doing these things it relies on the political, legal, social, and cultural resources open to it under a liberal regime. It ought then to play by the rules of the liberal game and exposes itself to censure if it disregards these rules in its efforts to shape the public debate.

In nonliberal societies, contemporary Catholicism serves as a liberalizing force. Here there is a convergence between the church's efforts to carry on its religious and social mission and to find and maintain an appropriate place in the larger culture and society and liberal demands for an open society and for judicial protection of human rights. At the same time, the church has to exercise a certain caution in championing liberal values and processes and has to assist a common search to find ways of building these values and processes into existing political and cultural traditions.

In its universal teaching activity, the church will continue to commend the legal and political framework offered by a liberal democratic regime even while it criticizes the economic and culture deficiencies of liberalism and its frequent blindness to religious values. In this area the church will need to refine its concept of good in order to arrive at a new synthesis that will be both coherent and flexible and that will move beyond the amalgam of Thomism and international humanitarianism that currently seems to be dominant in its argument.

The area where the church will exhibit the most resistance to liberal ideas and practices is in its own internal life. Here the traditional commitment to ideas of hierarchical order and doctrinal uniformity, a distrust of societies and movements that many in the church regard as corrupted by the moral laxity and materialist consumerism condoned, if not promoted by liberalism; and the iron law of oligarchy along with normal bureaucratic resistance to the decentralization of teaching and decision-making in the church all combine to make any systematic application of liberal principles to the inner life of the church extremely difficult. At the same time, resistance to liberalism on this front will generate considerable tensions because of the active participation of many church members in liberal politics and because of the church's continued commendation of many liberal values to the world. These tensions are currently felt most strongly where institutions under the sponsorship and control of the church and so within this final area of engagement are also participants in a liberal society and so within the first area of engagement.

The diversity of these areas of interaction between liberalism and Catholicism is, I would argue, a permanent barrier to a simple, enduring resolution of the conflicts between liberalism and Catholicism. Catholicism's appropriation of the principles of a liberal constitutional and political order, while it is not merely a pragmatic accommodation and represents a genuine development within the Catholic tradition, remains, from the liberal standpoint, incomplete. On the one hand, it provides a basis for a common alliance against dictatorial and tyrannical regimes; on the other hand, it is subject to being overridden by competing values, especially those values connected with a religious understanding of human sexuality and family life. Thus it falls between being a *modus vivendi* and a comprehensive agreement on principles.

Each area requires nuanced understanding and is liable to generate controversy. However, the nuanced understanding that is involved is not merely theoretical, but is also political. For the church sees itself as promoting a humane transformation of society. For a variety of reasons, both church leadership and church members are unwilling to acknowledge the political character of what they are doing. Reminding ourselves of this point assists us in seeing that Catholic social teaching has to be assessed not merely as a theoretical construction in political philosophy but also as a series of political utterances intended to position the church in regard to various political disputes. Because the teaching relies heavily on philosophical categories, because the church is often reluctant to be drawn explicitly into partisan conflicts in which Catholics can be found on opposing sides, and because most of the major documents are addressed to an international audience, the implications of the teaching for the resolution of current political disputes are often less than clear. The church is usually content to say that it gives moral direction and does not offer specific political guidance, though individual church leaders, not least the present pope, have shown themselves increasingly ready to denounce political regimes for specific evils such as the abuse of human rights. But the result is that Catholic social teaching often hovers in a region between the normative inquiries of ethical and political theory and the more empirical and historical studies of the social sciences. It often seems to lack the rigor and point characteristic of the best work in both these areas.

As a Catholic academic, I have mixed reactions to this phenomenon, since I believe that the academic discipline of careful philosophical analysis is enlightening and clarifying for the formation of public policy and since I regard tight and careful argument as intrinsically valuable. At the same time, I recognize the decisive importance of casting both moral values and political arguments in terms that can be widely shared in a democratic society and in the international community. I also believe in the urgency of the task of leading diverse regimes to more humane and wise policies and in the practical priority of this task over the intellectually absorbing work of achieving a theoretical reconstruction of the moral foundations of liberal democracy. I take it that the general direction of Catholic social teaching and practice in the second half of this century has responded to these urgent priorities, particularly as the church has moved during the last thirty years to take an active stance of advocacy for the poor in the Third World. I also believe that Catholicism and liberalism share a commitment to establishing the principles and discovering the resources that will enable us to realize a pluralistic, humane society that is distinguished for its sensitivity to the diversity of values cherished by its citizens and to the pressing needs of the people who lack the inner and outer resources to participate effectively in the arena of debate or in the market. In the fashioning and continuing renewal of such a society, I believe that Catholicism and liberalism have much to teach and to learn from each other. This process of shared learning and communication was in its infancy when this university was founded 200 years ago; it flourishes now even as the university does; and I pray as a matter of both religious commitment and civic obligation that it may continue to do so over the coming hundreds of years.

Notes

1. For a comparative interpretation of the French and American revolutions, see Robert R. Palmer, *The Age of the Democratic Revolution,* 2 vols. (Princeton, NJ: Princeton University Press, 1959–64).

2. The standard account of Carroll's life is that by Peter Guilday, *The Life and Times of John Carroll* (New York: Encyclopedia Press, 1922).

3. Pius IX, *Syllabus errorum,* in *Church and State Through the Centuries: A Collection of Historic Documents with Commentaries,* ed. Sidney Z. Ehler and John B. Marrall (London: Burns & Oates, 1954), pp. 284–285.

4. Ibid, pp. 282–284.

5. See William Lee Miller, *The First Liberty: Religion and the American Republic* (New York: Knopf, 1987) for a religiously sensitive view of issues around the First Amendment, which is neither Catholic nor dogmatically liberal.

6. Vatican Council II, *Dignitatis Humanae.*

7. John XXIII, *Pacem in terris,* 9.

8. Ibid, 12.

9. Ibid, 29.

10. Immanuel Kant, *Critique of Practical Reason,* tr. Lewis W. Beck (Chicago: University of Chicago Press, 1949), p. 175.

11. John XXIII, *Pacem in terris,* 12.

12. Ibid, 14.

13. Ibid, 25.

14. Ibid.

15. Joel Feinberg, *Social Philosophy* (Englewood Cliffs, N.J.: Prentice-Hall, 1973), pp. 83–88, 95–97.

16. John XXIII, *Pacem in terris,* 16.

17. Ibid, 24.

18. Ibid, 16. See Elizabeth McKeown, "The Seamless Garment: The Bishops' Letter in the Light of the American Catholic Pastoral Tradition," in *The Deeper Meaning of Economic Life*, ed. R. Bruce Douglass (Washington, D.C., Georgetown University Press, 1986), for an interpretation of Catholic social teaching which stresses the central place given to the family.

19. Ibid, 46; citing Leo XIII, *Immortale Dei*, 120.

20. Ibid, 52.

21. Leo XIII, *Immortale Dei*, in *Church and State Through the Centuries*, pp. 302–303.

22. Ibid, p. 303.

23. Vatican II, *Gaudium et spes*, 74.

24. Ibid.

25. See also Paul VI, *Populorum progressio* 30–31, a passage whose interpretation by the Latin American bishops is assessed in John Langan, S.J., "Violence and Injustice in Society," *Theological Studies* 46, (1985): 685–699.

26. John Courtney Murray, *We Hold These Truths: Catholic Reflections on the American Proposition* (New York: Sheed and Ward, 1960), pp. 56–63.

27. St. Augustine, *De Civitate Dei*, XIX, 21.

28. St. Thomas Aquinas, *Summa Theologiae*, I–II, 96, 2.

29. The notion of human dignity is presented as common ground to both human reason and divine truth in *Pacem in terris*, 9–10. It also plays a fundamental part in the argument of the U.S. bishop's pastoral letter of 1986, *Economic Justice for All*.

30. See, for instance, Vatican II, *Gaudium et spes*, 12–22, and the public teaching of John Paul II.

31. See, for a general account of the nature of this problem, John Langan, S.J., "Can There Be a Human Rights Problem in the Church?" *The Jurist* 46 (1986): 14–42.

32. John Paul II, *Sollicitudo rei socialis*, 20.

33. Ibid, 21.

34. Paul VI, *Populorum progressio, 23*.

35. Ibid, 58.

36. Ibid, 26.

37. John Paul II, *Sollicitudo rei socialis*, 15.

38. U.S. Catholic Conference, *Economic Justice for All*, 68–78, 186–215.

39. John Paul II, *Sollicitudo rei socialis*, 28.

40. Ibid.

41. Ibid.

42. Ibid.

43. Ibid, 41.

44. For a general discussion of the function of this notion in moral theology, see Richard A. McCormick, S.J., "Ambiguity in Moral Choice," in *Doing Evil to Achieve Good*, ed. Richard McCormick and Paul Ramsey (Lanham, Maryland: University Press of America, 1985).

45. Richard Brandt, *A Theory of the Good and the Right* (Oxford: Clarendon Press, 1979) offers a critique of irrational desires from a nonreligious standpoint.

46. This notion of "creative destruction" is fundamental in the appraisal of capitalism given by Josef Schumpeter in his *Capitalism, Socialism, and Democracy* (New York: Harper & Brothers, 1943).

47. This notion figures in an interpretation of the political aspects of *Gaudium et spes* in John Langan, S.J. "Political Tasks, Political Hopes," in *Questions of Special Urgency*, ed. Judith Dwyer (Washington, D.C.: Georgetown University Press, 1986), pp. 99–121.

48. U.S. Catholic Conference, *The Challenge of Peace*, 16; *Economic Justice for All*, 27.

7

Moral Conflict and
Political Consensus

Amy Gutmann and Dennis Thompson

When citizens reasonably disagree about the morality of a public policy, on what principles can they agree to conduct their public life? The hope of liberal political theory, and the basis of the most common solution to the problem of moral conflict in a pluralist society, is that citizens can still agree on principles that would remove decisions about the policy from the political agenda. Liberals typically invoke higher order principles (such as neutrality or impartiality) that are intended to transcend disagreement on specific policies: these principles purport to determine which issues are appropriate subjects for public policy and which are not. When there is no reasonable basis for resolving the moral conflict on an issue of policy, the principles preclude state action of the issue, and leave each citizen free to act on the basis of his or her own morality (to the extent possible without state action). A consensus on these principles thus insulates the political process from fundamental moral conflict.

We want to challenge, at least in part, this familiar liberal way of dealing with moral conflict. The consensus on these higher order principles that liberals propose is not sufficient to eliminate moral conflict from politics, and a more robust set of principles is necessary to govern the conflict that inevitably and legitimately remains. The higher order principles that constitute the core of the consensus, we suggest, must permit greater moral disagreement about policy and greater moral agreement on how to disagree about policy.

Two kinds of higher order principles should be distinguished, corresponding to different purposes that the consensus is supposed to serve. First, there are what may be called *principles of preclusion,* which serve the more familiar purpose of determining which policies deserve a place on the political agenda in the sense of being a legitimate subject for legislation. These principles preclude fundamental moral conflict by denying certain reasons moral standing in the policy-making process. Policies that cannot be justified by the appropriate reasons are precluded, typically by means of a written or unwritten constitution. We argue that any justifiable principles of preclusion will dispose of fewer issues and reasons than modern liberals usually assume. Although any adequate principles will not be morally neutral and thus will exclude some reasons and policies, they will also open up the political agenda to more moral disagreement than liberal theories usually allow.

Second, there are what may be called *principles of accommodation,* which govern the conduct of the moral disagreement on issues that should reach the political agenda. Liberal theorists have given these principles less attention because they assume that most fundamental moral disagreement is legitimately beyond the scope of government action. As long as the principles of preclusion do their job, liberals assume, the principles of accommodation will not have much moral work to do. Procedural principles (such as majority rule) regulate public policy disputes, and interpersonal principles of minimal moral content (such as toleration) take care of disputes outside the public forum. But if, as we suggest, the principles of preclusion do not preclude so much after all, the principles of accommodation assume greater importance than they usually have been accorded in liberal theory. We claim that such principles are essential for dealing with the problem of moral disagreement, and that they should go beyond the idea of toleration. They should be understood as resting on the idea of mutual respect, which is a prerequisite of democratic deliberation.

Section 1

Religious controversy has traditionally been regarded as the paradigm of moral conflict that does not belong on the political agenda, and it continues to play that role in much recent liberal theory.[1] The assumption is that, if the principles of preclusion can banish religious conflict from politics, then they might also dispose of other significant moral conflicts, such as controversies over abortion, pornography, or surrogate parenting. But in its more familiar form the argument for religious toleration does not serve to eliminate even religious conflict from politics. In its Lockean form, the argument for religious toleration can serve this purpose, but the premises of the Lockean argument open up the agenda to many other kinds of moral conflict.

The more familiar, modern version of the argument for religious toleration assumes a skeptical attitude toward religious belief and requires that the state be neutral toward all religions. It proceeds in three steps. The first step characterizes the nature of the moral conflict: in a pluralist society, citizens disagree about what is the true religion, and even whether there is any true religion at all. There is no rational way, no set of principles or forms of reasoning, that could, even among reasonable people, determine that one particular religion is true (even relatively true for a particular society at a particular time). This establishes the *skeptical premise.*

The second step is to show that the nature of the conflict requires the state to be neutral or impartial. Since no religion has any rational claim to truth, the state should not favor one religion rather than another, either in the effect of its actions or in its rationale for them. This is the *neutrality premise.*[2]

The third step is to demonstrate that neutrality implies that the state should not act on religious issues. Any action by the state requires justification, in a way that inaction does not, because action is an exercise of coercion against citizens. Since there is no justification for favoring any religion, neutrality thus implies inaction. This is the *inaction premise*. The three premises lead to the conclusion that the state should exclude religious questions from the political agenda. Citizens collectively should tolerate all religions, and individually practice their own as they wish.

Although this is the form of the argument that is supposed to be applied to other issues besides religion, it does not work well even for religion. We can see where it goes wrong by comparing it at each step with the Lockean form of the argument for toleration, which though now less familiar is potentially a stronger defense of toleration. The Lockean argument does not begin with a skeptical premise—and for good reason.[3] The claim that religious truths are unknowable and therefore that no religious party has a right to impose its "truths" on any other proves too much. Many religious citizens could not accept it without abandoning their religious beliefs, or at least without abandoning an important belief about those beliefs—namely, that the beliefs are true. If the only way to establish toleration is to forswear religious truth, then many citizens not only in Locke's day but also in ours would be inclined to forgo toleration.

The skeptical claim also proves too little, because even if religious truths are unknowable, it does not follow that the state can impose a policy of toleration on citizens who are deeply committed to furthering their religion by saving souls. Toleration, religious citizens might reasonably argue, is no truer—its truth is no more knowable on the basis of reason alone—than their religious beliefs.

Instead of the skeptical premise, the Lockean argument introduces what might be called a *validity* premise. Although citizens reasonably disagree about matters of religion, and although there may be no way at any particular time to persuade even reasonable people to follow the true religion, it may be the case that there is a true or valid religion, consistent with, if not knowable by, reason.[4] Any policy of toleration must not only be consistent with this possibility but should positively encourage the discovery and promotion of true religious belief.

Notice that this premise, while presupposing the possibility of religious or moral truth, is not so stringent as some more recently proposed criteria that otherwise share the same presupposition. In an important article on moral conflict in politics, Thomas Nagel suggests that to justify state action we must satisfy a higher (ethically based) standard of objectivity: the reasons for the policy must be true from "a standpoint that is independent of who we are."[5] Nagel's standard seems to exclude too much, however, not only the fundamentalist's belief that God sanctions racial discrimination, but also the liberal's belief in human equality (which underlies those coercive state policies that Nagel rightly wants to defend). It would also preclude the conflict over whether the fetus is a person (without which there would be no meaningful public debate over the legislation of abortion). None of these beliefs seems to be justifiable from a standpoint independent of who we are ("a common, objective method of reasoning"[6]); yet they are not equally acceptable (or unacceptable) starting points for public deliberation.

The Lockean argument rejects the neutrality premise in the modern argument for toleration—again for good reason. The purpose of toleration is not to provide equal opportunity for every religious group to flourish, or to make it equally likely that every religion will attract the same number of adherents or increase its congregation at the same rate. This seems impossible as some religions depend more on state support than others for fulfilling their purposes. Nor does neutrality or impartiality as a moral standard hold any appeal if we can all come to embrace the true religion. If we could be sure that the state would promote the true religion, then we should not want the state to remain neutral or impartial between truth and falsehood. But as a matter of historical and political fact, we have good reason not to trust the state to promote the true religion.[7] Instead of neutrality, the Lockean argument appeals to the *distrust of government* to defend the second step of the argument. The state should not be permitted to favor one religion over another because it is just as likely to favor the false as the true religion.

Finally, although Locke might sympathize with the presumption in favor of inaction, the Lockean argument does not invoke the presumption to defend inaction on religion. In this respect, the argument is more modern than more recent liberal arguments that do rely on the presumption. It should perhaps be even clearer in our time that in Locke's that the failure of the state to act can subject citizens to as much coercion and violation of their rights as a decision to act. Neither action nor inaction by the state should have a privileged status in moral justification. In place of the inaction premise, the Lockean argument introduces a substantive view about the nature of religious belief. The state must not try to command faith by the force of its laws because faith cannot by its very nature be commanded. Faith follows rational persuasion; it is not an act of will that a person chooses to bring into conformity with the dictates of authority.[8] (The secular analogue, which we develop below, holds that democratically formed, collective moral judgments by society must be a matter of deliberation: citizens should choose, deliberately, the principles of public morality.) In place of the premise of inaction, the Lockean argument offers a premise of *rational deliberation*.

Some religions, of course, do not accept the view that faith follows rational persuasion, and the Lockean premise will not satisfy their adherents. Were the rationale of religious toleration neutrality, we should criticize a state policy of toleration for not being neutral between citizens who believe that faith can be coerced and those who do not. But the Lockean argument does not claim neutrality among all religions. It is meant to be impartial among those religions that accept the voluntary nature of faith, but it is not impartial between religion and irreligion. For those whose religions are or can be understood as being consistent with the claim that religious belief should not be coerced, the argument offers a religious reason for excluding religion from politics. For those whose religion actually requires state coercion, the argument offers only a political reason for excluding religion from politics—the distrust of the state. On the Lockean argument, then, principles of exclusion rest on different grounds for different citizens. The principles are also historically contingent in that they are more likely to be acceptable in a society in which only a minority practice religions that by their nature require the assistance of state coercion.

Understood in this way, the Lockean premises offer a more plausible (if less general) justification for keeping religious issues off the political agenda than arguments based on skepticism and neutrality. Can they also serve as a general justification for principles of preclusion? We believe so, but if so the principles thus justified will not preclude as much nonreligious moral conflict as contemporary liberals claim to exclude by the more familiar argument for religious toleration. The Lockean premises will exclude some issues that liberals wish to exclude but admit many others. An example of each will show why.

A policy favoring racial discrimination, it is now generally agreed, deserves no place on the political agenda. Such a policy is not an option that legislatures or citizens should seriously consider, and if they were to do so, we would expect courts to prevent its adoption. Why should racial discrimination be banished from the political agenda and nondiscrimination established as a matter of constitutional right? There are many good reasons for rejecting racial discrimination as a policy or practice, but the argument for completely precluding its consideration for purposes of policymaking must be of a different, stronger kind. Skeptical or neutralist arguments are not sufficient for this purpose, since they imply that racial discrimination, like religion, is a position about which people reasonably disagree. The problem is especially striking when racial discrimination is combined with religious belief. The skeptical argument implies that since some religions sanction racial discrimination on grounds that cannot be rationally refuted, we should agree to disagree on this matter, leaving citizens free to discriminate or not according to the dictates of their religions.

To preclude racial discrimination from reaching the agenda, we need to show that it fails to satisfy the validity premise in the Lockean argument, suitably extended beyond the case of religious conflict. We need an argument showing that the defense of racial discrimination is not a *moral* position at all. If it is not, then no one can claim that, like religious belief, it is a position about which reasonable citizens might morally disagree. It will fail to satisfy the equivalent of the validity premise in the Lockean argument; we do not assume that it is a position whose validity anyone should seek to discover or establish in our society.

How might one try to show that a position favoring racial discrimination is not in this respect a moral position at all? Some reasons offered in favor of the policy would be disqualified on their face; those that refer to interests based on the self-interest of whites fail to accept a moral point of view at all. Other reasons might adopt a more general (and seemingly moral) perspective—for instance, the claim that white supremacy benefits blacks more than would social and political equality. These reasons also fail (in a different way) to qualify as moral reasons. They can usually be shown to be rationalizations because the nonmoral basis on which they rest is so tenuous. The alleged benefits of white supremacy are either undefined so narrowly as to exclude relevant considerations, such as the noneconomic prerequisites for living a dignified human life. Or they appeal to empirical evidence but reject all accepted methods of challenging the evidence.

Other reasons may appeal to nonmoral premises that do not purport to make empirical claims in the usual sense—for example, the claim that the laws of nature or God speaking literally through the Bible forbid the mixing of races. These kinds of appeals may be rejected because their basic premises are implausible (and therefore denied even by many people who accept these authorities): if God speaks literally through the Bible, why does so much of the Bible defy literal reading, even on fundamentalist accounts? But the primary reason why such appeals to authority must be rejected as moral reasons is that they close off any possibility of publicly assessing or interpreting the content of the claims put forward by the authority. It cannot constitute a moral reason to appeal to an authority whose dictates are closed to reasonable interpretation. To argue otherwise would place no limit at all on the claims that could be made in the name of morality. An appeal to authority certainly can count as a reason, but only when its dictates are open to interpretation by publicly acceptable reasons or methods of inquiry.

No doubt there are other bases on which to deny moral status to claims in favor of racial discrimination, but these should be enough to indicate the kinds of threshold requirements that we should be seeking to determine whether a position satisfies the Lockean validity premise, whether it counts as a moral position at all and therefore whether it should be precluded from the political agenda. The example of racial discrimination suggests that at least three kinds of requirements are necessary for a position to count as a moral one.[9]

First, there is the familiar (though still controversial) requirement of the moral point of view: the argument for the position must presuppose a disinterested perspective that could be adopted by any member of a society whatever his or her other particular circumstances (such as class, race, or sex). Satisfying this requirement distinguishes a moral position from one is that is merely prudential or self-regarding.[10] Persons whose positions satisfy this requirement in effect declare that they are prepared to enter into a moral discussion. *Second,* any premises in the argument that depend on empirical evidence or logical inference should be in principle open to challenge by generally accepted methods of inquiry. This requirement ensures that the claims will be accessible to others in the moral discussion. *Third,* premises for which empirical evidence or logical inference is not appropriate should not be radically implausible. They might be so in two ways, either by implying the rejection of other significantly more plausible beliefs widely held in the society, or by appealing to authorities whose claims cannot be challenged by those who doubt them. This requirement also helps keep the moral discussion relatively open to many points of view.

Reasonable people, of course, can disagree about what should count as a moral position, but this kind of disagreement seems more susceptible to rational resolution, if only because it abstracts from the reasons and passions that inhere in particular moral conflicts. The abstraction should not be regarded as neutral or formal: it expresses a substantive view about the nature of morality in political contexts—specifically, how citizens should collectively arrive at moral positions. The preclusion requirements reflect (as do the principles of accommodation we discuss below) an ideal of moral deliberation in a democratic process; they constitute part of the conditions necessary to sustain moral discussion among free and equal citizens.[11] Therefore, even if they do not resolve any particular moral conflict, they remain valid as the only basis on which we can hope to arrive at reasonable resolutions of substantive moral conflict in the future.

If a policy of racial discrimination can be precluded from reaching the agenda only in something like the way we suggest, then many other moral conflicts that many liberals would like to set aside will stubbornly resist banishment. Abortion is the paradigm of such a dispute, and unlike a conflict about racial discrimination both sides appear to satisfy the threshold requirements for a moral position. Both sides argue from different plausible premises to fundamentally conflicting public policies. Pro-life advocates believe the fetus to be a human being, a person in the generic sense of the term. Their principled basis of opposing legalized abortion is the right of an innocent human to live. Pro-choice advocates believe the fetus to be only a potential person. Their principled basis for championing legalized abortion is a women's freedom of choice with regard to her own body. Both sides can agree on the general (incompletely specified) moral principles that innocent people have a right to live and that women have freedom of choice with regard to their own bodies. But they arrive at radically different conclusions about abortion because they cannot agree on whether the fetus is a full-fledged person, whether the right to life extends to the obligation of women to realize the human potential of a dependent fetus, and whether women have freedom of choice with regard to their bodies even if the life of an innocent person is at stake.

Insofar as evidence is relevant to the dispute, both sides make claims that are susceptible to accepted methods of inquiry. The pro-life advocate appeals to established scientific facts about fetal development, and the pro-choice advocate refers to testable claims about the effects of pregnancy and child-bearing on women. And insofar as the premises are based on other kinds of claims (such as whether a fetus is a human being), those of neither side are radically implausible. Roger Wertheimer has convincingly argued that pro-choice and pro-life advocates can agree on all the facts about fetuses (and the circumstances of women who bear them) and still disagree in their beliefs as to whether the fetus is a person. Different plausible beliefs lie at the base of the best arguments for and against the legalization of abortion.[12] Reason itself does not "point in either direction: it is *we* who must point it, and *we* who are led by it. If you are led in one direction rather than the other, that is not because of logic, but because you respond in a certain way to certain facts [about the fetus]."[13]

Abortion thus satisfies the requirements of a genuine moral disagreement: the strongest cases both for and against abortion satisfy the three threshold require-ments for a moral position. Abortion therefore cannot be precluded from reaching the political agenda on the basis of the generalized version of the first Lockean premise of validity. Nevertheless, it might be supposed that a generalized version of the more familiar argument for preclusion, based on the premise of governmen-tal inaction, will work for abortion even though it does not work for religion. Wertheimer presents just such an argument in its most forceful form. Must abortion be excluded from the agenda on grounds of a presumption favoring governmental inaction? Wertheimer thinks that it must. In the face of ultimate moral conflict, Wertheimer argues, the government must not prohibit abortion. His argument essentially has three steps: (1) governments cannot restrict freedom unless they can justify their restrictions rationally; (2) neither of the two sides in the debate is more rationally justifiable than the other; and (3) therefore, the government cannot legitimately restrict the freedom of women to have an abortion.[14]

But the argument does not work here any better than it did in the case of religious toleration. By the same reasoning that Wertheimer uses to establish government inaction, one could show that legalizing abortion is illegitimate. From the perspective of those who perceive the fetus as a person, legalization ends the life of the fetus and therefore restricts its freedom absolutely. Without accepting one of the competing views of the fetus, this restriction on freedom is no more or less justified than restricting the freedom of women. Wertheimer's argument depends on giving decisive moral weight to the fact that the government need not act to make abortion legal.[15] But there is no decisive reason to favor government inaction under conditions in which human life is arguably at stake. The premises of the familiar argument are as inconclusive in the case of abortion as they were in the case of religious conflict, and even less plausible.

We have argued that both sides in the abortion controversy satisfy the conditions for a moral position and that therefore abortion fails the first Lockean premise favoring exclusion from the political agenda. But do either of the two other Lockean premises help preclude the abortion controversy? The second premise—distrust of the government—does not provide the basis for exclusion if there is good reason to trust the government as much as other agents on an issue. Both sides to the abortion controversy already (reasonably) agree that the government must be trusted with the task of prohibiting murder; there is no more trustworthy agent that can effectively carry out this task. The central question is then whether the government should or should not consider abortion to be murder. Distrusting the government to answer *this* question correctly does not favor one side or the other in the abortion controversy (unless one adds the presumption in favor of inaction, which we have already rejected).

The third Lockean premise, favoring rational deliberation, rather than preclud-ing the abortion controversy, would seem to imply that *it should* be a subject for collective moral discussion and decision. In the absence of other reasons for preclusion (such as there were in the case of religion and racial discrimination), this premise suggests that the issue falls within the scope of public policy, even if we collectively decide that abortion should be left to individual moral choice.

The principles of preclusion we have sketched provide an adequate (if underdeveloped) basis for determining whether moral conflict should reach the political agenda. The abortion controversy is the paradigm of a moral conflict that should not be precluded although modern liberal theory would preclude it. Racial discrimination is the paradigm of a moral conflict that should be precluded, although for reasons different from those offered by modern liberal theory.

Other controversies resemble one of the two paradigms to varying degrees. Capital punishment resembles abortion in that each side at its best seems to hold a position that merits respect. Each can offer reasons for its position that satisfy the threshold conditions of a moral position. Both argue from a disinterested perspective, a concern for preventing unnecessary death, but they give different weights to the risks involved (executing the innocent and protecting victims), and the premises underlying their different weightings are plausible, though their disagreement may not ultimately be resolvable by either moral argument or empirical evidence.

Laws against homosexuality and other policies that discriminate on the basis of sexual orientation resemble the case of racial discrimination. The basis for such policies fail the test of a moral position. Proponents of such policies sometimes adopt a disinterested point of view. But the common claims that homosexual sex causes various kinds of harms have not been supported with solid empirical evidence. Insofar as the case for these discriminatory policies rests on some perception of homosexual sex as unnatural, the position violates the third requirement of a moral position. Nor has a consistent argument been constructed on plausible premises to show that homosexual sex cannot be understood as part of the human condition.

These examples are meant to be merely suggestive. The task of elaborating the principles of preclusion is complex, requiring detailed consideration of subtle features of the moral positions and at the same time considerable refinement of the principles themselves. But the principles we have sketched and the paradigmatic examples of abortion and racial discrimination should be sufficient to suggest the possibility of moving beyond the conventional approaches of neutrality and toleration.

More generally, it is becoming less plausible to deal with fundamental moral conflict by taking the disputes off the political agenda and leaving the decisions to each individual. Many questions that were once regarded as purely a matter for individuals to decide in private have inescapably become questions of public significance. Political theories that cope with irreconcilable disagreement by a (hypothetical) social agreement to disagree on these questions—letting each individual decide—seem increasingly evasive. They offer a false impartiality in place of social recognition of the persistence of fundamental conflicts of value in our society.

Although it would be worthwhile to develop the principles of preclusion more fully, their role, if our argument so far is correct, is less significant than most liberals have assumed. If we are right that more moral conflict should reach the agenda and become the legitimate subject of legislation, then the critical problems concern the processes by which citizens conduct moral deliberation, and the moral reasons they should give in choosing among the substantive policies on the agenda.

Another reason these processes are so important is that it is through collective moral deliberation over time that citizens can (and should) decide which particular positions come to deserve a place on the political agenda. The preclusion principles are sensitive to changes in social and political attitudes. Perhaps citizens 100 years ago should have regarded discrimination against homosexuals as failing to meet the standards of a moral position at all, but citizens today have stronger grounds for taking this view. Because of the nature of social practices and the relative lack of public debate about the subject, many citizens at an earlier time may not have had an adequate opportunity to explore the full implications of their arguments. Furthermore, those who morally opposed discrimination could not themselves be so confident of their position, until they had tested their moral views over time in various circumstances and subjected them to the experience and evidence that is now more widely available. They come to see that, after ample opportunity for argument, the defenders of discrimination offer little more than expressions of personal preference. Even if there is nothing inherent in a moral view itself that renders it beyond the pale of moral discourse, it may be disqualified, as discrimination against homosexuals is coming to be disqualified, by our common recognition of the moral vacuity of the case for it.

Section 2

In seeking principles for political consensus in the face of fundamental moral disagreement, we need to attend not only to the nature of the positions but also the way in which people hold or express positions. Morally respectable positions can be defended in morally disrespectful ways. It is the role of the principles of accommodation to restrain those ways. These principles govern the relations among citizens who hold morally legitimate though fundamentally opposed positions on public policy. They suggest how citizens who disagree about an issue should treat each other with regard to that issue and related issues even when the policy debate results in legislation and the state takes a position favoring one side of the dispute. The principles are best conceived as expressing a virtue that lies at the core of moral deliberation in a democracy—*mutual respect*.

Like toleration, mutual respect is a form of agreeing to disagree. But mutual respect demands more than toleration. It requires a favorable attitude toward, and constructive interaction with, the persons with whom one disagrees. It consists in a reciprocal positive regard of citizens who manifest the excellence of character that permits a democracy to flourish in the face of (at least temporarily) irresolvable moral conflict.[16]

Mutual respect is a distinctively democratic kind of character—the character of individuals who are morally committed, self-reflective about their commitments, discerning of the difference between respectable and merely tolerable differences of opinion, and open to the possibility of changing their minds or modifying their positions at some time in the future if they confront unanswerable objections to their present point of view. The significance of this kind of character, and the justification for giving it a privileged place in dealing with moral conflict in a democracy, can finally be established only through a detailed interpretation of its specific virtues in a political context.[17] We present the outline of such an interpretation below, but two general considerations that tell in its favor can be mentioned.

First, mutual respect seems to be necessary to keep open the possibility of resolving, on a moral basis, any significant dispute about public policy that involves fundamental moral conflict. If citizens do not practice mutual respect as they try to come to agreement on a morally disputed policy, or as they try to live with the disagreement that remains after the disputed policy is adopted, they are forced to turn to nonmoral ways of dealing with moral conflict. They are driven to count on procedural agreements, political deals, and threats of violence—all of which obviously stand in the way of moral deliberation. The underlying assumption is that we should value reaching conclusions through reason rather than force, and more specifically through moral reasoning rather than through self-interested bargaining. Citizens and officials, we assume, can learn how to take each other seriously as moral agents. They can enter the discussion in the political forum with the purpose of discovering principles on which the society as a whole can act, rather than with the aim of devising arguments by which they can advance their own interests.

The presumption in favor of reason is itself contestable, but it should not be contested on grounds that it grants a higher value to political procedures than to moral substance of outcomes. Mutual respect makes possible, at the level of political decision, the deliberate choice of substantive moral values for the society as a whole. It is the moral value of choosing moral values, then, that (partly) justifies the prominence of moral reasoning in the political process. (In this respect, its justification recalls the Lockean premise that presumes that faith cannot be commanded.)

Second, mutual respect can contribute not only to social good but also to individual virtue. Persons who practice mutual respect are disposed against the premature moral skepticism, and the concomitant ennui and indecision, that afflict those who treat the existence of conflicting opinions as proof of the arbitrariness of all moral judgments. ("You have your opinion and I have mine, and who's to say who's right?") They are also less inclined toward moral dogmatism, and its accompanying anger and arrogance, that is common among those who treat moral disagreement as a sure sign of the ignorance or depravity of their opponents. ("Either you're for killing babies or you're against killing babies," declared Nellie Gray, the leader of a March for Life in Washington.[18] "Either you're for the liberation of women or you're against it" is the analogous dogmatism of pro-choice advocates.)

Being reciprocal, mutual respect makes two general kinds of demands of persons—the first specifying how one presents one's own moral position; and the second, how one regards others' moral positions. The principles of accommodation, which spell out these demands, thus require that citizens affirm the moral status of their own position and acknowledge the moral status of their opponent's position.

Although the principles refer to the way that opinions are held and expressed, their object is not mainly a matter of style or rhetoric, but rather of attitude and conduct as manifested in public actions. What they seek is not only speech but also action, and not only action but also action in cooperation with others over time. Their object is a family of dispositions, which comprise an excellence of public character that we expect democratic citizens to exhibit.

The first set of principles—calling on citizens to affirm the moral status of their own positions—involve a kind of moral or characterological integrity. There are no doubt many ways that citizens could demonstrate such integrity, but at least three seem important in politics. *First,* we expect citizens and officials to espouse their moral positions independently of the circumstances in which they speak. This is consistency in speech, and is a sign of political sincerity: it indicates that a person holds the position because it is a moral position, not for reasons of political advantage. There is of course no completely reliable way to tell if such a principle is satisfied. It is difficult enough in private life to judge sincerity; in the more distant relations of public life, sincerity becomes so hard to confirm that we (perhaps too easily) assume that hypocrisy is all there is. But we should be able to find more reliable criteria for recognizing, or at least providing good grounds for suspecting, insincerity. Politicians who continually shift their positions according to political advantage give us good grounds for doubting that they honestly accept on moral grounds any of the positions they espouse.

We should not think much of the moral seriousness of someone who expressed his moral position, however consistently, but never acted on it. We therefore need a *second* principle that requires that one should act in ways consistent with the positions one holds. This is the most familiar form of integrity—consistency between speech and action. The pro-choice advocate who prevents his daughter from having an abortion over her strong objection, the staunch opponent of legalized abortion who helps his daughter obtain an abortion—both fall short of acting in ways that warrant the respect of their fellow citizens. *Failing* to act may also be culpable. We legitimately expect people who accept positions of public responsibility to act according to their professed beliefs unless constrained by some overriding duty of office. Disrespect is due a politician who in a campaign emphasizes his concern over abortion but, once elected to office, fails (out of laziness or lack of leadership) to work for the policies implied by the position he advocated.

Finally, we might reasonably question the moral status of someone's position on a particular issue, even if he spoke and acted on it consistently, if he were to refuse to recognize its consequences for other related issues. Hence the need for a *third* principle: citizens should accept the broader implications of the principles presupposed by their moral positions. This is integrity of principle. Those who oppose abortion out of respect for fetal life should be equally strong advocates of policies to ensure that children are properly fed. Sometimes there may be good reasons for denying the apparent implications (perhaps because other more weighty moral considerations may block the natural inference). But if so, the burden should be on those who would deny the implications. If a pro-life advocate opposes the program of Aid to Families of Dependent Children on grounds that it is inefficient and mismanaged, then he should also seek alternative public policies that would go at least as far in protecting the health and welfare of poor children.

The second set of principles of accommodation, which call on citizens to acknowledge the moral status of the positions they oppose, also seeks to develop aspects of democratic character. They parallel the three principles prescribing forms of integrity, but since they look outward toward one's judgments of others, they may be thought of as forms of magnanimity.

First, acknowledging the moral status of a position that one opposes requires, at a minimum, that one treat it as a moral rather than a purely political, economic or other kind of nonmoral view. This acknowledgment in speech begins with the recognition that an opponent's position is based on moral principles about which reasonable people may disagree (provided that it meets the preclusion conditions for reaching the political agenda). An illustration of this kind of acknowledgment is the appeal in the House by a congressman opposing a motion that would deny government funding for abortions in the case of rape and incest:

> Let me at the outset say that I understand the depth of feeling of those who support the motion and who feel that abortion should be permitted only when the life of the mother is in danger. I understand the sincerity with which those who advocate that position come to the floor.
>
> Now, I know that obviously that [our] position [in favor of funding abortions in cases of rape and incest] is one that morally is inconsistent with the position of those who are supporting the motion, but I suggest to you it is certainly an understandable, defensible position, and one which I would hope those who do not like abortion would nonetheless understand. . . . I would hope that they would at least acknowledge that there is . . . moral controversy.[19]

In the debate that followed, many members in the tone and content of their arguments did in fact acknowledge the moral nature of the controversy.[20]

This debate stands in contrast with an earlier one in the House, also on abortion funding, in which members manifested less respect for the moral seriousness of their opponents. At one point in that debate, a congressman argued against abortion funding on the grounds that it would increase the federal deficit: "If we are going to pay off this debt, somebody has got to be born to pay the taxes to pay it off."[21] This prompted the next speaker to throw away her prepared remarks, and attack him for ignoring the moral issue: "We are talking about matters of life. . . ."[22]

There are of course many other ways of denying the moral status of an opponent's position—perhaps the most rampant is claiming that a position is politically motivated—but what they all seem to have in common is the refusal to give moral reasons for rejecting the position. We show respect for persons by joining with them in serious and sustained moral discussion on the issue in question and other issues that divide us. In such discussion, we not only state publicly our reasons for rejecting an opponent's positions, but we also invite and consider carefully responses to our objections.

Mutual acknowledgment in this kind of moral discussion could turn out to be a merely formal, ritualistic expression of mutual respect, unless there is some real possibility that each side may be moved by the reasons the other gives. Therefore, a *second* principle (paralleling the requirement of integrity in action) is needed to keep open the possibility that citizens could come to adopt and act on the position of their opponent. It requires citizens to cultivate a disposition toward openness. We should try to break personal and institutional habits that discourage our accepting the position of our opponent at some time in the future, or at least of modifying our own position in the direction of that of our opponent. Both the political mind and the political forum should be kept open to reconsideration of decisions already made and policies already adopted.

The disposition toward openness does not imply that political change is good in itself, or even that an open mind is the most virtuous form of character. It is, or should be, compatible with affirming one's own moral views strongly and consistently. We should be seeking a balance between holding firm convictions and being prepared to change them if we encounter objections that on reflection we cannot answer. Maintaining this delicate balance is no doubt psychologically (as well as intellectually) demanding, but the personal and political dangers of a psychologically simpler path, succumbing to moral dogmatism on the one hand or moral skepticism on the other, are greater.[23]

Although the disposition toward openness is elusive especially in politics, we can sometimes detect its absence or presence even in the statements of public officials. Consider the difference in emphasis in statements by Joseph Califano and Mario Cuomo on the question of abortion. Writing about his struggle with the abortion issue during his tenure as Secretary of Health, Education and Welfare, Califano commented:

I concluded that it was not sufficient simply to express my view clearly and consistently, but that it was also essential *to communicate the certainty with which I held it.* Any hedging would only encourage those who disagreed, to hope for a change that would not be forthcoming.[24]

In a nationally publicized speech at Notre Dame, Governor Mario Cuomo defended his position on the legalization of abortion this way:

I . . . [am] eager for enlightenment, eager to learn new and better ways to manifest respect for the deep reverence for life that is our religion and our instinct. I hope that the public attempt to describe the problems as I understand them, will give impetus to the dialogue in the Catholic community and beyond, a dialogue which could show me a better wisdom than I've been able to find so far.[25]

Because the contexts differ, we cannot be sure that the statements actually show a difference in the views or dispositions of the two speakers, but on its face Cuomo's speech shows a greater commitment to openness than does Califano's comment. Cuomo seems more inclined to consider the possibility of changing his mind on the abortion question. At the least, his speech invites further discussion and calls for continuing the dialogue on the issue. It holds open the possibility of moral change, and thus manifests moral regard for the position that it opposes.

Cuomo's speech is characterized not only by openness, but also by a commitment to seek a common perspective at a deeper level of morality ("reverence for life") that could transcend moral differences at the level of policy. This is an instance of a *third* form of magnanimity, another way of acknowledging the moral status of others' positions: in justifying policies on moral grounds, we should seek the rationale that minimizes rejection of the position we oppose.[26] While the corresponding (and compatible) requirement of integrity calls on us to accept the broader implications of our positions, this principle of magnanimity tells us to avoid unnecessary conflict in characterizing the moral grounds or drawing out the policy implications of our positions. The principle encourages what we may call an economy of moral disagreement at both foundational and policy levels of political argument.[27] It does not ask us to compromise our moral understandings in the interests of agreement but rather to search for significant points of convergence between our own understandings and those of citizens whose positions, taken in their more comprehensive forms, we must reject.

Some of the best work in practical moral philosophy can be interpreted as seeking such an economy. In one of the most widely cited philosophical analyses of abortion, Judith Jarvis Thomson succeeds in narrowing the range of disagreement between pro-life and pro-choice advocates to cases where pregnancy is largely voluntary.[28] By means of several hypothetical examples, she shows that even people who perceive the fetus to be a person should acknowledge that abortion may be justified in circumstances where pregnancy is the result of forced intercourse. That is part of the point of her well-known example of the unconscious violinist with kidney failure, who has been plugged into your circulatory system against your will. The violinist's survival depends on his remaining plugged into you for nine months, but he does not have a right to remain attached to you if you object.[29] The example is meant to suggest sometimes it may be morally permissible (though not admirable) to kill an innocent person even if your own life is not at stake. The example should convince even people who perceive the fetus to be a full-fledged person that it is not obviously unjust for women who become pregnant through no fault of their own (for example, by rape or incest) to be legally free to obtain abortions.

The political distance remaining between pro-life and pro-choice advocates is, of course, still great. In the vast majority of cases in which women seek abortions, where pregnancy is not the result of force, Thomson's arguments leave pro-choice and pro-life advocates radically opposed. Even in this treacherous territory of rationally irresolvable disagreement, there is still some prospect for further accommodation. For example, the grounds on which governments decide the questions should comply with the economy of moral disagreement. If the government decides to permit (or even fund abortion), it should be on grounds that acknowledge as far as possible the moral legitimacy of the pro-life position.

To some extent, the Supreme Court in *Roe v. Wade* did just that. Although the Court did not admit as a constitutional argument the claim that fetuses are persons, the majority opinion emphasized that the state has an interest in protecting the *potential* of life.[30] This emphasis moved the rationale for the decision closer to the conclusions of a pro-life position, particularly in the later stages of fetal development, and did so without abandoning the premise that fetuses are not persons. The Court, with consistency, allowed states to ban abortion in the third trimester, on the grounds that the state's interest in potential life is compelling once the fetus is viable. If medical technology advances and viability extends to earlier stages of pregnancy, then the Court's rationale, on this logic, should give increasing protection to fetal life. Otherwise, states are required to protect a woman's right to an abortion.

Because the Court did not let this logic prevail, it did not move as far as it might have in the direction of mutual respect. In its discussion of the second trimester of pregnancy, the Court introduced a consideration that is required by neither pro-life nor pro-choice premises: the paternalistic claim that the state has a compelling interest in protecting the health of pregnant women even against their own will.[31] Not only is the Court's justification of the second trimester criterion incompletely argued and inconsistently applied, but it also ignores a crucial question. If viability extends into earlier phases of fetal development, should states be permitted to regulate abortions in the second trimester as well as in the third? The answer implicit in the opinion seems to be that paternalistic protection of adults deserves more constitutional weight than paternalistic protection of potential life, even when that life is imminently actual.

Yet the Court never gives any legal or moral argument for this priority, and it is difficult to imagine how such a priority could be justified. The Court's reliance on this paternalistic argument renders its judgment more divisive and less open to change through rational deliberation than a public philosophy would prescribe. We should direct a similar criticism at Congress were it to decide to fund abortion on grounds, for example, that the removal of a fetus is morally equivalent to ordinary surgery.

Not only legislators and judges, but citizens should also be expected to practice the economy of moral disagreement. They ought to be able to agree, for example, that someone's views on abortion should not affect how she is treated in other respects. A pro-lifer ought not to favor denying a woman who has an abortion access to other essential medical care. A pro-choicer ought not to refuse pro-lifers the right to speak against abortion even in front of an abortion clinic.

Officials and citizens can also minimize the areas of their public disagreement by promoting policies on which their principles converge, even if they would otherwise place those policies significantly lower on their own list of political priorities. Although pro-choice advocates may think publicly funded programs that help unwed mothers care for their own children are less important than pro-life proponents do, pro-choice advocates should join in actively promoting these programs and other policies that are similarly consistent with the principles of both sides. By trying to maximize political agreement in these ways, we do not end serious moral conflict, but we affirm that we accept significant parts of the substantive morality of fellow citizens to whom we may find ourselves deeply opposed in other respects.

The politics of mutual respect is not always pretty. The deliberation that takes place among citizens and public officials under the principles of accommodation may be quite robust. Citizens may find it necessary to make extreme and uncompromising statements, and to refuse to cooperate with opponents. These strategies may be justified when, for example, they are necessary to gain attention for a legitimate position that would otherwise be ignored, and therefore to promote mutual respect in the long run. Even if it does not promise a comprehensive common good, a philosophy of mutual respect does seek agreement on substantive moral values for the society. By thus raising the moral stakes of politics, it may at least in the short run increase moral conflict in politics.

Mutual respect, as expressed through the principles of accommodation, thus requires an effort to appreciate the moral force of the positions of people with whom we disagree. But at least as important as these individual efforts are the demands on political institutions. To fulfill those demands, we may need to consider changes in our institutions, and perhaps the creation of new ones.

The principles imply that the forums in which we conduct our political discussion should be designed so as to encourage officials to justify their actions with moral reasons, and to give other officials as well as citizens the opportunity to criticize those reasons. Legislators, for example, might act more like judges by assuming a regular responsibility to explain in writing in principled terms the basis for their decisions. To encourage the virtue of openness, we could ensure that our institutions permit reconsideration of important moral decisions and policies at regular intervals. Although unlimited opportunities to reopen questions would of course paralyze government, some of the existing barriers to fundamental changes may be too high. The procedures for amending the Constitution, for example, make the possibility of future change in some major policies seem hopelessly remote. To promote an economy of moral disagreement, we might fashion more broad-based political organizations that permit citizens who hold different moral positions to work together on other causes whose goals they share. In this respect, a fluid and open party system would be more desirable than a political structure dominated by single-issue groups.

The merits of these particular institutional suggestions would have to be considered in the context of many different political factors, and other changes may turn out to be more constructive.[32] The point of the suggestions is to emphasize that the principles of accommodation do not impose duties merely on individuals, but also carry implications for institutions. Mutual respect is a political virtue, and as such it is shaped by the institutions in which it is practiced.

Section 3

Practicing the virtue of mutual respect as we propose here would create a broader kind of political consensus and thus expand the scope of what may be called the public philosophy—those set of moral principles on which reasonable citizens should agree, whatever moral principles they hold privately. Such a public philosophy would embrace, not only principles that protect basic rights (such as nondiscrimination) and principles that justify certain procedures (such as majority rule), but also principles that govern the conduct of moral relations in public life.

This kind of public philosophy would avoid the dichotomy that has come to dominate contemporary discussions of political theory, which pose a choice between basing politics on a comprehensive conception of the good or limiting politics to a conception of procedural justice. We can and should avoid choosing either of these approaches exclusively. The quest for agreement on a conception of the good (the aim, for example, of some communitarian theories[33]) underestimates the significance and legitimate persistence of fundamental moral disagreement. In a pluralist society, comprehensive moral theories neither can nor should win the agreement of all citizens. A public philosophy for such societies must reject the unqualified quest for agreement because it must renounce the claim to comprehensiveness. This is part of the point of interpreting the principles of preclusion in the way that we do: we recognize that the political agenda will never be free of fundamental moral disagreement. Deliberating about the substantive moral values underlying policy does not guarantee that citizens will agree on a coherent set of those values, or on many values at all.

The rejection of comprehensiveness as an aim, as we have argued, does not imply skepticism, moral or metaphysical. On the contrary, it reflects the core commitment to a conception of politics that is conducive to moral deliberation and to a conception of persons whose convictions are guided by their moral deliberations. Like the Lockean premise that posits that religious belief should not be commanded, the foundation of mutual respect presupposes that moral choices, and in particular collective moral choices, should be made deliberately. In opening forums of political decision-making to a wide range of legitimate moral disagreement and defending practices within those forums that cultivate mutual respect among citizens, mutual respect supports a political process that promotes moral learning. Citizens put their moral beliefs to the test of public deliberation, and strengthen their convictions or change their minds in response to the arguments in which they engage under conditions governed by the principles of accommodation.

This process goes beyond the proceduralism that many liberals favor. Unlike theories that would minimize the moral content of politics, a public philosophy of mutual respect accepts the need to promote substantive moral principles in politics—principles that could become part of a public morality for the society as a whole. Although the policy prescriptions of mutual respect may be less comprehensive, the prescriptions for political deliberation are more comprehensive, and more demanding, than other moral doctrines. In cultivating the virtue of open-minded commitment among citizens and in encouraging an economy of moral disagreement in politics, mutual respect orients the deliberations of citizens and public officials toward a view of the common good—a common good that is compatible with continuing moral disagreement. This common good is constituted partly by those substantive rights and obligations on which many moral philosophies converge and partly by a public search for additional moral agreement.

A public philosophy of the kind we are urging aims at both less and more than the "overlapping consensus" that John Rawls describes as the political foundations for justice.[34] A public philosophy aims at *less* than Rawls's theory by permitting, under certain conditions, disagreement on aspects of the basic structure itself. Political agreement may be undesirable even when the basic structure of a society is at issue (as it is in the abortion controversy, in which the question of who should count as a member of society is in dispute). In deference to the demands of mutual respect, the policy prescriptions of a public philosophy are in this respect less comprehensive than those of most moral doctrines, including Rawls's. Mutual respect does not guarantee that all public policies produced by the process it governs will fit the conventional liberal program.

But mutual respect also aims at *more* than Rawlsian justice because it continues to seek agreement on substantive moral principles—even comprehensive ones— that could guide citizens and public officials acting within the basic structure. Rawls "removes from the political agenda the most divisive issues, pervasive uncertainty and serious contention about which must undermine the bases of social cooperation."[35] He leaves citizens to dispute in public primarily those moral views that potentially unite them.[36] In an argument with non-Catholics about nuclear deterrence, Catholics could appeal to their own theology, but only insofar as they rely on principles that can be presented as consistent with the fundamental principles of their opponents. "We do not state more of our comprehensive view than we think would advance the quest for consensus."[37] Appealing to distinctively Catholic principles would not serve the important goal of achieving an overlapping consensus. Similarly, insofar as the Catholic doctrine on abortion serves politically to divide citizens on this issue, the Rawlsian position counsels political silence (though of course it does not require it). Comprehensive moral theories contribute constructively to politics on his view only to the extent that they serve as a source of common principles.

By contrast, mutual respect requires citizens to strive not only for agreement on principles governing the basic structure, but also for agreement on practices governing the way they deal with principled disagreements, whether about the basic structure or ordinary policies. The agreement on these practices is possible because citizens who seriously disagree over policies such as the legalization of abortion, capital punishment, and pornography can share other substantive standards: they can recognize that their own moral commitment might turn out to be wrong even though they now have good reason to believe them to be true; they can value public deliberation as a critical means of subjecting their moral commitments to critical scrutiny (and possibly changing them in the future); and they can give serious consideration to opposing points of view as a manifestation of their appraisal respect for morally reasonable people. Because we should agree on how to be morally governed in our political behavior even when we morally disagree on fundamental political issues, a public philosophy should be more comprehensive than Rawls suggests.

In the pursuit of principles of mutual respect, we move from seeking agreement on the level of legislation or the basic structure to the level of political deliberation. A public philosophy emphasizing mutual respect articulates a consensus on the conditions for political discussion of enduring moral disagreement. This shift in the level on which agreement is sought is significant, both theoretically and practically. Theoretically, this kind of public philosophy expresses as complete a conception of politics as is possible within a morally pluralistic society. It seeks agreement on how publicly to deliberate when citizens fundamentally (and reasonably) disagree, rather than on how to purge politics of disagreement. Practically, a public philosophy reminds citizens of the collective risks they run if they individually continue merely to disagree in politics without also searching for ways to foster respect for the moral differences that give rise to moral conflict. A public philosophy incorporating the principles of preclusion and accommodation that we have suggested would direct practical efforts as much toward methods of dealing with irreconcilable disagreements as toward the means of resolving them.

A political consensus on a public philosophy of mutual respect could create and sustain a political discourse that manifests more than mere toleration of moral disagreement in politics and at the same time preserves a plurality of moral principles. A fully developed public philosophy of this kind would help us decide what moral conflict should be precluded from politics, and what political practices we should promote to accommodate that conflict. Such a philosophy has yet to be developed, but its theoretical form and its practical value in politics should be clear.

Notes

1. E.g., John Rawls, "Justice as Fairness: Political not Metaphysical," *Philosophy & Public Affairs* 14 (Summer 1985), pp. 248–51); Thomas Nagel, "Moral Conflict and Political Legitimacy," *Philosophy & Public Affairs* 16 (Summer 1987), pp. 223–27; and David A. J. Richards, *Toleration and the Constitution* (New York: Oxford University Press, 1986), pp. 67–162.

2. For a more thorough discussion of several relevant meanings of neutrality and their application to a procedural theory, see John Rawls, "The Priority of the Right and Ideas of the Good," *Philosophy & Public Affairs* 17 (Fall 1988), pp. 260–64.

3. The argument we present is in its essentials found in Locke's *A Letter Concerning Toleration*, James Tully, ed., (Indianapolis, Ind.: Hackett Publishing Co., 1983), pp. 23–39. We call the argument Lockean, however, to indicate that we do not claim that every element of our reconstruction, especially our applications to twentieth-century problems, is precisely faithful to Locke's intention or even his text. Also, we ignore a number of arguments that were important for Locke and his contemporaries, for example, the argument against tolerating atheists and Catholics. The claim that people who do not believe in God cannot be trusted to keep promises and that people who owe allegiance to the pope cannot be trusted to obey a secular authority are distinct from those that underlie Locke's general defense of toleration.

4. Locke, *A Letter Concerning Toleration*, pp. 23–25.

5. Nagel, "Moral Conflict," p. 229.

6. Ibid., p. 235.

7. Locke, *A Letter Concerning Toleration*, pp. 27–28.

8. Ibid., pp. 23, 26–29, and 38.

9. The best short analysis, which goes beyond the formal criteria that are usually advanced to identify a moral position, is Ronald Dworkin's "The Concept of a Moral Position" in his "Lord Devlin and the Enforcement of Morals," in Richard Wasserstrom, ed., *Morality and the Law* (Belmont, Calif.: Wadsworth, 1971), pp. 61–67.

10. A wide range of substantive positions satisfy this requirement. For example, an "ethic of care," a morality that admits greater obligations to closely related people than to distantly related people or to humanity more generally, can be adopted by all members of a society, regardless of their class, race, or sex. The commonly drawn contrast between an "ethics of principle" and an "ethics of care" is *not* between a moral point of view and an amoral one.

11. For a helpful discussion of the foundations of the deliberative ideal, see Joshua Cohen, "Deliberation and Democratic Legitimacy," in Alan Hamlin and Philip Pettit, eds., *The Good Polity: Normative Analysis of the State* (Oxford: Basil Blackwell, 1989), pp. 17–34. Also see Charles Larmore, *Patterns of Moral Complexity* (Cambridge: Cambridge University Press, 1987), esp. pp. 59–66; and Bernard Manin, "On Legitimacy and Political Deliberation," *Political Theory* 15 (August 1987), pp. 338–68.

12. Roger Wertheimer, "Understanding the Abortion Argument," in Marshall Cohen et al., eds., *The Rights and Wrongs of Abortion* (Princeton, N.J.: Princeton University Press, 1974), pp. 23–51.

13. Ibid., p. 41.

14. Ibid., pp. 50–51.

15. Or else his argument depends on a stronger (and less defensible) interpretation of the first step:

that governments cannot restrict freedom unless they can justify their restrictions rationally to those *already rational* beings whose freedom is restricted. This stronger claim is itself morally suspect unless one already believes that a human life is not at stake and therefore a government need not rationally justify sanctioning the termination of human life, it need only rationally justify restricting an already rational person's freedom. (The same argument would render it wrong to make infanticide illegal.) The stronger interpretation is suspect unless one already accepts the conclusion that logically follows, that abortion ought to be legal.

16. In contrast to what has been called recognition respect (what we owe all persons simply by virtue of their being persons), mutual respect is a form of appraisal respect; it expresses a positive appraisal of a person for manifesting some excellence of character. This "enables us to see that there is no puzzle at all in thinking both that all persons are entitled to respect just by virtue of their being persons and that persons are deserving of more or less respect by virtue of their personal characteristics" Stephen L. Darwall, "Two Kinds of Respect," *Ethics* 88, no. 1 (October 1977), p. 46; also pp. 38–39, 45.

17. On the significance of some of these qualities for democratic character, see Albert Hirschman, "Having Opinions—One of the Elements of Well-Being?" (Paper presented at the Annual Meeting of the American Economic Association, New York, December 1988).

18. Quoted in Joseph A. Califano, Jr., *Governing America* (New York: Simon & Schuster, 1981), p. 84.

19. Remarks of Congressman Bill Green (Republican, New York), *Congressional Record,* September 9, 1988, H7351.

20. However, Congressman Green's opponents did not draw the conclusion that he wished them to draw from the existence of moral controversy: that "the decision as to what should happen to the product of that rape that is best left to the woman's own conscience . . . (ibid.)." In effect, he was evoking a version of the neutrality argument to try to remove the issue from the political agenda.

21. Remarks of William Dannemeyer (Republican, California), *Congressional Record* (September 22, 1983), p. H7319. Although Dannemeyer also said that the "economic consequences of the moral issue should not be permitted to resolve the matter," his entire speech was devoted to the "fiscal consequences."

22. Representative Barbara Mikulski (Democrat, Maryland), ibid.

23. For insights into the significance of openness for democratic character, see Hirschman, ibid.

24. Califano, *Governing America,* p. 68 (emphasis added). Califano also comments that he should do all he could to avoid "unnecessary provocation."

25. "Religious Belief and Public Morality: A Catholic Governor's Perspective," September 13, 1984, pp. 17–18, xerox. We are grateful to Ken Winston for calling our attention to the significance of this passage.

26. The requirement of an economy of moral disagreement appears to resemble Larmore's "universal norm of rational dialogue," which he explains as follows: "When two people disagree about some specific point, but wish to continue talking about the more general problem they wish to solve, each should prescind from the beliefs that the other rejects, (1) in order to construct an argument on the basis of his other beliefs that will convince the other of the truth of the disputed belief, or (2) in order to shift to another aspect of the problem, where the possibilities of agreement seem greater" (*Patterns,* p. 53). There are, however, important differences between Larmore's understanding and ours. On our understanding of mutual respect, people who disagree (but wish to continue talking) need not prescind from publicly professing beliefs that others reject. Nor should they "retreat to neutral grounds." Instead they should search for common grounds (and their search should satisfy the standards of mutual respect). An economy of moral disagreement aspires to a mutual commitment to substantive moral principles that are not necessarily neutral either with respect to prevailing conceptions of the good life or even to the specific controversy. It should also be clear from the place of an economy of moral disagreement within a broader public philosophy that the recommendation to prescind from invoking values at odds with some citizen's beliefs is contingent upon those beliefs meeting the threshold requirements of a respectable moral position.

27. The search for an economy of moral disagreement should not be identified with Rawls's search

for an overlapping consensus. In our view, an economy of moral disagreement is not a defining feature of a political theory. It is only one form that respectful accommodation of moral conflict may take in a pluralistic society in those cases in which conflicting moral perspectives fortuitously converge in their practical implications.

28. Judith Jarvis Thomson, "A Defense of Abortion," in Cohen et al., *Rights and Wrongs of Abortion*, pp. 3–22.

29. Ibid., pp. 4–5.

30. Ibid., pp. 162–64, *Roe v. Wade*, 410 U.S. 113 (1973).

31. Thomson, "A Defense of Abortion," pp. 163–64.

32. For some examples of characteristics of legislative institutions, especially the Congress, that encourage and discourage deliberation, see Jane Mansbridge, "Motivating Deliberation in Congress," in Sarah Baumgartner Thurow, ed., *Constitutionalism in America*, vol. 2 (New York: University Press of America, 1988), pp. 59–86.

33. See, for example, Alasdair MacIntyre, *After Virtue* (Notre Dame: University of Notre Dame Press, 1981), esp. pp. 6, 20–21, 189; and Michael Sandel, *Liberalism and the Limits of Justice* (New York: Cambridge University Press, 1982), esp. p. 183.

34. John Rawls, "The Idea of an Overlapping Consensus," *Oxford Journal of Legal Studies* 7 (Spring, 1987), pp. 1–25.

35. Ibid., pp. 17, 20–21.

36. Rawls recognizes that some questions properly on the political agenda will be controversial, because they are so important that differences over them "have to be fought out, even should this mean civil war" or presumably because they are as yet unresolvable by a political conception of justice. In both cases, however, the aim of a political conception of justice, on Rawls's account, is to create an overlapping consensus and thereby decrease political controversy (ibid., p. 13).

37. Ibid., p. 14.

8

Bringing the Good Back In

William M. Sullivan

A Statement of the Issue

We live in a period marked by a major revival of the theory of philosophic liberalism. Examples are more than plentiful: the general enthusiasm for the free market and the considerable vogue of Chicago School economics both in and beyond the academy; the prominence of public finance theory in schools of public administration; the current *éclat* attached to rational choice theory; the importance of the contractarian theories of Rawls and Nozick in political philosophy. These recent developments continue classic liberalism's historic concern to enhance for individuals the plasticity of life, especially in regard to the constraints of social institutions and cultural norms. Proponents of liberal theory seem to agree that liberalism is committed at least to the defense of individual freedom of choice—so-called "negative liberty"—and, as they see it, a strong consequent aversion to positive specifications of the public good.

For over a decade we have also experienced an upsurge in a mode of political philosophy and ethics styled by some as "communitarian." A large and growing number of authors have produced striking and powerful criticisms of philosophic liberalism. Criticism of philosophic liberalism is the common stance connecting such otherwise diverse thinkers as Alasdair MacIntyre, Michael Walzer, Roberto Mangabeira Unger, Charles Taylor, Michael Sandel, Thomas Spragens, and John Dunn, to name only a few. These critics have challenged the adequacy of liberal theories of political, ethical, and social order. They argue that an adequate notion of social life must rely upon shared understandings more extensive than those countenanced by liberal theories.

Individualist liberals have a ready response to this criticism. Defenders of classic liberalism frequently argue that public agreement concerning the ends of collective action must be tightly restricted to those agreements which do not "privilege" or benefit some conceptions of the ends of life over others. In the interests of defending individual freedom, liberals have argued that public decision-making should be guided by principles which are "neutral" among various conceptions of what is worth pursuing in life beyond the defense of the private freedom of individual choice. Perhaps because religious commitments to ultimate values have often been the issues at hand, liberals have frequently characterized all conceptions of common ends as "metaphysical" commitments which necessarily imperil the freedom of those who do not subscribe to them.[1]

In this chapter I argue that this last claim, and the familiar arguments to which it has given rise, are unwarranted overgeneralizations from certain real but historically particular situations. Contemporary democratic life is characterized by the increasing interpenetration of private and public ends, and I argue that this development ought to be facilitated rather than opposed by political philosophy, including liberal theory itself.

My intention is to take up the "communitarian" critique outlined above, and develop it by proposing the potential gains for democratic life which the notion of the common good can provide. This understanding of the common good need not entail "metaphysical" commitments as this term is often understood. The sense of "metaphysical" in question—which is not uncontested—connotes a complete and final knowledge of the ultimate nature of things which bears upon the conduct of life. By contrast, the conception of the common good espoused here is open to discursive examination, argument, and testing. It is intended to be a flexible and inclusive notion. This does not guarantee that consensus can be reached, nor does it exclude reference to religious or otherwise ultimate commitments. But it does require that in the political realm consensus be achieved by means of discursive argument and deliberation rather than by the imposition of claims held as authoritative on other grounds.

According to this conception, the common good is a consensus on values to be publicly striven for. But the consensus is more political and practical in nature than ultimate and theoretical. The understanding of the common good I am proposing is then an intermediate one. It stands midway between claims about the ultimate ends of collective life and the liberal dogmatism which ignores the possibility of a practical, political understanding of the common good. I want to associate this middle position with a tradition of political thought I will call social liberalism.

While classic individualist liberals have long eschewed political argument about collective ends, social liberals have insisted upon the indispensability of some common interpretations about ends for the achievement of key liberal commitments such as the ideal of rational self-determination. Social liberal thinkers thus anticipated many of the arguments of contemporary communitarians.

I have in mind thinkers such as T. H. Green and the New Liberals in Great Britain, Emile Durkheim and his school in France, and Josiah Royce, John Dewey, and George Herbert Mead in the United States. Significantly, these thinkers, like Hegel before them, looked to a critical appropriation of classical political philosophy and biblical religion in formulating their positions. Social liberals argued that rational self-determination is a collective social achievement which can be secured only where the development of supportive institutions and ethos becomes a primary focus of public effort.

Social liberals argued their case in a broadly historical way. In this they differed markedly from the leaders of the contemporary liberal revival who prefer a more formalistic, atemporal style. T. H. Green, for example, viewed human society as a collective educational enterprise. For Green, the classic liberal notion of the free human person endowed with rights is the outcome of a development in which the individual comes to make himself an object of his own concern. But this development is only made possible by the mutual recognition afforded by social life. In other words, the capacity for personhood could develop only in contexts supporting reciprocal recognition.

Individuals, in the sense of self-determining persons, require certain institutional patterns and practices of social interrelationship for their very being. As these patterns determine what individuals can become, those things which the members of society understand as important for the life of persons become the prerequisites for individuality. In this way moral individuality has been the outgrowth of a certain understanding of the common good.

For Green, the growth of inclusiveness in these institutional patterns describes moral progress. It has resulted from historically emerging agreements about the importance of the higher types of human desires and capacities. Integrity, courage, responsiveness to the value of the whole, and a willingness to sacrifice for these ideal goods are the practical prerequisites for expanding the understanding of who counts in life. In this sense moral progress means the development of the virtues, seen as collective and not simply individual understandings of the good. In each era, then, the opportunities for individual growth are tied to the moral and institutional possibilities of the social order. A society can be measured by how fully it embodies a sense of a common good which enables persons to pursue their self-realization in ways that are both genuinely their own and yet harmoniously related to and sustained by the pursuits of others.

The strength of the so-called communitarian critics of individualistic liberalism derives in part from their restatement of this claim of the social liberals. The force of the claim is that classic liberal theories, whether contractarian, utilitarian or denotological, depend upon a more concrete social ethos or ethic than they explicitly acknowledge. According to the critics, the classic liberal principle of respect for individuals is part of the collective self-understanding of liberal societies, and thus a social achievement.

In this view, broad collective understandings guide individuals, even in liberal societies like the United States whose cultures are characterized by a high degree of individualism. More to the point, only a shared social ethic can provide the mutual confidence on which secure public discourse depends. Without such confidence, as Bernard Williams has argued, the rational calculation of the contractarians and utilitarians becomes impossible in practice.[2] And it is this shared confidence which provides the practical basis for the central liberal value of respect for persons.

Critics of classic liberalism hold that this social ethic is dependent upon its embodiment in certain normative social practices. A widely shared social ethic, in turn, provides the common interpretations which define, as the practices it interprets sustain, common identities and purposes. As a social ethic enables individuals to recognize their own and their fellow citizens' dignity through the support their common goals receive in public life, it is the practical matrix for the notion of individual rights.

If this characterization of the "communitarian" critique is correct, the opposition between liberals and "communitarians" is misunderstood when it is viewed as an argument over the degree of "community" desirable in modern societies. This is particularly the case when "community" is understood as connoting a heavy patina of "emotional warmth" and general *Gemütlichkeit*.[3] The real issue concerns the nature of public life under modern conditions. It is better stated as a question about the cultural and institutional requirements for the widely agreed upon goal of effective democracy. In other words, the question concerns the conditions for the democratic direction of modern societies through broadly based citizen participation and public argument.

The current argument between liberals and "communitarians" is thus an old one. Its origins lie in the historical development of the autonomous legal order, the market economy, and other features of what we now term modernity. Seen this way, the fundamental issues are, I think, two. First, how should we understand modern social life? Do any actual societies answer to the descriptions provided by liberal theory? Can any actual societies sustain themselves entirely and exclusively on the bases supposed by liberal theory? Is the legal order of rights and contract, on the one hand, and the moral order of duty and private conscience on the other, enough? Or does even a social order organized according to these liberal principles not in fact depend upon the support of a denser social ethic than that described by liberals?

The second issue is normative. Can an individualist liberal conception of social life guide public discourse toward enhancing an institutional and ethical context conducive to the flourishing of both rational autonomy and mutual trust? This question is interdependent with the first in that an answer to either question will entail a consistent answer to the other. But this interdependence between the empirical and the normative has not always been thought to be the case, particularly by liberals. It was once a matter of argument. Liberals typically bolstered their position by claiming for it valid status according to the cognitive criteria of modern science. The theorists of the social contract have sought to endow their principles with a self-evident clarity independent of any antecedent loyalties or beliefs.

The notion of the "state of nature" has historically been a central notion for liberal political thinking. In the state of nature unassociated individuals who nonetheless need to cooperate for survival arrive at certain terms of contract. This paradigm functioned as the analogue to the basic elements and conditions postulated by natural scientific theories in their explanations of physical systems. Like the natural sciences, liberal political theory aimed to produce compelling, even self-evident accounts of the reasons underlying social arrangements. These accounts, in order to be judged rational by scientific standards, strove to invoke no social or cultural loyalties beyond those "impartial" norms which would seem reasonable to unassociated but self-interested beings in the state of nature. By these procedures, liberals aimed to provide an unassailable foundation for the "natural rights" of individuals independently for any social or cultural membership. This conception of political and moral rationality continued to be taken for granted by liberal theorists as recently as John Rawls's "veil of ignorance" in the "original position" (or state of nature) which served to secure the impartiality and rationality of his theory of justice.

Recently, however, many liberals, including John Rawls, have joined many of their academic colleagues in taking an interpretive turn. The move away from reliance upon a presumably self-validating and universal method of reasoning toward an acknowledgment that rationality is always embedded in contingent cultural understandings radically revises the way liberals now view their own commitments. In the revised account liberalism is presented straightforwardly as a moral-political understanding in conscious contrast and competition with others. Here the factual and normative questions become tightly joined. Compared to the older positivistic conception, this updated hermeneutic liberalism troubles some supporters as well as critics. By acknowledging that the liberal understanding of social life is one historical development among others, hermeneutic liberalism seems, from the standpoint of the canons of a self-justifying rationality, to raise the problem of philosophic relativism, thereby adding a new complexity to the defense of classic positions.[4]

This interpretive turn in political philosophy provides a new and encouraging context within which to reconceive the argument between the critics and defenders of classic liberalism. By bringing descriptive and normative discourse closer together, the new context highlights the ways in which political theories serve to interpret and to some extent to constitute the understandings which actually guide activity in the public realm.

Seen this way, political theory becomes implicated in the world it seeks to describe and thereby receives both warrant and responsibility for contributing to the public discussion of social life. I want to argue that recent changes in both American moral understandings and political practice reveal the need to bring discourse about the common good into the center of public life. But such discourse need not involve intractable arguments over ultimate principles. On the contrary, I will argue that it is the limitations of the liberal language of individual rights which has exacerbated such seemingly unresolvable arguments as those over affirmative action and abortion, and that a political rather than ultimate conception of the common good may provide our most effective resolution to these conflicts.

A Changed "Political Space"

While the argument between individualist liberals and their critics is an old one, it is not accidental that it has reemerged with particular intensity at this historical juncture. The crucial historical catalyst was the change in the American cultural and political world accomplished during the 1960s and its aftermath. That period saw the climax and then the beginnings of the dissolution of the global preeminence of the United States sometimes called the American Century. As the postwar consensus began to unravel, the United States experienced an extraordinary political and cultural effervescence. Old, submerged currents of thought surfaced along with novel cultural currents. The revival of both classic liberal political philosophy and of neo-laissez-faire economics both date to the aftermath of the 1960s, while important elements of the "communitarian" critique can be identified in the cultural wave of that time.

During the early years of the 1960s, government assumed officially what it had already taken on in practice: responsibility for the performance of the national economy. Simultaneously, the momentous political battle for the full inclusion of black Americans changed forever the moral and legal order of the U.S. in a more inclusive direction. The movement for civil rights spawned a wave of political concern with solidarity and the issue of social justice. The era's extraordinary prosperity also opened a host of new cultural possibilities for individual self-realization. Many of these cultural developments took political forms, most notably in the women's movement.

The enduring effect of this ferment was to generate a host of new responsibilities for government. Not only in efforts to pursue racial justice, but in many other ways Americans today find themselves deeply dependent upon the national government. In the economic realm even entrepreneurial progress such as the boom of the semiconductor industry has been dependent upon federal, often military, research and development. Increasingly, Americans see what were formerly private difficulties and sufferings as matters of public responsibility, as with job-related injury, cancer or AIDS.

Theodore Lowi was correct when he noted at the end of the 1960s that this new governmental intervention involved more than traditional issues such as fairness of competition and had expanded to embrace a concern of the overall social, and increasingly, the natural environment. The problem, as Lowi saw it, was that this expansion of intervention was proceeding without clear legal or constitutional grounding, thereby producing a diffuse sense of illegitimacy. Lowi's proposed remedy was to follow F. A. Hayek in calling for a retreat from interest-group bargaining and market regulation toward a conception of the "rule of law" based upon the liberal notion of individual rights. Such a public philosophy would attempt to restore legitimacy by pulling back from an interventionist state.[5]

However, there is substantial evidence that the efforts to subject social outcomes to public jurisdiction have come to enjoy widespread public support.[6] Besides producing a host of new claims upon government, these changes have given rise to expanded ethical claims. To use the Rawlsian language, our "settled moral convictions" have been growing and changing dramatically during the past two decades. Lowi is still importantly correct in one respect. All this has created major problems for traditional liberal conceptions of law and government. However, retreat to the proceduralism of the classic liberal state is not the only alternative.

The issue can be profitably illuminated through Sheldon Wolin's notion of "political space." Wolin argued that each political society must "structure its space" in both the physical and metaphorical senses. "Political space" refers to the institutional arrangements of a political society which "serve to mark out paths along which human motions can proceed harmlessly or beneficially."[7] Beginning early in the century, but taking a quantum leap since the 1960s, the tendency in the United States has been away from a public order describable largely in terms of liberal reciprocity. Gradually U.S. political space has taken on a new configuration which embodies an increasing sense of collective responsibility for the outcomes of social life. The issue is whether the classic liberal interpretations of the situation can effectively make sense of this change in a way that is capable of guiding institutional reconstruction.

These developments of the past several decades reveal major inadequacies in our inherited language of the public. The doctrine of individual rights and contract cannot by itself give effective and stable institutional realization to the new moral convictions about collective responsibility. It is this situation which gives more than academic currency to the current debate between liberals and communitarians. It is also the situation which makes a renewed development of social liberalism our best practical as well as theoretical hope for resolving public confusion and conflict.

The theoretical key to that development is the transformation of political space structured on classic liberal lines into one centered on a discourse about the common good. Or, put another way, liberalism needs a political understanding of the common good. American culture possesses the resources to develop one, drawing from its republican and religious heritage and recasting this in the form of social liberalism. Such a development ought to be welcomed by liberals since, as I will try to show, it would represent progress toward expanding and stabilizing liberal goods such as respect for persons and rational liberty.

The Need for a Common Good

The point of enriching the language of public life in this way is to amplify our social capacities to interpret and debate the common purposes on which our increasingly interdependent world depends. In the theoretical realm, this development means moving beyond "thin" liberal theories of the good and an ethics of pure reciprocity. These place arbitrary and dogmatic limits upon public moral and political discourse at a time when the need is for a broadening of the terms of public debate and public philosophy. The liberal tradition will be significantly transformed but also strengthened by this development.

If the expanding sense of collective capacity and responsibility requires more extensive public discussion of common goals, then the heritage of classic liberalism does not serve us well. This is because the liberal conception of political space rests upon two fallacies. The first is the dogmatic limitation upon giving public sanction to collective interpretation of the ends of an increasingly interdependent social life. The second, correlated fallacy is the notion that institutions are merely devices for individual use. According to this fallacy, individuals can expect to use institutions with impunity, much as they might use the post office, without that use resulting in any significant effect on the identity and purposes of the user.

These widespread fallacies, formulated in much liberal theory as well as political thinking, often impede and sometimes render self-defeating the liberal goal of rational self-determination. This is because the truncated public language of liberalism shuts down public debate prematurely or renders it incomprehensible to many participants. The effort of philosophic liberalism to erect a conceptual *cordon sanitaire* to prevent infection of the public realm by interpretations of the ends of action, especially religious interpretations, has played a historically useful role in destroying despotisms. However, the contemporary United States is paying a high cost for continued reliance upon that early modern creed whose once admirable simplicity of formulation has, in our era, grown simplistic.

Institutions are not simply devices, as a moment's sociological reflection shows. Institutions are recognized patterns of interaction which define an order of mutual recognition in which individual identities are formed, as a family gives sense and purpose to the lives of its individual members by enabling them to realize themselves as spouses, parents, and children. In this way institutions, as liberals such as John Stuart Mill and Alexis de Tocqueville well understood, shape individuals.[8] Because institutions assign responsibility and sanction accountability, they are the indispensable practical basis for any normative order. Because they are collective realities, institutions generate and sustain common norms and goals.

In the public sphere, as in the legally private realm, the workings of institutions, including the law and the courts, create common meanings which prescribe the proper conduct of life. They define, for example, what it is to be fair in exchange, to be a family, and what the responsibilities of the individual are to all classes of others. However, the abstract language of rights, divorced from the meanings and ends in which rights are inevitably embedded in practice, can make it hard to grasp the impact of law upon understandings of the good actually operative in the society.

To establish the inadequacy of the liberal language of rights for dealing with the problems of modern social interdependency, one could cite a variety of public issues. But none so poignantly illustrates the problem as the continuing failure to effectively institutionalize the goal of racial equality.

The civil rights movement of a quarter century ago profoundly reshaped the national consciousness. Racial equality became an uncontested part of the moral consensus and a basic legal commitment. The great burst of freedom made possible by open housing and antidiscrimination legislation enabled millions of black Americans to leave overcrowded urban ghettos and poorly paying occupations. Yet as the fortunate and determined entered the broad American middle class, those left behind found themselves unable to get a start in a labor market less in need of unskilled workers.

The isolation of the urban underclass was a peculiarly perverse and unwanted outcome of the successes of the struggle for civil rights. At the same time, well-intentioned efforts to compensate for the past evils of racism through mandatory school busing and affirmative action produced not only gains for many black Americans, but bitterness and distrust among some whites, confusion among many more. It has seemed that the gains of the civil rights era are slipping away despite our best efforts to hold on to and advance them. What has gone wrong?

Part of the problem has certainly been the changing nature of the American economy, which has worked against many poor urban blacks. The patchy, ad hoc character of the nation's welfare system is also probably to blame for the persistence of the underclass, while there has been an unmistakable willingness to ignore their plight on the part of a large segment of officials and the more secure citizenry. But in the cases of affirmative action, busing, and the like, the very way in which these efforts have been understood and carried out is unmistakably a significant part of the problem. The difficulty stems from the exclusive reliance on the liberal understandings of individual "rights" in order to address complexly interdependent problems of social and economic participation.

In the American liberal polity, modern civil rights legislation has been construed as an effort to specify the intent of the post–Civil War constitutional amendments. The purpose of the Reconstruction amendments was to redress the wrong of slavery and, equally importantly, to enable the freedmen to enter the economic, social, and political mainstream without hindrance. The intent of initiatives such as affirmative action was to continue and extend these achievements, taking into account the lack of progress during the century since Reconstruction.

The notion has been that compensatory action, such as mandated quotas in hiring for certain occupations or admissions to certain kinds of schools, becomes justified when it is possible to prove a pattern of discrimination in the past which has worked to exclude members of certain groups from the ordinary and fully equal participation in those institutions. Rights in this perspective may indeed function as "trumps." But the history of a variety of legal contests shows that the determination of whose "rights" have been truly violated, and who should receive what compensatory remedy, has been tortuous indeed. The goal of full legal and social integration has been maddeningly elusive. At no point have we as a nation been able to formulate clearly what arrangement of institutions and resources would be necessary to achieve the kind of society which could embody our ideal of racial equality.

Progress in securing the goals of civil rights for all has proven frustrating. But institutionalizing the new freedoms in the spheres of private life first explored in the movements of the 1960s has produced no more satisfying solutions. As with civil rights, effecting a workable, stable consensus on the rights of women has, after a first blush of enthusiasm, proven equally resistant to resolution. Here a recent work in comparative jurisprudence has proved particularly enlightening. It also suggests a practical direction toward the resolution of some of these issues, a direction which can serve as an example of the future of social liberalism.

A Comparative Perspective

It has long been a commonplace among liberal apologists that discussion of common ends is inherently divisive and so best kept to the private rather than public realm. And certainly recent American experience with public debate concerning fundamental moral and social values such as marriage and divorce, abortion and changing medical technologies, has been anything but encouraging. Given this record, the contention of Mary Ann Glendon in *Abortion and Divorce in Western Law* that several West European nations have managed to handle these problems less contentiously by explicitly making them objects of public argument and goal-setting is, at the least, striking.

While Glendon's study deals with comparative law and its associated institutions, she insists, against much American tradition, that law is not simply a tool or device. It is also, and perhaps more importantly, a principal means by which a society understands and shapes itself. This, then, is an approach which resonates with the interpretive turn in contemporary political philosophy. Law, Glendon argues, is both interpretive and constitutive. A legal system is "part of a distinctive way of imagining the real," in Clifford Geertz's words, and specifically a way by which "social data are reconstructed as legal facts and concepts." However, law also contributes to shaping social reality, so to speak, in its own image. Glendon asks us to consider "what sorts of meaning" family law is creating, and "what sort of family is it helping to constitute?"[9]

By taking a comparative perspective Glendon is able to highlight some surprising differences between American and West European adjustments to the changes the past several decades have worked in sexual and family life on both sides of the Atlantic. As she summarizes: "At present we lead the developed world in our extreme liberty of abortion while we lag behind the countries to which we most often compare ourselves in the benefits and services we provide to mothers and to poor families, and in the imposition and collection of child support obligations" (p. 53). In regard to divorce, the United States is again unique "in its relative carelessness about assuring either public or private responsibility for the economic casualties of divorce," casualties who are overwhelmingly women and children.[10]

At the same time, the United States is marked by a far higher degree of public acrimony than any West European nation about the issues of abortion and family law, including such matters as day care and child support as well as divorce. Glendon notes that even countries such as West Germany and Spain, which have strong pro-life and pro-abortion groups as well as a history of major political involvement on the part of religious bodies, have developed enduring compromises on a matter which in the U.S. continually threatens to erupt into violence and constitutional crisis. By turning abortion into a constitutional issue in the *Roe v. Wade* decision, the U.S. Supreme Court brought litigation and public argument to a premature halt, before any effective moral consensus could be established. The result, according to Glendon, is that "the main avenue left open for political activity with respect to the abortion issue is then the cumbersome process of constitutional amendment."[11]

What is it about the American legal and political process that has made it so difficult to achieve civil compromise and lasting civic peace on these issues? Ethnic and religious diversity aside (the West Europeans are not always more unified on these matters than we), a substantial part of the answer lies in the relative poverty of a legal tradition that does not relate the notion of individual rights to any conceptions of collective or common goods.

Unlike the *Roe v. Wade* decision, the West German and Spanish abortion laws are not framed as a balancing of individual rights. Instead of pitting the right to life of the fetus against a woman's right to privacy, choice or control over her body, these European laws emphasize a commitment to an order of public values. Glendon notes that in their review of the abortion laws, the German and Spanish courts refused "to hold that a fetus has legal rights. Rather, the court said that unborn life is a public good protected by the court."[12] The German and Spanish laws, then, do not outlaw all abortion; neither do they authorize abortion on demand. Instead they define potential human life as a public good and seek to protect that good by requiring that there be some extenuating circumstances for abortion.

This is a definition of the situation not likely to please the pro-abortion cause. However, both in language and in practice, Glendon notes, these circumstances are given a generous interpretation, far too generous to satisfy many pro-life advocates. The point, however, is that these European laws result from and contribute to a compromise, one which, because it is an argument about social values, also helps to refine and legitimate a consensus on certain common good. They acknowledge "an important ideal of a large segment of the population, while accommodating in practice to some extent those who do not or cannot live up to that ideal." Such laws clearly reflect political debate, so that they "let us know, too, why the winners did not obtain everything they sought."[13]

Law, then, is not only a system of social regulation nor a mere reflection of social consensus. It is an active part of the larger public process through which a society defines its identity. The case that Glendon makes is that law is educative of attitudes and expectations. In their approaches to the legal treatment of divorce and abortion the West European nations are doing more than patching together unsatisfactory political compromises riddled with inconsistency. Instead, Glendon insists, "a conversation is going on about the right way to live." The aim of legal reformers has been to "maintain a widely shared ideal in the law . . . while accommodating the opinions and behavior of those who do not share or cannot live up to the ideal." These efforts have used "law-making as an occasion for dialogue" by "preserving a sense of responsibility and social context along with regard for individuals and their rights."[14]

To all this a classic liberal might raise a fundamental objection. Does not this endorsement of public value consensus make those societies less free by violating the liberal prohibition upon non-neutral principles of political judgment? But this objection is inconsistent with liberal practice. Liberal jurists and legislators have often effected reorganizations of public life so as to privilege certain conceptions of character and the "good life" over others. In the last century, as legal historians have shown, the language of rights was used to extend market relations into areas of society previously outside commercial relations. This was carried out quite explicitly to foster the benefits expected to follow from the application of laissez-faire economics.[15]

In the case of family law in the contemporary United States, Glendon shows that a similar process has been underway. Recent reforms in family law have redefined the understanding of marriage so that, at law, the relationship exists "primarily for the fulfillment of the individual spouses" so that "if it ceases to perform this function, no one is to blame and either spouse may terminate it at will." All this is in keeping with the liberal notion that individual freedom of choice is the overriding good to be advanced by the law. It is instructive to notice, however, that "children hardly appear" except as "rather shadowy characters in the background."[16]

The result, whether intentional or not, is that children, like many women, find themselves alone, outside any sustaining network of enforceable responsibilities. In effect, conceptions of marriage that do not regard it as simply an easily dissolved contract between consenting parties receive neither hearing nor support in a crucial part of the public realm. The social cost of such single-minded liberalism is, as noted, largely borne by women and their children.

The point of this example is not to dismiss all reforms of family law that have expanded equality and individual freedom of contract. Rather, the difficulty arises precisely from the fact that in family law the liberal case has not been advanced as a set of claims about what ought to be publicly affirmed about the goals and obligations of marriage as an institution. Exclusive reliance upon the language of rights focuses attention, as might be expected, upon individuals rather than institutions. The result is that American "family policy" develops implicitly, making the social implications of concern with individual liberty difficult to grasp and often simply unexamined.

What difference might an explicit consideration of the goods involved in "family policy" make? Glendon cites the West German Constitution's endorsement of marriage and the family as enjoying "the special protection of the state." But the same Constitution also stresses that each individual has the right "to the free development of his personality" and that "men and women have equal rights."[17] Here we encounter contrary aims within the same framework. The point, however, is that "the fact that not all of these important values can be fully implemented simultaneously" does not render incoherent either the German Constitution or public debate over family policy. Instead, the articulation of these contrasting goals seems to remind judges, legislators, and the public that these values all must be kept in play.

In such a context, one might argue, it is more rather than less likely that conceptions important to some groups will continue to receive a hearing and a place in legal decisions.

It also seems likely that the very practice of having to keep the competing values in mind works to promote efforts at accommodation and synthesis, rather than head-on collisions of immutable principles.

Finally, we might notice that where the common good can be discussed and defined through the medium of public values, historical memory is kept alive and old purposes can be both criticized and reaffirmed. By contrast, consider the shameful record of the U.S. Supreme Court's interpretation of the Fourteenth Amendment at the end of the last century. The amendment, drafted to defend the rights of freedmen was first interpreted to free business corporations from legal obligations on the reasoning that corporations could be considered "persons" under the amendment. As we know, it was a painfully long time until the aims of Reconstruction were once again brought to bear in the interpretation of the amendment.

By contrast, in its finding on the abortion law the West German Constitutional Court could note that underlying their basic or constitutional law "are principles for the structuring of the state that may be understood only in the light of the historical experience and the spiritual-moral confrontation with the previous system of National Socialism." The court went on to stress that because of this historical fact, the law "demands unconditional respect for the life of every individual human being, even for the apparently socially 'worthless', and which therefore excludes destruction of such life without legally justifiable grounds."[18]

How might our own constitutional and social history have been affected if the Reconstruction amendments could have been framed and interpreted with reference to "the historical experience and the spiritual-moral confrontation with the previous system" of slavery? A political space structured by consideration of the common good could hardly avoid focusing on just such historically and culturally specific issues. This is not the least reason to bring the common good back in.

Toward a New Vision

Political and moral theories gain currency, in part, because they are able to interpret the problems of their times in ways judged by their contemporaries to be more satisfactory than opposing theories. These judgments are themselves always partial, contestable, and incomplete. This is so because the cogency of the arguments mounted by any theory reflects how plausible that theory's premises appear to those party to the debate. Because we always argue within a contingent institutional context, a theory's success in interpreting the social world is, apart from its sheerly logical features, always influenced by what its historical context makes comprehensible and plausible.

As we have seen, the American polity is marked by a growing recognition of public responsibility for social outcomes. This development represents a moral interpretation of social interdependency. That interpretation concludes that because we collectively can and do affect individual life chances, then we collectively must assume a responsibility to do so in an equitable manner. But the examples of the efforts to secure civil rights for all and the conflicts over family policy show that Americans are at odds over what constitutes equity in these cases.

It has proven difficult to get consensus by arguing over "rights" alone. A major reason for the intractable nature of these conflicts in the U.S. emerges in high relief from consideration of Glendon's comparative data. In the American arguments over rights there is an implicit debate being joined about the proper order of social relationships between the races, within marriages, and between adults and children. Especially in the arguments about abortion and divorce, these disputes involve substantive disagreements over the kinds of lives the law should legitimate and which it should not. These are arguments about virtues and the ends of life. While "metaphysical" and religious commitments are involved in virtually all of these conflicts, Glendon's comparative data suggest that nevertheless there may be innovative ways beyond our apparent impasse.

The rigidity and absolute quality which the social contract theory gave to natural rights has made constructive public argument difficult in the area of family law. Both sides in the abortion controversy quickly resorted to rights claims in order to "trump" their opponents. The increasing vehemence with which the two camps have asserted the priority of their respective claims—the woman's right to privacy versus that of the fetus to juridical personhood—has not enhanced the credibility of philosophic liberalism as a language of public deliberation. Abortion is one controversy in which a long period of arguing has failed to enhance mutual respect among the participants. Neither has it advanced a process of social learning. There has been fear on both sides that, should rights become in any sense "discussable," majority tyranny is just around the corner. This fear has helped to keep alive the hope that social contract theory can provide a rational basis for rights which can be demonstrated independently of historical or social context.

Unfortunately for this attempt, the notion that individuals possess powers that ought to be respected always requires interpretation. The idea of natural right has played a key role in defining American identity since the Declaration of Independence. Rights help establish individual identity by specifying what capacities must be recognized by others and what corresponding duties to respect such rights become binding upon all. But rights must be distinguished from mere preferences. This requires some consensus about the things which can legitimately be called necessary for personhood under particular conditions. Thus, when rights and duties are unclear or in dispute, as at law and in much political argument, interpretation becomes essential.

The liberal appeals to abstract liberty or equality provide only thin principles of interpretation. This is suggested by the courts' frequent turns to history, traditional usage, and moral consensus in order to specify the meaning of liberty or equality in their decisions. In cases of severe conflict, such as family policy, where consensus is in doubt, tradition far from univocal and the exact meaning of equality vague, successful public deliberation may require a shift in the way the issues are put.

Rights claims might be seen as affirmations of the society's struggle to discern and realize a more inclusive understanding of itself and its possibilities. Such public argumentation is not wholly foreign to American practice. A common end, such as mutual defense or obedience to law—or promotion of social goods such as life, the family, and racial equality—provides a context for civic self-interpretation. It makes it possible to discuss for what reasons and under what circumstances all have a duty to work for such an end as well as who should be excused and for what reasons.

A political notion of the common good, then, could serve as a framework within which to structure public arguments in a new way. By requiring participants in the public argument to demonstrate how their proposals can enable all of us to live decently together, the idea of the common good offers a significant advantage over a discourse based upon individual rights advanced in abstraction from the defining goods of the political association. Over time, such a framework could help individuals and groups to reinterpret their interests in ways more conducive to the discovery and forging of agreements.

A more explicit focus upon social values as a framework for discussion does not preclude irreconcilable conflicts. However, it would make it possible to acknowledge particular claims within, and even as required by, the common adherence to general principles. Casting political debates as arguments about the common good would also work to bring a coherence to public arguments which is presently lacking. By effectively requiring all participants to state their positions in terms of general agreements, the process of debate about a common good works to bind differing parties together within a common frame of principles. This much is clear from Glendon's examples. Generalizing the point, one could expect that with a more explicit use of the common good to structure public argument, disagreement would become both more intelligible to all parties and more limited in scope.

The likely result is a greater degree of common understanding. Such a heightened awareness of those commitments which are shared across differences can provide the basis for mutual respect even across the cleavages and interest and belief, since it is those shared commitments that make the differences intelligible. The long-term result could be a more inclusive yet morally comprehensible society, one in which an effective culture of public argument would be both a means and an end of political life.

If the social order we inhabit were fully organized according to the principles of philosophic liberalism, an argument like Glendon's would be very hard to mount. That it has intelligibility and plausibility in the American context indicates, perhaps, that a potential exists for an expansion of our political space beyond the constrictions of classic liberalism. To make a concluding argument, I want to bring into the conversation one of the century's most influential liberal thinkers, Walter Lippmann.

Writing just prior to the Second World War, Lippmann argued that the several centuries' long expansion of the division of labor attendant upon the market economy was rapidly making of the planet one interrelated "great society." The task, Lippmann argued in a book by this name, was to transform this chaotically interdependent world system into a "good society."[19] By this phrase Lippmann meant a society in which economic and social relations would be ordered by rationally comprehensible laws embodying equity and freedom.

Lippmann called for an institutional order which could make comprehensible the moral significance of interdependence, and which could develop the ethical life necessary to sustain such an order. He looked to classical philosophy as well as biblical religion as sources for the idea of a "higher law," but he located this higher law in the "progressive discovery of men striving to civilize themselves. Its scope and implications," he emphasized, "are a gradual revelation that is by no means completed."[20] One essential of progress toward this good society must be the development of the capacity for political deliberation, including the interpretation of social developments and their directions. It is this capacity that American democracy at present needs most to develop. It is what John Dewey, a twentieth-century social liberal even more aware of the collective dimensions of liberal goals than Lippmann, called "social intelligence."

Lippmann's invocation of the search for "higher law" may sound strangely "metaphysical" for so ardent a liberal. But his emphasis upon the "progressive discovery of men striving to civilize themselves" resonates with Glendon's interpretation of European legal developments. Lippmann also seems to anticipate Lowi's observation about the difficulties attendant upon expanding public responsibility without increasing public comprehension and argument.

Lippmann located the achievements of the liberal tradition within a larger narrative. In his later work, *Essays In The Public Philosophy*, Lippmann spoke of the "traditions of civility" which "permeated the peoples of the West and provided a standard of public and private action which promoted, facilitated and protected the institutions of freedom and the growth of democracy."[21] Yet, oddly for a liberal, Lippmann presented as his first example of the importance of this tradition for the present a repudiation of the absolute right to property proclaimed by liberals such as Blackstone (and Locke). "The ultimate title," wrote Lippmann, "does not lie in the owner. The title is in 'mankind,' in *The People* as a corporate community . . . ownership is a grant made by the laws to achieve not . . . private purposes but the common social purpose."[22]

Lippman's narrative reunited the liberal concern for personal freedom with the priority given the common good by the civic tradition. In Lippman's story, liberal purposes appear as important means by which the common good has been made more inclusive and individual dignity more secure. Yet, Lippmann uses the property example to note how the notion of the common good is once again needed, only now to protect individuals and society from the damaging effects of the liberal property system itself. Lippmann provides a powerful exposition of the strengths of the liberal tradition while pointing up its important limitations in our present context. By arguing that liberal societies need to recover the meaning of the common good if they are to remain civil, Lippmann provides a useful example of how we might incorporate the liberal virtues of tolerance and inclusivity within a wider civic vision.

We might say that Glendon's examples of the active role of law in the search for a political common good provides an instantiation of Lippmann's "progressive discovery." The motive for seeking more comprehensive viewpoints is not so much a wish to compromise for the sake of peace as it is the desire to include for the sake of justice. The notion of reason implicit in this search for the common good is a practical one. Yet it is also close to the classical conception of reason which the Greeks called *theoria*. Unlike the modern notion of "theory" which promises control over what is known, classical reason meant "to have been given away to something that in virtue of its overwhelming presence is accessible to all in common . . . the more what is desirable is displayed for all in a way that is convincing to all, the more those involved discover themselves in this common reality; and to that extent human beings possess freedom in the positive sense, they have their true identity in that common reality."[23]

The effort to develop a conversation about the common good could create the constituency for bringing juridical accountability to broadened public responsibilities. While the social liberals, who wrote during the heyday of free market capitalism, tended to identify ethical purpose with state action, the need today is to expand our sense of the public. The "big state" developed earlier in the twentieth century does not in every way suit this purpose, even though many of its managerial functions are probably here to stay. But the novel task for our own time is to redesign our institutions. We need the state to serve not so much as a force of command as the provider of civic infrastructure for the promotion of public life. Such is the possibility disclosed by the civic vision: a public space structured by a free society's argument about the common good.

Notes

1. See, for example, Isaiah Berlin's claim to this effect in his *Four Essays on Liberty* (New York: Oxford University Press, 1969).

2. Bernard Williams, *Ethics and the Limits of Philosophy* (Cambridge MA: Harvard University Press, 1985), pp. 170–3. It is instructive in this connection to note T. H. Green's apparent awareness of this problem. See especially his *Lectures on the Principles of Political Obligation* [1895] (London: Longmans, 1963).

3. For example, see Charles E. Larmore, *Patterns of Moral Complexity* (Cambridge: Cambridge University Press, 1987), pp. 92–93 and 104–7.

4. See: John Rawls, "Justice As Fairness: Political Not Metaphysical," *Philosophy and Public Affairs*, vol.14, no.3 (Summer 1985) pp. 237–251.

5. See: Theodore Lowi, *The End of Liberalism: The Second Republic of the United States*, 2nd. ed. (New York: W. W. Norton, 1979).

6. For an analysis of data supporting the claim of a widening sense of public responsibility, see: Ronald L. Jepperson and David H. Kamens, "The Expanding State and the U.S. 'Civic Culture': The Changing Character of Political Participation and Legitimation in the Post-War U.S. Polity," (Paper presented at the Annual Meeting of the American Political Science Association, 1985).

7. Sheldon Wolin, *Politics and Vision: Continuity and Innovation in Western Political Thought* (Boston: Little, Brown, 1960), p. 16.

8. See: Stephen L. Elkin, *City and Regime in the American Republic* (Chicago: University of Chicago Press, 1987).

9. Mary Ann Glendon, *Abortion and Divorce in Western Law: American Failures, European Challenges* (Cambridge, MA: Harvard University Press, 1988), p. 9. See also: Richard Stith, "New Constitutional and Penal Theory in Spanish Abortion Law," *American Journal of Comparative Law*, vol.35, no.13 (Summer 1987), pp. 513–58.

10. Ibid., p. 105.

11. Ibid., p. 45.

12. Ibid., p. 38.

13. Ibid., p. 109.

14. Ibid.

15. See: Morton J. Horowitz, *The Transformation of American Law: 1780–1860* (Cambridge, MA: Harvard University Press, 1977); also see: Michael Barzelay and Rogers Smith, "The One Best System? A Political Analysis of Neoinstitutionalist Perspectives on the Modern Corporation," in Warren J. Samuels and Arthur S. Miller, eds., *Corporations and Society: Power and Responsibility* (New York: Greenwood Press, 1987), pp. 82–104.

16. Glendon, *Abortion and Divorce*, p. 108.

17. Ibid., p. 56.

18. Ibid., p. 30.

19. Walter Lippmann, *The Good Society* (Boston: Little, Brown and Company, 1943).

20. Ibid., p. 347.

21. Lippmann, *Essays in the Public Philosophy* (Boston: Little, Brown, 1955), p. 99.

22. Ibid., p. 93.

23. Hans-Georg Gadamer, "What Is Practice?" in *Reason in the Age of Science*, Frederick G. Lawrence, trans., (Cambridge, MA: MIT Press, 1981), p. 77.

9

"Lopp'd and Bound": How Liberal Theory Obscures the Goods of Liberal Practices

Stephen G. Salkever

Introduction

The founding texts of the tradition of liberal political philosophy are intransigently antiteleological. Both Hobbes and Locke, distancing themselves from what they see as the scientifically sterile and politically incorrect Aristotelianism of the schools, insist that there is no *summum bonum,* but as many human goods and conceptions of virtue as there are separate individuals. While both speak of natural law, it is clear that neither means by this an innate and direct link between human reason and the cosmic order. For Locke especially, the question of the definitive human good ceases to be an appropriate theme for theoretical science or philosophy and becomes a matter of religion or faith, or rather of a faith divorced from reason.

Further, both base this claim not only on enmity to the schools and to cosmic teleology, but in a reconception of the nature of substance, including animal species, thus rejecting the concept of an intelligible human species good, or *ergon,* that forms the basis for the naturalistic virtue-oriented political philosophy of Plato and Aristotle. Humanity can no longer be known by its characteristic way of life—for example, as a rational animal, however "rationality" might be understood—but, as Locke asserts in the rational parrot vignette in the *Essay Concerning Human Understanding,* rationality or any other teleological attribute (relating to the animal's way of life as a whole) is at most no more definitive of the creature's being than that it is "a body, so and so shapes" *(Essay,* Book 2, Chapter 27). Given the inadmissibility of conceptions of the good, Hobbes and Locke establish the basis for liberal political authority and for theoretical critique in the idea of a contract among rational individuals for the protection of their natural rights.

*For helpful comments on earlier drafts of this essay, I am indebted to the conference participants and to Bob Dostal, Peter Euben, Bill Galston, Jane Hedley, David Paris, and Adam Sloane.

The development of liberal theory has continued the early rejection of any teleological[1] ground, instead anchoring politics either in utilitarian notions of general welfare, or in claims about fundamental rights independent of utility. But over time, claims about fundamental rights have lost their self-evident character, and doubts have arisen concerning both the moral power and the ontological assumptions of utilitarianism. At present, liberal theory faces a sustained challenge from a revived civic humanism or classical republicanism, which claims that liberal theory's concentration on individual rights and interests has obscured the extent to which individual human identities are constituted by participation in political life.[2] In order to respond adequately to this challenge, liberal theory seems required, willy-nilly, to explain itself in terms that violate its traditional neutrality concerning ways of life by articulating some notion of the liberal virtues to match the republican encomium to committed citizenship.[3] Does the attempt to formulate liberal conceptions of the virtues risk abandoning the core of liberal theory, or even of the liberal regime as such?

The argument of this essay is that it does not. My claim is that if we consider liberal theory not as a self-generating and timeless set of rules and principles but as an attempt to understand and defend the liberal political culture that emerged from feudal society in seventeenth and eighteenth-century Europe and the United States, we will see that neutral-principles liberal theory does not adequately respond to the problem posed in Tocqueville's remark that "a new political science is needed for a world itself quite new."[4] This new liberal world is hard to characterize—since it is the one in which we still live—but unless we make the attempt we are doomed either to treat liberal theory in an ahistorical vacuum, or simply to ignore the problematic relationship of liberal theory to the liberal political tradition. Like all cultures or traditions, liberalism is directed toward certain goods. Provisionally, I suggest that liberal politics is distinguished from other regimes by its simultaneous devotion to three different—and sometimes conflicting—goods or aspirations: the good of political autonomy or self-government, the good of individual freedom or of tolerating an indefinite (though not infinite) variety of ways of life, and the good of material productivity or comfortable living.

These liberal goods are embodied in the characteristic institutions of the liberal regime—a representative government based on nearly universal suffrage, a legal/constitutional order that protects individual rights, and a free commercial market in goods and services. Since these goods and institutions are not reducible to a single measure, they will often be in tension with each other in all possible combinations, the claims of the market opposing those of individual rights and of self-government, and so on. A liberal regime can be successful only if it maintains this tension and prevents any one of its central elements from swallowing the others and transforming the liberal regime into a capitalist market, or a totalitarian state, or a society of narcissistic individuals.[5] Liberalism can avoid these nightmares only if liberal individuals pursue their plural goals *in a certain way,* that is, only if the people who live in and by liberal institutions display particular virtues, particular habits of the mind and heart. In particular, given the plurality of liberal goods and the liberal stress on independent living, the inclination and the ability to choose thoughtfully among a variety of opportunities—to act deliberatively—would appear to be a key liberal virtue. But whatever qualities are required for a successful liberal polity, we would expect liberal theory to identify them and to call attention to activities or practices in any given liberal society that tend to promote or to block the development and expression of liberal virtues and ways of living.

In practice, however, liberal political philosophy has systematically rejected the possibility of a fundamental theoretical defense for certain virtues and ways of life. The argument of Section 1 of this chapter is that early modern liberal theory was strongly though not explicitly teleological in spite of its overt ban on teleology, and that the liberal institutions which are the point of departure for this theorizing similarly rely on strong intuitions about virtues to be supported and vices to be controlled as well as on principles of rights or equality. In Sections 2 to 4, by means of a discussion of two contemporary liberal practices, law and higher education, I argue that rights- or utility-based liberal theorizing about such liberal institutions tends to weaken as well as to misconceive them, thus undermining those practices the theory intends, however critically, to defend. The reason for this anomaly is not to be found in any internal shortcoming of neutral-principles liberalism, but in a basic misunderstanding of the appropriate relation of theory to practice, of the proper function of liberal theorizing within the liberal polity. Finally, in Section 5, I suggest that if theorizing is understood as an aid to deliberation and dialogue rather than as a potential substitute for them—if the image of theorizing is the questioning teacher rather than the ideal conflict-resolving legislator or judge—the arguments for theoretical neutrality and against teleology lost much of their force. My argument is that liberal theorizing can recover this more appropriate sense of its task insofar as it is open to a stylistic reorientation in the direction of the preliberal political philosophy of Plato and Aristotle.

Classical Liberal Theory and Neutral Principles

Classical liberal theory tends to associate claims about virtues and good lives with traditional repression and oligarchy; similarly, a familiar (since Marx's *On the Jewish Question*) left critique of liberal theory is that it is not really neutral at all, but that liberal principles of justice serve as a screen to conceal the ascendancy of established or aspiring capitalist entrepreneurs within liberal society.[6] This predicament gives rise to what David Paris calls the "either too much or too little" quandary that afflicts all efforts at discovering core liberal principles or values. If such principles are truly neutral among virtues or beliefs, then they are of little use for the purposes of critique or defense—the reason why we theorize about politics in the first place—but insofar as they possess evaluative power they are open to the charge that they are only apparently neutral, and in fact conceal the extent to which they endorse the interests of some individuals and groups at the expense of others.[7]

A brief look at John Locke provides an example of the structure of the theoretical account of liberal politics, in which a commitment to neutrality seems to sit uneasily with a preference for commercial activity, and the suggestion that the economy should be the central concern of politics. In considering the Lockean argument, we can see the beginning of the persistent tendency for theoretical discussions—whether honorific or accusatory—of whether liberal practices truly live up to liberal goals to concentrate exclusively on two aspects of liberal practice, the market economy and the extent to which state institutions respect individual privacy, and to ignore those liberal institutions (for example, courts, universities, churches) that are more directly concerned with endorsing certain ways of life or virtues.

For Locke as for Thomas Hobbes, moral and political philosophy must be entirely neutral relative to the perpetual conflict among human preferences; no desires or ways of life are in themselves good or bad:

> [T]he various and contrary choices that men make in the world do not argue that they do not all pursue good; but that the same thing is not a good to every man alike. This variety of pursuits shows, that everyone does not place his happiness in the same thing, or choose the same way to it. . . . And therefore it was a right answer of the physician to his patient that had sore eyes:—If you have more pleasure in the taste of wine than in the use of your sight, wine is good for you; but if the pleasure of seeing be greater to you than that of drinking, wine is naught.[8]

The only possible answer to the question of the human good is thus *anthrōpos metron*. But this theoretical argument for neutrality, developed at length in the *Essay,* is not in accord with Locke's defense of liberal politics in the *Second Treatise* and the *Letter Concerning Toleration*. I take the central argument in Locke's evaluative explanation of liberal politics to be the following hypothesis: If you want a comfortable and secure life, then consent only to the authority of a representative government that protects and regulates property (including life and liberty) by standing laws. Such an argument is not, obviously, addressed to all human beings regardless of their preferences among ways of life. It presupposes a preference for a comfortable life (rather than a luxurious, or glorious, or patriotic, or holy life, to name a few alternatives), yet cannot explicitly and theoretically defend this preference—to do so would be to come into direct contradiction with the theoretical neutrality among lives and preferences established so painstakingly in the *Essay*. Thomas Hobbes finds himself in the same difficulty, and responds by hinting that there is in fact universal agreement about the human good and the human virtues:

> Now the science of virtue and vice is moral philosophy, and therefore the true doctrine of the laws of nature, is the true moral philosophy. But the writers of moral philosophy, though they acknowledge the same virtues and vices; yet not seeing wherein consisted their goodness; nor that they come to be praised, as the means of peaceable, sociable, and comfortable living, place them in a mediocrity of passions: as if not the cause, but the quantity of a gift, made liberality.[9]

In this quarrel with a caricature of Aristotle, Hobbes accepts the need to defend liberal virtues by grounding them in a liberal conception of the flourishing life, but at the same time implies that this conception itself—peaceable, sociable, and comfortable living—is utterly nonproblematic and thus in no need of theoretical defense or critique.

Locke's response to this quandary is, like Hobbes's, to adopt an impressive variety of rhetorical strategies seemingly designed to persuade readers to accept the liberal preference for comfort without demanding theoretical justification. These include scriptural reference meant to show that the biblical God has a clear preference for industry, comfort, and the conquest of nature for the sake of increased productivity *(Second Treatise,* Chapter 5, sections 31–35); citation of an older natural law tradition to identify these goals as intrinsically rational (in spite of Locke-the-empiricist's clear commitment to an instrumental conception of rationality);[10] and vigorous deployment of animal imagery to suggest that individuals who prefer other goals or ways of life to the orderly pursuit of peace and comfort are not human beings at all, but either sneaky polecats and foxes or great devouring lions *(ST,* sec. 93). Just as Hobbes seeks to exclude those "needy men and hardy" who hope to mend an ill game by causing a new shuffle *(Leviathan,* Chapter 11) from his audience's conception of shared humanity, so Locke repeatedly implies throughout the *Second Treatise* and the *Letter* that the normal and mature human desire is to preserve property (sec. 87), to seek "safety and security" (sec. 94) and "comfortable, safe, and peaceable living one amongst another, in a secure enjoyment of their properties" (sec. 95), to seek "safety, ease, and plenty" (sec. 101), to avoid a condition that is "very unsafe, very unsecure" (sec. 123), to enjoy "their properties in peace and safety" (sec. 134), and "to secure their peace and quiet" (sec. 137). Other passionate desires are only marginally or abnormally human; speaking of the willful and restless tyrant, Locke warns against someone who seeks "the satisfaction of his own ambition, revenge, covetousness, or any other *irregular* passion" (sec. 199, emphasis added). The liberal preference for a peaceable and comfortable life is established subliminally, as it were, by repetition that appears to seek the reader's complicity, rather than by an explicit argument that would risk contradicting the neutrality condition.

For Hobbes as for Locke, the business of government is to establish the possibility of a comfortable life, not "a bare preservation, but also all other contentments of life, which every man by lawful industry . . . shall acquire to himself."[11] Given the goal of a comfortable (rather than a luxurious or a necessitous)[12] life and the virtues and passions that support it, Locke's conclusion is that the most important business of government is "the increase [in value] of lands and the right employing of them" *(ST,* sec. 42), or "procuring, preserving, and advancing" human interests in "life, liberty, health, and indolency of body; and the possession of outward things, such as money, lands, houses, furniture, and the like."[13] Principally, this means a concern with money and commerce, because *these* are the means of increasing the human value of the world *(ST,* sec. 48). Locke's position does not necessarily endorse a laissez-faire economy, nor does he celebrate the unlimited pursuit of private gain; as Hannah Arendt says, " 'bourgeois freedom' is frequently and quite wrongly equated with the freedom to make more money than one actually needs."[14] Nevertheless, Lockean theory requires that the main focus of political concern be on the economy, and not the moral education or political life of the citizenry.

But this silence about moral education does not have to reflect moral neutrality; rather, it indicates confidence that the preference for the comfortable life is so obvious to his readers as not to require explicit justification. Locke's confidence on this score flows from a striking assumption about the progressive character of human history that dominates liberal theory for the next two hundred years. This is the belief that the maturity and infancy of the human face can be known by comparing the central features of European social life with the social organization of the American Indians:

> The equality of a simple poor way of living confining their desires within the narrow bounds of each man's small property made few controversies and so in need of many laws to decide them: And they wanted not of justice where there were but few trespasses. . . . Thus we see that the *kings* of the *Indians* in *America,* which is still a pattern of the first ages in *Asia* and *Europe,* whilst the inhabitants were too few for the country, and want of people and money gave men no temptation to enlarge their possessions of land, or contest for wider extent of ground, are little more than *generals of their armies;* and though they command absolutely in war, yet at home and in time of peace they exercise very little dominion, and have but a very moderate sovereignty.[15]

The social life of the Indians is free from domestic quarrels, close to nature, held together by friendship and trust, marked by equality; and yet no one could choose this way of life (any more than a rational adult can choose infancy). "In the beginning, all the world was America," but now Locke and his readers share the conviction, without need for any argument, that "a king of a large and fruitful territory there feeds, lodges, and is clad worse than a day labourer in England."[16] The need for a government of laws and for neutral principles of justice arises only in a world of commerce and inequality; but for all its difficulties, that modern European world is by consensus not merely preferable, but simply more real than the only visible alternative.

A hundred years later in America, Thomas Jefferson narrows the questions of the best life in precisely the same way, by presenting it as an alternative between noble and romantic childhood and the real world of adult (European) maturity:

> Societies exist under three forms, sufficiently distinguishable: 1) without government, as among our Indians; 2) under governments wherein the will of everyone has a just influence, as is the case in England in a slight degree and in our States in a great one; 3) under governments of force, as is the case in all other monarchies and in most of the other republics. . . . It is a problem, not clear in my mind, that the first condition is not the best. But I believe it to be inconsistent with any great degree of population.[17]

A more elegant yet still nostalgic view of Indian life as a reminder of the possibilities of a lost historical childhood is Tocqueville's celebration: "The Indian knew how to live without wants, to suffer without complaint, and to die singing." American Indians are practically the moral equivalent of the European aristocracy, yet even better since without shameful hierarchy: "the Indians, all poor and all ignorant, are also all equal and free . . . there was in their manners a habitual reserve and a sort of aristocratic courtesy."[18] A strong sense of a radical and generally progressive break between the traditional prelude, whether represented by feudal aristocrats or American Indians, and the modern commercial world rules out the need for any theoretical consideration of the question of the best life; history takes the place of teleology, or at any rate the version of morally charged history uniformly adopted by liberal theorists[19] (as well as by their opponents, Rousseau, Hegel, and Marx) makes teleological theorizing unnecessary. The presumed superiority of the commercial over the traditional life papers over the need to consider virtues and vices directly—since traditional vices (like avarice) can in fact produce the greatest public goods, so long as they are controlled by properly conceived rules of justice and right:

> So vice is beneficial found,
> When it's by justice lopp'd and bound.[20]

Given consensus on the desirability of comfort and material security, the question then becomes how to organize and resolve interest conflicts according to just laws, rather than how to promote the development and successful public expression of virtue.

Within this moral consensus, liberal theory aims at protecting individual freedom against the threat of tyrannical oppression. This freedom is generally understood as the opportunity to pursue one's own sense of the good in one's own way, and it is to be protected by establishing a private space within which individuals can determine their lives. This conception of freedom as individual opportunity is controversial, but it is already familiar to Aristotle as being one of the characteristic beliefs of democracy,[21] and indeed liberal beliefs and democratic structures seem to go together—it is appropriate for people who live on a basis of an equality of birth to be seriously concerned with the necessary conditions for living well, and to worry that talk about virtues will lead to the reimposition of an oppressive hierarchy. Insofar as Locke's argument in the *Second Treatise* is characteristic, the claim of the liberal theorist is that the pursuit of private interest will ordinarily lead to public benefit. This is not intrinsically a screen for projects of unlimited acquisition; rather, it presupposes a certain *style,* or certain virtues, of acquisition and development of property as being typical. This style, that of the rational, industrious, and peaceable producer, is not treated as problematic or needing discussion or justification, however; Locke appears to assume that once individual opportunity is freed from tyrannical restraint, these virtues will automatically follow. Locke's liberal theory is thus not mere proceduralism, nor is it neutral with respect to ways of life or virtues—he does not propose a solution to human conflict that will be a "machine that would go of itself"[22] nor a political system that will be a foolproof guarantee of natural rights even for a Kantian nation of intelligent devils: "the Commonwealth . . . embraces indifferently all men that are honest, peaceable and industrious."[23] The problem is that he neither explains nor justifies the virtues that his understanding of the structure of a legitimate political order presupposes.

But the liberal theorist's goal of a government of just laws rather than virtuous people is only apparently neutral, since all laws favor some ways of life over others, as Aristotle notes in *Politics* 3: "one might say that it is foolish for the authoritative element to be a human being instead of the law . . . but insofar as the law is either oligarchic or democratic, what difference does it make concerning these perplexities?" (1281a34–38). Aristotle does in the end prefer a government by laws (requiring rotation in office) to a government in the hands of any person or group (barring the unlikely appearance of a genuinely godlike prince), but not because he thinks this will achieve public neutrality relative to ideas of the good life, but as a necessary (though never foolproof) check against inevitable human partiality (1286a–1287a).

Unless we are willing to assume that the most widely shared aspirations of the last three hundred years of Western European humanity somehow constitute an unquestionable moral norm for human conduct, it is difficult to avoid the conclusion that the search for the perfectly neutral rule of justice in liberal theory is a futile attempt to escape from the consequences of what Hannah Arendt calls the irreducible plurality of the human condition by hypothesizing a moral point of view that is presumably neutral among ways of life, whether a state of nature, an uncoerced speech situation, or an original position. But if the unexamined assumption of the progressive advantage of West over East is no longer acceptable or sufficient—and this difficulty is suggested by, among other things, the various communitarian challenges to liberal theory—liberal theory faces a crisis concerning its ground. The attempts to meet this challenge without teleological argument, by trying to ascertain the core "values" or opinions about justice rooted in the liberal tradition,[24] seem not to provide sufficient critical distance, at least if we assume that one function of theorizing is to provide a way of criticizing as well as comprehending the practices within which we live. At the same time, the possible appeal of teleology should not blind us to the fact that nothing could be more illiberal than some proposed theoretical legislation of a standard set of liberal virtues or an overly detailed image of a New Liberal Man. I think, however, that there is a third alternative.

Liberal Practices and their Virtues:
The Question of Theory and Practice

This alternative begins by recognizing that there is more to liberalism than liberal theory, and that liberal practices and institutions, including the market economy, are not morally neutral but embody definite opinions about human goods and virtues, at the very least insofar as institutional definitions of success imply definite conceptions of the good life and of virtues and vices. These goods include but are not limited to the life of comfortable security adopted as normal by liberal theory; at the very least, the independent significance of the goods of self-government and of individual liberty must also be noted. While the eventual meaning of a regime is not the same as the motives that bring it into existence, we can clarify our picture of liberal goods by reflecting on the historical origins of liberalism. Rogers Smith's account of the genesis of the liberal project serves as a good point of departure here:

> Liberalism is properly identified with the emancipating aspirations of the En-
> lightenment and its concerns for universal human rights, religious toleration,
> the promotion of commerce and the sciences, and rejection of the theocratic
> and martial medieval ethos. It found expression in the political agenda of the
> lower gentry and middle classes in England and America, who fought from the
> seventeenth century on against repressive religious and intellectual ortho-
> doxies."[25]

In other words, liberalism as a regime is characterized by not one but a bundle of aspirations, which in particular cases and perhaps even in general are not always consistent with one another: a free commercial market, domestic and international peace, economic development, widespread intellectual enlighten-ment, toleration of a wide variety of religious and moral beliefs (the thoroughly secular state), and representative and republican political institutions. What gives this bundle sufficient unity to allow us to refer to it as a single regime is the intention to establish the material and institutional conditions within which individuals can make lives for themselves without the deadening obstacles offered by political or economic or cultural (race, status, ethnicity, gender) sources of oppression. This formulation contains what is attractive about neutrality—its opposition to arbitrary hierarchy—but to speak of "making a life for oneself" differs from "neutrality" in drawing out attention to a way of life as a whole, something that develops over time and in a certain physical and psychological context, rather than asking us to concentrate primarily on particular moments or events abstracted from the problems of human development. It also calls attention to the way in which institutions and practices help shape preferences and characters, rather than simply aggregating already formed preferences or distributing resources among presumably rational agents.[26]

In considering the virtues of some liberal practices, I will use American examples, partly because of my own limits. It should also be noted, however, that any attempt to speak of the virtues of liberal practices will probably have to choose between focusing on the practices of one particular country or paying too much attention to the one internationally liberal institution, the economic market, and the tendency of theorists to reduce all liberal practices to elaborations of the market is something I want to resist here. The case of America is also interesting for other reasons—because of Tocqueville's sense that America is an exception that sets the norm for liberalism by being the first Western nation without a traditional aristocracy, and because (and this Tocqueville did not foresee) it is the first liberal polity to be faced with the fact of extensive ethnic and racial diversity, thus raising in an especially immediate and acute way the question of whether we can talk about liberal virtues without violating our egalitarian heritage and the liberal commitment to toleration and diversity.

By examining briefly two American practices, courts of law and places of higher education,[27] I want to show that in addition to the clear virtue preferences in the rhetoric of liberal theorists, the assertion that liberalism is not neutral regarding virtues is supported in practice by liberal institutions that by their definitions of institutional success reinforce some moral habits and ways of life and penalize others. I am thinking here of institutions like the market (which depersonalizes exchange), law courts, deliberative assemblies, religious groups, colleges and schools. Tocqueville's *Democracy in America* is the model of theoretical sensitivity to the way such practices shape character in subtle and indirect ways. Too often, both liberal and antiliberal theorists have, with Marx and Weber,[28] assumed a world in which otherwise independent and scattered individuals are linked solely and sporadically by the economic market, and that the central determining features of the liberal regime are thus the international market and the rapid decline in significance of all national institutions (or their hidden complicity with market forces)—Alasdair MacIntyre and Richard Rorty are the latest examples of this.[29] But exclusive focus on the market prevents a serious examination of liberalism's neutrality toward the good by looking past those noneconomic and noninternational practices that might embody substantive goods, thereby consigning them to the margins of political life as conceived by both liberal and antiliberal theory.

The theoretical focus on the presupposed hegemony of the market blinds theorists both to the variety of liberal practices within different countries and to the noneconomic consequences of market practices. Since it is assumed that the function of the market is either to distribute goods efficiently, or to corrode national culture (or both), it becomes difficult to evaluate claims like Emerson's in 1844 in which he places the function of trade in the following way: "The philosopher and lover of man have much harm to say of trade; but the historian will see that trade was the principle of Liberty; that trade planted America and destroyed feudalism; that it makes peace and keeps peace, and it will abolish slavery."[30] Emerson expected to see "trade" decline, and other systems of social coordination replace it; an important question today would be the extent to which the market is shaped by other institutions, and why public opinion, in America at least, tends to regard the market as a more just arbiter of interest conflicts than the political system in spite of a widespread public distrust of concentrated wealth.[31] Answers to these questions are not obvious, and require a historian of the Tocquevillian kind rather than theorists who move too quickly to identify a central pacemaker, whether an institution or principle or rule, thus not only neglecting but undermining those practices its categories exclude.

My argument, then, will be that liberal practice has not been well served by liberal theory, that liberal theory not merely ignores the virtues implicit in legal and educational institutions, but that such theory tends to interpret these institutions in terms that obscure and even oppose the practice of particular liberal virtues.[32] But this is not to say that theory and practice are two separate realms, or that one must distinguish sharply between liberal words and thoughts and liberal deeds (as if nontheoretical practice were either thoughtless or speechless). A better way of thinking about the relationship is to conceive of theory as a part of practice as a whole, much in the way that I think Aristotle understands the relationship between *politikē* (which includes both political philosophy and social sciences) and *pronēsis* (or practical judgment).[33] That is, practical philosophy or theory is one of the elements that make up liberal practice in two senses: as a separate enterprise, located primarily in universities, and, more fundamentally, as the universalizing moment or aspect in the activity of practical deliberation, in thinking about how we should act in particular situations. The question of the relation of theory to practice then becomes: How should this aspect or moment be related to the activity of deliberation, or to liberal practice as a whole? The question has two separate parts: substantively, What kind of a perspective is needed for adequate theorizing? Should theory establish a neutral perspective? A universally transcendent one? Should it remind us of the character of the moral consensus of our society? Or ask us to recall what we know of human needs and virtues? And second, what is the relationship of the theorizing moment—whether neutral, transcendent, uniquely consensual, or teleological—to the goal of deliberation: Should theory provide a rule for resolving the conflicts that give rise to deliberation (as for Mill and Rawls), or should it play some other, less controlling, role in informing deliberation?

Liberal individualist theory, on my view, not only fails to defend liberal institutions properly, but in fact tends to undermine the work of these institutions—such as American courts and colleges—that support liberal virtues. It does this by conceiving the goals of these institutions in terms of impersonal neutral principles, such as efficiency and equality, and then treating the institutions as projects devoted to living up to these standards. But both courts and colleges can plausibly be said to pursue very different projects, projects aiming at supporting certain virtues and ways of life that are threatened by demands that they conform to the requirements of *justice,* that is, by the requirement that actions and policies be justified on grounds of some neutral principle or else be subject to the accusation of creating or reinforcing unjustifiable privilege.

In effect, liberal theory insists that institutions constituted by the goal of forming and supporting good characters must be explained and evaluated as if their function were simply the just distribution of some valuable resource. In law, this distortion takes the form of the twin critiques of judicial decision by law-and-economics adherents, who insist that the only legitimate judicial activity follows the principle of social wealth maximization, and by critical legal theorists who, applying a principle of equality that by definition cannot be satisfied by the institutions of bourgeois society, insist that judicial activity is oppression masked in the forms of procedural fairness. In higher education, the relevant critiques are those from economists applying the "gatekeeper" model to explain educational behavior in terms of efficient (or discriminatory) training of workers and officials; the related conception of the research university, which views the function of higher education as the production and dissemination of knowledge; and a principle of equality of opportunity, which considers less the function of universities and colleges than the problem of access to them.

The Internal Goods of American Law

At least since Tocqueville, observers of American politics have been struck by the surprisingly important role played by the courts in American politics, surprising in that there seems to be no constitutional sanction for this role. Indeed, the two leading political institutions in what Skowronek calls the nineteenth-century "state of courts and parties" appear to have evolved their roles independently of any before-the-fact specification.[34] Part of the reason for the lack of discussion of the important role of the courts can be traced to the discomfort of early modern liberal theorists with the idea of a politically active role for common law judges. For Locke, the legislature must be the source of that dispute resolution for which civil society is instituted, and the judiciary is to be entirely subordinate to the legislature—not one of the three major functions of government at all. Hobbes is explicitly hostile to judge-made law, linking it with a mindless devotion to following old practices rather than applying rational principles of justice. "[T]here is no judge. . . . but may err in a judgment of equity; if afterward in another like case he find it more consonant to equity to give a contrary sentence, he is obliged to do it. . . . Princes succeed one another: and one judge passeth, another cometh: nay, heaven and earth shall pass; but not one tittle of the law of nature shall pass." Only reasonable customs (that is, those that accord with the Hobbesian law of nature, "Do not that to another, which thou thinkest unreasonable to be done by another to thyself") are to be accounted law, and the judgment concerning what is reasonable belongs not to the judge but to the sovereign: "And our lawyers account no customs law, but such as are reasonable. . . . But the judgment of what is reasonable, and of what is to be abolished, belongeth to him that maketh the law, which is the sovereign assembly, or monarch."[35]

Judge-made law based on comparisons of present with past cases viewed in the light of the judge's sense of community standards of conduct corresponds to Hobbes's conception of prudence, an unscientific form of judgment to be shunned in politics, both because it "is but a memory of succession of events in times past" rather than genuine and precise casual knowledge, and because there is no way of distinguishing real from fake prudence: "[s]igns of prudence are all uncertain; because to observe by experience and remember all circumstances that may alter the success, is impossible."[36] There is thus no basis for the authority of an independent judge, since no person's judgment is better than any other's; the theoretical liberal conclusion is drawn by Montesquieu, that in a nonoppressive republican government there is absolutely no room for judicial discretion:

> The more the government approaches a republic, the more the manner of judging becomes fixed. . . . In despotic states, there is no law: the judge is himself his own rule. In monarchies there is law: and where it is precise, the judge follows it; and where it isn't, he tries to find its spirit. In a republican government, it is the nature of the regime that the judges follow the letter of the law. There is then no citizen against whom one could interpret the law when his goods, his honor, or his life are at stake.[37]

In a sense, the conclusion of early modern liberal theory is that an active and independent judiciary poses a threat to liberal equality by substituting one individual's sense of good and bad conduct for neutral rules of justice. *Spoudaios metron* (the serious person is the measure [of right and wrong]) makes sense from an Aristotelian point of view, but not to the liberal theorist.

And yet, in the most advanced of the nineteenth-century liberal democracies, Tocqueville notes that, "An American judge, armed with the right to declare laws unconstitutional, is constantly intervening in political affairs." And since "[t]here is hardly a political question in the United States which does not sooner or later turn into a judicial one," it is not surprising to Tocqueville that "the spirit of the law, born within schools and courts, spreads little by little beyond them . . . till finally the whole people have contracted some of the ways and tastes of a magistrate." While Tocqueville saw American lawyers and judges as introducing an "aristocratic" note into American politics because of their professional love of authority and an "ordered life," he understood their influence in the democratic republic to be important and healthy; so long as judges retained a degree of independent political power, they might help resist the dangerous internal tendency in democracy to degenerate into the novel and debased regime of the industrial or capitalist aristocracy.[38]

For Tocqueville, unlike Montesquieu, the function of the courts, at least in American politics, was not simply administering impartial justice, but rather contributing to the development of habits of mind that would defend the liberal public good, the democratic republic, by calling attention to what Madison called the "permanent and aggregate interests of the community."[39] Madison, of course, seems to reject the notion that any special institution is needed to help protect permanent interests (and not only the rights of minorities) against present and perhaps momentary majority factions, holding in *Federalist* 10 that the great extent of the republic will be sufficient to "lop and bound" impulsive passions and hastily conceived interests. But in *Federalist* 63, in making the case for the Senate, and more generally for the virtues of representative government, Madison says that such an institution is necessary not as a source of impartiality simply, but as a body that has as its task the deliberative interpretation of the common good, "as a defence to the people against their own temporary errors and delusions":

> As the cool and deliberate sense of the community ought in all governments, and actually will in all free governments ultimately prevail over the views of its rulers; so there are particular moments in public affairs, when the people stimulated by some irregular passion . . . may call for some measures which they themselves afterwards will be the most ready to lament and condemn. In these critical moments, how salutary will be the inference of some temperate and respectable body of citizens.[40]

But representation in the end is no more sufficient protection for this "cool and deliberate sense of the community" than is the extended commercial republic. Hamilton, in his defense of an independent federal judiciary in *Federalist* 78, argues that the ratification of a written constitution would establish a voice in American politics that is more authoritative than the law-making voice of the people's representatives. To interpret this fundamental voice, and to carry forward its conversation with the legislature, an independent judiciary is required as "an intermediate body between the people and the legislature, in order, among other things, to keep the latter within the limits assigned to their authority."[41]

Hamilton's doubts about democracy are well known, but the argument he makes here must not be dismissed as mere antidemocratic rhetoric. The realization that unchecked legislative supremacy might be as despotic as any absolute monarchy became increasingly widespread in the years following the American revolution, and led to a new emphasis on the importance of a separation of powers and calls for an independent judiciary, among Jeffersonians as well as Federalists.[42] The foundation for this independent judiciary was at first sought in a "higher" law or in Lockean natural rights, but by the early 1800s this ground was replaced by the notion of popular consent or sovereignty as expressed not by the election of representatives, but in the general sentiments of the written constitution, the argument made by John Marshall in *Marbury v. Madison* and *McCulloch v. Maryland*. Leslie Goldstein argues persuasively that in the years between 1776 and 1800 a novel sense of liberal constitutionalism arose in America, one in which "the significance attached to the concept of 'government by consent of the governed' rose dramatically, even as that concept itself took on a transformed meaning. This process was accompanied by a notable decline of the outlook that it was appropriate for judges to strike down statutes on the basis of unwritten law, *and* by a dramatic increase in the acceptance of judicial review."[43] Goldstein's hypothesis appears counter-intuitive only if we assume, with rights-based liberal theory, that the only basis for a liberal critique of particular laws and policies must be some principle of fundamental rights or of equality, rather than a voice that finds a basis in the written constitution for expressing a sense of American public identity, of the public good or aspiration, which incorporates but it not limited to the enunciation of such principles.

This understanding of the function of American law as an interpretive community within the liberal polity has been most fully developed by James Boyd White. White's contention is that "the law is best regarded not so much as a set of rules and doctrines or as a bureaucratic system or as an instrument for social control but as a culture, for the most part a culture of argument." In legal practice, the role of ideal lawyer or judges is to give voice to their sense of the meaning of the culture as presented to them in the sharply focused context of a case or controversy, and in terms set by the materials of statutes, constitutional provisions, and earlier judicial opinions. As White argues, legal activity is loosely analogous to reading a text, but from the inside, as it were: "How would the ideal reader contemplated by this document, indeed, constituted by it, understand its bearing in the present circumstances? This requires an understanding of the text in its cultural and political context, in light of the accepted meanings of words and with an understanding of the major purposes of the text, of its types and examples. It thus requires one to be an expert reader of the culture itself."[44] Insofar as these readings are bound by theoretical requirements to conform to neutral principles or rules of justice, the practice becomes severely limited against its own implicit intention—against its role within democratic political culture.[45]

The language of the law thus provides one way in which the question of goods and virtues can be articulated within liberal culture. This does not mean that legal conversation about these matters has followed a simple and straightforward course, nor that legal institutions should be treated as off-limits to theoretical critique. Morton Horowitz argues that American judges in the first half of the nineteenth century, far from acting as Tocquevillian checks on the emerging power of capitalist enterprise, transformed traditional common law conceptions and interpreted Constitutional intent in the light of a particular conception of the needs of an expanding commercial society, one that favored active entrepreneurship over the quiet enjoyment of one's own:

> In the process, the conception of property gradually changed from the eighteenth century view that dominion over land above all conferred the power to prevent others from interfering with one's quiet enjoyment of property to the nineteenth century assumption that the essential attribute of property ownership was the power to develop one's property regardless of the injurious consequences to others.[46]

This was surely not a jurisprudence that followed neutral principles; nor, however, was it mere capricious invention or undemocratic ideology. The record of opinion and dissent left by the courts of the early republic became materials for later reassessment of the judgment that commerce was the primary element of the American public good, a view that began to lose its hold with post–Civil War demands for government regulation of commercial practices both from within (for example *Munn v. Illinois)* and without (for example, the Granger movement) the practice of law.

In a variety of other areas, the conversation within the courts can be seen as a series of considerations of the question of the human good arising from particular situations, often calling attention to the character of American identity by focusing on the ways of groups at the margins of society—the debate over the character of American patriotism in *West Virginia Board of Education v. Barnette,* the discussion of how to weigh the virtues of law-abidingness and rationality in *Yoder v. Wisconsin.* There is much disagreement about goods and virtues within the tradition, but this is not a mark against the practice of law unless we assume that there must be a single clear objective good out there before we can speak of goods and virtues at all. The liberalizing element in American legal practice is not that it achieves correct and final solutions to legal questions (recollecting *Dred Scott* and *Lochner* are sufficient to establish that), but that by its method of approaching and resolving such questions it makes authority accessible without dissolving it, opening such authority to future reflection and critique, both within the court system and in representative institutions.[47] The internal liberal good of this practice lies not in achieving undeniable and final correctness, but in arguing in such a way as to encourage further argument: "The best judge, like Socrates, exposes himself to refutation. The most important achievement of judicial writing is . . . the manifestation in performance of a serious, responsible, and open mind, faithful to the sources of authority external to the self even while contributing to their transformation."[48]

But the imprecision of this norm has been a source of concern, and not only to liberal theorists. At least since the 1820s, there has been a strong movement within the legal profession to establish "the scientific character of law" for the sake of separating legal problems from other social problems, and to make the practice of law technical and autonomous: "the attempt to place law under the banner of 'science' was designed to separate politics from law, subjectivity from objectivity, and laymen's reasoning from professional reasoning."[49] A similar impulse is visible in contemporary claims that judicial decisions can be ultimately understood and evaluated in terms of clearly defined rules, such as the law-and-economics rule that "people should always act in whatever way will be financially least expensive for the community as a whole," or, more narrowly and plausibly stated, "that wealth maximization [is] an ethically attractive objective to guide common law adjudication."[50] This approach makes it possible to treat legal issues in such a way as to yield precise answers, but only by a very narrow interpretation of the public good—that the good of the community, or the good aimed at by the common law, is its overall wealth.[51] While this theoretical reconstruction of the law as applied economics aims at transforming obscure subjectivity into precise characterization through bringing to bear the model of a commercial market abstracted from any cultural context, the critical legal studies movement reaches for the same goal via the path of Marxist ideology critique or Nietzschean unmasking.[52] The practical results of this theorizing are equally troubling; once conventional legal practice as a whole is seen as a screen for unjustifiable domination, it appears impossible to return to serious engagement in this practice. Having dissolved any internal conception of the goods of legal practice, the theorist-practitioner must speak ironically, not to say cynically: "I know the language I speak is inherently oppressive, but. . . ."; or, "I know the language I speak is childishly clumsy and archaic, but. . . ." While neutralist attempts to establish a consensual conception of fundamental equality or rights may narrow the sense of function or purpose implicit in the legal tradition unnecessarily, the lops and bounds established by legal economics and critical legal theory are so defoliating as to force a choice between atheoretical participation in the tradition or an escape from practice into theory.

The Internal Goods of
Liberal Education in America

A remarkably similar difficulty about theorizing the goods implicit in a liberal practice (one that, like the law, opens authority to reflection and critique) exists today in theoretical discussions of higher education in America, and especially of the peculiarly American way of carrying out the concept of a liberal education.[53] As with law, liberal theory tends to conceive the function of higher education in terms of neutral rules or principles of utility, or productivity, or equality—either in terms of some notion of economic efficiency or social utility maximization, as in the economist's metaphor of the university as "gatekeeper," or in terms of the production and dissemination of scholarly knowledge, or in terms of the extent to which such education does or does not conform to some principles of democratic equality.[54]

The first reference in the West to liberal education or the liberal sciences is in

Aristotle's *Politics* (Book 8, 1337b5–21), where it is described as an education
appropriate to the life and work of a free human being, one who is neither a slave
nor yet works strictly for wages. The passage is brief and far from elaborate, but
in it Aristotle associates the adjective "free" or "liberal" with three things: there
are liberal works or deeds *(erga),* liberal persons, and liberal sciences *(epistemai).*
Liberal education employs those sciences (especially music) that equip the free
person to act well in situations not governed by compulsion or necessity. It is
thus an education to prepare the young for "leisure" in a very special sense; not
for idle play or relaxation, but for the work that belongs to a free person, as
opposed to the toil imposed on a slave or an alienated laborer.[55]

At its beginning, then, the idea of liberal education is not morally neutral, but
closely tied to a particular sense of the human virtues. Whether this classical
conception of the virtues is compatible with modern liberalism is not only a
genuine question, but one answered largely in the affirmative by the American
politicians and educators of the early republic,[56] who established colleges on the
classical model in substantial numbers in the first fifty years of independence.
Nevertheless, this question is obscured for us by the fact that the classical liberal
theorists of the seventeenth century strongly opposed (for good reasons) the kind
of liberal education they found institutionalized in Western European universities,
and developed in response a very different conception of the purpose of university
education, one bequeathed to us as their theoretical heirs. Thomas Hobbes's
discussion of "the use of universities" is a good example. For Hobbes, the function
of the university is not to develop liberal habits of mind but to disseminate true,
or scientifically ascertained, knowledge, especially knowledge of the science of
moral philosophy expounded in *Leviathan.* Most people, Hobbes says, fall into
one of two classes: those who are either too poor or too greedy to care about
anything but their labor (Aristotle's *banausoi),* and those too rich or too lazy to
care about anything but "sensual pleasures" (Aristotle's *truphē).*[57] Such people
don't think for themselves, and accept on faith the opinions of others who give
the appearance of cleverness, chiefly divines and lawyers. These latter, in turn,
learn what they know from attending the universities, or by reading books
published by eminent university men. The universities, then, are to become
centers for the broadest dissemination of scientific knowledge, the institution that
mediates the discoveries of scientists such as Hobbes to an incurious public, and
promotes, as far as possible, the replacement of prudence by applied science in
political calculation.[58] The exercise of prudent or deliberate judgment was, of
course, precisely the sort of free person's work contemplated by liberal education
on the Aristotelian model.

During the course of the nineteenth century, American higher education saw
the neutralist conception of the function of the university favored by liberal theory
overtake and surpass the character-oriented practice of liberal education. Part of
this change was due to failures of the classical colleges themselves, whose
achievements consistently fell lamentably short of their aspirations. In many

places, the curriculum was maintained out of habit rather than choice, the quality of teaching—and certainly the social status of teachers—was often low, and campus violence was not infrequent.[59] But this failure cannot be separated from the fact that the explicit goal of the colleges—to form minds capable of political leadership without reference to any professional specialty—suggested to many a yearning for an aristocracy on the model of old England (in spite of the significant numbers of poor young men and women who found their way to colleges such as Amherst and Mount Holyoke), and a threat, or at any rate an annoyance, to the new American aristocracy of commercial enterprise.[60] Finally, with the establishment in 1876 of Daniel Gilman's Johns Hopkins, a new model of American higher education came to the fore, one modelled on the patently successful nineteenth-century German research university rather than on vague recollections of an inappropriately English or a remotely Greek past.

The professor in the new university was a scholar or investigator, rather than a teacher of the young, and the institution itself was constituted by the goal of advancing specialized knowledge (and incidentally national or institutional prestige) through research: "The new academic professional thought of himself as an 'investigator' devoted to advancing the frontiers of knowledge through research, and his loyalties when to his 'field' rather than to the classroom dedication that had made the older type of college teacher seem a mere schoolmaster."[61] The appeal of this new conception of the function of higher education is not hard to understand; not only could teachers now redefine themselves as scientists, they could proceed with their work as though its value had no connection with any debatable notion of the good human life or the virtues.

The major theoretical defense of this conception of the university as the proper residence of science (including under this term both the natural and the "historical and cultural" sciences) is Max Weber's "Science as a Vocation."[62] Weber's argument begins by asserting the necessary specialization of modern scholarly inquiry, and argues that the meaning of specialized science is the chain of progressive discovery within particular specialties (137–138). This does not mean simply a general increase in knowledge of the world—for Weber, our knowledge of the everyday apparatus of our technologized world is much less than that of the ordinary savage (recall Locke and Jefferson on the North American Indian here)—but rather implies the "knowledge or belief" that everything in the world is knowable and calculable if one has learned the proper method, that there are no mysterious incalculable forces: "This means that the world is disenchanted" (139). Scholarship then is a collection of methods for arriving at the truth about a world without magic, which for Weber is to say that science has nothing at all to tell us about the meaning of the world or how we should live in it (142). This is not only true of scholarship in the natural sciences, but of scholars in the *Geisteswissenschaften* as well: "They teach us how to understand and interpret political, artistic, literary, and social phenomena in terms of their origins. But they give us no answer to the question whether the existence of these cultural phenomena have been and are *worth while*" (145, Weber's emphasis). The identification of teleology with mystification links Weber back to the Hobbesian origins of liberal neutrality, and he seems at first even more faithful than Hobbes to his reductionist presuppositions in claiming that modern scholarship can give life no guidance (or supply no "values") other than helping us face inconvenient facts, or teaching us to calculate and control the means for achieving whatever we happen to desire. Yet as was the case with Hobbes and Locke, the preference for a certain way of life and conception of virtue lies close to the neutralist surface. Again as with the early theorists, its content is supplied by an unexamined value-supplying contrast with the world of historical childhood; for Weber, the virtue of the scholarly life is to be able to bear the fate of the times—the disenchanted world—"like a man" (155).[63] The disenchantment from the thrall of ancient authority gives research its place within the liberal regime, in spite of the fact that it "is the affair of an intellectual aristocracy" (134); what is impossibly wrong with the classical college from this point of view is not its elitism,[64] but its unquestioning attachment to an oppressive and illiberal canon of "cultural phenomena."

The great triumph of the German model in American education is beyond dispute; the recent coinage of the term Research University to designate our most prestigious places of higher learning testifies to this hegemony. We have seen the flowering of Daniel Gilman's vision of a university whose chief purpose is specialized graduate training and where the main point of undergraduate education is to pay the freight for the work of the graduate departments.[65] And yet if we consider its Weberian justification, we may well wonder whether it is entitled to its present eminence within the liberal theory of education. The persuasiveness of that justification must appear at least questionable to us in the light of our very justified doubts about the adequacy of the Western moderns versus savages contrast on which it relies in the absence of any careful reflections on human virtues and the human goods.[66]

One way to pursue this question is to bring to mind the continuing practice of something like the older model of liberal education directed at forming the capacity to deliberate as it exists and sometimes flourishes at a number of American colleges, and even within some research universities. What I have in mind here is the practice of organizing undergraduate studies around the goal of educating young people to deliberate well, to be able to think clearly about ends and means in situations calling for answers when no precise solutions or rules for reaching such solutions exist. The traditional method for such education is literary, in an extended sense: by responding actively to difficult and puzzling texts (in a variety of genres), by trying to imagine wholes where there seem to be only pieces of thought and word, students learn to be more articulate about ordinary confusion and about their lives as a whole. Such a goal is, I think, neither neutral nor illiberal, neither a concern with *Wissenschaftlich* facts nor an indoctrination in "core values" or "the best that has been thought and said," neither von Humboldt nor Newman and Arnold (nor Confucius), but something more peculiarly liberal and American. Eva Brann's statement of the nature of this third alternative is worth quoting at length:

> These two separate enterprises [scholarly research and the transmission of traditional culture] are both good and necessary for something, but not for the education as such of citizens in a republic. For that, another mean is needed, which I shall term *inquiry*, an activity in which teaching and learning are not quite separable. It might be called Socratic if the *imitatio Socrati* were not a piece of temerity. It is devoid of any intention to add to the collectible store of information; it has no relation at all to the newness or oldness of knowledge, being altogether intent on thinking things anew rather than on thinking new things. Positively, it is an intention—much more dependent for its realization on desire than on talent, and therefor potentially universal—to be thoroughly aware of what one does and says and thinks. It becomes actual teaching insofar as the intention is skillfully converted into an orderly public process.[67]

Teachers at liberal arts colleges of all descriptions will, I think, have little trouble recognizing this intention and recalling the never-ending debates over how best to translate it into curricular structure.[68] Often, such education works through a close reading of well-known Western texts, but if that reading is true to its intention students will not be encouraged to revere these works as Monuments of Our Culture, but to criticize, question, push, and tear at them as a means toward developing habits of self-reflection and self-critique.[69] As with the case of American law, the difficulty lies not in creating a new and teleological educational practice, but in finding ways of theorizing about an existing tradition of education for thoughtful citizenship that are adequate to assessing the worth of particular local efforts. But as we have seen, the most prominent liberal modes of theorizing the function of higher education tend through their neutrality to obscure the presence of this very active, though persistently undervalued, liberal practice.

Whatever their roots in preliberal European history, the two American institutions that have been considered here, the law and the liberal arts college, have in common a particular attitude toward authority[70] that is peculiarly liberal. They both operate through an active encounter with authoritative texts that serve in part to constitute the modern liberal regime, at least as much as popular sovereignty or our unwillingness to regard any individual as superior by virtue of inherited status. But both institutions seek to develop a sense of the accessibility of authority, and of the good citizen's role in continuing the dialogue with our legal and literary context. While neither practice yields to the temptations of apparent impartiality provided by the rules of the market or of scientific progress, neither seeks simply to celebrate their written sources but to use them to stimulate the growth of independent reason. In this, I think, we can see a striking difference between the goods of these liberal practices and the idea of the good citizen's relationship toward authority presented by many of the communitarian critics of liberalism. In reflecting on this difference between liberalism and communitarianism we can, I think, begin to get a sharper picture of the look of the characteristic liberal virtues.

The communitarian critic of liberalism, from Marx to MacIntyre, finds fault with the liberal tendency to treat the "unencumbered self" as somehow prior to the forms of social life which in fact constitute its individuality. For the communitarian, the liberal self, floating above contextual commitments, is a fundamentally empty and self-deceiving conception, one that makes the typical liberal error of ignoring or concealing the extent to which our lives are constituted by the communities in which we live. The difficulty with this critique is that unless it subscribes to some concept of substantial historical progress in the mode of Hegel and Marx, the communitarian ignores or conceals the problem of distinguishing among better and worse communities, thus exhibiting a quandary which mirrors the perplexity inherent in liberal theory's neutrality. As Leo Strauss says in his discussion of Carl Schmitt, "he who affirms the political as such, is neutral towards all friend-foe groupings. . . . Thus the affirmation of the political as such proves to be liberalism preceded by a minus sign."[71] But a consideration of liberal practices suggests that another conception of liberal freedom is available, one that avoid the neutrality of both individualism and communitarianism. One might say, for example, that the liberal commitment to freedom of religion, to the belief that religion must be freely chosen, means that whatever religion has formed me must be held open to continual challenge and reconsideration.[72] Liberal religion is freely chosen not in the sense that faith is selected from a spiritual buffet, but in the sense that liberal society requires individuals to hold their religious and other commitments open to continual dialogue and challenge; religion is freely chosen in the sense that it is professed openly in the midst of continual dialogue with alternative ways of life and modes of belief. This is much like Gadamer's notion of a dialogic or hermeneutic attitude toward the world as one in which individual "readers" always remain open to the possibility of being persuaded against their deepest, most self-constituting beliefs by the texts they encounter. This commitment to and even joy in self-consciousness and self-scrutiny is a different sense of the good life from either zealous sectarian dogmatism or essentially *passive* toleration or neutrality. The liberal virtue here is the ability to maintain a balanced tension between moments of commitment and of doubt.[73]

This liberal conception of the good life is thus inseparable from a kind of ironic stance toward oneself, an unwillingness to take any one of my present beliefs or commitments too seriously. The term "irony" can mean many things; all would agree that speech is ironic when it contains a meaning different from its literal or apparent sense, but there are many kinds of difference. In speaking of Socratic irony as a kind of liberal intellectual virtue, I do not mean irony either as a deceitful way of tricking your enemies, or as infinite self-reflexive negativity. These are both nineteenth-century antiliberal senses of "irony," conceptions that flow from the thought of Hegel, Kierkegaard, and Nietzsche. As I understand

Socratic irony, it is less strategic than the first of these and less bombastically enervating than the second; rather, it is, as Wayne Booth says, the knowledge "that all literal statements mislead," and that "the true philosopher lives in self-corrective dialogue, in which the inadequacies of one attempt lead inevitably to another one, and then yet to another."[74] As I use the term here, irony is the virtue of human self-consciousness, a sort of mean between cynicism (the mode of slaves and tyrants) and prophecy (the mode of priests and kings).

This ironic attitude is by no means necessarily a paralyzing condition—*aporia* doesn't immobilize permanently, and Socrates appears to be a paralyzed and paralyzing stingray only to those with immature souls like the virile young Meno or Callicles. Socrates' life may seem an unlikely example of liberal virtue, though I think Eva Brann is acute in suggesting that, in a sense, "Socrates is indeed the aboriginal American,"[75] but several important American figures could illustrate as well this combination of self-irony and active power. Arguably the greatest of American presidents, Abraham Lincoln, spoke the language of the Bible throughout his public speeches, yet consistently refused to make public professions of faith, as in this story recounted by John Diggins: "Asked during a campaign whether he believed in 'the truths of the Scripture,' he denied that he had ever denied them without exactly saying that he had, or presently would, affirm them."[76] Consider also Emily Dickinson, whose poetic voice is constituted by the ironic layering of skeptical verse on top of the common meter rhythms of Isaac Watts's Calvinist hymns. One might say that a similar tension marks the relationship between the two documents which form the official American public voice—one of which (the Declaration of Independence) calls on God and Providence as our foundation and support, while the other (the Preamble to the Constitution) makes no reference to divinity whatsoever, but presents only the openness of "We the people," and rather than asserting self-evident truths about inalienable rights, establishes instead the ground for a fundamental law that is permanently open to revision. This is by no means to claim that American politics have been perfectly liberal in deed or even in aspiration—the Constitution institutionalizes, at least for a while, the exclusion of women, blacks, and Indians from citizenship—but only to show that the core of American politics provides an example of a political structure that encourages self-doubt and reflection without defeating action or the emergence of new forces in political life.

My argument has been that institutions like judicial review and liberal education continue to serve as supports for the virtues and voices that define at least this American version of liberalism. We hardly live in a desert of MacIntyre's soulless bureaucracy or Bloom's mindless relativism,[77] nor are all our institutions at a loss to articulate the goods that define their place in liberal culture, and to imagine that we do in the manner of some communitarian critics is to mask problems that are real but neither insoluble nor tragically endemic to liberal society. Liberal theorists, on the other hand, tend to forget that what justice lops and bounds is not only vice (or individual interest), but the authority of liberal practices as well.

The question that remains is: Why has it been so difficult for liberal theory to overcome its attachment to neutrality and to present a case for the goods of liberalism?

What Practice Needs From Theory:
Legislation or More Talk?

The liberal theorist's attachment to neutrality and resistance to teleological theorizing (or "virtue ethics") cannot simply be diagnosed as a bad habit, or a case of the language of liberal theorizing outlasting the experiences (the feeling of an unproblematic superiority of European to Indian life) that underlie it. There are serious practical objections to teleology,[78] and I want to take up three of the most important here: that virtue theory is appropriate only within a homogeneous society, one totally unlike the pluralistic (in aspiration) liberal polity; that unprincipled virtue theory is too weak to provide sufficient resistance to unjust and oppressive laws; and that virtue theory is too strong, legislating morality in clear opposition to the liberal commitment to dialogue and debate. I will conclude by suggesting that these objections flow from a misconception of the appropriate relation of theory and practice.

The view that virtue theory presupposes a relatively closed and homogeneous society with firm traditions holds that Plato and Aristotle were able to theorize the Greek virtues only because there happened then and there to be a relatively stable consensus about virtue, so that the philosophers could assemble their theories from existing raw materials. But this runs against the way in which Plato and Aristotle are both deeply critical of some of the central aspects of their culture's conception of the good, such as the Greek tendencies to identify virtue and virility, to view the political life as the only respectable career for a male, and to attribute substantial virtue to inherited ethnic Greekness and natural slavishness to barbarians.[79] This critical orientation is missed by those who begin by presupposing, with Hegel and MacIntyre, that theories must take not only their point of departure but their first principles from the culture context in which they are located. Still, it must be granted that even when Plato and Aristotle are clearly critical of Greek practice, they tend to temper their critique and stop short of proposing radical cultural change—consider Socrates' advice to obey the laws always in the *Crito,* and Aristotle's to us shocking restraint in not taking up the question of the extent of unnatural slavery in the *Politics.*

This leads to the second objection to virtue theory, that its weakness is such that it "fails to do justice to justice,"[80] to individual rights and the possibility of oppressive laws and customs. The need for theoretically grounded principles of right and justice appears so strong that Iris Murdoch, a virtue theorist and a profound critic of Kantian neutrality, says that such principles are good and necessary in politics even though utterly inadequate in ethics.[81] Much interesting recent work in extending the language of the virtues to political considerations has come from feminist theorists who aim at reconceiving political life in terms of the virtues of focused care and attentiveness associated with practices and institutions that have traditionally been identified as women's work.[82] But here, too, the project of introducing the language of virtue into political theorizing has been attacked on grounds that it runs afoul of the fundamental equality of political life,[83] or that it fails to establish a sufficiently powerful principle of critique.[84]

The Greek virtue theorists were not without experience of the weakness of philosophy in the face of tyrannical inclination, as the reader of Plato's *Seventh Letter* can testify. But this did not lead them to attempt to reformulate practical philosophy with an eye to its empowerment, perhaps because they thought that there were other and more effective ways of opposing injustice than theoretical principle. In the first book of the *Republic,* Socrates raises the question of the meaning of justice (thus himself problematizing what might otherwise have been an effective restraint against unjust inclinations), and dismisses easily the neutral principles of keeping promises and helping friends/harming enemies. But when the concept of justice is itself attacked by Thrasymachos, who asserts that not justice but its opposite *(pleonexia,* the quest for unlimited acquisition and enjoyment) is best, Socrates does not respond by setting forth an adequate rule of his own. He does two things instead: first to orient the discussion away from justice and toward the more fundamental question of the good life; and second, to defeat Thrasymachos' claim for *pleonexia* by showing that it is incompatible with certain practices constituted by knowledge, of the sort that we might call professions. One cannot be a successful doctor or musician (or lawyer or college teacher) and follow the rule of *pleonexia*—to do so would be to fail to accept the internal goods of these practices and so to be excluded from them (349b–350a). Thrasymachos is a teacher of oratory, a member of a profession with its own internal goods, and he is thus not inclined to continue to defend a motive that is inconsistent with his life. The successful check against *pleonexia* and tyrannical longing here is not Platonic theory, but Socrates' timely reminder of the internal good of a Greek practice. The other great Platonic defender of tyranny and injustice, Callicles of the *Gorgias,* has no such professional commitment, and so proves much less susceptible to Socratic refutation and agreement than Thrasymachos. Callicles is a politician; Socrates' only recourse seems to be to try to make him ashamed of what he is. Aristotle's analysis of the problem of the causes of and cures for injustice in *Politics* 2 is similar: for injustice motivated by economic need, the remedy is a better economic public policy; for injustice motivated by *pleonexia,* better institutional habituation in moral virtue; only for the greatest crimes, those motivated by the longing for pleasures that are entirely under our control, is theorizing the indicated treatment, but surely this theorizing is a continuous activity, rather than a well-formulated principle of justice. Bringing this line of reflection forward to the present, we might say that the best safeguard against oppression can never be theory as such, but will instead be those institutions and practices which sustain the liberal virtues. The role of theory is not to replace but to inform and refresh these institutions, perhaps in the sense that Socratic theorizing in the *Gorgias* might be said to aim more at challenging and influencing Gorgias' oratorical practice than at saving Callicles' soul.[85]

But the oldest and still perhaps the deepest liberal objection to the possibility of a teleological liberal theory is that such a theory despotically closes off the question of the good, and thus violates the central liberal commitment to form a world in which people can make their own lives. Surely one can think of antiliberal teleological theories that do just that; but this is not the only available model, and I would argue that the best teleological theorizing, that of Plato and Aristotle, does nothing of the kind. In the *Politics,* Aristotle's theoretical interventions into Greek political disputes all take the form of orienting practice deliberation toward the *question* of the best life—without determining in advance how such a reorientation might affect subsequent practical deliberation. Similarly, Plato's Socrates presents himself to us as the true practitioner of political theory *(Gorgias),* and yet he spends his political time not in urging one form of legislation or another, nor in telling people how to live (Socrates is not Apollodorus), but in turning the citizens' thoughts from the question of power toward the question of virtue *(Apology)* or the good life, prodding and problematizing their self-conception, rather than legislating their lives. This indirect connection of teleological theory to action is also suggested by the account of the political activity of the true and theoretical *politikos* in the *Statesman* (305c–d). This person does not rule directly or even act *(prattein)* at all, but rather remains behind the scenes in a democratic polity, intervening by supplying a beginning *(archein)* to a trio of professional practices, those of generals, judges, and democratic orators. The connection between theory and practice here is not the provision of a powerful rule or principle (or image of the good) that can settle all conflicts over how to act.

Why is this idea of a nondeductive connection between theory and practice so foreign to modern theorizing? We can, I think, begin to get a sense of why modern theory finds ancient indirection strange and finally unattractive by looking at an eighteenth-century work that expresses the contemporary need of concerned citizens of the secular liberal state to discover in a theorist or a theory the Legislator who can replace the vanished God. This longing for clear and ultimate solutions is the subject of an unfinished essay by the young Jean-Jacques Rousseau, published some years after his death under the title, "An Allegorical Fragment or Fiction on Revelation."[86] Rousseau here presents a parable in the form of a dream of "the first person who attempted to philosophize." The dream narrative unfolds a horrible vision of a city governed by the priests of a cult of deities of (almost) unspeakable grossness and viciousness. None of the oppressed citizens dare, or care, to expose the deformity of the idols of the city until an old man, Socrates without the name, plays a clever trick on the priests by feigning blindness, unmasks evil, and exposes the false gods. This man, seized and condemned by the wicked priests, chooses not to escape his fate but rather to "die like a philosopher" in order to prove to witness that he had not lived as a mere sophist. But just before his death he, like Socrates in the *Crito,* makes a very clear homage to the same cult he had unmasked, leaving his assembled followers in a state of aporetic bewilderment. At just that crucial moment, a clear voice announces the appearance of "the son of man," a figure who easily and without paradox and irony destroys the evil cult once and for all and announces the coming of a new and perfect order.

Rousseau's expectation is typical of modern theorists, who hope or affect to hope with one degree of seriousness or another that theory might provide us with an act of comprehensive legislation rather than simply continue to raise questions about the grounds of our authoritative practices and institutions. But this latter conception of the function of theory is, I think, more in keeping with the teleological tradition in political philosophy and, at any rate, more appropriate to the substantive goals or goods of liberal politics. Theory as problematizing critique is neither as powerfully curative nor as dangerous as theory as legislation—it is an altogether more modest conception of the work of practical theorizing. But this is no drawback so long as the practice or polity that concerns us is one that while highly criticizable is yet not deeply and incorrigibly flawed. Practical philosophers need not be legislators unless we assume with Rousseau, Marx, Nietzsche, Heidegger, and MacIntyre that contemporary practice is wholly bankrupt and in need of radical transformation. But my reading of the practices of liberal education and the law suggests that this is simply not the case—and I think similar conclusions would be drawn if we paid attention to internal statements of the goods of other liberal institutions—such as science,[87] or literature and the arts, or religion.

Another image of the manner in which theory might speak to practice is presented in Thomas More's *Utopia.* The prickly Raphael Hythloday, back from a voyage to the theoretically perfect land of Utopia, says there is no sense in using his theoretic knowledge to advise princes, since they won't listen to him. "There is no place for philosophy in the council of kings," Hythloday says. But More replies thus:

> "Yes, there is," I said, "but not for this scholastic philosophy which supposes that every topic is suitable for every occasion. There is another philosophy that is better suited for political action, that takes its cue, adapts itself to the drama in hand, and acts its part neatly and well. This is the philosophy for you to use. When a comedy of Plautus is being played, and the household slaves are cracking trivial jokes together, you propose to come on stage in the garb of the philosopher, and repeat Seneca's speech to Nero from the *Octavia.* Wouldn't it be better to take a silent role than to say something wholly inappropriate, and thus turn the whole play into a tragi-comedy? You pervert and ruin a play when you add irrelevant speeches, even if they are better than the play itself. So go through with the drama in hand as best you can, and don't spoil it all simply because you happen to think another one would be better.
> "That's how things go in the commonwealth, and in the council of princes. If you cannot pluck up bad ideas by the root, if you cannot cure long-standing

evils as quickly as you would like, you must not therefore abandon the common-wealth. Don't give up a ship in a storm because you cannot direct the winds. And don't arrogantly force strange ideas on people who you know have set their minds on a different course from yours. You must strive to influence policy indirectly, handle the situation tactfully, and thus what you cannot turn to good, you may at least make less bad. For it is impossible to make all institutions good unless you make all men good, and that I don't expect to see for a long time to come."[88]

This is to say that the goal of practical philosophy is not to *resolve* controversy, but to encourage and educate it by pushing public discussion in the direction of a more adequate consideration of the desirability of certain ways of life and conceptions of virtue. But in order to do this well, the acting theorist needs an acute sense of the particular drama which seems to offer a role. On this view, the experience that gives rise to the need for practical theorizing is not a desperate need for an unquestionable foundation, but rather the sense that even in generally tolerable lives we can make mistakes about what is good for us, individually and as political communities.[89]

This view of the proper business of theory coheres with one plausible way of characterizing the goal of liberalism itself—as neither the passive and evaluatively neutral toleration of all differences, nor the peaceful resolution of all conflicts arising from individual differences, but rather as an active engagement in open argument (argument that is not bound by strict rules or theory-determined methods for reaching conclusions) for the sake of developing the habits of inquiry and self-examination and the virtues needed for success in the business of making a life for oneself. This goal is seldom made explicit but is contained in the liberal commitment to encouraging unrestricted *talk* (or a wide variety of different kinds of talk)—a commitment missing from and perhaps even excluded by liberal individualist theory, which is generally more anxious to curtail the oppressive potential of dialogue, or to replace dialogue's indefiniteness with precise and nondialogic modes (neutral principles or utilitarian calculations), than to envision the indirect moral benefits of relatively open-ended and unpredictable practical discussion.

One of the important tasks of liberal theory would be to say more about how to characterize and evaluate such talk. Rorty's notion of "carrying on the conversation" is not an adequate metaphor for this version of the liberal good because it implies a homogeneous and friendly social club and thus makes liberal politics appear superficial relative to the lives we lead; nor is the Millian image of a social laboratory appropriate, because it wrongly suggests the existence of certain definite "scientific" practical truths or theorems to be discovered, and because it presupposes a single very clear method or algorithm for discovering them, and so makes discussion merely instrumental; nor is Holmes's marketplace of ideas[90] a good metaphor, since it also treats discussion as concerned with means only, rather than as at least partly constituting the end of liberalism—as the activity through which the individual capacity for reflective self-government, for making lives of our own is institutionalized. This very general conception of the liberal *telos* is not unlike Aristotle's characterization of living as living *kata prohairesin (Politics* 3, 1280a31–34), living according to thoughtful or deliberate choice, an aspiration not prominent in either narrowly liberal or communitarian thought.

In the end, what is required is not an ideal theory or theorist; perhaps the notion of a separate social role of Moral or Political Theorist (as opposed to the Lawyer or College Teacher or Scientist who theorizes) is itself an unfortunate thing. What practice needs from theory is not an answer to questions of action choice, nor even an absolute and precise answer to the questions of action choice, nor even an absolute and precise answer to the question of the nature of the human virtues or goods. Instead, the theoretical moment in deliberation might better be conceived as the point at which we remind ourselves of the *problem* of human virtue and of the variety of possible theoretical solutions. The gain for practice is that our subsequent deliberation will have more of a "fore-chosen" cast, be more *kata prohairesin*. This is finally to say that liberal theorizing adequate both to meet the communitarian attack on liberalism and to sharpen reflection on the problems and possibilities of various liberal practices must not only revive and extend early modern liberal theorizing,[91] but will need to find its theoretical point of departure—its theoretical home—not in the endless manufacture and refinement of theories of justice but in the theoretical politics of the Platonic Socrates, *philologos* (lover of discourse) as well as *philosophos* (lover of wisdom).

Notes

1. For convenience and clarity, I want to reserve use of the term "teleology" for theories whose fundamental point of evaluative reference is some conception of the good human being (rather than a principle such as rights or equality, or an event such as pleasure); thus utilitarianism, while consequentialist, is not teleological in this sense.

2. For good recent summaries of the liberal/republican argument, see Michael Sandel, "The Political Theory of the Procedural Republic," *Revue de Métaphysique et de Morale* 93 (1988) 57–68, and Amy Gutmann, "Communitarian Critics of Liberalism," *Philosophy and Public Affairs* 9 (1985), 308–322.

3. See, for example, William Galston, "Defending Liberalism," *American Political Science Review* 76 (1982), 621–629, and "Liberalism and Public Morality," in *Liberals on Liberalism,* ed. Alfonso J. Damico (Totowa, NJ: Rowman and Littlefield, 1986), 129–147; George Kateb, "The Moral Distinctiveness of Representative Democracy," *Ethics* 91 (1981), 357–374; and Amy Guttmann, *Democratic Education* (Princeton: Princeton University Press, 1987), Chapter 1.

4. Alexis de Tocqueville, *Democracy in America,* ed. J.P. Meyer, trans. George Lawrence (Garden City, NY: Anchor Books, Doubleday & Company), p. 12.

5. Liberalism is not, of course, the only regime constituted by a tension between several equally central goods. Consider, for example, the relationship in Confucian China between humanity or benevolence on the one hand and devotion to the rites or ceremoniousness on the other. If the rites are performed without benevolence, or if benevolence is practiced without concern for the rites, the regime is corrupted.

6. See also MacIntyre, *Whose Justice? Which Rationality?* (Notre Dame, Ind.: Notre Dame University Press, 1988); Samuel Bowles and Herbert Gintis, *Democracy and Capitalism: Property, Community, and the Contradictions of Modern Social Thought* (New York: Basic Books, 1986), argue that just as the liberal emphasis on political equality leads to failure to notice the consequences of economic inequality, so the state socialist emphasis on economic equality undervalues the significance of inequalities of political power.

7. Paris, "Educational Reform in a Liberal Society: Creating a Liberal Character," (Paper presented at the American Political Science Association meetings, August 1986).

8. *Essay Concerning Human Understanding,* ed. by Alexander Campbell Fraser, 2 vols. (New York: Dover Publications, 1959), Book 2, chap. 21, vol. 1, pp. 350–351.

9. Hobbes, *Leviathan,* ed. Michael Oakeshott from the edition of 1651 (Oxford: Basil Blackwell, n.d.), chapter 15, p. 104.

10. Compare *Second Treatise,* ed. Richard Cox (Arlington Heights, Ill.: Crofts Classics, Harlan Davidson, 1982), chapter 2, section 6 with *Essay,* vol. 1, pp. 141–142.

11. *Leviathan,* Chapter 30, p. 219. Spinoza's characterization of the goal of politics in terms of comfort and the supposedly universal desire "to live as far as possible securely beyond the reach of fear" is quite similar. See *Theological-Political Treatise,* trans. R.H.M. Elwes (New York: Dover Publications, 1951), pp. 47, 73, 202.

12. The meaning of Locke's (and Hobbes's) repeated use of the term "comfort" is nicely glossed by Joyce Appleby in her discussion of the important function of the term in the political vocabulary of American republicanism a century after Locke: "Because so much has been made of the Puritan work ethic in America, it is worth pointing out that the Republicans [i.e., the Jeffersonians in the 1790s] did not extol those pristine virtues of thrift and frugality. What opened before their eyes was the prospect of the widespread enjoyment of comforts. Indeed, the word comfort sprang into use in these years. Luxuries conjured up an aristocratic economy of elite consumption and plebian toil while necessities brought to mind the penury of age-old limits. Comforts, on the other hand, could be generally aimed at and enjoyed without harm to others." Appleby, *Capitalism and a New Social Order: The Republican Vision of the 1790s* (New York: New York University Press, 1984), p. 91. Tocqueville uses the category in much the same way: "It will always be easy theoretically to divide each people up into three classes. The first class is composed of the rich. The second of those who, without being rich, are in all respects comfortably off. The third class includes those with little or no property." *Democracy in America,* p. 209.

13. *A Letter Concerning Toleration,* ed. James H. Tully (Indianapolis: Hackett, 1983), p. 26.

14. Arendt, "Thoughts on Politics and Revolution," in *Crises of the Republic* (New York: Harcourt Brace Jovanovich, 1972), 199–233, p. 221. Hobbes is explicitly opposed to an absolute property right *(Leviathan,* Chapter 29, p. 215), and worries about undue concentrations of great wealth (p. 217).

15. Locke, *Second Treatise,* Chapter 8, sections 107–108, emphasis in text.

16. Ibid., Chapter 5, sections 49 and 41, emphasis in text.

17. Jefferson, Letter to James Madison, January 30, 1787, in *Selected Writings: Jefferson,* ed. Harvey C. Mansfield (Arlington Heights, Ill.: Crofts Classics, AHM Publishing Corporation, 1979), p. 67.

18. Tocqueville, *Democracy in America,* pp. 28–29. On the theoretical aspects of the tragic confrontation between liberal America and the North American Indians, see Ralph Lerner, "Reds and Whites: Rights and Wrongs," in Lerner, *The Thinking Revolutionary: Principle and Practice in the New Republic* (Ithaca: Cornell University Press, 1987), pp. 139–173.

19. For example, J.S. Mill's *On Liberty* begins by saying that the reach of the neutrality principle ('the sole end for which mankind are warranted, individually or collectively, in interfering with the liberty of action of any of their number is self-protection. . . . His own good, either physical or moral, is not a sufficient warrant") extends only to "any member of a civilized community." We may, Mill says, "leave out of consideration those backward states of society in which the race itself may be considered as in its nonage." As with Locke, Mill makes this distinction only to say that from this point on he can speak as if the European were the only possible human being: social maturity is "a

period long since reached in all nations with whom we need here concern ourselves." *On Liberty*, ed. David Spitz (New York: W.W. Norton, 1975), chapter 1. Mill seems blissfully unaware of the significance of his "we"—not only in the way it excludes, but also in the way it affirms a social solidarity at odds with Mill's liberal theory. For a wonderful example of the way a talented Chinese observer saw through the surface of the individualism of Mill, Spencer, and Adam Smith to "misread" them as something like communitarians, see Benjamin Schwartz, *In Search of Wealth and Power: Yen Fu and the West* (Cambridge, Mass.: Harvard University Press, 1964).

20. Bernard Mandeville, *The Fable of the Bees*, ed. Irwin Primer (New York: Capricorn Books, 1962) ll. 425–426, p. 38.

21. *Politics* 6, 1317b.

22. Michael Kammen. *A Machine That Would Go Of Itself: The Constitution in American Culture* (New York: Random House, 1986).

23. *Letter Concerning Toleration*, p. 54. In the *Letter*, Locke likewise assumes certain practices and virtues of the normal citizen: that "All men know and acknowledge that God ought to be publicly worshipped," (p. 38), and that every tolerable church ought to preach the virtues of "Charity, Meekness and Toleration and diligently endeavour to allay and temper all that Heat, and unreasonable averseness of mind, which . . . any man's fiery Zeal for his own Sect . . . has kindled against dissenters" (p. 34).

24. John Rawls, "Justice as Fairness: Political Not Metaphysical," *Philosophy and Public Affairs* 14 (1985), 223–251, and Ronald Dworkin, *Taking Rights Seriously* (Cambridge, Mass.: Harvard University Press, 1978), pp. 180–183. For interesting discussion, see John R. Wallach, "Liberals, Communitarians, and the Tasks of Political Theory," *Political Theory* 4 (1987), 581–611.

25. Rogers M. Smith, "The 'American Creed' and American Identity: The Limits of Liberal Citizenship in the United States," *Western Political Quarterly* 41 (1988), 225–251, pp. 229.

26. For an excellent discussion of the formative character of institutional life and the difference it makes to empirical political analysis, see Stephen L. Elkin, *City and Regime in the American Republic* (Chicago: The University of Chicago Press, 1987).

27. These practices evolved, to be sure, from preliberal ancestors. But my contention is that the goods and virtues American courts and colleges promote—in particular, the habits of independent deliberation and judgment—are sufficiently different from those which defined the work of their feudal predecessors that these practices must be understood as liberal, rather than as vestiges of an older order.

28. Max Weber, as much as Marx, sees the unlimited triumph of the spirit of acquisition at the expense of all other practices as a central fact of the modern age: *The Protestant Ethic* is the story of the unintended creation of an all-consuming monster, "the tremendous cosmos of the modern economic order. This order is now bound to the technical and economic conditions of machine production which today determine the lives of all the individuals who are born into this mechanism, not only those directly concerned with economic acquisition, with irresistible force . . . material goods have gained an increasing and finally an inexorable power over the lives of men as at no previous period in history." *The Protestant Ethic and the Spirit of Capitalism*, trans. Talcott Parsons (New York: Charles Scribner's Sons, 1958), p. 181.

29. In *Whose Justice? Which Rationality?* (Notre Dame, Ind.: University of Notre Dame Press, 1988), MacIntyre identifies the market as the central institution of the liberal tradition (p. 336), and claims that by concealing its traditional status from itself liberalism opens into the "rootless cosmopolitanism" (p. 388) of internationalized modernity. For a celebration of these same traits, see Ronald Rorty, "Postmodernist Bourgeois Liberalism," *The Journal of Philosophy* 80 (1983), 583–589, and "Thugs and Theorists: A Reply to Bernstein," *Political Theory* 15 (1987), 564–580.

30. Ralph Waldo Emerson, "The Young American," in *Ralph Waldo Emerson: Essays and Lectures*, ed. Joel Porte (New York: The Library of America, 1983), 211–230, p. 221.

31. Robert E. Lane, "Market Justice, Political Justice," *American Political Science Review* 80 (1986), 383–402.

32. My contention is that the problem caused by this tension between liberal theory and liberal practice over the virtues is that liberal theory, in particular the analytic heirs of classical liberal theory,

lacks the resources to articulate and defend the virtues of liberal practice, among them what Cora Diamond calls "the human good of articulateness, of having the words one needs." Diamond, "Losing Your Concepts," *Ethics* 98 (1988), 255–277, p. 270. Michael Ignatieff makes a similar point: "Freedom is empty as long as we are trapped in physical necessity. Freedom is also empty if we lack a language in which we can choose the good." *The Needs of Strangers* (New York: Penguin Books, 1986), p. 136.

33. Aristotle's formulation is that *politikē* and *phronēsis* are the same *hexis*, but a different essence. *Nicomachean Ethics* 6, 1141b23–24. I argue for the part to whole interpretation of Aristotle in Chapter 2 of my *Finding the Mean: Theory and Practice in Aristotelian Political Philosophy* (Princeton: Princeton University Press, 1990).

34. Stephen Skowronek, *Building a New American State: The Expansion of National Administrative Capacities 1877–1920* (Cambridge: Cambridge University Press, 1982), pp. 1–35.

35. *Leviathan*, Chapter 26, pp. 181, 177, 174.

36. Ibid., Chapter 46, p. 436, and Chapter 5, p. 30.

37. *De L'Esprit Des Lois* (Paris: Garnier Freres, 1961), Volume 1, Book 6, Chapter 3, p. 82.

38. Tocqueville, pp. 269–270, and 555–558.

39. *Federalist*, Number 10, in *The Federalist*, ed. Jacob E. Cooke (Middletown, Conn.: Wesleyan University Press, 1961), 56–65, p. 57.

40. Ibid., Number 63, 422–431, p. 425.

41. Ibid., Number 78, 521–530, p. 525.

42. See Gordon S. Wood. *The Creation of the American Republic, 1776–1787,* Chapter 11. In Jefferson's words, "All the powers of government, legislative, executive, and judiciary, result to the legislative body. The concentrating these in the same hands is precisely the definition of despotic government. It will be no alleviation that these powers will be exercised by a plurality of hands, and not by a single one. 173 despots would surely be as oppressive as one." *Notes on Virginia*, Query 13, in *Selected Writings*, p. 30. On the widespread support for some kind of judicial review at the Constitutional Convention of 1787, see John Agresto, *The Supreme Court and Constitutional Democracy* (Ithaca: Cornell University Press, 1984), pp. 56–64.

43. Leslie Friedman Goldstein, "Popular Sovereignty, the Origins of Judicial Review, and the Revival of Unwritten Law," *Journal of Politics* 48 (1986), 51–71, p. 53 (emphasis added).

44. James Boyd White, *When Words Lose Their Meaning: Constitutions and Reconstitution of Language, Character, and Community* (Chicago: The University of Chicago Press, 1984), Chapter 9, pp. 267 and 271–272.

45. Much of the energy for the criticism directed at the practice of judicial review stems from an unexamined, and I think untenable, equation of "the democratic process" and "the electoral process" or the sovereignty of present majorities. A prominent example is John Hart Ely, *Democracy and Distrust* (Cambridge, Mass.: Harvard University Press, 1980). For a well-argued critique of this view, see Sotirios A. Barber, *On What the Constitution Means* (Baltimore: The Johns Hopkins University Press, 1984).

46. Morton J. Horwitz, *The Transformation of American Law, 1760–1860* (Cambridge, Mass.: Harvard University Press, 1977), p. 99.

47. The case against judicial finality and for understanding the Court as one voice among several in American political dialogue is made by Barber, *On What the Constitution Means,* and by Agresto, *The Supreme Court and Constitutional Democracy,* Chapter 5, who sees the existence of this dialogue as a way out of the pointless debates about judicial activism and self-restraint.

48. *When Words Lose Their Meaning*, pp. 269–270. An argument that the Supreme Court at its best provides an exemplary model for liberal democratic deliberation is made by Frank Michelman, "The Supreme Court, 1985 Term—Foreword: Traces of Self-Government," *Harvard Law Review* 100 (1986), 4–77. An argument that a function of one aspect of judicial review—Equal Protection adjudication—is to establish norms for public deliberation is made by Cass Sunstein, "Public Values, Private Interests, and the Equal Protection Clause," *The Supreme Court Review* 5 (1982), 127–166.

49. Horwitz, *Transformation of American Law*, p. 257.

50. Ronald Dworkin, *Law's Empire* (Cambridge, Mass.: The Belknap Press of Harvard University Press), p. 276.

51. The broader formulation is Dworkin's statement *(Law's Empire*, p. 286) of the position whose best-known exposition is by Richard Posner, *The Economic Analysis of Law* (1977); the narrower is from Richard Posner, "The Ethical and Political Basis of the Efficiency Norm in Common Law Adjudication," in *Law, Economics, and Philosophy*, ed. Mark Kuperberg and Charles Beitz (Totowa, NJ: Rowman & Allanheld, 1983), 81–101, p. 81. In criticizing this position, Bruce Ackerman says that, "When Richard Posner, for example, was pressed to explain the evil of slavery, the best he could do was to assure us that, so long as the dollar value of our labor as free persons is higher than our dollar value as slaves, we have nothing to fear from the great god Efficiency! . . . Within our legal culture, it seems far *less* controversial to say that slavery is wrong because it denies each person's fundamental right to equal respect, than to say that it is wrong only so long as it is inefficient." *Reconstructing American Law* (Cambridge, Mass.: Harvard University Press, 1984), pp. 91–92. Ackerman's neutralist alternative is a clear improvement over Posner's solution, but it is not, however, the only possibility; one might also argue in cases like *Brown v. Board of Education* that the institution of American slavery was not only a matter of extreme and unjust oppression (and acknowledged as such by the Founders), but that it also maintained abnormal over a very long period of time several kinds of wretched lives—the lives of the masters as well as the slaves—such that remedial policy measures are of central importance to the maintenance of a liberal public identity.

52. Roberto Mangabeira Unger, one of the founding fathers of CLS, defends the liberal (he would say "superliberal") credentials of the movement in *The Critical Legal Studies Movement* (Cambridge, MA: Harvard University Press, 1986). For a strong liberal critique, see Rogers M. Smith, "After Criticism: An Analysis of the Critical Legal Studies Movement," in Michael W. McCann and Gerald L. Houseman, eds., *Judging the Constitution* (Glenview, IL: Scott, Foresman and Company, 1989), pp. 92–124.

53. In the discussion that follows, my debt to Eva Brann's superb *Paradoxes of Education in a Republic* (Chicago: The University of Chicago Press, 1979) will be apparent.

54. For critical discussion of the "gatekeeper" model, see Gutmann, *Democratic Education* pp. 181–195. The same foundation supports all three—the economic, the technocratic, and the populist—neutralist interpretations of higher education: the idea that the function of higher education is to increase the supply of instrumental knowledge either for society as a whole or for individuals, and not to shape preferences and habits.

55. "Arts are *banausic,* or narrowly industrial, insofar as the worker does not realize his own ideas but by a mere routine produces a useful object in a mode that is the prototype of what Marx calls *alienation*." Brann, *Paradoxes,* p. 60. For discussion of the Aristotelian understanding of the function of liberal education in Greek context, see Carnes Lord, *Education and Culture in the Political Thought of Aristotle* (Ithaca: Cornell University Press, 1982).

56. There were dissenters from the consensus on the benefits of the classical curriculum, pre-eminently Thomas Jefferson, whose University of Virginia founded in 1824 marked the first step in the direction of a more varied and more directly scientific and work-oriented program of studies. While not all the early colleges were denominational in character, many were, and many of these were evangelical in their orientation, but by no means necessarily illiberal in their conception of the virtues. See, for example, the inspiring account of Mary Lyon and the founding of Mount Holyoke College in Helen Lefkowitz Horowitz, *Alma Mater: Design and Experience in the Women's Colleges from Their Nineteenth Century Beginnings to the 1930s* (Boston: Beacon Press, 1986), pp. 9–27.

57. Luxury. Aristotle comments on the ineducability of the very rich in *Politics* 3, 1295b 13–18.

58. *Leviathan,* Chapter 30, pp. 224–225. My summary cannot do justice to one of the wittiest passages in a very witty book.

59. For a sober though by no means unfriendly account, see Gerald Graff, *Professing Literature: An Institutional History* (Chicago: The University of Chicago Press, 1987), pp. 19–35.

60. Ibid., pp. 20–22.

61. Ibid., p. 62.

62. In *From Max Weber: Essays in Sociology*, ed. and trans. by H.H. Gerth and C. Wright Mills (New York: Oxford University Press, 1946), pp. 129–156. References in parentheses in the next paragraph are to this edition. We could better call attention to the significance of Weber's essay for us, as well as to its strangeness, by translating the title, "Wissenschaft als Beruf," as "Scholarly Research as a Calling."

63. Part of the appeal of value-free German *Wissenschaft* to nineteenth-century American teachers of the humanities was the way it transformed their professional gender from female (schoolteachers) to male (scientists): The "reputation for effeminacy would have to be effaced from the modern languages before they could become respectable in the university. One of the attractions of Germanic philology would be that as a hard science its manliness was not in question." Graff, *Professing Literature*, p. 38.

64. Commercial and scientific elites seem perfectly compatible with liberal theorizing as well as liberal practice, once they are envisioned as marks of the way members of the liberal consensus differ from the savages.

65. The emphasis of the most American undergraduate curricula is not on liberal education as such, but on a "strong major" plus electives, a system which frees the researcher-professor from concern with the undergraduate's education, and at the same time enjoys a privileged ideological status as "the curricular counterpart of classical American Liberalism." W.M. Hexter, L.A. Babb, E.W. Bruss, H. Hawkins, M.A. Peterson, J.M. Upton, *Education at Amherst Reconsidered: The Liberal Studies Program* (Amherst, Mass.: Amherst College Press, 1978), p. 19.

66. It has appeared questionable to a number of critics, both German and American, both conservative and left of center. See especially Friedrich Nietzsche, *On the Advantage and Disadvantage of History for Life*, and Jürgen Habermas, "The University in a Democracy: Democratization of the University," in *Toward a Rational Society: Student Protest, Science, and Politics*, trans. Jeremy J. Shapiro (Boston: Beacon Press, 1971), 1–12.

67. *Paradoxes of Education in a Republic*, p. 106.

68. For a very interesting reconstruction of one such college's discussions of this process over the period of 150 years, see Hexter et al., *Education at Amherst Reconsidered*.

69. This kind of teaching occurs more often in less prestigious institutions than in elite colleges and universities, and most often in that least prestigious of academic settings, the Freshman English classroom. See Wayne Booth, "Reversing the Downward Spiral: Or, What is the Graduate Program For?" *Profession 87* (Modern Language Association of America, 1987), 36–39.

70. In speaking of authority here I have in mind the account by Hannah Arendt, "What Is Authority?" in *Between Past and Future: Eight Exercises in Political Thought* (New York: Penguin Books, 1977), 91–141. Arendt's notion refers to the Roman experience of a community constituted by a common sense of foundation, and inclined to treat that foundation as superior to any present power, out of a motive distinct from either compulsion or rational persuasion. The notion that authority refers to texts we all as persons follows from Gadamer's conception of prejudices as "biases of our openness to the world." Hans-Georg Gadamer, *Philosophical Hermeneutics*, trans. and ed. by David E. Linge (Berkeley: University of California Press, 1977), p. 9. The concept of accessible or legible authority, authority respected yet open to criticism, I owe to Richard Sennett, *Authority* (New York: Random House, 1980). It suggests the Gadamerian (and, I think, Aristotelian) insight that the task of practical reason is not to construct an alternative to authority, but to distinguish between legitimate and false authorities. See *Truth and Method*, pp. 245–253, and "On the Scope and Function of Hermeneutical Reflection," pp. 32–35.

71. Leo Strauss, "Comments on *Der Begriff des Politischen* by Carl Schmitt," reprinted in Strauss, *Spinoza's Critique of Religion*, trans. E.M. Sinclain (New York: Schocken Books, 1965), 331–351, pp. 349–350.

72. My point here is a response to what I take to be the critique of the liberal attitude toward religion in Robert N. Bellah, et al., *Habits of the Heart*, especially pp. 227–228, where one finds communitarian umbrage taken at the Gallup poll finding that 80% of Americans think that an individual should arrive at his or her own religious beliefs independent of any churches or synagogues.

73. Leo Strauss formulates this in the following way, speaking of a stylized conflict between Athens

and Jerusalem, between a people without authority and a people wholly constituted by divine authority: "It seems to me that this unresolved conflict is the secret of the vitality of Western civilization. . . . The very life of Western civilization is the life between two codes, a fundamental tension. There is therefore no reason inherent in Western civilization itself, in its fundamental constitution, why it should give up life. But this comforting thought is justified only if we live that life, if we live that conflict. No one can be both a philosopher and a theologian nor, for that matter, some possibility which transcends the conflict between philosophy and theology, or pretends to be a synthesis of both. But every one of us can be and ought to be either one or the other, the philosopher open to the challenge of theology or the theologian open to the challenge of philosophy." Strauss, "Progress or Return? The Contemporary Crisis in Western Civilization," *Modern Judaism* 1 (1981), 17–45, pp. 44–45.

74. Wayne C. Booth, *A Rhetoric of Irony* (Chicago: University of Chicago Press, 1974), p. 275.

75. "In his unpretentious dignity and purposeful openness, at least, Socrates is indeed the aboriginal American—and in his deeper aspects he *should be* naturalized." *Paradoxes of Education in a Republic,* p. 105 (emphasis in text). Gerald M. Mara argues on the basis of a sensitive reading of the *Theaetetus* and the *Protagoras* that the theory and practice of dialogue provided by Plato's Socrates gives us a model for liberal toleration. "Socrates and Liberal Toleration," *Political Theory* 16 (1988), 468–495.

76. John P. Diggins, *The Lost Soul of American Politics* (Chicago: The University of Chicago Press, 1986), p. 326.

77. Allan Bloom says that in the contemporary university, "*All* the students are egalitarian meritocrats." *The Closing of the American Mind* (New York: Simon and Schuster, 1987), p. 90 (emphasis in text). Eva Brann's response is, "If that were true, and a group held a belief without exception, one would indeed be driven, willy-nilly, to the thought of a domination by a supra-individual spirit, that is, a congenital psychic infection by history. In fact it is probably false. In my experience there are always some students who are acutely if reticently proud of the advantages accruing from the right sex, religion, and social status, while those who do believe that 'each individual should be allowed to develop his special and unequal talents' without reference to those factors might, I put it to Mr. Bloom, not just generationally *believe* it but also individually *think* it; it is certainly what *I* think." Review of *The Closing of the American Mind, The St. John's Review* (1988), 71–79, p. 76.

78. There is, of course, also a substantial theoretical objection to teleological theorizing (that it is "metaphysical" and hence false), but I cannot consider that here. I do discuss this in *Finding the Mean,* Chapter 1; the Aristotelian argument there is that while we can never know the internal *telos* of any animal species (including human being) with certainty and precision, we can distinguish between more and less plausible accounts of those *teleis,* and that this level of accuracy is all that is required for carrying out the appropriate work of practical theorizing.

79. I make a case for this reading of Plato and Aristotle in "Women, Soldiers, and Citizens: Plato and Aristotle on the Politics of Virility," *Polity* 19 (1986), 232–253. It is also possible that we overestimate the homogeneity of Greek or even Athenian culture as part of our tendency to dichotomize modernity and tradition. See L.B. Carter, *The Quiet Athenian* (Oxford: Clarendon Press, 1986).

80. Ruth Anna Putnam, "Reciprocity and Virtue Ethics," *Ethics* 98 (1988), 379–389, p. 389. This is in general a valuable summary of the main practical objections to teleology.

81. Iris Murdoch, *The Sovereignty of Good* (New York: Schocken Books, 1971), pp. 80–81.

82. A central effort here, building on Murdoch's critique of neutrality, is Sara Ruddick, "Maternal Thinking," *Feminist Studies* 6 (1980), 342–367. See also Jean Bethke Elshtain, "Antigone's Daughters," *Democracy* 2 (1982), 46–59, and "Reflections on War and Political Discourse: Realism, Just War, and Feminism in a Nuclear Age," *Political Theory* 13 (1985), 30–57.

83. Mary Dietz, "Citizenship With a Feminist Face: The Problem With Maternal Thinking," *Political Theory* 13 (1985), 19–37.

84. Jean Grimshaw, *Philosophy and Feminist Thinking* (Minneapolis: University of Minnesota Press, 1986). For an instructive discussion of both the promise and difficulty of extending "the ethic of care" to political discourse, see Joan Tronto, "Beyond Gender Difference to a Theory of Care," *Signs* 12 (1987), 644–663.

85. Consider the similar possibility suggested by the reference to Isocrates at the end of the *Phaedrus*.

86. In Rousseau, *Oeuvres Completes,* ed. Bernard Gagnebin and Marcel Raymond, 4 vols. (Paris: Gallimard, 1969), volume 4, 1044–1054.

87. For a thoughtful critique of the twin dangers of treating science as a monolithic absolute on the one hand and a pure social construction on the other, see Evelyn Fox Keller, *Reflections on Gender and Science* (New Haven: Yale University Press, 1985). Keller summarizes her case for a reformed conception of objectivity on pp. 177–179.

88. More, *Utopia,* trans. Robert M. Adams (New York: W.W. Norton, 1975), Book 1, pp. 28–29. For an interpretation of More as Platonic critic of utopian theory, see Eva Brann, " 'An Exquisite Platform'; *Utopia," Interpretation* 3 (1972), 1–26.

89. According to Socrates in the *Theaetetus,* our ordinary experience of error is the experiential ground of inquiry, and is the reason we cannot be content with *anthropos metron*—neutrality about the good doesn't square with our experience of being wrong ourselves (170a–b) and of *poleis* whose laws do not serve their interests (177d).

90. Dissent in *Abrams v. U.S.* 250 U.S. 616, 630 (1919).

91. On the contemporary importance of considering these theorists with an eye not prejudiced by nineteenth-century antiliberalism, see John Keane, ed., *Civil Society and the State* (London: Verso, 1988).

10

Aristotelian Social Democracy

Martha Nussbaum

"No Citizen Should Be Lacking in Sustenance"

Aristotle spoke about the human being and good human functioning. He also spoke about the design of political institutions in the many areas of life that should, as he saw it, fall within the province of the lawgiver's concern. He connected these two levels of reflection through a certain conception of the task of political planning. That task, as he saw it, is to make available to each and every citizen the material, institutional, and educational circumstances in which good human functioning may be chosen; to move each and every one of them across a threshold of capability into circumstances in which they may choose to live and function well. The aim of this chapter is to give a philosophical outline of a political conception based upon these elements in Aristotle, to describe the relationship of this conception to some forms of liberalism, and to explain why I find it a valuable and promising political conception. As my title indicates, I believe that this conception provides the philosophical basis for a certain sort of social democracy—one that shares a number of important features with some forms of liberalism that have been defended in the recent debate, but one that also breaks with liberalism at some crucial points.

We can begin investigating this conception by reading three passages from Aristotle's *Politics:*

1. *Politics* 1330b11. The things that we use most of and most frequently where our bodies are concerned, these have the biggest impact on health. Water and air are things of that sort. So good political planning should make some decisions about these things.

2. *Politics* 1329b39 ff. We must speak first about the distribution of land and about farming. . . . For we do not believe that ownership should all be common, as some people have urged. We think, instead, that it should be made common by way of a use that is agreed upon in mutuality. At the same time, we believe that no citizen should be lacking in sustenance and

support. As for the common meals, everyone agrees that they are a valuable institution in a well ordered city. . . . And all citizens should participate in them, but it is not easy for poor people both to bring in the required contribution and to manage the rest of their household affairs. . . . Then we must divide the land into two portions—the one to be held in common, the other to belong to private owners. And we must divide each of these two portions in half again. Of the commonly held portion, the one part will be used to support the cost of religious festivals, the other part to subsidize the common meals. Of the privately held portion, one part will be on the frontiers, the other part near the city. Each citizen will be given two lots, in such a way that all have a share in both sorts of land. That way is both equal and just.

3. *Politics* 1255b20. Political government is government of free and equal citizens.

Our first passage makes a quick transition. From the fact that water and air are of great importance for health, a central part of good human functioning, it is inferred directly that the adequate provision of these resources (by which is meant, we later see, a clean public water supply and healthy air) is the job of government.

Our second passage makes a similar move, with an even more striking result. The argument seems to go as follows. Participation in the common meals is a valuable part of social functioning. But a system of unqualified private ownership will produce a situation in which the poor are unable to join in, so that they will lose out on a valuable part of citizenship. (We shall examine this premise in a moment.) Nor, for reasons not given in this passage (and we shall discuss these reasons later) is a system with no private ownership altogether acceptable. Aristotle's conclusion: We want a system that includes some private ownership, but that also guarantees that no citizen will be lacking in sustenance—both with respect to common meals and, presumably, with respect to other valued functionings. The solution chosen is an extraordinary one, even from the point of view of the contemporary welfare state. For it is clear, first of all, that fully half the city's land will be held in common. Half of the product of this part will subsidize civic festivals (including, for example, the festivals at which tragedies and other music will be performed—so this looks above all like a subsidy for education). The other half will directly subsidize the participation of all citizens in the common meals.

Aristotle here tells us his own solution to a problem he has discussed before. Common meals, he has argued, are a very important part of the provision of nourishment for all, and also of civic participation and sociability (1272a19–21). In Sparta, each citizen is required to pay a subscription to join, out of his private property. The citizen who is unable to pay is excluded, not only from the common meal, but, as a penalty for failing to join, from all civic participation (1271a26–37, 1272a12–21). Aristotle has criticized this system, praising instead the arrangement in Crete which he calls "more common to all"—for the common meals there are subsidized out of publicly held produce and cattle, as well as by a tariff paid in by dependent noncitizen farmers in the surrounding area. Here, in his own ideal city, he follows the Cretan model, but goes even further. For, since he omits the tariff from noncitizen dependents, he is required to devote an extremely large proportion of the city's land to the common project.

But matters do not end there. For Aristotle has told us, as well, that there will be a "common use" of the land that *is* still privately held. What does he mean by this? The passage refers back to one in Book II, in which Aristotle tells us that the lawgiver must make sure that citizens make their property available to others, not only to personal friends, but also for "the common use of all." He gives some examples: "In Sparta, for example, men use one another's slaves as if they were their own, and one another's horses and dogs. And when they are on a journey, if they need food, they take it from the farms in the area" (1263a30 ff.). Aristotle does not tell us there how the lawgiver will effect this result. What is clear is that things in Aristotle's city will be arranged, through and through, with a view to the full sustenance of every citizen at all times. Even where private property is permitted, it is to be held only provisionally, subject to claims of need. This complex result is defended on grounds of both justice and equality.[1]

Finally, our third passage defines government of a political sort—the sort Aristotle is describing in our first two passages—as a government "of free and equal citizens." It becomes clear elsewhere that this "of" has a double sense: for both ruler and ruled are, in fact, to be free and equal, and they are to be the same people, taking turns in exercise of office.[2]

What we see, then, are three elements. First, we have a conception of good human functioning. (This is incompletely specified here, but we see that it includes both good functioning of body and good social interacting.) Second, we have a conception of political rule, which involves full support for these functionings ("no citizen should be lacking in sustenance") and insists that this support is to be done in such a way as to treat citizens as free and equal. Third, we have a sketch of institutional arrangements that both preserve some private ownership and circumscribe it, both by a scheme of common ownership and by a new understanding of private ownership as provisional, subject to claims of need. There are many difficulties in understanding the concrete details of what will go on. But this much appears evident.

My aim is to articulate the connections among these three elements, showing how a certain view of good human functioning gives rise to a political conception, through an understanding of political rule. We must ask, first of all, how the Aristotelian conception defends the need for a substantial theory of the human good prior to the selection of a political structure. A large part of our task will then be to examine this account of good human functioning and to ask how the Aristotelian conception arrives at it. I shall argue that the account of good human functioning is based upon a conception of the human being. I shall call this conception the "thick vague conception of the human being," and the associated conception of good functioning the "thick vague conception of the good," in order to distinguish it from conceptions of the good used in some liberal theories. By this name I mean to suggest that it provides a (partially) comprehensive conception of good human functioning (in contrast to Rawls's "thin" theory), but at a high level of generality, admitting of multiple specifications. I shall argue that this conception of the human being is not metaphysical in the sense in which it is frequently taken to be by liberal theorists who contrast their own conceptions with Aristotle's. It is, instead, an ethical-political account[3] given at a very basic and general level, and one that can be expected to be broadly shared across cultures, providing focus for an intercultural ethical-political inquiry. We shall then see how choice figures in the Aristotelian conception, and ask how political rule is understood to be a rule of free and equal citizens. We shall ask what room this conception allows for pluralism in the specification of ends. All this will put us in a position to describe its relationship to the liberalisms of John Rawls and Ronald Dworkin, and also to some of the theoretical underpinnings of Scandinavian social democracy.

Context and Motivation

Before we continue further, I must make some prefatory remarks. First, about the use of Aristotle. I shall call this conception Aristotelian, and I shall refer for illumination to arguments and example of Aristotle's. I believe, in fact, that the conception is in most essential respects Aristotle's, and I have defended it as such in three other essays, each dealing with a different aspect of the conception. "Nature, Function, and Capability: Aristotle on Political Distribution" (hereafter NFC) deals with the general idea that political arrangement must be based upon a view of good human functioning, and that its aim is to produce capabilities to function. The two other essays deal with the conception of the human being. "Non-Relative Virtues: An Aristotelian Approach" (NRV) examines the way in which this conception claims to organize a nonrelative debate about human ends across societies. "Aristotle on Human Nature and the Foundations of Ethics" (HN) argues that the conception of the human being is evaluative and ethical/ political, rather than metaphysical in the sense that some recent writers have claimed.[4] All of these essays contain detailed textual argument; and all (especially NFC and HN) examine strains and apparent or real inconsistencies in Aristotle's account. Here I shall do little of that. Instead, I aim to give a perspicuous philosophical picture of the conception, showing how its different parts fit together and how it provides us, here and now, with an attractive political alternative. If the reader is not convinced by the textual arguments of the other papers, she can just call it Conception X, and assess it anyway. At times, too, I shall be abbreviating philosophical arguments that are developed at greater length in the other essays, in order to present an overview of the conception. I shall say when I am doing this, and I hope that it will produce clarity rather than the opposite. Notes will provide fuller textual references, and comments on Aristotle's relation to the developing view.

Second, I must say a word about my own context in relation to the current liberalism debate. I wrote the first and the final drafts of this chapter in Finland, at an institute for the study of foundational issues in development economics. Most of my work on the Aristotelian conception during the past three years has been done here, in connection with a project that attempts to investigate conceptions of "the quality of life" for developing countries.[5] This context gives me, I feel, a somewhat peculiar relation to the liberalism debate, for two reasons. First, because much of the debate, as it is being carried on in some of the literature that provides the background for our conference, is American in focus and even in argument. It frequently conceives of liberalism as a tradition deriving from the American founding and from its Enlightenment backing; and it asks about problems that are, in many cases, specific to American political life.[6] I shall not altogether ignore these questions. But the reader should be warned that my statement of the problems is not very much shaped by them. And if I seem to defend alternatives that have no relationship to what is at all plausible or within the range of alternatives currently offered on the American political scene, the cause of this is not so much utopianism, or detachment from political reality, as it is detachment from that particular set of alternatives and immersion in a different set of alternatives.

This brings me to a second difference between my approach and that of many recent writers on liberalism. In most of the contemporary debate, the nation-state is taken as the basic unit, and inquiries about distribution concern the basic structure of this unit. John Rawls, in his most recent writings, explicitly states that his results could not be used either to deal with issues of international justice or to approach questions of justice in societies far removed from liberal democratic traditions deriving from the Enlightenment.[7] My view is that this pessimism is both unjustified and dangerous. Especially in light of the increasing interaction among diverse societies and the frequency of communications, cross-cultural debate about questions of justice is both possible and actual. It seems to me to be an advantage in a philosophical view if it can both explain this debate and provide a framework for its continuation and enhancement (see NRV). And it is urgent that this discussion should develop further. Many of the most urgent problems of justice and distribution that face human beings who live within nation-states are problems that are now, in their very nature, international problems, requiring worldwide communication and common effort for their effective solution. Aristotle may have been able to think of water and air as problems that each city can face on its own; now they are urgent problems for all human beings together, and in common. So are the related problems of hunger and famine, and the urgent question of preserving the ecology of the planet.[8] If we are so much as to survive as a species and a planet, we clearly need to think about well-being and justice internationally, and together. It seems to me that a view of justice that does not take account of this situation, and attempt to provide a framework to address it, is incomplete, and somewhat anachronistic. A great merit of the Aristotelian conception, with its emphasis on human functioning, is, by contrast, that, while it asks about institutions starting from the viewpoint of the single polity, it also insists on using basic conceptions that are shared and shareable by human beings in many times and places, conceptions on the basis of which, it is claimed, a conversation across political boundaries could also be organized (NRV).

And in fact, this would seem to be a merit of the Aristotelian conception from the point of view of Rawlsian liberalism itself. For Rawls insists, as does Aristotle, that the goal of philosophical theorizing in politics is not simply theory, but also, and more urgently, practice. The people engaging in inquiry are imagined by Rawls, as by Aristotle, to be searching for a conception of justice by which they can live, and live together. They are not looking for a detached good "out there," but for something that they can bring about in their lives.[9] It would then seem that if a necessary condition of the viability of a conception of justice in today's world is its ability to provide a basis for international dialogue, Rawls should be just as interested in the fulfillment of that condition as is Aristotle. The antecedent of this conditional may be controversial; but I believe that the evidence for it mounts every year.

The Priority of the Good and the Task of Political Arrangement

The Aristotelian conception believes that the task of political arrangement cannot be understood or well performed without a rather full theory of the human good and of what it is to function humanly. The task of political arrangement is, in fact, defined in terms of such a theory. Aristotle writes, "It is evident that the best *politeia* is that arrangement according to which anyone whatsoever might do best and live a flourishing life." His criterion for excellence in a political arrangement is that the people involved should be enabled, by that arrangement, to choose to function well and to lead a flourishing life, insofar as the polity's material and natural circumstances permit.[10] But this means, he argues, that we cannot understand what good arrangement is, or which arrangements are good, without having, first, an account of good human functioning in terms of which we can assess the various competitors. He concludes, "A person who is going to make a fitting inquiry into the best political arrangement must first get clear about what the most choiceworthy life is—for if this is unclear, the best political arrangement must remain unclear also" (*Pol.* 1323a14–17).

This priority of the good is the most conspicuous difference between the Aristotelian conception and all major liberal theories. But the difference is actually not easy to grasp; and it is a far more subtle difference than has sometimes been supposed. So we must do more work to understand exactly what the Aristotelian conception requires in this regard. We shall proceed in two stages. In this section we shall develop a general account of Aristotle's idea of the priority of the good, by examining his arguments against two alternative views. We then try to situate these arguments in the contemporary debate, giving some examples to show just what is at stake. In the next section we examine the Aristotelian theory of good itself, asking just how far away it is from "thin" theories of the good that a liberal could accept, and how it is used in assessing political arrangements.

The Aristotelian conception argues that the task of political arrangement is both *broad* and *deep*. *Broad,* in that it is concerned with the good living not of an elite few, but of each and every member of the polity. It aims to bring every member across a threshold into conditions and circumstances in which a good human life may be chosen and lived. It is *deep* in that it is concerned not simply with money, land, opportunities, and offices, the traditional political distributables, but with the totality of the functionings that constitute the good human life.[11] It opposes itself to three other conceptions of the relationship between an idea of the good and a political arrangement—all of which have their analogues in contemporary liberal theory. It needs to be stressed that liberal theories, too, give priority to a certain sort of conception of good: for, as Rawls says, we need to know what we are distributing and to know that these things are good.[12] So the question is, how does each conception conceive of the account of good that is to be used in defining the task of political arrangement itself, prior to the selection of distributive patterns and principles?

Aristotle's first opponent defines the good of an arrangement in terms of the total (or average) opulence it produces. The view does not ask what this opulence does for and in people's lives; it also does not ask how the opulence is distributed. Aristotle mentions an example of this sort: the view that the good city is the wealthy city, no matter what this wealth is doing and who has it. And he frequently alludes to political views that have this tendency, finding them in regimes such as that of Sparta.[13] A contemporary example of this sort of view is the tendency to measure economic development in terms of GNP (total or average) and to rank countries accordingly, where development is concerned, without asking any further questions.

The Aristotelian objection to this view is that it treats as an end in itself something that is only a tool. And it imagines that there is no limit to the goodness of money and possessions whereas in fact (according to the Aristotelian) they have no value, beyond what they do for and in the lives of human beings. Since no major liberal theorist in philosophy defends such a crude measure of the good in connection with the choice of political principles, I shall spend no more time on this opponent—beyond noting that, despite its crudeness, it is widely used by liberal democratic governments, especially when it is not the lives of their own citizens that are in question, but those of distant strangers.

The second group of theories still thinks of money and possessions as good. But it asks about their distribution, as well as their total or average amount. A simple example of this type of theory in the ancient world, and a direct ancestor of contemporary liberalisms, is the theory ascribed by Aristotle to Phaleas, according to which a political arrangement is good just in case it distributes property and money equally among the citizens. (Phaleas apparently said nothing about how to promote growth in the total of goods, or about whether one might tolerate some inequalities in order to achieve this result.)[14]

More sophisticated versions of this type of view can be found in the liberal political theories of Dworkin and Rawls. Dworkin defends equality of resources as a criterion of good distribution, and thus of good arrangement.[15] Rawls's theory of the good has by now become extremely complex, and we will need to return to it later on. But we can begin with the core of the theory, in its initial statement. In *The Theory of Justice,* then, Rawls argued that we need, prior to the selection of principles of justice, a "thin theory" of good, "restricted to the bare essentials." The list of "primary goods" is, as Rawls conceives it, a list of things of which rational individuals, whatever else they want and plan, desire "as prerequisites for carrying out their plans of life." "Other things being equal, they prefer a wider to a narrower liberty and opportunity, and a greater rather than a smaller share of wealth and income."[16] An index of primary goods (above all, at that stage, of wealth and income)—and not, for example, an index of capability or activity— is used in order to judge which people in the society are the "worst off," what counts as an improvement in someone's condition, and so forth. Rawls's second principle of justice permits inequalities only if they improve the condition of the worst off, so defined.

The basic intuitive idea used by the Aristotelian conception to argue against this is the idea that wealth, income, and possessions simply are not good in themselves. However much people may actually be obsessed with heaping them up (and Aristotle devotes much critical attention to this "chrematistic" tendency), what they have really, when they have them, is just a heap of stuff. A useful heap, but a heap nonetheless, a heap that is nothing at all unless it is put to use in the doings and beings of human lives.[17] But this means that to answer any of the interesting questions about their distribution—how much we should give, to whom, under what institutional structures—we need to see them at work in human functioning, seeing which of the important functions of human beings they promote or impede, and how various schemes for their arrangement affect these functionings.[18] They all "have a boundary, like tools: all are useful *for* something" (*Pol.* 1323b7–8). The right amount and the right ordering can be seen only be taking a stand on the question, "What *for*?"

Several more concrete observations can be added to support this general argument. First, the Aristotelian insists that more is not, in fact, always better, where wealth and income are concerned. At any rate, we have no right to assume that this is so, in advance of developing a theory of good living. If something has worth in itself, then more of that thing is probably always better. But once we grant that wealth and income are not like that, but are means, albeit of a very versatile sort, it seems inconsistent to assert confidently that more is always better.[19] This is a heretical and a deeply peculiar thought, to those brought up in liberal capitalism. It seems as if more cannot help being better. To Aristotelianism, by contrast, the thought is not peculiar, but obvious and central. The Aristotelian really does not see any point in heaping these things up more and more, either for herself or for others. Too much wealth may produce excessive competitiveness, or excessive focus on technical and managerial tasks, distracting people from social interaction, from the arts, from learning and reflecting. If this is so, then Aristotle is quite prepared to say, so much the worse for wealth. And he entertains perfectly seriously the possibility that wealth might have these bad results.[20]

Second, the Aristotelian recognizes wide individual variation in the functional role of the instrumental goods. In Aristotle's famous example, the right amount of food for Milo the wrestler, given his activity level, size, and occupation, is an amount that would be too much for most people. On the other hand, Milo would be very badly off, from the point of view of functioning, if he had an amount of food that is just right for a small sedentary philosopher. Again, as Aristotle prominently recognizes, the needs of pregnant women for food and other goods associated with health are very different from the needs of a nonpregnant woman. We might add that the protein needs of a child are altogether different from those of an adult. Again, a person with mobility problems, or a missing limb, will require a much larger subvention in order to be minimally mobile than will a person with no such deficiency.[21] If we look further into social context, still more variety appears. Children from disadvantaged minority groups need more money spent on them, if they are really to have access to education, than do middle-class children: we can see this by looking at what they are able to do and to be. Again, as things currently are, women need more support in terms of child care and so forth, if they are to work as they choose, than do others who do not face similar social obstacles.[22] All this is one more reason why the Aristotelian wishes to make the central question not, "How much do they have?", but rather, "What are they able to do and to be?" And she wishes to say that government has not done its job if it has not made each and every one of them capable of functioning well—even if it has given them many *things*.

Rawls's current reply to this point[23] is, first, to insist that we should leave out of account, for the time being, those who have deficiencies so severe that they are not "normally cooperating members of society." This reply seems obscure: for it appears that "normally cooperating" is specified in terms of the two moral powers,[24] excluding only those with severe mental (or moral?) deficiencies. And yet the objection was made, above all, in connection with differences in physical need. It would surely be odd to define a one-legged person as not a normally cooperating member of society. And, as we have said, even among people who could not be construed as suffering from deficiency, there are many and wide differences, at least some of which the legislator ought to take into account. The idea that there is such a thing as a normal body with normal needs is a myth that the Aristotelian, with that view's emphasis on contextual particularity, avoids.

Rawls's second strategy (one shared by Dworkin) is to regard the allotment of primary goods as like insurance.[25] We give, *ex ante,* equal *expectation* of primary goods, though *ex post* a person who has an accident may in fact get more. We reply that accidents are not the only sources of variation in functional need, and probably not the most important. Some of our examples, and many that could be imagined, rest on uninsurable differences. So it seems, at least to me, that Rawls has not yet met the objections he has received on this point.

Turning now from the subject of individual variation to our third objection, we must insist that in any actual and conceivable contemporary structure of allocation, decisions are in fact made one way or another about which resources are allocated, about how and through what channels they are allocated, and about the areas of human life in connection with which they will be allocated. Governments do not, in fact, completely stay out of the business of choosing to support certain human functions rather than others. No modern state simply puts income and wealth into the citizens' pockets; instead, programs are designed to support certain areas of life—health, education, defense, and so forth. Any other approach would produce confusion. Even to answer the question "Which things that we have to hand are the useful and usable resources?" requires *some* implicit conception of the good and of good human functioning. In particular, decisions about how and whether plants, minerals, and animals are to be taken for use requires a conception of good human functioning in relation to other species and to the world of nature. In short: to answer any of the interesting, actual political questions about resources and their allocation through programs and institutions, we need to take some stand, and do all the time take a stand, on the Aristotelian question, "What human functions are important? What does a good human life require?"[26]

Finally, a list of functionings can show us one very important thing that an account of good based on wealth and resources alone cannot show us. It can show us where tensions and conflicts might be present in the ends that human beings try to promote. I am thinking here not of conflicts between persons, as when A's pursuit of A's good conflicts with B's pursuit of B's good. I am thinking of conflicts among the demands of generally agreed components of the good life, as when certain sorts of industrial or scientific progress may come to be in tension with ecological or health-related values, or where the demands of work may compete with the function of child care. Here, first of all, we want to know about these conflicts and who faces them, since these people—for example women or men who combine a full-time career with family responsibilities—will usually need extra resources and support systems if they are to live as well as people without such conflicts. Simply giving them an equal amount will not do enough; and we will not even find out about their problems if we concern ourselves with resources without having a view of the good. Beyond this, the promotion of the good of all citizens, in cases where pervasive conflicts exist among components of the good, will require deep reflection about the good and about how resources and institutional arrangements might mitigate conflict. It will also require reflection about which conflicts government should attempt to mitigate and which are signs of a tragic tension within the good itself, not to be mitigated without a loss in richness of life. These reflections must take place prior to decisions about the allocations of amounts of resources, and even prior to decisions about which things are resources that we may use. In some cases, reflection on conflict may lead to large-scale institutional changes, changes that would not even have been imagined had the exercise been confined to the provision of equal amounts of resources all round.[27]

These are some of the Aristotelian's arguments against the Rawlsian liberal. All have their basis in Aristotle's own arguments, as we have seen, and most of them are explicitly stated by Aristotle himself. But Aristotle's third opponent must now be confronted. This is, of course, the utilitarian, whose approach dominates much of the contemporary scene in economics and public policy.[28] The utilitarian agrees with Aristotle that resources are valuable because of what they do *for people*. But she is a liberal, or a quasi-liberal, in wishing to leave the decision about goodness to each person. In particular, she wishes to make it a function of the satisfaction of desires or preferences that people happen, as things are, to have. She rejects the idea that any more objective account of good human functioning is either necessary or desirable.

The central difficulty with this proposal is one that is recognized both by the Aristotelian conception and by many liberal conceptions, including Rawls's.[29] It is the fact, frequently emphasized by Aristotle,[30] that desire is a malleable and unreliable guide to the human good, on almost any seriously defensible conception of good. Desires are formed in relation to habits and ways of life. At one extreme, people who have lived in opulence feel dissatisfied when they are deprived of the goods of opulence. At the other extreme, people who have lived in severe deprivation frequently do not feel desire for a different way, or dissatisfaction with their way. Human beings adapt to what they have. In some cases, they come to believe that it is right that things should be so with them; in other cases, they are not even aware of alternatives. Circumstances have confined their imaginations. So if we aim at satisfaction of the desires and preferences that they happen, as things are, to have, our distributions will frequently succeed only in shoring up the status quo.[31]

The Aristotelian takes desire seriously as *one* thing we should ask about, in asking how well an arrangement enables people to live. But she insists that we must also, and more insistently, ask what the people involved are actually able to do and to be—and, indeed, to desire. We consider not only whether they are asking for education, but how they are being educated; not only whether they perceive themselves as reasonably healthy, but how long they live, how many of their children die, how, in short, their health *is*.[32]

In all of this, the Aristotelian approach understands the job of government to be, as we have said, both broad and deep. It takes cognizance of every important human function, with respect to each and every citizen. But now we must introduce an extremely important qualification. The conception does not aim directly at producing people who function in certain ways. It aims, instead, at producing people who are *capable* of functioning in these ways, who have both the training and the resources to so function, should they choose. The choice itself is left to them. And one of the capabilities Aristotelian government most centrally promotes is the capability of choosing: of doing all these functions in accordance with one's very own practical reasoning.[33] We shall see in the next sections that leaving this place for choice is an absolutely essential part, for the Aristotelian, of promoting truly *human* functioning, in every sphere. In short: the person who is given a clean public water supply can always put pollutants into the water she drinks. The person who has received an education is free, later on, to waste it. The person who has good recreational facilities may fail to take advantage of them. The government aims at capabilities, and leaves the rest to the citizens.[34]

Many questions need to be raised here; and we shall return to this issue. For now, we should simply notice how much this qualification narrows the gap between the Aristotelian and the liberal. For it was the liberal's desire to create a context of choice for individuals that made her stop with the thin theory of good. The Aristotelian's claim is that stopping with such a thin theory neither shows the point of those instrumental goods nor gives sufficient guidance to promote their truly human use. And we can now add that such a thin theory may actually not show the legislator how to produce the capability of choosing, a human function that has institutional and material conditions like any other.

Two examples will clarify this point and give a general illustration of the differences between the Aristotelian theory and its various opponents. Let us imagine, first, the worker whom Marx described in his *Economic and Philosophical Manuscripts of 1844*. This worker performs a monotonous task in a large industrial enterprise over which he himself has no control. He is not prosperous; in fact, he is needy. But material need is only one part of his problem. The other part is that, being removed from choice and control over his work activity, he has been alienated from the fully human use of the food he has, and of his senses more generally. "In his human functions," Marx writes, "he no longer feels himself to be anything but an animal."[35]

In assessing the situation of this worker, the utilitarian, the liberal, and the Aristotelian will all ask different questions. The utilitarian will ask how he feels about his life and what he desires. It certainly seems possible that if things are bad enough with him, he will turn out to be far less dissatisfied than he ought to be, given his situation. He may lack the energy of desire and imagination to conceive of a better way and aspire to it. This deformation of desire was, for Marx, one of the worst features of such situations. So the utilitarian question will be unlikely to lead on to a radical criticism of his material situation, or to a redistribution aimed at giving him a very different one.[36]

By contrast, the liberal's questioning about resources or primary goods will be likely to go somewhat further. For the liberal will ask not just how he feels, but what resources he actually commands. And this will certainly lead, in the theories of both Rawls and Dworkin, to a strong criticism of the worker's material situation, insofar as he is deprived, and to a redistribution that is aimed at giving him a more substantial amount. On the other hand, it is less likely that this liberal questioning about resources will lead to any far-reaching criticism of the relations of production that are, according to Marx, the primary impediment to this worker's truly human functioning. If he has enough things, the liberal judges that things are well enough with him, and that he has received equal treatment. The liberal characteristically does not probe more deeply, looking for impediments to good functioning in the structure of the worker's daily modes of interaction with others, asking whether his life is such that he is capable of using the resources he is given in a truly human way.[37]

The Aristotelian, by contrast, asks, and asks in a very wide-ranging way: What is this worker able to do and to be? What are his choices? What are his modes of interaction with his work and with other human beings? What is he able to imagine and to enjoy? How is he eating and using his senses? And how do the institutional and work-related conditions of his life promote or impede these functionings? The job of government, on the Aristotelian view, does not stop until we have removed all impediments that stand between this citizen and fully human functioning. This job will, then, frequently involve a great deal more than reallocation of resources. It will usually involve radical institutional and social change.[38]

Take, again, the women in a village in Bangladesh, as described in the impressive study *A Quiet Revolution,* by Marty Chen.[39] These women had low status in their community, in every area. They were less well nourished than males, less educated, less respected. Let us consider their situation where just one question, the question of literacy, is concerned.

A desire-based approach, which has frequently been used in this and related cases, argues that if these women do not demand more education and a higher rate of literacy, there is no reason at all why government should concern itself with this issue. Polls are taken; women express satisfaction with their educational status; no further effort is made. As Chen's account makes clear, this approach looks very short-sighted once one considers the weight of the cultural forces pressing these women not to demand more education (and also not to *feel* that they want more); once one considers, as well, the absence, in their daily lives, of paradigms of what education could do and be in lives similar to theirs, the absence of any experience of the alternative they are asked to consider. Sometimes the combination of ignorance and cultural pressures actually prevents the formation of the desire for education; sometimes it prevents only the public expression of the desire. In both cases, a utility-based approach to public policy will be unable to criticize the status quo, no matter how unjust, on reflection about the full range of human possibilities, that status quo might seem.

As Chen describes the history of this problem, the next approach tried was, in fact, a liberal approach, practiced both by an international development agency and to some extent by the local government. This approach consisted in giving the women of the village ample educational resources, in the form of adult literacy materials. (Already, notice, this approach took a stand about what functions and what resources were the important ones for these people, giving them literacy materials rather than simple cash. In this sense it ceased to be a purely liberal approach. It also ceased to be a purely liberal approach when it gave these women more, on account of the special impediments they faced in functioning, than was given to males who lacked these impediments.) But this approach had little impact on the women's functioning. This was so because no attempt was made by the development agency to study their way of life in depth, asking what role literacy played and might play in it, how it might fit in with their other functions, and also what special impediments their current way of life created for the good use of educational resources. Merely handing some resources to the women did not go far enough. For example, it did not begin to address, or even describe, the many conflicts in functioning that a literate woman would be likely to encounter in that society.

The failure of this liberal project prompted a transition to what seems to be a more Aristotelian approach. The researchers began to look at the women's lives in greater depth, asking what, over all the major functions and over a complete life, the women were able to do. This led to a searching inquiry, carried out in women's cooperatives, in partnership between the local and the foreign women, into the role of education in their functioning, and its relationship to other valuable functionings. This brought about the beginning of many complex and interrelated transformations in women's role in the village, transformations involving the whole structure of gender relations and relations of production. The Aristotelian argues that this kind of inquiry is the only kind that goes deep enough.[40] Without such an inquiry into the goodness and full humanness of various functionings, and into the special obstacles faced by deprived groups, the most valuable sort of social change could not have begun. Simply making enough things available was not enough. But to do more we need a conception of the good.

The liberal argues that citizens have been treated as free and equal if they have been given equal amounts of all-purpose resources (Dworkin), or if inequalities can be justified as being for the good of the worst off (Rawls). The Aristotelian also holds, as we have seen, that political rule is a rule of free and equal citizens. But she holds that citizens have been treated as free only if they have been given the necessary conditions for the exercise of choice and practical reason (among which will be education, political participation, and the absence of degrading forms of labor). And they have been treated as equals only if the whole life of each one of them has been considered with rich imagination[41] and, as a result, each one has been given whatever he or she needs in order to be in a position of capability to live a rich and fully human life, up to the limit permitted by natural possibilities.

The Thick Vague Conception of the Good

But if we are to give priority to the good, we must have a conception of the good. And this is where the liberal becomes apprehensive. For it appears that any substantial notion of the good that might be used by political thought will be biased in favor of some projects that citizens might choose, and hostile toward others. Such a conception will, it seems, therefore be objectionably paternalistic in its tendency to support some ways of life rather than others. Liberals suspect, furthermore, that the Aristotelian's decision to base her substantial conception of the good on an account of the human being will import metaphysical elements that are controversial among the citizens, and thus will prove unable to ground a political consensus.[42] So the Aristotelian must show what her concept of the good is, how much determinate content it has, how (using what background concepts) it is derived, and what political work it can do.

The Aristotelian uses a conception of the good that is not "thin," like Rawls's "thin theory"—that is, confined to the enumeration of all-purpose means to good living,[43] but "thick"—dealing, that is, with human ends across all areas of human life. The conception is, however, vague and this in a good sense. It admits, that is, of many concrete specifications; and yet it draws, as Aristotle puts it, an "outline sketch" of the good life.[44] It draws the general outlines of the target, so to speak. And yet, in the vague guidance it offers to thought, it does real work. The Aristotelian proceeds this way in the belief that it is better to be vaguely right than precisely wrong; and that, without the guidance of the thick vague theory, what we often get, in public policy, is precise wrongness.

The thick vague theory is not, in the sense that worries liberals, a metaphysical theory. That is, it is not a theory that is arrived at in detachment from the actual self-understandings and evaluations of human beings in society; nor is it a theory peculiar to a single metaphysical or religious tradition. Indeed, it is (as I argue in HN) both internal to human history and strongly evaluative;[45] and its aim is to be as universal as possible, to set down the basis for our recognitions of members of very different traditions as human across religious and metaphysical gulfs. The theory begins, as we shall see, from an account of what it is to be a human being. But this account, far from being based on "metaphysical biology" (as some critics of Aristotle have held),[46] is actually based on the commonness of myths and stories from many times and places, stories explaining to both friends and strangers what it is to be human rather than something else. The account is the outcome of a process of self-interpretation and self-clarification that makes use of the story-telling imagination far more than the scientific intellect. In HN I describe this process as occurring within a single community whose members wish to clarify to themselves and to their children the meanings they have found in living as human beings. But an equally important part of such stories, as I try to show in NRV, is that they are recognitions of humanness across distance. Aristotle wrote, "One can see in one's travels to distant countries the ties of recognition and affiliation that link every human being to every other" (EN1155a21–2). The vague thick theory is a set of stories about such ties. In this way, it is a most general and preliminary evaluative theory: for it recognizes that certain aspects of human life have a special importance. Without them, we would not recognize ourselves or others as the sort of beings we are; and they provide the basis for our recognition of beings unlike ourselves in place, time, and concrete way of life as members of our very own kind.

The basic idea of the thick vague theory is that we tell ourselves stories of the general outline or structure of the life of a human being. We ask and answer the question, What is it to live as a being situated, so to speak, between the beasts and the gods, with certain abilities that set us off from the rest of the world of nature, and yet with certain limits that come from our membership in the world of nature? The idea is that we share a vague conception, having a number of distinct parts, of what it is to be situated in the world as human, and of what transitions either "up" or "down," so to speak, would turn us into beings no longer human—and thus (since on the whole we conceive of species identity as at least necessary for personal identity) into creatures different from ourselves. Frequently this conception is elucidated (and perpetuated) by myths, especially myths of nonhuman yet anthropomorphic creatures, either bestial or godlike,[47] who force our imaginations to ask, "Why, if these creatures resemble humans, don't we count them as human?" In this way, we learn something about ourselves.[48]

Take, for example, the countless stories told by the ancient Greeks about the Olympian gods—beings who look like human beings, who have most of the same desires, but who are also immortal and, to a certain extent, invulnerable. Imagining them, we ask what our sense of the great gulf between their way of life and ours tells us about the role of certain natural limits in making us the beings we are. Take, again, the Cyclopes, beings who have human shape and form, but who live in isolation from community and who lack all sensitivity to the needs of others, all sense of commitment and affiliation. What do we learn about our own self-understanding, when we notice that our stories treat such creatures as nonhuman monsters?

This is the way the exercise proceeds. (In HN I develop in detail some concrete examples.) And the great convergence across cultures in such storytelling, and in its singling out of certain areas of experience as constitutive of humanness, gives us reason for optimism that if we proceed in this way, using our imaginations, we will have, in the end, a theory that is not only the parochial theory of our local traditions, but also a basis for cross-cultural attunement. In fact, it would be surprising if this were not so, since the question we are asking is: What are the features of our common humanity, features that lead us to recognize certain others, however distant their location and their forms of life, as humans and, on the other hand, to decide that certain other beings who resemble us superficially could not possibly be human? The question we ask directs us to cross boundaries.[49]

The list we get if we reflect in this way is, and must be, open-ended. For we want to allow the possibility that some as yet unimagined transformation in our natural options will alter the constitutive features, subtracting some and adding others. We also want to leave open the possibility that we will learn from our encounters with other human societies to revise certain elements in our own standing account of humanness, recognizing, perhaps, that some features we regarded as essential are actually more parochial than that. We must insist that, like most Aristotelian lists,[50] our working list is meant not as systematic philosophical theory, but as a summary of what we think so far, and as an intuitive approximation, whose intent is not to legislate, but to direct attention to certain areas of special importance. And the list is not only intuitive, but also heterogeneous; for it contains both limits against which we press and powers through which we aspire. This is not surprising, since we began from the general intuitive idea of a creature who is both capable and needy. We shall return to this point, showing how it affects our political use of the list.[51]

Here, then, as a first approximation, is a kind of story about what seems to be part of any life that we count as a human life.

Level A of the Thick Vague Conception:
The Constitutive Circumstances of the Human Being
(or: the Shape of the Human Form of Life)

Mortality.

All human beings face death and, after a certain age, know that they face it. This fact shapes more or less every other element of human life. Moreover, all human beings have an aversion to death. Although there are many circumstances (varying among individuals and from culture to culture) in which death will be preferred to the available alternatives, it is still true that in general human beings wish to live and, like Lucretius's "first mortals" (prior to any culture) leave with fear and grief "the sweet light of life."[52] If we did encounter an immortal anthropomorphic being, its way of life would be so different from our own that we could hardly regard it as a part of the same kind with us. The same would be true if we encountered a mortal being that showed no tendency to avoid death or to seek to continue its life.[53]

The Human Body.

We live our entire lives in bodies of a certain sort, whose possibilities and vulnerabilities do not as such belong to one human society rather than another. These bodies, similar far more than dissimilar (considering the enormous range of possibilities) are our homes, so to speak, opening to us some options and denying others. We are so used to our bodies that we tend to forget how different from other bodies and conceivable bodies (and from the condition of bodilessness) they are, how far and how deeply they demarcate our possibilities. The fact that any given human being might have lived anywhere and belonged to any culture is a great part of what grounds our mutual recognitions; this fact has a great deal to do with the general humanness of the body, its great distinctness from other bodies. The experience of the body is culturally shaped; but the body itself, not culturally variant in its requirements, sets limits on what can be experienced, ensuring a lot of overlap.[54]

There is of course much disagreement about *how much* of human experience is rooted in the body. Here metaphysics enters into the picture in a nontrivial way. So in keeping with the general nonmetaphysical character of the list I shall include at this point only those features that would be agreed to be bodily even by metaphysical dualists. I shall discuss the more controversial features (perceiving, thinking, etc.) as separate items, taking no stand on the question of dualism.

1. *Hunger and thirst; the need for food and drink.* All human beings need food and drink in order to live; and all have comparable, though varying nutritive requirements. Being in one culture rather than another does not make one metabolize food differently. Furthermore, all human beings have appetites that are indices of need. Appetitive experience is to some extent culturally shaped; and sometimes it is not parallel to the body's actual level of need. And yet, we discover enormous similarity and overlap. Moreover, human beings in general do not wish to be hungry and thirsty (though they might choose to fast for some reason). Aristotle remarks that if we discovered someone who really did not feel hunger and thirst at all, or, feeling them, did not care about eating and drinking, we would judge that this person was "far from being a human being."[55]

2. *Need for shelter.* A recurrent topic in myths of humanness is the nakedness of the human being, its relative fragility and susceptibility to heat, cold, the elements in general. Stories that explore the difference between our needs and those of furry or scaly or otherwise protected creatures remind us how far our life is constituted by the need to find refuge from the cold, or from the excessive heat of the sun, from rain, from wind, from snow and frost.[56]

3. *Sexual desire.* Though less necessary as a need than the needs for food, drink, and shelter, sexual desire is a feature of more or less every human life. Aristotle includes it among the desires whose complete absence would be the sign of a being far from human. It is, and has all along been, a very

strong basis for the recognition of others different from ourselves as human beings.

4. *Mobility*. We are, as the old story goes, featherless bipeds—that is creatures whose form of life is in part constituted by the ability to move from place to place in a certain way, not only through the aid of tools we have made, but also with our very own bodies. Human beings like moving about, and dislike being deprived of mobility. An anthropomorphic being who, without disability, chose never to move from birth to death would be hard to view as human; and a life altogether cut off from mobility seems a life less than fully human.

Capacity for Pleasure and Pain.

Experiences of pain and pleasure are common to all human life—though once again their cultural expression and perhaps, to some extent, the experience itself, will vary. Moreover, the aversion to pain as a fundamental evil is a primitive and, apparently, unlearned part of being a human animal. A society whose members altogether lacked that aversion would surely be considered to be outside the bounds of humanness.[57]

Cognitive Capability:
Perceiving, Imagining, Thinking.

All human beings have sense-perception, the ability to imagine, and the ability to think, making distinctions and, as Aristotle famously says, "reach(ing) out for understanding."[58] And these abilities are regarded as valuable. It is an open question what sorts of accidents or impediments to individuals in these areas will be sufficient to make us judge that the form of life is not human, or no longer human. But it is safe to say that if we imagine a tribe whose members totally lack sense-perception, *or* totally lack imagination, *or* totally lack reasoning and thinking, we are not in any of these cases imagining a tribe of human beings, no matter what they look like.

Early Infant Development.

All human beings begin as hungry babies, aware of their own helplessness, experiencing their alternating closeness to and distance from that, and those, on which they depend. This common structure to early life—which clearly is shaped in many and varied ways in different social arrangements—still gives rise to a great deal of overlapping experience that is of great importance for the formation of emotions and desires, and that is a major source of our ability to see ourselves in the emotional experiences of those whose lives are otherwise very different from our own. The merits of one or another psychoanalytical theory of infancy can be debated; that there is some general overlapping structure of deep significance cannot be. And the work of Freud on infant desire and of Melanie Klein on grief, loss, and other emotional attitudes has, despite the presence of *some* culture-specific material, still succeeded in mapping some part of the territory of our common humanity. If we encountered a tribe of apparent humans and then discovered that they never had been babies and had never, in consequence, had those experiences of extreme dependency, need, and affection, we would, I think, have to conclude that their form of life was sufficiently different from our own that they could not be considered part of the same kind.[59]

Practical Reason.

All human beings participate (or try to) in the planning and managing of their own lives, asking and answering questions about what is good and how one should live. Moreover, they wish to enact their thought in their lives—to be able to choose and evaluate, and to function accordingly. This general capability has many concrete forms, and is related in complex ways to the other capabilities, emotional, imaginative, and intellectual. But a being who altogether lacks this would not be likely to be regarded as fully human, in any culture.[60]

Affiliation with Other Human Beings.

As Aristotle claimed, all human beings recognize and feel a sense of affiliation and concern for other human beings. (Here the conceptual and the empirical are closely linked: we recognize other humans, and our concept of the human is shaped, in an open-ended way, by what we find ourselves able to recognize.) Moreover, we value the form of life that is constituted by these recognitions and affiliations—we live to and with others, and regard a life not lived in affiliation with others to be a life not worth living. (We may want to spell this out further: for it is Aristotle's view that we define ourselves in terms of at least two sorts of affiliation: intimate family relations and social or civic relations.)

*Relatedness to Other Species and
to Nature.*

Human beings recognize that they are not the only living things in their world: that they are animals living alongside other animals, and also alongside plants, in a universe that, as a complex interlocking order, both supports and limits them. We are dependent upon that order in countless ways; and we also sense that we owe that order some respect and concern, however much we may differ about *what* we owe, to whom, and for what reasons. Again, a creature who treated animals exactly like stones and could not be brought to recognize some problem with that would probably be regarded as too strange to be human. So, too, would a creature who did not care in any way for the wonder and beauty of the natural world. (Here, perhaps, we are in the process of watching some part of our kind become other than what a human being has usually been taken to be; perhaps we shall someday be called upon either to change our conception of humanness or to acknowledge a fundamental gulf in forms of life among humans.)[61]

Humor and Play.

Human life, wherever it is lived, makes room for recreation and laughter. The forms play takes are enormously varied and yet we recognize other humans, across many and varied barriers, as the animals who laugh. Laughter and play are frequently among the deepest and also the first modes of our mutual recognition. Inability to play or laugh is taken, correctly, as a sign of deep disturbance in an individual child; if it is permanent the consequence may be that we will prove unable to consider the child capable of leading a fully human life. An entire society that lacked this ability would seem to us both terribly strange and terribly frightening. We certainly do not want a life that leaves this element out; and on the whole we want more of it than circumstances permit us to have.[62]

Separateness.

However much we live for and to others, we are, each of us, "one in number," proceeding on a separate path through the world from birth to death. Each person feels only his or her own pain and not anyone else's. Each person dies alone. When one person walks across the room, no other follows automatically. When we count the number of human beings in a room, we have no difficulty figuring out where one begins and the other ends. These obvious facts need stating, since they might have been otherwise; we should bear them in mind when we hear talk of the absence of individualism in certain societies. Even the most intense forms of human interaction, for example sexual experience, are experiences of responsiveness, and not of fusion. If fusion is made the goal, the result is bound to be bitter disappointment. And this is so no matter how much society may try to hold us together. Plato's *Laws* discusses the aim of doing everything possible, "by hook or by crook," to make "common even what is by nature private, such as eyes, ears, hands, so that they will seem to see and hear and feel in common." It never works.[63]

Strong Separateness.

Because of separateness, each human life has, so to speak, its own peculiar context and surroundings—objects, places, a history, particular friendships, locations, sexual ties—that are not the same as those of anyone else, and in terms of which the person to some extent identifies herself. Though societies vary a great deal in the *degree* of strong separateness they permit and foster, there is no life, short of a life of total imprisonment, and perhaps not even that life, that really does fail to say the words "mine" and "not-mine" in some idiosyncratic and non-shared way. What I touch, use, love, respond to, I touch, use, love, respond to from my own separate point of view. The items I call "mine" are not exactly the same as those called that way by any other person. On the whole, human beings recognize one another as beings who wish to have some separateness of context, a little space to move around in, some special items to use and hold and cherish.[64]

This is an open-ended list. One could subtract some items and/or add others. (A comparison of this list with the list in NRV will show me doing this.) But it is a thick vague starting point for reflection about what the good life for such a being might be.

Notice that the list is already evaluative: it singles out some items, rather than others, as the most important items, the ones in terms of which we identify ourselves. We say that a life without these items or structures is not recognizable as human; and, given that any life we can coherently wish for ourselves or for others will have to be, at least, human (see HN),[65] it sets an outline around our aspirations. But it does this in two different ways. For, as I said and as we can now see, the list is composed of two different sorts of items: limits and capabilities. As far as the capabilities go, it is clear that calling them part of humanness is making a very basic sort of evaluation. It is to say that life without this item would be too lacking, too impoverished, to be human at all. *A fortiori,* it could not be a good human life. So this list of capabilities is a kind of ground-floor, or minimal conception of the good.

With the limits, matters are more complicated. For we insist that human life, in its general form, consists in a struggle against these limits. Humans do not wish to be hungry, to feel frustration or pain, to die. (Separateness is extremely complex, both a limit and a capability.) And yet, we should not assume that the evaluative conclusion to be drawn is that we should try as hard as possible to get rid of the limit altogether. It is characteristic of human life to prefer recurrent hunger plus eating to a life with neither hunger nor eating; to prefer sexual desire and its satisfaction to a life with neither desire nor satisfaction. And even where death is concerned, human beings probably do not, when they think most clearly, wish to lose their finitude completely; or, if they vaguely do so, it is at the cost of embracing a transition to a wholly different form of life, with different values and ends, in which it is not at all clear that the identity of the individual could be preserved. So the evaluative conclusion has to be expressed with much caution, in terms of what would be a humanly good way of countering the limitation.[66]

This brings us to the second stage of our thick vague conception. For now we are in a position to specify vaguely certain basic functionings that should, as constitutive of human life, concern us. We shall actually introduce the list as a list of the related capabilities, rather than of actual functionings, since we have argued that it is capabilities, not actual functionings, that should be in the legislator's goal.

Basic Human Functional Capabilities

1. Being able to live to the end of a complete human life, as far as is possible; not dying prematurely, or before one's life is so reduced as to be not worth living.

2. Being able to have good health; to be adequately nourished; to have adequate shelter; having opportunities for sexual satisfaction; being able to move about from place to place.

3. Being able to avoid unnecessary and non-useful pain, and to have pleasurable experiences.

4. Being able to use the five senses; being able to imagine, to think and reason.

5. Being able to have attachments to things and persons outside ourselves; to love those who love and care for us, to grieve at their absence; in general, to love, grieve, to feel longing and gratitude.

6. Being able to form a conception of the good and to engage in critical reflection about the planning of one's own life.

7. Being able to live for and to others, to recognize and show concern for other human beings, to engage in various forms of familial and social interaction.

8. Being able to live with concern for and in relation to animals, plants, the world of nature.

9. Being able to laugh, to play, to enjoy recreational activities.

10. Being able to live one's own life and nobody else's.

10a. Being able to live one's own life in one's very own surroundings and context.

This is a list of functional capabilities that are very basic in human life. The claim is that a life that lacks any one of these, no matter what else it has, will be regarded as seriously lacking in humanness. So it would be reasonable to take these things as a focus for concern, if we want to think how government can actually promote the good of human beings. The list provides a minimal theory of good. It is not meant to suggest that these are unrelated items; for in obvious ways they interact with one another, and interpenetrate one another. An example of interaction is the relationship between moving about and nourishing oneself. Aristotle notices that the two have to be looked at together, in the sense that our characteristic mode of nutrition, unlike that, for example, of sponges, requires moving from here to there. In this sense the two are made for one another. An example of interpenetration is the relationship between separateness and all of the others: whatever we do, we do as beings who are, each of us, "one in number," separate and distinct, tracing distinct paths through space and time.

At the same time, we must also notice that it is basic to the whole structure and motivation of the list that it is a list of *separate* components, components that may in principle conflict with one another as well as offering one another cooperation and mutual support. Concern for other species may or may not fit well with our efforts to feed ourselves, to be mobile, to be healthy. Our care for those close to us may or may not be harmoniously related to our cognitive self-development. The approach to the list through myths and stories promises that we will go on exploring the various items in many different imagined combinations, seeing how they support one another and where they conflict. And the whole approach being suggested here insists, throughout, on recognizing a plurality of good things, things distinct from one another in quality. The ethical and political situation the list puts us in is thus very much like the situation depicted in the polytheism of Greek religion. There are many divinities—that is to say, for our purposes, many areas of human life that claim our attention and reverence.[67] The quality of a life must be evaluated along all of these distinct dimensions. And yet the "gods" do not always agree—that is, one strand in our common humanness may not be harmoniously related to another, given the circumstances of life.

The Architectonic Functionings

We now notice a special case of interpenetration, one that is fundamental for our understanding of the list as a whole, and its political implications. Two of the human functions organize and arrange all of the others, giving them in the process a characteristically human shape. These two are: practical reason and affiliation. All animals nourish themselves, use their senses, move about, and so on—and all of this as beings one in number. What is distinctive, and distinctively valuable to us, about the human way of doing this is that all these functions are, first of all, planned and organized by practical reason, and, second, done with and to others.

These two functions are not simply two among others. They are the two that hold the whole enterprise together and make it human.[68] Human nourishing is not like animal nourishing, nor human sex like animal sex, because human beings can choose to regulate their nutrition and their sexual activity by their very own practical reasoning; and also because they do so not as solitary Cyclopes, (who would eat anything at all, even their own guests), but as beings who are bound to other human beings by relationships of mutual attention and concern. We may sometimes find in a putatively human life activity that lacks this humanizing character. Of the worker in his example, Marx writes:

> It is obvious that the *human* eye gratifies itself in a way different from the crude, non-human eye; the human *ear* from the crude ear, etc. . . . The *sense* caught up in crude practical need has only a *restricted* sense. For the starving man, it is not the human form of food that exists, but only its abstract being as food; it could just as well be there in its crudest form, and it would be impossible to say wherein this feeding-activity differs from that of animals.[69]

But the point is that this life is less than human, *a fortiori* surely not a good human life. Practical reason is both ubiquitous and architectonic. It both infuses all the other functions and plans for their realization in a good and complete life. And the same is true of affiliation. We do whatever we do as social beings; and the kind of deliberative planning we do for our lives is a planning with and to others.

At this point, we should return to Rawls. For we find Rawls's liberalism partially converges with the Aristotelian conception at this point. In Rawls's account of the person and the person's moral powers, and in his stipulation that principles are being selected for a life that is going to be shared with others, we find an approximation to our own requirements that a human life should be according to practical reason and affiliation. Rawls, like the Aristotelian, is prepared to rule out the conceptions of the good that do not make room for choice and practical reason: in this sense, as he explicitly says, there is an element of perfectionism in his theory. His recent work spells this out in even more detail, in terms of the two distinct moral powers. And he insists, further, that the political conception chosen must be such as to support the development of the moral powers in the citizens. Where affiliation is concerned, once again Rawls is Aristotelian. For he stipulates that the conception must be one by which citizens can live together in community, and he imagines the citizens as sociable beings, beings whose fundamental interest is to live with and toward others.[70]

But then it appears problematic that Rawls stops where he does, and refuses to move further in the direction of the Aristotelian theory. For the Aristotelian claim (which Marx endorses and develops) is surely a plausible one: that powers of practical reason are powers that require, for their development, institutional and material necessary conditions that are not always found. One would then suppose that citizens who value the moral powers in themselves and in others, and whose aim it is to select a conception of justice by which they can live well together in community, would take thought for those conditions, and think of good political principles not simply as principles regulating the distribution of the instrumental "primary goods" but, instead, as principles for the adequate realization of these and other fully human capabilities in the citizens. And this approach, as we have suggested, would seem to lead in the direction of a more sweeping reconsideration of labor relations, educational institutions, and other aspects of the form of life of the citizens than is promised in Rawls's "thin theory" of the good.[71]

Rawls's failure to move further in this direction is perhaps explained by his Kantianism. Perhaps he really does not think of the moral powers as interdependent with circumstances in the world, and in need of support from the world.[72] This tendency to separate the realm of morality from the empirical world shows up, in fact, in Rawls's failure to bring together the "thin theory" of the good embodied in the enumeration of primary goods with the theory of good embodied in the account of the two moral powers, saying how and whether the primary goods are understood as providing support for the moral powers.[73] We will return to this topic. But in order to deal with it well, we need to pursue in more detail the Aristotelian conception of the task of politics.

The Task of Politics, in Relation to the Thick, Vague Conception

The task of Aristotelian politics is to make sure that no citizen is lacking in sustenance.[74] With respect to each of the functionings mentioned in the thick vague conception, citizens are to receive the institutional, material, and educational support that is required if they are to become capable of functioning in that sphere according to their own practical reason—and functioning not just minimally, but well, insofar as natural circumstances permit. Politics examines the situations of the citizens, asking in each case what the requirements of the individual for good functioning are, in the various areas. Both the design of institutions and the distribution of resources by institutions is done with a view to their capabilities.

The Aristotelian aim should be understood along the lines of what has been called *institutional*, rather than *residual*, welfarism. That is, politics does not just wait to see who is left out, who fails to do well without institutional support, and then step in to bail these people out. Its aim is, instead, to design a comprehensive support scheme for the functionings of all citizens over a complete life. Aristotle's common meal plan, we recall, did not simply assist the poor. It subsidized the entire common meal program for all citizens, so that nobody could ever come to be in a situation of poverty with respect to that program. In a similar way, the Aristotelian conception (and Aristotle himself) promotes a comprehensive scheme of health care and a complete plan of public education for all citizens over a complete life,[75] rather than simply giving aid to all those who cannot afford private health care and private education. This way is defended as more equal and more just.

The Aristotelian uses the available resources to bring all citizens across a threshold into a condition in which good human functioning, at least a minimal level, can be chosen. In NFC, I give a more extensive account of this aim, in terms of levels of capabilities. To summarize briefly, the Aristotelian program aims at producing two types of capabilities: internal and external. Internal capabilities are conditions of the person (of body, mind, character) that make that person in a state of readiness to choose the various valued functions. External capabilities are internal capabilities plus the external material and social conditions that make available to the individual the option of that valued function. Internal capabilities are promoted, above all, by schemes of education, by health care, by appropriate labor relations. But over and above this the legislator must work to make sure that a capable individual has the chance to function in accordance with that capability: and this calls for another, slightly different, set of concerns with labor, and with the circumstances of personal and social life.[76]

In all of these areas, as I have said, treating citizens as free and equal means moving all of them across the threshold into capability to choose well, should the available resources at all permit this. The focus is always on getting more to cross the threshold, rather than further enhancing the conditions of those who have already crossed it. This is so for two reasons. First, because that is what it is to treat citizens as free and equal. Second, because, as we have noted, once a person has crossed that threshold, more is not necessarily better. The limit of money's usefulness in human life is set by its role in getting an individual across the threshold into good living; after that, more of it is not clearly better, and may well be worse. Good living may admit of degree: it may be that there are resources that will further enhance good functioning for someone already above the threshold. But, first of all, these are not likely to be found in the sphere of money and property, but, far more likely, in the sphere of education, and other goods that an individual who already has reached a certain level of capability can be expected to pursue on his or her own, given that capability. Thus if once the political structure makes available to each and every citizen education sufficient to bring them across the threshold—whatever we decide that ought to be—getting further still is something that they can reasonably be left to pursue on their own, and that they will be in a good position to pursue, given their already achieved capability level.

It should be noticed in what follows that the Aristotelian conception does not introduce a distinction corresponding to Rawls's distinction between the basic structure of society—in constructing which we are permitted to use only the thin theory of good—and the legislative stage, in which fuller information may be used.[77] For the Aristotelian, it would not be very clear how one might draw any such distinction, or what, in terms of it, ought to count as basic. Educational policy and structure, population policy,[78] a scheme of labor relations—all of these would presumably belong to a later legislative stage in Rawls's scheme; and yet for the Aristotelian they are absolutely basic, at least as basic, and perhaps more so, than the scheme of offices and concrete judicial and deliberative institutions. The Aristotelian finds choices in all of these areas important in making it possible for citizens to live well; and she sees no way of doing any of them well without consulting the entirety of the thick vague theory of good.[79]

If we now examine our list of basic capabilities, remembering that what we aim at in each sphere is the capability to function, in that sphere, according to both practical reason and affiliation, we can begin to imagine what the conception requires. It requires comprehensive health care; healthy air and water; arrangements for the security of life and property; protection of the autonomous choices of citizens with respect to crucial aspects of their medical treatment. It requires sufficient nutrition and adequate housing; and these are to be arranged so as to promote the choices of citizens to regulate their nutrition and their shelter by their own practical reason. (This would, for example, lead one to place emphasis on health education, drug education, and so forth.) It requires the protection of the capability of citizens to regulate their own sexual activity by their own practical reason and choice. (Here once again, support for educational programs would seem to play a crucial role.) It would require protection from assaults and other preventable pains. For the senses, for the imagination, and for thinking, it would require, beyond medical support, education and training of many kinds, aimed at the fostering of these capabilities; and the protection of the arts, as essential for the good functioning of imagination and emotion, as well as sources of delight. For practical reason, it would require institutions promoting a humanistic form of education, and the protection of citizen choices in all contexts, including the context of designing the political conception itself. For affiliation and the emotional life, it would require support for rich social relations with others, in whatever way it will emerge, through argument, that the institutional and political structures can best support and protect these relations. It would require reflective policies promoting due respect for other species and for the world of nature. It would require the provision both of recreational facilities and of forms of labor that permit the choice of recreation and enjoyment. And finally, for separateness, and for strong separateness, it would require protection of a sphere of noninterference around the person, larger or smaller, so that, according to practical reason and in relationship with others, each person can choose, in his or her own context, to lead his or her very own life.

The idea is that the entire structure of the polity will be designed with a view to these functions. Not only programs of allocation, but also the division of land, the arrangement for forms of ownership, the structure of labor relations, institutional support for forms of family and social affiliation, ecological policy and policy toward animals, institutions of political participation, recreational institutions—all these, as well as more concrete programs and policies within these areas, will be chosen with a view to good human functioning.

It would require more than one *book* to make arguments in each of these areas, saying what alternatives the Aristotelian would be likely to choose. But in order to give an idea of the depth at which the conception operates, designing the most basic things with a view to the good, we can make some preliminary comments about four areas: labor, property, political participation, and education. In each case I shall draw on Aristotle himself, who gives us a better idea than anyone else of what the Aristotelian conception requires.

Labor.

Aristotle notices a fact that frequently gets obscured from view in discussions of this sort, including most liberal discussions. This is, that some forms of labor are incompatible with good human functioning. Because they are monotonous and mindless, and demanding in their time requirements, they leave the worker less than fully human, able to perform other functionings only at a less than fully human level. Aristotle may have had too extreme a view about what forms of labor were like this (see NFC); but it is the beginning of progress to recognize that some in fact are. And Marx was especially indebted to Aristotle for his own reflections on this point.[80] Liberal discussion usually assumes that if we give people enough money and commodities, and guard against some especially flagrant abuses (abuses that count, for example, as diminutions of basic liberties), things will go well enough, and people will be able, at the close of the working day, to get on with their conceptions of the good, whatever they are. (This is especially true of liberal Kantianism, which tends, as we have said, to think of the moral personality as impervious to damage from the world.) The Aristotelian makes no such assumption.[81] The conception calls for a searching examination of the forms of labor and the relations of production, and for the construction of fully human and sociable forms of labor for all citizens, with an eye to all the forms of human functioning. Only that will count as treating people as both free and equal.

Property.

Land, money, and possessions are just things, and have no intrinsic worth. Thus there is no absolute right to property in the Aristotelian conception. The claim citizens have is to sustenance in their various essential functionings: to being brought across the threshold into capability for good human functioning. And the question about property must simply be, what form or forms of ownership best promote this situation? Best promote, that is, not only good functioning but the equal distribution of good functioning, in the sense that every citizen is to move across the threshold. In addressing himself to this question, Aristotle never seriously considers the possibility that all ownership should be private. This he considers highly divisive, inimical to sociability, and subversive of the stability and security of the polity. He considers, as we have seen, various combinations of common and private ownership, schemes where some private ownership is combined with common use, and also (as the agrarian nature of his polity requires) schemes in which some of the commonly owned land is held by individuals who are in charge of developing it.[82] What he asks in assessing these various forms is, what makes human functioning best? Or to take his other way of putting the question, what is it to treat citizens as free and equal?

It is important to notice that in defending *common* ownership Aristotle is not defending *state* ownership. Common ownership is in a very real sense ownership by all the citizens in common, and not by some remote bureaucratic entity. The Aristotelian conception must take thought for this distinction and its practical realization, since it is especially difficult to foster common ownership under modern conditions of size and population; and yet especially important to foster it, insisting on this distinction.[83]

Although Aristotle barely mentions the idea that there should be no common ownership, he does take very seriously indeed the idea that there should be no private ownership. This idea had been defended, of course, by Plato; but it was obviously attracting interest in other quarters as well.[84] Aristotle argues against it. And his arguments are of interest to us: for they show us exactly what role property plays, and fails to play, in the Aristotelian conception. There seem to be two areas in which Aristotle believes that some private property-holding will promote fully human functioning. One is the area of strong separateness. Aristotle believes that it is a basic human good that each person should go through life surrounded by a context that is, in part, just his or her own, into which nobody else can interfere. Property is a part of that context. This argument derives from older Athenian traditions: for Athenians prided themselves on the fact that they enjoyed a certain latitude and non-interference in their private dealings.[85] What is worth noticing is that the support for private property provided by this argument is contingent and controversial. If someone can show the Aristotelian that the particular kind of context of non-interference that separate functioning really requires does not, in fact, include private ownership, then the defense of private property, thus far, collapses. And Aristotle's insistence on common use—that it ought to be possible for a needy person to help herself to your crops, without penalty and with good will—shows that in any case he did not defend private ownership in the form in which most contemporary thought defends it.[86]

His other argument connects property with sociability, through an observation about human psychology. In *Politics* II, criticizing Plato, Aristotle observes that the thought that something is all your own makes a person care for something, and take responsibility for it, far more and more intensely than the belief that the thing in question is owned by many. Thus including some private ownership in the city will be useful, as an incentive to concerned, responsible, and energetic activity. Just as in a household with too many servants taking care of the tasks no task gets done well (he observes), so in a Platonic city no socially valuable task will be well looked after.[87] Similar arguments for a measure of private enterprise have recently been advanced in some contemporary socialist and communist countries. Here again, as with the first argument, we see that private property is supported only through a contingent instrumental argument, which will fall if at some time its psychological premises prove false.

Political Participation.

The Aristotelian conception is one in which all citizens share in ruling, as well as in being ruled. This is essential to the conception of what it is to treat citizens as both free and equal. More concretely, each citizen is a citizen in virtue of having two sorts of capability in the political sphere: legislative capability and judicial capability (see NFC).[88] But we must now ask why this is so according to the conception we have described. A welfarist conception need not be democratic, clearly. And since the Aristotelian aims at producing capabilities to function humanly, rather than at protecting natural rights, we need to ask in virtue of what argument this form is arrived at.

Aristotle's arguments are rather direct, since planning the conception of the good that shapes a citizen's life is a job that goes on, in part, in the political sphere. The argument is then, first, that good functioning in accordance with practical reason requires that every citizen should have the opportunity to make choices concerning this plan.

Aristotle's second argument cannot be set out in full here. It is, that in setting out fully and adequately the list of basic functionings that constitute the thick vague conception, we need to divide sociability into two parts, requiring for fully good human functioning both close personal relationships (friendships, family relationships) and also relationships of a political kind, the function that is constituted by playing one's role as a citizen alongside other citizens. The arguments that support this are set out in detail in *The Fragility of Goodness,* ch. 12.[89] They have a particular poignancy, since Aristotle, as a resident alien at Athens, had personal friendships without having political relationships. He is then judging, in effect, that his own life lacks something that is essential for fully good human functioning.

Finally, Aristotle appeals to the conception of political rule as a rule of free and equal citizens.[90] They are not free if they are treated despotically by a ruler and have no share at all in rule. Nor are they treated as equals if they are relegated to subordinate functionings while some king lords it over them. This does not mean that there is no room in government for expertise; nor does it mean that citizens can never delegate functions of some sorts to experts. It does mean that citizens should be judged by citizen juries selected in some representative way; and it means that some sort of democratic legislative body, either direct or representative, should make the major decisions concerning the conception. Citizens are not forced or required to participate. They are given what Aristotle calls "empowerment" (*exousia*). In Athenian terms, their names are in the lottery, although when a name comes up the person can always decline the function. This is Aristotle's way of respecting practical reason in the design of specifically political institutions.

Education.

No part of the political design occupies the Aristotelian as much as education. Education is required for each of the major functionings; and it is required, as well, for choice itself, as the Aristotelian insists. One distinctive sign of the Aristotelian conception, with its intense focus not only on functioning but also on truly human functioning within the various spheres of life, will be its tendency to make education a, perhaps the, central focus of planning, and to judge success in this aspect to be the hallmark of a successful political design (cf. *EN* II.1, *Pol.* VIII.1, and other refs. in NFC).[91]

The Aristotelian approach will be to specify vaguely certain capabilities that we wish to develop in citizens through education, and then, as Aristotle puts it, to behave like good doctors (EN X.9), looking responsively at the needs and circumstances of the varied groups of citizens and designing the structures of education in such a way as to bring them to those capabilities.[92] He envisages a combination of a more or less uniform public structure with a more flexible private education provided in and by the family. But there would be many other ways in which this combination of intimacy with community might be captured. The central point is that the Aristotelian will at each step look at what the citizens are actually able to do and be in virtue of their education, and will measure its success accordingly. It will not assume that merely providing resources for education is sufficient, especially where adverse circumstances exist, but will use imagination to design programs that will make it possible for disadvantaged groups to take full advantage of resources.

But the issue of education cannot usefully be discussed further without confronting, at least in a preliminary way, two of the most difficult issues it raises, issues on which the gap between the liberal and the Aristotelian appears to be especially wide. These are the issue of pluralism and the issue of choice.

Pluralism and Choice

The liberal's central motivation for operating without a "thick" conception of the good is to leave room for a pluralistic society, and to respect the equality of citizens as choosers of their own conceptions of the good, favoring no conception over any other. As we have noted, Rawls narrows the list of available conceptions considerably through his insistence on the two moral powers. But in the respects that are most important to someone thinking about the history of American democracy, Rawls's conception leaves the most divisive choices open. Citizens are not told what religion they must have, or even whether to have a religion. They are not told what forms of sexual conduct to adopt, or what professions to pursue, what recreations to enjoy. The liberal view about Aristotelianism is that it always involves opting for a single conception of good rather than a plurality; and that in the process it tells people what they should be, asking them (as Dworkin puts it) to live the life that a supremely wise man thinks would be best for them.[93] This is actually to remove their moral autonomy, and thus, from the liberal's point of view, to treat them *unequally*.

There is no issue to which the Aristotelian should be more sensitive than this one, since her ability to convince contemporary citizens of the merits of her view depends very much on the way these charges are answered. The first thing she must insist on is that her conception of the good, while thick, is in fact vague. That is, it is designed to admit of plural specifications, in a number of different ways. First of all, the constitutive circumstances of human life, while broadly shared, are themselves realized in different forms in different societies. The fear of death, the love of play, relationships of friendship and affiliation with others, even the experience of the bodily appetites—these never turn up in a vague and general form, but always in some specific and historically rich cultural realization, which can profoundly shape not only the conceptions used by the parties in these areas, but also their experience itself, and the choices they will make. To take just one example, developed at length in NRV, the sexual appetite will be both differently talked about and differently experienced in a society that does not contain several of the salient beliefs around which sexual discourse and experience are structured in our society, such as the belief in the moral salience of the gender of the object, the belief that each person has an inner sexual orientation that is relatively permanent and morally assessable, and so forth.[94] Nonetheless, as NRV went on to argue, we have in these areas of our common humanity sufficient overlap to sustain a common discourse, focusing on a family of common problems. And frequently the common discourse will permit us to criticize some conceptions of the grounding experiences themselves, as at odds with other things human beings want to do and to be.

When it comes to choosing a conception of good functioning with respect to these problems, we can expect an even greater degree of plurality to become evident. And here the Aristotelian conception wants to retain plurality in two significantly different ways: what we might call the way of plural specification, and what we might call the way of local specification.

Plural specification means just what its name implies: that the political plan, while operating with a definite conception of the good at a vague level, operates with a sufficiently vague conception that, while much is ruled out as inappropriate to full humanity, there is a great deal of latitude left for citizens to specify each of the components more concretely, and with much variety, in their lives as they plan them.[95] Some conceptions of the good are indeed ruled out by the insistence on our list of functions. But many alternatives are left in. For corresponding to each of the vague functions there is an indefinite plurality of concrete specifications that may be imagined, in accordance with circumstances and tastes.[96] Many concrete forms of life, in many different occupations, display functioning in accordance with all the major capabilities. And once we have imagined forms of labor that are not (as Aristotle thought all manual labor must be) oppressive to humanity, we will be able to describe a wide and open-ended number of concrete forms of employment, recreation, and so forth, answering to varied talents and tastes.

Where religion is concerned, the Aristotelian conception follows the lead of Aristotle himself. For if we examine his list of the virtues and consider what, from the point of view of Greek traditions, is missing, we notice a very striking omission. The virtue of piety, and proper behavior toward the gods, receives no discussion at all.[97] I believe that this is closely connected with the political nature of the list: the point is, that the lawgiver is to take no thought for this virtue in the design of institutions, beyond, apparently some supporting of specifically civic festivals. In part this protects the separate choices of citizens in that sphere: this was already in some ways an Athenian tradition. In part as well, it protects the cross-cultural character of politics for the concerns of the lawgiver are to be those that are broadly shared and shareable, whereas religion is seen as a sphere of local particularity. Our Aristotelian conception then, makes no special provision for religion, regarding it as one of the ways in which citizens may choose to exercise their powers of thought, emotion, and imagination; it protects the separateness with which they do this, and fosters a climate of non-interference.

In education, the Aristotelian aims at the cultivation of certain powers of mind, but she realizes that these general powers are developed in many different ways, by many different concrete courses of study. Here she will be likely to allow students a certain flexibility, increasing as their capability for choice increases, and structured in accordance with the assessment of the background and needs of the students in each case.

This brings us to the way of local specification. Aristotelian practical reasoning is always done, when well done, with a rich sensitivity to the concrete context, to the characters of the agents and their historical and social circumstances. This means that in addition to the pluralism we have described the Aristotelian must also consider a different sort of plural specification of the good. For sometimes what is a good way of promoting education in one part of the world will be completely ineffectual in another. Forms of affiliation that flourish in one community may prove impossible to sustain in another. In such cases, the Aristotelian must aim at some concrete specification of the general good that suits, and develops out of, the local conditions. This sensitivity will help the Aristotelian to answer the charge of paternalism.[98]

And yet we insist that the Aristotelian does not simply defer to local traditions, for example, where gender relations are concerned. She assesses them against her vague conception of the good. Comparing the current conditions with the vague conception, she imagines a possible transition from the current ways to some specification of the vague conception that fits that history and those circumstances. This is, in fact, what happened in our example from Bangladesh. Once the parties abandoned the idea that they could realize the good in Bangladesh in much the same way they might have in Europe, they were able to join with the local women to assess the current situation, to compare it with a possible transformation of that situation in which the women would realize a greater scope and dignity of activity, and to imagine specific forms of education that would assist, in those concrete circumstances, the transition from the current state to the state of greater capability.

Here we have a case in which cultures with radically different traditions in the areas in question confronted one another, with excellent results. These results were possible because the parties (Western women and rural women) recognized one another as fellow human beings, sharing certain problems and certain resources, certain needs for fuller capability and certain possibilities for movement toward capability. They were possible, as well, because both parties approached one another with the resources of imagination, emotional responsiveness, and humor, not simply with scientific facts and calculations— making possible a fully human interaction. (The prose of Chen's account, with its rich descriptive and evocative character, manifests the characteristics of mind that the Aristotelian approach needs to use in order to be fully rational.) Perhaps, too, the results were possible because the women did not identify so deeply with their current ways of life that they refused the invitation to imagine something different. Dissatisfaction and reflection in this way support and increase one another. But above all the confrontation was possible because the Aristotelian approach is not a paternalistic approach, as Dworkin and others have alleged, one that simply tells distant people what wisdom requires. It is an invitation to participate in a reflective adventure. And the claim is that the "thick vague conception" is only as valuable and as lasting as is its role in guiding such adventures. The parties are provided with a map of possibilities, or rather initiated into a dialogue about such a map—and then, after imaginative reflection, they are asked what they would choose.

Things will not always be so easy—though, indeed, it is not as if the issue of women's education is, in fact, a simple obvious issue, with a simple policy outcome. It is among the most divisive and the most urgent issues in the developing world, and it is great credit to the Aristotelian view if it can direct reflection about it. There will, however, be other questions that will prove still more deeply divisive, as traditions confront one another, and as each confronts its own internal diversities and conflicts. A society whose entire way of life rests upon adherence to policies that deprive members of a certain race, or class, or gender of the good human life will not be eager to endorse either the contents or the procedures of the Aristotelian list as essential for all human beings. Does this count against the Aristotelian conception?

Here the Aristotelian has three points to make. First, it can almost certainly be shown that the thick vague conception *is* endorsed by the opponent as central in his own life, and in other related lives for which he cares. He lives in such a way as to endorse it, even while he denies its importance, in debate, for others whom, by discourse and interaction, he implicitly recognizes as human beings. Second, the opponent's failure to endorse the full Aristotelian conclusion is (in this case of inconsistency, and in other related cases) explained by his failure to reflect and imagine, not by his successfully performing the Aristotelian procedure but arriving at different results. Sustained and searching reflection and imagining would have revealed the inconsistencies we have mentioned. And reflection, in modifying beliefs, would, sooner or later, modify the relevant emotions and desires. It should not count against the Aristotelian conception that people who fail to work through its procedures do not concur in its results (or, through it, agree with one another). Third, the conception is not intended to answer every difficult question. There will be many issues on which citizens disagree—especially when conceptions themselves are unclear or in process of evolution (as in the case of abortion)—where the Aristotelian list pronounces no decisive verdict for either side. The conception (as we shall see further below) directs government to protect the privacy of citizens in many areas. But it remains an open question, and one that should be settled in and through the evolution of reflective debate, how far and into what areas that protection extends.

There is much more to be said here, and most of it will have to be said concretely. But the claim is that the Aristotelian conception provides a richer and more promising starting point for further work on divisive social issues than do the thinner conceptions used by many liberalisms—and also than the fully determinate conceptions used by many forms of conservatism and communitarianism.

It is frequently charged that there is, in the kind of social democracy imagined in the Aristotelian conception, a deep tension between the value of well-being (and of public care for well-being) and the value of choice. As government more and more fully supports well-being, with a more and more comprehensive (if vague) conception of the good, it more and more removes from citizens the choice to live by their own lights. In much of the recent debate about the adequacy of welfarism in Scandinavia, for example, this tension is frequently alleged, and constraint on choice is assumed to be a result of the very structures that support functioning.[99]

The Aristotelian conception insists that this tension is, to a great extent, illusory. Human choice is not pure spontaneity, flourishing in spite of the accidents of nature.[100] The Aristotelian uses (and defends with argument) a more naturalistic and worldly conception of choice, according to which, as we have said, both the capability to choose good functioning within each sphere and the capability of choosing at all, quite generally, have complex social and material necessary conditions, conditions that are not likely to exist without strong government intervention. Marx's worker is not choosing to work as he works, even if he lives in a liberal capitalist democracy. Women in many, in fact almost all, parts of the world have not chosen the lives they lead, since frequently they have no conception, or a deficient conception, of alternatives and a confined list of possibilities. Choice is not only not incompatible with, but actually requires, the kind of governmental reflection about the good, and the kind of intervention with laissez-faire, that we find in Aristotelian social democracy.

In Aristotelian social democracy, citizens exercise choice in four ways. First, in every area of life, given the material and institutional provisions of the plan, they become capable of choosing to function well in that sphere (or not to, should they choose that). Second, given the political structure of social democracy, they also choose the plan: they are at every stage to feel not like sheep but like active participants. (This means that every effort should be made to dispel the idea that a large remote bureaucracy is doing the planning, and to encourage citizen participation. This is at the core of a certain disaffection with social democracy in Scandinavia; and we should guard against it.) Third, as we have said, citizens have choice in the sense of having many available options within the vague conception, given its vagueness.[101]

And finally, separateness and strong separateness have been read here to require the protection, around each citizen, of a sphere of privacy and non-interference within which what goes on will not be the business of political planning at all, though politics will protect its boundaries. What is in this sphere and how far it extends are matters for political argument; but the Athenian interpretation of this idea was that it included almost all speech, above all political speech, most of family and sexual life, and most, though not all, of one's dealings with personal friends.

An adequate account of this fourth sort of choice is absolutely essential, if the Aristotelian conception is to satisfy some of the strongest intuitions to which the liberal appeals. The conception needs a scheme of basic rights in order to give further definition to the concept of strong separateness. But we should notice that these rights will not be construed as the natural and more or less *a priori* starting point for political thought, as in some liberal conceptions (though not in all).[102] They will be justified with reference to the role they play in protecting a way of life that citizens have agreed to be good for them as human beings.

In this area the Aristotelian must diverge from Aristotle. For while Aristotle attaches significance to some parts of the Athenian tradition of citizen freedom—for example, to the privacy of the family and to the absence of restriction on political speech and participation—it must be admitted that the general question, "How far may government regulate people's daily lives, and in what ways?" had little interest for him.[103] He devotes to it no sustained analysis. Furthermore, some of his concrete recommendations are likely to horrify most liberals. Pregnant women are required to do exercise every day for their health. Abortions for population control are, in certain cases, not just permitted but required, as are certain types of infanticide. Ages for marriage and child-bearing are regulated by a stern scheme of incentives and disincentives.[104] It is all very well to point out that the urgency of problems of infant mortality and population control in his society explains these paternalistic injunctions; but this does not either explain or excuse the absence of sustained philosophical reflection on the limits of the law.

It seems to me that this type and this degree of paternalism are not intrinsic to the Aristotelian conception. In fact, I believe that a more consistent development of its basic intuitions about strong separateness and choice would be in the direction of a scheme of basic rights of the person. And I suspect that even Aristotle himself felt able to interfere so much in these cases because he was dealing above all with women, whom he did not admit as free and equal citizens,

and with children, who did not yet have adult citizen rights. He himself recognized
that the status of citizen called forth a greater restraint.

The issue of choice is deep. We cannot deal with it fully without a more
extended account (part of which I have tried to provide elsewhere) of what
it is to be an animal that chooses, and what it is to educate a child to become
such an animal. But it seems to me clear that the issue of choice is not all
on the side of the liberal, by any means. Indeed, the Aristotelian can turn the
liberal's charge back against him, arguing that there is a deep tension between
liberal *non*-intervention and the value of choice, since frequently the liberal
does not permit himself to do enough restructuring to make people really
capable of choosing.[105]

The Measurement of Welfare in Scandinavia

I have already made certain comparisons between the Aristotelian conception
and the Scandinavian social democracies. Now we can make the comparison
more concrete by describing a fascinating convergence. For in fact the strategies
by which both the Finnish and the Swedish governments have inquired into the
well-being of citizens replicate or parallel, to a surprising degree, the Aristotelian
approach and even the Aristotelian vague conception.[106]

The central intuition of the Scandinavian approach to welfare measurement is
that the human being is an active being who pursues good functioning in a number
of different areas. Each of these components is irreducible to any other; therefore
any good measure of how well people are doing will be a plural measure. The
quality of life will be assessed along all of these dimensions. Furthermore, what
we look for when we look at the lives of citizens (argues Robert Erikson, a
leading Swedish theoretician of the approach) is for their "capacity . . . to control
and consciously direct (their) living conditions; i.e., the individual's level of
living will be an expression of his 'scope of action'." In order to assess the lives
of citizens in this way, government researchers "must take a stand on which the
most central areas of human life are, the areas where it is most essential that the
individual can direct his living conditions."[107]

This approach, as Erikson and others insist, is fundamentally opposed to what
had been the dominant approach to the measurement of welfare prior to their work
namely an approach that measures quality of life by measuring the satisfaction of
desires or preferences. Feelings of satisfaction, argues Erik Allardt, pioneer of
the Finnish approach, are unstable and unreliable as measures of how well people
are doing. What we should do instead, he insists, is to look at what they are
actually able to do, what their functionings and choices actually are in many
different areas. Allardt gave his major book on welfare measurement the active
title *Having, Loving, Being* in order to indicate both the breadth of his concern
and its active character.[108]

The list of components of good living used by the Swedish researchers included, as Robert Erikson reports the following items:[109]

Components	Indicators
1. Health and access to care	Ability to walk 100 meters, various symptoms of illness, contacts with doctors and nurses
2. Employment and working conditions	Unemployment experiences, physical demands at work, possibilities to leave the place of work
3. Economic resources	Income and wealth, property, ability to cover unforeseen expenses up to $1000 within a week
4. Knowledge and educational opportunities	Years of education, level of education reached
5. Family and social integration	Marital status, contacts with friends and relatives
6. Housing and neighborhood facilities	Number of persons per room, amenities
7. Security of life and property	Exposure to violence and thefts
8. Recreation and culture	Leisure time pursuits, vacation trips
9. Political resources	Voting in elections, membership in unions and political parties, ability to file complaints

(Erikson notes that in an earlier survey questions were asked about diet and nutrition; but Swedish citizens resented such questions as an intrusion on privacy.)

The resemblance of this list to the Aristotelian list is striking though not surprising, given what we have said about the universal character of the thick vague conception. (In fact, more or less identical conceptions turn up in assessments of quality of life currently being used in medical practice and medical ethics.) The list is, from our point of view, somewhat unrefined. Some of the indicators are actual functionings, some resources for functioning, some capabilities. Had Erikson examined these distinctions further, more clarity might have been achieved. (In some cases, however, he can justify the shift as the result of reflection on a problem. For example, he deliberately decided that, given the subtle obstacles to the political participation of minority groups and women, one could not be convinced that an individual had actually been rendered fully *capable* of participating except by the fact that he or she *did* participate.) Some components of interest to us are omitted. The parallel Finnish survey, for example, asked about the citizens' relationship to nature and to animals, and about a wider range of social interactions.[110] And some of the items included are of unclear relevance: for example, it is unclear in what direction marital status is supposed to be an indicator of quality of life! Finally, some of the questioning does not go deep enough. The full quality of labor relations cannot be ascertained by these questions; there is no attempt to ask whether the holding of private property is in fact always a positive indicator of quality of life. But despite these flaws, the survey surely has more power than many comparable measures to inform government of the really important things, the things with which its work is most centrally concerned.

The results of the survey were used in the way recommended by the Aristotelian conception. Where the data showed a lower level of capability in some area or areas for some identifiable subgroup of the population—women and elderly people figured prominently here—the government set to work to imagine a response, aiming at the fuller integration of these groups into good human living. Erikson concludes his study by contrasting Swedish social democracy with the liberalisms of other Western nations:

> I would suggest that poverty is the main welfare problem to social liberalism while inequality is the main problem to social democracy. . . . To social democracy state activities are not only a supplementary mechanism, but one on par with the market. In an institutional welfare state a redistributive model of social policy includes provisions to cover basic needs for all citizens.

This contrast is perhaps somewhat unclearly expressed; for liberalism is very much concerned with equality, in its own way. Erikson's point is perhaps better expressed by saying that liberalism and social democracy are concerned with equality in different ways.[111] Liberalism focuses above all on giving resources. (And as Erikson notes, this is frequently connected with a willingness to rely on the market, except where poverty or severe hardship is produced.) In social democracy the concern for equality is a concern for equal capability to live well over a complete life. Government activity provides comprehensive and not just supplementary support, operating with a partially comprehensive conception of the good.

Aristotle and the Liberal

This has been a sketch. And much more work remains to be done to elaborate its parts, and to show the relationship of each part to various claims made by different versions of liberalism. But instead of beginning that larger task here, I want instead, in concluding, to focus once again on the basic intuitive idea of the Aristotelian conception, contrasting it as clearly as possible with some of the intuitive underpinnings of Rawls's Kantian liberalism.

Rawls's Kantian constructivism uses an idea of the person that is in many respects a Kantian idea. The person[112] is characterized above all by the two moral powers and not, for example, by needs, or vulnerabilities. The basic structure of society is seen as an expression of the parties' moral personhood in the arrangement of the available resources. Persons are understood to need resources for the various things they do and choose; in this sense Rawls's Kantianism is empirical. But their need and their dependency is not exactly the focus of the conception's intuitive idea, nor of its account of the moral powers themselves. This interpenetration between person and nature is not imagined as going very deep, in the sense that once necessary things are to hand, all is well. No deeper consideration of the structure of relatedness between persons and things—or, indeed, persons and one another—is called forth by the Kantian idea of the person. For although Rawls's is indeed an empirical Kantianism, it retains some part of the Kantian tendency to separate the moral realm from the natural, and to think of moral personality as creating a realm of its own, a realm to some extent distinct from and independent of the natural realm. I am saying this vaguely, since it is only vaguely that I have been able to get at these intuitive features of liberal Kantianism. But I think that the Kantianism does important work here, and that we must focus on it if we are to understand at a deep level the difference between the two conceptions.

The Aristotelian conception, by contrast, begins from the intuitive idea of a being who is neither a beast nor a god. This being comes into the world (the single world there is, the world of nature) characterized both by certain basic powers and by amazing neediness—by rich neediness, we might say, borrowing a phrase from Marx, in the sense that the very powers of this being exist as needs for fulfillment and claim, for their fully human development, rich support from the human and the natural world. This being's good must always be pursued as a system of complex relations of dependence between the agent and unstable items in the world, such as friends, loved ones, food, water, a city of fellow citizens. Government is "a sharing for the sake of the good life,"[113]—that is, a complex series of cooperative stratagems devised to protect and support citizens in their eating, moving, loving, and choosing, so as to convert their basic powers into fully human capabilities for choices of functioning. Human activity always goes on in complex interdependence. The task of politics must be to imagine forms of interdependence that are human rather than slavish, and to forge those circumstances, where possible, in the world.[114]

Notes

1. On the distinction between ownership and use, see *Politics* II.5 as a whole; for an excellent discussion of the history of this distinction in Greek political thought, see Newman (1887), commentary on II.5.

2. *Pol.* 1332b25–7; cf. 1325b7, 1334a27–9.

3. It is not possible to make a sharp distinction between the ethical and the political in discussing Aristotle's views, since for him the task of politics is to secure to all the citizens the conditions of a complete good human life, and an essential element in the complete good life is political activity (see below). Thus Aristotle explicitly describes his ethical writing as a part of political inquiry. This is an important difference between his views and various forms of liberalism; we shall study its implications below.

4. Nussbaum (1988, 1990a, 1990c).

5. The institute is the World Institute for Development Economics Research (WIDER), Helsinki, a branch of the United Nations University. For the work that has been done so far in the project on defining the quality of life, see Nussbaum and Sen (1990).

6. Thus Rawls explicitly limits his discussion to the conceptions of "a modern constitutional democracy" (Rawls (1985) 224), and his discussion of the relevant historical issues focuses on the Enlightenment and debates over toleration—thinking clearly, above all, of the English and American versions of these debates, and not about the rather different histories even of other European democracies, for example those of Scandinavia. Dworkin's discussion is even more explicitly American: in Dworkin (1985) he refers to many concrete examples from the current American debate, provisionally defining liberalism in terms of positions on these issues.

7. Rawls (1971) 8 ff. limits the discussion to the principles that should govern the basic structure of a single society; he opposes the application of the principles discovered in the original position to questions of justice between nations. In Rawls (1985) the scope of the discussion has contracted further, since now the results are said to hold only for the basic structure of society in a group of nations that share a certain history and certain traditions: "Whether justice as fairness can be extended to a general political conception for different kinds of societies existing under different historical and social conditions, or whether it can be extended to a general moral conception, or a significant part thereof, are altogether separate questions. I avoid prejudging these larger questions one way or another" (225).

8. See Brundtland (1987) for an eloquent statement on this issue; on hunger see Dreze and Sen (1990); on women's issues, and on the general question of justice in relation to national boundaries, see O'Neill (1990).

9. Aristotle: cf. *EN* (*Ethica Nicomachea*) 1103b26–31, 1179a18–20, 1179a33–b4; for discussion and further references see Nussbaum (1986a). For Rawls's statements on this issue, see especially Rawls (1980) 516–19, 554 ff. See also Rawls (1971) 46–53.

10. *Politics* 1323a 17–19. For a full discussion, and other references, see NFC.

11. For textual references and discussion, see NFC and also Nussbaum (1988a). Cf. esp. *Pol.* 1323a17–19, 1324a23–5, 1325a7, *EN* 1103b2–6.

12. Rawls (1971) 396. For further development of the view of primary goods, see Rawls (1982) and (1988).

13. See especially *Politics* I.8, VII.1. On the excessive attention to wealth in Sparta, *Pol.* 1270a11 ff., where the large inequalities of resources produced by the Spartan system are also criticized. For a typical example of Aristotle's attitude to money—as necessary in order to avoid the constraints of poverty, but productive of excessive luxuriousness if present in too large a quantity, see *Pol.* 1266b 24–6. It is interesting to note that *isotēs,* the Greek word for "equality," also means a "middle" amount; and when Aristotle says that there should be *isotēs* of resources, he plays on this double meaning (1266b24), contrasting the "equal" with the deficient and the excessive.

For contemporary discussion of these issues, see Nussbaum and Sen (1990): especially the papers by Sen and Cohen.

14. On Phaleas, see *Pol.* 1266a39 ff., and for discussion see NFC.

15. See Dworkin (1981, 1985).

16. Rawls (1971) 396. Rawls (1982, 1988) refine and expand the list, making it far more heterogeneous and focusing less attention on wealth. Thus the latest version of the list in Rawls (1988) divides primary goods into five categories: (1) basic rights and liberties; (2) "freedom of movement and free choice of occupation against a background of diverse opportunities"; (3) "powers and prerogatives of offices and positions in the political and economic institutions of the basic structure"; (4) income and wealth; (5) the social bases of self-respect. Rawls suggests he is willing to add other goods, "for example, leisure time, and even certain mental states such as the absence of physical pain." On the one hand, this alteration of the list addresses some of the Aristotelian's criticisms, since it now includes a number of human capabilities that the Aristotelian, too, regards as basic human goods. But insofar as it does so, the new list seems to depart from the original notion of "primary goods," the notion of all-purpose means that are neutral among conceptions of the good. Rawls (manuscript) shows that he still wishes to maintain the original conception, against Sen's more Aristotelian proposal;

thus there now seem to be considerable tension and ambiguity in the position. In NFC I discuss the original list proposed in (1971), criticizing it from an Aristotelian position.

17. See *Pol*. VII.1, and the discussion in NFC. Here the Aristotelian conception and Aristotle are explicitly and fully together.

18. See Sen (1980, 1987); I compare Sen's conception to Aristotle's in NFC.

19. Cf. *Pol*. VII.1, and note 13 above.

20. See especially *Rhet*. II.15–17, discussed in Nussbaum (1986) 339–40. The bad effects of wealth include insolence, arrogance, and a mercenary attitude to other valuable things.

21. On Milo, see *EN* 1106b3, and the discussion in "The Discernment of Perception" in Nussbaum (1990). For Sen's statements of similar points, see (1980, 1984, 1987). Aristotle discusses the nutritional and exercise needs of pregnant women at *Pol*. 1335b12 ff.

22. On women's capabilities and the support they require, see Sen (1984, 1985). The relationship between Sen's views and Aristotle is discussed in NFC. Aristotle does not take exactly this view of women, since he does not consider them at all capable of living a fully good human life under any circumstances; but he does say that they should have what is required for living the sort of good life that is open to them; and throughout the *Politics* he manifests concern for the nutrition and development of women. On children, he explicitly commits himself to the idea that each child should get whatever it, as an individual, needs in order to flourish—cf. EN 1180b7 ff., where this idea is used to defend the role of the family in education.

23. See Rawls (1988) and especially Rawls (manuscript).

24. On the moral powers, see Rawls (1980).

25. See Rawls (manuscript); Dworkin (1981).

26. Throughout *Politics* II, Aristotle repeatedly points to the many ways in which regimes, whether or not they have a *theory* of the good, nonetheless commit themselves, through their policies, to some definite conception of the good.

27. Here the Aristotelian view develops a point that Aristotle's own emphasis on the plural and noncommensurable nature of the components of the good life makes natural; and to some extent Aristotle himself recognizes the possibility of such conflicts—see Nussbaum (1986) ch. 11 and "Discernment of Perception" in Nussbaum (1990). But he does little with this point, and tends on the whole to believe that the claims of the different components will be in harmony. For some further observations on this point, see Nussbaum (1990b).

28. For ancient analogues to various aspects of the utilitarian position, see Nussbaum (1976) and (1986) ch. 4. Aristotle attributes to Protagoreans the view that all appearances are true (*Metaph* IV)— a view which, in the area of ethics, would have related implications.

29. See Rawls (1971) 258–65: "The upshot of these considerations is that justice as fairness is not at the mercy, so to speak, of existing wants and interests. . . . Both justice as fairness and perfectionism establish independently an ideal conception of the person and of the basic structure so that not only are some desires and inclinations necessarily discouraged but the effect of the initial circumstances will eventually disappear" (261–62). See also Rawls (1988).

30. The point is most frequently expressed as a criticism of the thesis that pleasure is identical with the good: cf. *EN* VII.11–14, X.1–4; cf. also the account of "bestial vice" and of desires malformed through bad experiences in *EN* VII.5, 1148b15 ff.

31. See Sen (1984, 1985, 1987), O'Neill (1990), and Allardt (1990). Speaking of the policies of the Finnish model of welfare research, Allardt writes: "To base the choice of welfare criteria entirely on the subjective views of the people themselves is therefore likely to lead to an unfruitful conservatism."

32. This question is not independent of desire (cf. NFC); for it is, in effect, to ask what they *would* desire if their education and knowledge of alternatives were above the threshold of what is required for practical reason and choice. Thus Dworkin (1985) is misleading when he suggests that a procedure of this sort asks what some ideally wise man would choose *for* others, as if this is a person they have no chance of being. In Aristotle's view, the good human life is in principle "common to many: for it is open to all who are not maimed with respect to excellence, as the result of a certain learning and

concern" (*EN* 1099b18–20). It is up to politics to create the conditions in which this learning can take place.

33. For further discussion of Aristotle's views on this point, see NFC and HN, with further textual references; and cf. Sen (1985).

34. This does not imply that it is easy to draw the line between capability and actual functioning, or to tell when the absence of a function results from choice, rather than from the absence of a capability. On this problem, see Williams (1987).

35. Marx (1844), in Tucker, pp. 88–89: see the discussion in NFC. Another section of this passage is cited and discussed below. On Marx's debt to Aristotle during this period, see de Ste. Croix (1981) especially 69 ff.

36. See the related discussion in Marglin (1974).

37. See Rawls (1971), Dworkin (1981, 1985). A much discussed limitation of Rawls's account of distribution is his assumption that the subjects of distribution are "heads of households" who will act on behalf of the interests of their families. On the limitations of this position where women's issues are concerned, see Okin (1987). Dworkin, unlike Rawls, explicitly assumes that ownership of resources will be private: see Dworkin (1981) pp. 283, 290. One might also note that (again, unlike Rawls) Dworkin appears to rely on actual uncriticized preferences, leaving the market mechanism to do the screening. Thus his view is less likely than is Rawls's to ask certain critical questions.

38. On Aristotle's sweeping rejection of all manual labor from the lives of citizens, see below n. 80 and accompanying text.

39. Chen (1986).

40. This example also shows how the Aristotelian approach insists on being sensitive to context and history, making judgments that suit all the particular features of the case and balancing an ongoing interest in the general conception with concrete perceptions. See "Discernment" in Nussbaum (1990) and the further discussion of Chen's example in Nussbaum (1990a). Both of these papers discuss Aristotle's own view about particular perceptions, with textual analysis and references.

41. On the faculties of the good legislator, see "Discernment" in Nussbaum (1990), and Nussbaum and Sen (1989).

42. Dworkin distinguishes his own view from a view that he finds both in Marxism and in various forms of conservatism, namely, the view "that the content of equal treatment cannot be independent of some theory about the good for man or the good of life, because treating a person as an equal means treating him the way the good or truly wise person would wish to be treated" (1985, pp. 191–92). Although he does not explicitly name Aristotle here, the description certainly coincides with some versions of Aristotle that are frequently accepted, especially through the Catholic tradition. Rawls is more explicit, contrasting his view with the "perfectionist" views of both Plato and Aristotle (1988, pp. 254, 272–73, cf. also 1971, pp. 25, 325). Admittedly, Aristotle's supporters frequently contribute to this situation, portraying his account of the good as metaphysical: see, in very different ways, MacIntyre (1981, though the view is different in 1987), Williams (1985). Williams's very interesting account of Aristotle on human nature is discussed in HN. For an example of the Catholic use of Aristotle to ground a sectarian metaphysical theory of the good, see Maritain (1943).

43. Note, however, that the theory has grown "thicker," and closer to Aristotle's; see above n. 16.

44. *EN* 1098a20–23; for full discussion of this passage, see HN.

45. For this terminology, see Charles Taylor (1989, 1990); compare the use of the idea of a "model of man" in Putnam (1987). It will be seen that the Aristotelian account of the human being, as I construe it, is closer to what Rawls calls a concept of the person than to what he calls a theory of human nature, in the sense that it is an evaluative conception, constructed within human society: see HN. But it is a conception of a being who is essentially embodied and dwelling in the world of nature—cf. below; in this way it is importantly distinct from Kant's conception of the moral agent.

46. See MacIntyre (1981), Williams (1985): both, in general sympathetic to Aristotle, find a serious difficulty for his account at this point.

47. On the role of reflection about beasts and gods in arriving at a conception of the human, see HN, Nussbaum (1986), and "Transcending Humanity" in Nussbaum (1990).

48. See HN for a further account of this procedure; on the way in which a sense of species identity sets bounds to aspiration and well-wishing, see *EN* 1159a8–12, 1166a19–23.

49. An obvious problem is that some agents who ask this question will arbitrarily exclude certain humans from humanity; and Aristotle himself is guilty of this, in his reflections on women and natural slaves. On how the Aristotelian approach can confront this difficulty, see HN; and also Nussbaum (1990b).

50. This is true of many lists that have sometimes been taken as closed and normative: for example, the list of the "four causes" in the *Physics;* usually Aristotle is explicitly open-ended about what his account has produced.

51. HN approaches the list by focusing on the two architectonic capabilities, and briefly describes the limits; NRV focuses on the limits, as they give rise to a unitary debate about the virtues. Here I try to put these pieces together.

52. Lucretius *De Rerum Natura* V. 989: cf. Nussbaum (1989).

53. Aristotle discusses mortality in *DeAnima* II.4, and in the discussions of courage in the ethical works. See also Nussbaum (1989) and "Transcending Humanity" in Nussbaum (1990).

54. On the role of the body in the conception of the human being, see also NRV; and on Aristotle's view of the unity of soul and body, see Nussbaum and Putnam (1990).

55. *EN* 1119a7–10. NRV holds that appetitive desire is culturally shaped, and pursues the implications. On cultural invariance in nutritive need, however, see Gopalan (working paper). Aristotle recognizes the political importance of nutrition throughout the *Politics:* see NFC, and refs. above.

56. The need for shelter is a central theme in Greek myths about the "human condition": see, for example, Protagoras' speech in Plato's *Protagoras,* and Aeschylus' *Prometheus Bound.* Aristotle does not very much stress this feature, but he takes its importance for granted. His preferred definition of "house" is "a covering that prevents destruction from rain and wind and heat" (*De Anima* 403b3–4—he is not as happy with the attempt to define it as "stones and bricks and timber"). *Politics* VII.11 discusses the selection of the city's location with a view to the health of the citizens, asking what winds are healthy, etc., and pursuing the question of a healthy water supply.

57. NRV discusses a Stoic argument that holds the belief that pain is bad to be a cultural artifact; this view seems highly implausible, although one should certainly grant that *conceptions* of the painful and the pleasant are shaped by cultural learning. Rawls now is willing to add the absence of pain to the list of primary goods: see above n. 13.

58. *Metaphysics* I.1; see the discussions in NRV and HN. HN discusses Aristotle's view that not every child born of two human parents is human: in the absence of a certain basic level of capability (see NFC) the judgment of species membership cannot be made, since being human is, as we have argued, an evaluative matter.

59. For a related account of the story of a human life, see Wollheim (1986); in NRV I discuss the views of Klein (1984) about the emotional life of the young child. According to all major ancient philosophers, Aristotle included, emotions are closely linked to belief, and can be changed by change of belief; in Aristotle's view they are partly constituted by beliefs. This being the case, there is a great deal of room for the cultural shaping of emotion, as Epicureans and Stoics were quick to point out. But given that all cultures hold some beliefs about the great importance of items external to the agent and difficult to control (i.e., there has never been a thoroughly Stoic culture), every culture will have some analogue of emotions such as grief, anger, love, and fear. On this see also Lutz (1988).

60. On practical reason and affiliation, see HN.

61. On this part of human life, see Allardt (1990), who convinced me that NRV had been defective in omitting it from the list. In one way, this element is very Aristotelian, since Aristotle insists throughout on thinking of the human being as an animal and a natural being among others, and on the beauty and interest of all natural creatures (see *Parts of Animals* I.5). On the other hand, it must be acknowledged that the ethical works do not take an interest in any ethical issues arising out of these facts; and the *Politics* tends to treat animals and plants as valuable only insofar as they subserve human ends. This seems to me an odd tension in Aristotle, perhaps to be explained by the early date of some parts of the *Politics,* before Aristotle's years of biological research. See, however, *Pol.* I.5, where he briefly considers the animals' own interests.

62. Aristotle's emphasis on this element is striking: see *EN* IV.6–8. Few moral philosophers place so much emphasis on this. Rawls is now prepared to consider adding leisure time to the list of primary goods (above n. 13): and to this the Aristotelian would no doubt say that the time itself is valuable as a space for a certain sort of human activity, namely what Aristotle calls *diagogē meta paidias* and *homilia emmelēs* (passing the time with play, and harmonious association, *EN* 1127b33 ff.).

63. This is based on the general Aristotelian requirement that substances be "one in number" and "separate": cf. *Metaph* V.7, VII 1, etc. For an excellent account of the position and its intuitive credentials, see Wiggins (1980). The Plato reference is to *Laws* 739c.

64. "Strong separateness" is defended by Aristotle in his criticisms of Plato in *Politics* II: see Nussbaum (1980). The separateness of persons is fundamental to Rawls's critique of utilitarianism: cf. (1971) 554 ff.

65. Here I leave to one side the very difficult problems connected with Aristotle's defense of the contemplative life in EN X.6–8; in (1986) Appendix to ch. 12 I argue that this passage is in a number of important ways inconsistent with the overall argument of the *EN*. It is especially inconsistent, it seems to me, with passages that insist on circumscribing aspiration and well-wishing by considerations of kind membership, explicitly ruling out the transition to the divine (above n. 48).

66. On confronting the limits, see Nussbaum (1989) and "Transcending Humanity" in Nussbaum (1990).

67. See Nussbaum (1986) chs. 2–3, Nussbaum (1990b).

68. See HN.

69. Marx (1844) in Tucker, pp. 88–89, discussed in NFC.

70. See Rawls (1980, 1985, 1988).

71. Despite Rawls's expansion of the list of the primary goods, he is still clearly opposed to this idea: see especially the discussion of "civic humanism" in (1988) 272–73.

72. There are, of course, other motivations: above all, the desire to find a conception that can win an "overlapping consensus" from citizens of different religious and ideological backgrounds: see, for example, (1988) 256.

73. In a fairly obvious way, the basic rights and liberties provide support for the moral powers; but this element in the list of primary goods is logically not parallel to, for example, income and wealth: for it is itself a set of human capabilities, not a tool whose point is seen only in connection with the capabilities. What Rawls does not investigate, it seems to me, is the role of goods like income and wealth in making possible the development of a person who will have the capability of choosing a conception of the good.

74. On this task, see the further discussion in NFC.

75. The notion of the complete life is central in Aristotle's conception of *eudaimonia*, and in his thought about what a human being is generally. Its political influence can be seen in his concern to provide for functions that are specific to a particular time of life (see *Pol*. VII.14). Compare Rawls's notion of the citizens as "normal and fully cooperating members of society over a complete life" (1988, p. 270).

76. See NFC; the line between internal and external is difficult to draw, and it is always hard to say when a failure to function is due to external circumstance, when to absence of inner capability, and when to the individual's choice. (On this problem see Williams [1987].)

77. Rawls (1971) 195 ff.

78. Aristotle is very much concerned with population policy, and criticizes previous legislators for not devoting enough time to this: see for example *Pol*. 1266b8 ff. Aristotle's concerns with the issues that are faced today by development economists have in general been too little described and emphasized in the literature: in part, because philosophers tend not to be interested in these issues, in part because of the still prevailing tendency to think of ancient Greece as the ancestor of modern Europe, rather than as a developing country. (See NFC 170–71).

79. On the importance of considering the list as a whole, see NFC n. 30, and cf. Sen (1987).

80. For Aristotle's views about manual labor, cf. NFC; Marx's own emphasis on leisure for workers was certainly very much indebted to Aristotle. Aristotle's view was that neither farming nor any form

of manual labor was compatible with the functions of the citizen. The Aristotelian conception should depart from Aristotle on this point, while not failing to press the Aristotelian question about the relationship between forms of labor and full humanity. Ancient Athenian political ideals contain a richer conception of the laborer: the plays of Aristophanes, especially, reflect a tradition that ascribes political value to the type of practical intelligence involved in the activities of the farmer and craftsmen. In our own political tradition, the poems of Walt Whitman provide helpful models; I discuss Whitman's relation to ancient Greek democratic traditions in "Discernment," in Nussbaum (1990).

81. See Nussbaum (1986) chs. 11–12.

82. See esp. *Pol.* II.9–10, VII.10.

83. For example, by encouraging worker-owned businesses and other forms of worker control.

84. See *Pol.* II.3–7, and Newman's commentary.

85. On Athenian traditions in this regard (with particular reference to Thucydides' portrait of Periclean ideals), see "Discernment" in Nussbaum (1990). The insistence of Athenians on the integrity and separateness of the body is especially striking: see Halperin (1989).

86. One might fruitfully compare to this housing policies that have been adopted in some socialist and social-democratic countries, giving the homeless certain rights toward unoccupied or luxury housing.

87. *Pol.* 1262a32–40.

88. Cf. *Pol.* 1275a22–23, 1275b18–20, 1276a4–5.

89. Nussbaum (1986): cf. *Pol.* III.5, VII.9–10.

90. On the development of the ancient Athenian conception of freedom and the free citizen, see Raaflaub (1985).

91. On education, see further in NFC. Rawls (1988) 268 allows the state to take a limited interest in education, insofar as children are viewed as future citizens. But note that his conception of the citizen is more circumscribed than is Aristotle's, and the state's concern with education will be correspondingly limited. (For example, the state will presumably not be able to concern itself with the role played by literacy and other forms of education in promoting nonpolitical types of functioning—although Rawls does allow it to take thought for the citizens' being "economically independent and self-supporting members of society over a complete life . . . all this from within a political point of view.")

92. In this connection, NFC discusses the approach to education embodied in Buck (1945).

93. See Dworkin (1985).

94. See Foucault (1984), Halperin (1989); the issue is discussed in NRV.

95. On the different types of further specification of ends, see NRV. Plural specification may be either individual or communal: societies too may choose among available options for instantiating a particular function. But very often the society's history, traditions, circumstances, and other ends will make the appropriate choice rather more circumscribed. This is how "local specification" (below) differs from "plural specification": in plural specification the idea is one of choosing from among a plurality of available options, in accordance with tastes; in local specification the idea is one of finding the appropriate way of instantiating a certain function, given awareness of one's traditions, circumstances, etc. Obviously the two interact and overlap in complex ways.

96. Here modern interests in individual self-discovery and self-expression move the contemporary Aristotelian away somewhat from Aristotle—but less than one might think, since Aristotle too values the contribution of diverse experiences of life (see *Pol.* III.15 on the analogy between deliberation and a public feast); and Aristotle, too, thinks of the good human life as a development and full expression of capabilities. On different ingredients of the modern sense of identity in this regard, see Taylor (1989).

97. Piety is typically one of the five main virtues in lists of virtues—along with courage, moderation, justice, and wisdom. See Plato's *Protagoras* for an example. But morality and religion are less distinct in Greece than they are for us, and there is little sense of the religious as a separate sphere of exalting spiritual experience. The gods protect spheres of value, and honoring the divine is above all acting so as to show respect for the valuable.

98. On education, see NFC and Buck (1945). For criticism of monolithic approaches to curricular planning, see Nussbaum (1987). For further discussion of local specification, see NRV.

99. See the essays in Graubard (1986).

100. See Nussbaum (1986) ch. 9.

101. It is especially important to notice that Aristotle believes it is possible to deliberate rationally not only about instrumental means to ends, but about the constituents of the end themselves—even about constituents of *eudaimonia*, the ultimate end. On this see Wiggins (1975), Richardson (1986).

102. Dworkin (1985), however, has an instrumental understanding of rights that comes closer to this aspect of the Aristotelian position.

103. See Barnes (1989).

104. See, for example, *Pol.* VII.16 on the regulation of marriage and pregnancy, VII.17 and VIII on the regulation of physical and cultural education. The issue is thoroughly discussed in Barnes (1989), with further references.

105. In this connection one might recall the well-known exchange on freedom between Margaret Thatcher and Neil Kinnock: she asserting that the policies of Labour would diminish citizens' freedoms, he replying that it was only on account of such policies that he and others like him had had the freedom to choose a university education.

106. See Allardt (1975, 1976, 1990); Erikson (1990), Erikson et al (1987), Galtung (1980), Graubard (1986), Vogal et al. (1988).

107. Erikson (1990).

108. Allardt (1975), discussed in Allardt (1990). The Finnish approach places greater emphasis on the delineation of valuable types of personal affiliation than does the Swedish approach, and also includes consideration of the individual's relationship to animals and the world of nature. Procedurally, it employs both objective and subjective indicators, though, like the Swedish approach, it focuses on the former, asking above all how individuals are actually doing. Another important contribution of this approach is its (very Aristotelian) use of the concept of a threshold of good living in each of the various areas, below which no individual should be: see Allardt (1990).

109. Erikson (1990).

110. See Allardt (1990).

111. See Sen (manuscript).

112. Notice that even the fact that the basic notion is that of *person* rather than that of *human being* is significant: on this difference, see Wiggins (1980), Williams (1985a). Kant, at least, intended the rational to be a genus of which the human (the "animal rational") was just one species: and morality to be based on rationality rather than on our specific humanness, far less on our animality.

113. See for example *Pol.* 1328a37–8.

114. I am especially grateful to Henry Richardson for encouraging me to develop these ideas in the first place, and for giving me extensive and searching criticisms; thanks are also due to Gerald Mara and the others present at the Georgetown conference for their helpful comments. I am grateful to Amartya Sen for discussion of the issues. Much of this work was done at WIDER, Helsinki (see n. 5); I gratefully acknowledge the support of the Institute during the period of writing.

Bibliography

Allardt, E. 1975. *Att ha, Att Älska, Att Vara. Om Wälfärd i Norden. (Having, Loving, Being. On Welfare in the Nordic Countries.)* Borgholm: Argos, 1975.
———.1976. "Dimensions of Welfare in a Comparative Scandinavian Study." *Acta Sociologica* 19: 227–40.

———.1990. "Having, Loving, Being: An Alternative to the Swedish Model of Welfare Research." In Nussbaum and Sen, 1990.

Barnes, J. 1989. Paper presented to the 9th Symposium Aristotelicum on the *Politics*. Published in the Proceedings of the Symposium, ed. G. Patzig.

Brundtland, G. H. 1987. *Our Common Future*. Report of World Commission on Environment and Development.

Buck, P. et al. 1945. *General Education in a Free Society: Report of the Harvard Committee*. Cambridge, MA: Harvard University Press.

Charles, D. 1988. Comments on Nussbaum 1988. *Oxford Studies in Ancient Philosophy*, Supplementary Volume.

Chen, M. 1986. *A Quiet Revolution: Women in Transition in Rural Bangladesh*. Dhaka: BRAC.

Chodorow, N. 1978. *The Reproduction of Mothering*. Berkeley and Los Angeles: University of California Press.

Dalenius, T. 198 . *Privacy in Surveys: a Scandinavian Problem*.

Dreze, J., and A. Sen, 1990. *Hunger and Public Action*. Oxford: Clarendon Press.

Dworkin, R. 1981. "What is Equality? Part 2: Equality of Resources." *Philosophy and Public Affairs* 10: 283–345.

———.1985. "Liberalism." In *A Matter of Principle*. Cambridge, MA: Harvard University Press: 181–204. Originally published in S. Hampshire, ed., *Public and Private Morality* (Cambridge: Cambridge University Press, 1978).

Erikson, R. 1990. "Descriptions of Inequality. The Swedish Approach to Welfare Research." In Nussbaum and Sen, 1990.

Erikson, R., E. Hansen, S. Ringen, and H. Uusitalo, eds. 1987. *The Scandinavian Model. Welfare States and Welfare Research*. London: M. E. Sharpe, Inc.

Foucault, M. 1984. *The History of Sexuality*, Vol. 2. Trans. R. Hurley. New York: Pantheon.

Galtung, J. 1980. "The Basic Needs Approach." In K. Lederer, ed., *Human Needs: A Contribution to the Current Debate*. Cambridge, MA: Oelgeshlager, Gunn, and Hain.

Gopalan, C. Forthcoming. "Undernutrition: Measurement and Implications." Paper prepared for the WIDER Conference on Poverty, Undernutrition, and Living Standards, Helsinki, July 1987. To appear in the Proceedings, ed. S. Osmani, Oxford: Clarendon Press.

Graubard, S. R., ed. 1986. *Norden: The Passion for Equality*. Oslo: Norwegian University Press. Original published in *Daedalus*.

Halperin, D. 1989. *One Hundred Years of Homosexuality and Other Essays on Greek Love*. New York: Routledge, Chapman and Hall.

Klein, M. 1975. *Love, Guilt, and Reparation and Other Works 1921–1945*. London.

———.1984. *Envy, Gratitude, and Other Works 1946–63*. London.

Lutz, C. 1988. *Unnatural Emotions*. Chicago: University of Chicago Press.

MacIntyre, A. 1981. *After Virtue*. South Bend: University of Notre Dame Press.

———.1987. *Whose Justice? Which Rationality?* South Bend: University of Notre Dame Press.

Marglin, S. 1974. "What Do Bosses Do? The Origins and Functions of Hierarchy in Capitalist Production," Part 1. *Review of Radical Political Economics* 6: 60–112.

Maritain, Jacques, 1943. *The Rights of Man and Natural Law*. New York: Charles Scribner's Sons.

Marx, K. (1844). *The Economic and Philosophical Manuscripts of 1844*. Trans. M. Milligan. In *The Marx-Engels Reader*, ed. R. C. Tucker, New York: 1978.

Newman. W. 1887. *Aristotle's Politics: Text and Commentary*. Oxford: Oxford University Press.

Nussbaum, M. 1976. "Consequences and Character in Sophocles' *Philoctetes*." *Philosophy and Literature* 1: 25–53.

———.1980. "Shame, Separateness, and Political Unity: Aristotle's Criticism of Plato." In A. Rorty, ed., *Essays on Aristotle's Ethics*. Berkeley and Los Angeles: University of California Press, 395–435.

———.1986. *The Fragility of Goodness: Luck and Ethics in Greek Tragedy and Philosophy*. Cambridge: Cambridge University Press.

———.1986a. "Therapeutic Arguments: Epicurus and Aristotle." In M. Schofield and G. Striker, eds., *The Norms of Nature*. Cambridge: Cambridge University Press.

———.1987. "Undemocratic Vistas." A review of Allan Bloom, *The Closing of the American Mind*. *The New York Review of Books:* November 5.

——.1988. "Nature, Function, and Capability: Aristotle on Political Distribution." *Oxford Studies in Ancient Philosophy,* Supplementary Volume: 145—183.

——.1988a. "Reply to David Charles." *Oxford Studies in Ancient Philosophy,* Supplementary Volume.

——.1989. "Mortal Immortals: Lucretius on Death and the Voice of Nature." *Philosophy and Phenomenological Research:* December.

——.1990. *Love's Knowledge: Essays on Philosophy and Literature.* New York and Oxford: Oxford University Press and Clarendon Press.

——.1990a. "Non-Relative Virtues: An Aristotelian Approach." In Nussbaum and Sen, 1990. An earlier version published in *Midwest Studies in Philosophy,* 1988.

——.1990b. "Reply to Onora O'Neill." In Nussbaum and Sen, 1990.

——.1990c. "Aristotle on Human Nature and the Foundations of Ethics." In J. Altham and R. Harrison, eds., a volume in honor of Bernard Williams. Cambridge: Cambridge University Press.

Nussbaum, M., and H. Putnam, 1990. "Changing Aristotle's Mind." In a volume of new essays on Aristotle's *De Anima,* ed. M. Nussbaum and A. Rorty. Oxford: Clarendon Press.

Nussbaum, M., and A. Sen, 1989. "Internal Criticism and Indian Rationalist Traditions." In M. Krausz, ed., *Relativism: Interpretation and Confrontation.* South Bend: University of Notre Dame Press: 299–325.

Nussbaum, M., and A. Sen, eds. 1990. *The Quality of Life.* Oxford: Clarendon Press.

Okin, S. M. 1987. "Justice and Gender." *Philosophy and Public Affairs* 16: 42–72.

O'Neill, O. 1990. "Justice, Gender, and International Boundaries." In Nussbaum and Sen, 1990.

Putnam, H. 1981. *Reason, Truth, and History.* Cambridge: Cambridge University Press.

——.1987. *The Many Faces of Realism.* La Salle, Ill.: Open Court.

Raaflaub, K. 1985. *Die Entdeckung der Freiheit.*

Rawls, J. 1971. *A Theory of Justice.* Cambridge, MA: Harvard University Press.

——.1980. "Kantian Constructivism in Moral Theory: The Dewey Lectures 1980." *The Journal of Philosophy* 77: 515–72.

——.1982. "Social Unity and Primary Goods." In A. Sen and B. Williams, eds., *Utilitarianism and Beyond.* Cambridge: Cambridge University Press: 159–86.

——.1985. "Justice as Fairness: Political Not Metaphysical." *Philosophy and Public Affairs* 14: 223–51.

——.1988. "The Priority of Right and Ideas of the Good." *Philosophy and Public Affairs* 17: 251–76.

——.Manuscript. "Reply to Sen." Now part of the revised Dewey Lectures.

Richardson, H. 1986. *Rational Deliberation of Ends.* Ph.D. diss., Harvard.

de Sainte Croix, G. E. M. 1981. *The Class Struggle in the Ancient Greek World.* London: Duckworth.

Sen, A. 1980. "Equality of What?" In *Tanner Lectures on Human Values,* I, ed. S. McMurrin. Cambridge: Cambridge University Press. Repr. in Sen (1982).

——.1982. *Choice, Welfare, and Measurement.* Oxford: Basil Blackwell.

——.1984. *Resources, Value, and Development.* Oxford: Basil Blackwell.

——.1985. *Commodities and Capabilities.* North-Holland.

——.1987. *The Standard of Living.* Tanner Lectures on Human Values 1985, ed. G. Hawthorne. Cambridge: Cambridge University Press.

——.Manuscript. *Inequality Reexamined.*

Taylor, C. 1989. *Sources of the Self: The Making of Modern Identity.* Cambridge, MA: Harvard University Press.

——.1990. "Explanation and Practical Reason." In Nussbaum and Sen, 1990.

Vogel, Joachim, et al. 1988. *Inequality in Sweden: Trends and Current Situation.* Stockholm.

Wiggins, D. 1975. "Deliberation and Practical Reason." *Proceedings of the Aristotelian Society:* 29–51. Repr. in Wiggins, *Needs, Values, and Truth,* Oxford: Blackwell, 1987.

——.1980. *Sameness and Substance.* Oxford: Basil Blackwell.

Williams, B. 1985. *Ethics and the Limits of Philosophy.* Cambridge, MA: Harvard University Press.

——.1985a. "Hylomorphism." *Oxford Studies in Ancient Philosophy* 4: 189–199.

——.1987. Comments on Sen, "The Standard of Living." in Sen, 1987.

Wollheim, R. 1986. *The Thread of Life.* Cambridge, MA: Harvard University Press.

11

The Search for a Defensible Good:
The Emerging Dilemma of Liberalism

R. Bruce Douglass and
Gerald M. Mara

Section 1

Liberalism not only values pluralism; it is itself highly pluralistic. Especially
now it presents itself as a complex mix of different tendencies. This is so even
if attention is confined just to the Anglo-Saxon variants, and as times goes by,
the more complex the mix seems to become. Largely because of the extraordinary
vitality that liberal theory has enjoyed of late, it presents the spectacle of an ever-
expanding array of diverse possibilities, with each new alternative acting as an
invitation to the creation of still others. From Rawls to Nozick to Ackerman to
Rorty, the "family" just keeps growing.

It is hardly to be expected, therefore, that an investigation which takes at all
seriously the self-understanding of contemporary liberalism will yield any simple
conclusions. Given the multiplicity of different versions of liberal teaching that
can be invoked, there is almost certain to be variation—and controversy—in the
way that the issues in question are addressed even among those who count
themselves as supporters. As the reader no doubt has already observed, even
among the contributors to this volume who see themselves advancing the liberal
cause, there is no small amount of disagreement about how to proceed in meeting
the challenge that talk about "the" good poses.

These differences notwithstanding, in at least one crucial respect there is
surprising unanimity. Despite the fact that liberal theorists have been urged of
late, especially by John Rawls,[1] to pursue a defense of liberal political theory not
dependent on anything approaching a comprehensive or full view of what is of
value in human life, the participants in this discussion are inclined to follow a
different path. More or less explicitly, they frankly acknowledge the impossibility—and indeed even the undesirability—of separating the analysis and defense
of liberalism as a political teaching from a distinctive stand on the matter of how
life ought to be lived. Whether the good in question be construed as commodious
living or the autonomy of a selective self or mutual respect or irony, repeatedly

the arguments encountered in these pages take for granted the necessity of basing the case for liberalism on some such commitment.

Nor is there much inclination evident, either, to treat the goods in question as obvious—or noncontroversial, as Rawls would say. The critics, such as Stephen Salkever and Kenneth Schmitz, obviously find much to question in the conception(s) of the good which they attribute to liberal theory. And the defenders end up conceding the point by the lengths to which they go in elaborating one or another defense or affirmation. Brian Barry, in pointing to the threat posed to liberal values by various enemies, provides the most obvious illustration. But those who invest themselves in the elaboration of a case for the extension of liberal theory and practice in one or another new direction also bear witness, by both the tone and the substance of what they have to say, to the fact that the basis for their claims is anything but uncontroversial. The entire drift of Bruce Ackerman's defense of his particular brand of neutrality, for example, reflects the sense that the appeal of the goods it is meant to serve cannot be taken for granted. And Amy Gutmann and Dennis Thompson build the case that they do for mutual respect because, once again, the value they wish to see placed on it is by no means universally shared, even in societies (such as the United States) where liberal ideas have been influential.

This is a recognition that we welcome, and it is one we take to be an important advance. The project of a moral and political theory which could accomplish the purposes that liberals have embraced and still remain neutral about the ends of human life we have long felt to be misguided, and the departure from that way of conceiving of the liberal project in the sort of thinking that finds expression in these pages we find salutary. Even though it entails a turning away from Rawls's notion that liberalism as a political theory can be defended as an overlapping consensus cutting across different and even incompatible conceptions of the good,[2] it bespeaks a self-critical clarity of intent which can scarcely help but render more coherent and intelligible what is actually at stake in the liberal project. The acknowledgment that there is no getting around the question of the good clears the way, moreover, for it to be taken up directly—which, in our judgment, is exactly the step that needs to be taken. If liberalism is indeed, Rawls's dissent notwithstanding, another partisan doctrine, with its own distinctive conception of the goods that should have priority in the ordering of our lives, then it should be defended as such. And liberals should address themselves to *that* task, above all.

Once this is admitted, however, problems arise—of just the sort that the proponents of liberal neutrality have had it in their minds all along to avoid. One is simply to specify, in defensible terms, what the good in question is. Given the variety of different branches that the liberal "family" today includes, this in itself is by no means easy. And beyond it lies, in turn, the even more formidable challenge of making the case for the priority of the good favored by liberals over the alternatives. This means, among other things, showing how it is that such partisanship can be reconciled with the value that liberals have historically prided themselves on placing on toleration. If priority is indeed attached to a particular way of life, how at the same time is it possible to be open to competing alternatives in the manner that liberals have professed to favor?

It is a tall order, and difficulty almost certainly attends any serious effort to meet it. But to date at least, it has not proved to be altogether unmanageable. For in point of fact there is already in liberal theory, both past and present, a response that, superficially at least, more than fits the bill, and it is for this reason, in turn, that we believe liberalism has been as successful as a political theory as it has in fact turned out to be.

The spirit of this response is succinctly captured in a characterization of the aims of the liberal project that Barry offered some years ago in a book-length critique of Rawls's *Theory of Justice.* Liberalism, he said, is an outlook on life that "exalts self expression, self-mastery and control over the environment, natural and social; the active pursuit of knowledge and the clash of ideas; the acceptance of personal responsibility for the decisions that shape one's life."[3] This same endorsement is put even more succinctly in his chapter in this volume when he praises liberalism for fostering "the spirit of critical thinking and the practice of autonomous decision making."[4] Thus conceived, the liberal good turns out, above all, to be a certain kind of freedom, and what an accent on this particular good allows—or *seems* to allow, at least—is a recognition of the right of others to live by their own priorities as they see fit. In the words of R. M. Hare, "[w]hat distinguishes the liberal is that he respects the ideals of others as he does his own. This does not mean that he agrees with them . . . nor does it imply that he lacks confidence in his own ideals . . . it is part of the liberal's ideal that a good society, whatever else it is, is one in which the ideals and interests of all are given equal consideration."[5] The openness that this entails has manifest attractions, and it is, we would propose, one of the principal reasons why liberalism has come to enjoy the appeal that it has. For it seems, ingeniously, to provide a way of both accepting and getting around the necessity of choice.

But, as Barry's claim implicitly demonstrates, the more carefully one examines what precisely is involved in pursuing the agenda that liberals typically have derived from thinking in these terms, the more evident it becomes that things are not quite what they initially seem. For the attribution of priority to freedom in the sense liberals typically envisage is in actuality not nearly so tolerant or neutral as it first appears, and the more experience we have with liberalism in this respect, the more obvious this becomes. The closer we come to realizing freedom in the liberal sense, the more evidence there is that it is purchased as a definite price. As its more realistic proponents (Barry among them) have been inclined to acknowledge all along, certain goods—and ways of life—are promoted at the expense of others. It goes without saying, for example, that the legislative agenda pursued by the ACLU is not equally conducive to the realization of the goods valued by all of the affected parties. And the freedom to exploit natural resources such as the Amazon rainforest would contribute to the realization of certain goods while being utterly destructive of others. So choice turns out, in fact, to be inescapable. And so does the need for justification. The obvious costs or exclusions that stem from the liberal exaltation of freedom would seem, in fact, to make a justification for offering this particular answer to what Barry sees as "the unanswerable but irrepressible question of the meaning of life"[6] more important than ever.

But such justification seems slow in coming, and one may wonder, still, after all that is said about the subject, whether anything like a body of argument adequate to the task has been or indeed even can be produced. For as the saga of the development of the liberal tradition plays itself out, the more evident it becomes how difficult it is to meet the challenge in question on the terms on which it has to be confronted. For once it comes to be acknowledged that the fiction of freedom's neutrality can no longer be sustained, the choice that presents itself to the liberal theorist is a stark one: either to continue to adhere to freedom as the primary good but face up squarely to the necessity of defending it as a partisan good in competition with other goods; or alternatively, to acknowledge the need for developing another way of thinking about the good that is somehow more inclusive of goods other than freedom but at the same time still in keeping with liberalism's historic identity and purposes.[7]

The very fact that such a choice has to be confronted, however, only complicates the problem. For the two options lead, perhaps inescapably, in very different (if not opposite) directions, and the more they are pursued, the more obvious this can be expected to become. For as freedom is pursued more vigorously, limits upon it begin to appear more and more as oppression, while any attempt to specify a liberal good other than freedom implies the potential if not the necessity of limiting freedom's influence. Thus, each path compounds the problem of justification by calling into question the most basic and fundamental assumptions of the other. There is a dilemma in the making here, and it promises, we believe, to pose as formidable a challenge as any that liberal theory has confronted in the past. Indeed, it could well turn out to be even more so. For what is at stake is the coherence of the liberal project every bit as much as its justification, and it is not at all to be taken for granted that it will be successfully addressed. This above all is the moral that we draw from the papers collected in this volume, and in the pages that follow we mean to show why this is the case.

Section 2

The claim that we are advancing about the priority attached to freedom in liberalism is hardly novel, of course. And given the nature of the themes that are characteristically invoked by liberal parties and regimes, it has a prima facie plausibility about it. It is not for nothing that the standard that is most often invoked by liberals in public life to judge the success of policies and institutions is the contribution they make to the realization of freedom. The good society in its liberal manifestation is, as its defenders consistently suggest, a society that cherishes and promotes the good of freedom.

It goes without saying, however, that the defense of the constitutional protection of civil and political liberties is one thing and the commitment to personal freedom in the sense Schmitz has in mind when he speaks of the "selective" self is quite another. And it is not at all necessary that a commitment to the one implies an attraction, much less a dedication, to the other. Liberals have long been among the staunchest supporters of the sort of public liberty that we associate with the invocation of the rights of citizens. But is it appropriate, also, to impute to them an inclination to seek the more fundamental opportunities for choice which Schmitz has in mind?

In this regard, as others, there is a lot more to liberalism than meets the eye. As Salkever in particular reminds us, liberal practice seems to reveal a preoccupation with a great deal more than just the single good of freedom and, in keeping with its own spirit, the deceptively simplistic designation "liberal theory" itself would seem to enclose a plurality of goods. Hobbes's fundamental commitment to individual survival, for example, and Bentham's mission to extend pleasures and limit pains are hardly identical. And together they appear remote, to say the least, from Mill's attachment to the fully developing individual and Rawls's elevation of the just, self-respecting human being who is both creatively active and socially aware. It would be foolish to claim that this chorus of different commitments can or should easily be reduced to the song of a single voice. However, for all of their variety they do have shared premises. And it is not implausible that those premises influence, perhaps decisively, the more particular and distinctive concerns to which they give expression. One, for example, is that politics is justifiable only by appeal to the well being, rights, or claims of individuals. Thus, the social science of the major liberal thinkers emerges, virtually without exception, as some form of methodological individualism.[8] In this respect, at least, Ackerman and Connolly are the heirs of Hobbes and Bentham. And this explanatory style has its evaluative counterpart in the recognition of the normative importance of the person as both the purpose and the limit of politics. In Robert Nozick's famous statement, no state or group of individuals should *dare* do more or less than further the voluntary and interactive choices of its members.[9]

By itself, though, this premise seems inclusive of much more than liberalism. It is not, for example, at all incompatible with a properly understood Aristotelianism in which the *polis* is prior *(proteron)* to each of us individually only because of the assistance which it offers in our endeavor to become virtuous or excellent representatives of our species.[10] However, this latter notion is challenged decisively by a second premise which is generally characteristic of the liberal argument. This is its rejection of teleology, or the claim that there is a discoverable excellence or optimal condition (be it simple or complex, precise or vague), which characterizes human beings *qua* human beings. Such early liberals as Hobbes and Locke rejected this concept of human excellence because of its incompatibility with materialism or empiricism. More contemporary liberal theorists, usually under the influence of Kant, see the identification of a human *telos* as subversive of the free rationality and autonomy which characterizes *human* beings.

To be sure, the differing grounds for these liberal denials of teleology result in the endorsement of often strikingly different alternatives. Salkever seems completely justified in finding the praise of commodious living at the heart of early liberal theory. Yet this tendency to rest content with the "delightful" enjoyment of civil interests is challenged by both Mill's implicit dissent from Benthamite utility and Kant's discovery of a rationality freer than heteronomous calculation. What both sets of alternatives and their parallel descendants have in common, however, is the insistence that the individual who justifies and limits politics is both able and entitled to choose his own course of action, his own life plan, without being constrained by some sort of excellence or perfection which is thought to be appropriate for members of the entire species. As important as the commitment to commodious living is to Hobbes and Locke, then, it is clear that they do not think of it as an independent good. For both men, the accumulation of property emerges as the most natural and constructive fruit of a free existence.[11] And when later liberals such as Kant, Mill, and Rawls, in contrast, dismiss a life dedicated exclusively to material comfort as servile, if not base, it is in large measure from a point of view committed, once again, to a certain kind of freedom. It is, as much as anything, the narrowness of a way of life absorbed in the production and consumption of material goods to which they object, and what they hold out as the corrective, in turn, is a respect for the plurality of the different types of goods that are in principle available to human beings.[12]

Moreover, even when liberal theorists contemplate imposing restraints upon the exercise of freedom or identifying various human excellences, they would appear to do so for the purpose of furthering a more complete realization of the life of freedom. Thus, when Mill and Bentham set limits on individual behavior for the sake of the general good, they construe the general good as aggregated individual satisfaction or individual expression.[13] Rawls's Kantian constraints on the selection of principles of justice are intended to exert a broadly regulative influence only, by setting formal limits or boundaries upon rather than by offering substantive goals or examples for the choices of rational and reasonable individuals.[14] Likewise, for both Mill and Rawls the excellences emerge as those qualities explicitly valued by expressive or autonomous persons. Just as Mill identifies desirability through inspecting the phenomenon of desiring, we may hypothesize that he assesses admirability on the basis of what is admired. Perhaps the educated and those of finer feeling identify the excellences as well as the higher pleasures.[15] Their preferences may well be the implicit basis for Mill's saying that it is better to be Pericles than either John Knox or Alcibiades.[16] Similarly, Rawls's free and equal partners to the original position determine the content of the virtues by deciding what qualities they rationally desire in one another.[17] Thus, the substance of the virtues selected seem more than incidentally related to the qualities required for intelligent choice and personal autonomy and responsibility.[18]

For all of the various goods which its better-known proponents espouse, therefore, there is still a definite uniformity and consistency to liberal teaching that can be traced to the one-sided priority attached to the good of freedom. To be sure, the variety is real because the various "lesser" goods in question are seen as contributing essentially to the life of freedom, and for this reason freedom is not a "dominant" end in the restricted Rawlsian sense.[19] But still, the priority of freedom limits the kinds of goods which can be reasonably endorsed. Perhaps the most important limitation for our immediate purposes is the resistance it imposes to anything resembling a teleological understanding of human excellence. It is no accident, for example, that Rawls sees any effort to defend the claim that forms of culture should help to realize human excellence as objectionably perfectionist.[20] Or that Mill praises the activities that he does *because* they are our own. Or that liberal theorists in general tend to see all deliberate attempts to influence character formation politically as species of oppression. What William Galston calls Locke's "ontological neutrality" in the *Letter Concerning Toleration*, the claim that "the coercive weapons at the disposal of civil society could not possibly achieve their purported end—the inculcation of true belief or faith," rests on the assumption that the *only* means for politics to affect private beliefs is through compulsion or manipulation.[21] Mill's similar attitude leads him to replace the commitment of the incomplete progressives with a very different perspective on liberty. "They have occupied themselves rather in inquiring what things society ought to like or dislike than in questioning whether its likings or dislikings should be a *law* to individuals."[22] This political distrust of teleology by liberals extends very clearly to this volume, in which Bruce Ackerman warns us against "all sorts of intolerant public pronouncements about the nature of 'human flourishing.' "

Section 3

There are innovations aplenty, to be sure, involved in the migration from the way of thinking that finds expression in the *Second Treatise of Government* to that of *On Liberty,* much less *A Theory of Justice,* but they do not entail any essential discontinuity in the way that the logic of liberty is understood. All along, it has been a matter of emancipating selves from the constraints imposed by pre-established values and identities, and the more recent emphasis on individuality simply reflects the extension of this tendency ever more deeply—and widely—into the constitution of the self. Locke himself may not have been inclined to place quite the same emphasis on self-*creation* that Mill or Rawls does, but the path down which he moves, especially in the *Letter Concerning Toleration,* clearly leads in that direction.

This is a project, moreover, which is manifestly still being worked out. As the chapters by Bruce Ackerman and William Connolly in this volume in particular illustrate, there is still a great deal more that could be done to expand the opportunities available to individuals for self-creation. In fact, what they have to say reflects, too, the sense that for all of the appeal which the idea of self-determination has come to have in modern societies, its fulfillment has really only begun. Both write with a sense, which is distinctly reminiscent of Mill, that the freedom for selves to be (and become) what they would choose to be is by no means to be taken for granted, and that indeed it continues to be a "fragile" good that is in constant danger of being overridden by one or another alien power. And the purpose of the enterprise in which they are engaged, in turn, is to deepen and enlarge the liberal commitment in precisely this direction.

This means, inescapably, a radicalization of what is at stake in the pursuit of freedom. Ackerman, for example, would seem to have in mind the possibility of extending the scope of conscious self-creation into practically every imaginable aspect of our existence, and the drift of what he has to say is to suggest that any infringement on the freedom to explore such opportunities which is not voluntarily adopted should be considered suspect. The point of the sort of neutrality he advocates is precisely to preclude any such thing from taking place. For if the exercise of power (and he has in mind, clearly, *all* forms of it) were ever actually to be required to be justified through the sort of dialogue he recommends, then presumably it would be virtually impossible for adults, at least, to fall involuntarily under the sway of other selves. Not just in public life, but in virtually every other domain as well, conscious, autonomous self-creation would unambiguously become the norm.[23]

The thing that is truly striking about this argument, moreover, is the single-mindedness with which the good of self-determination (and implicitly, self-creation) is treated as an end in itself. Although Ackerman notes in passing that there are other, even "better" things in life about which one might be concerned, the thing that clearly matters above all else in the sort of "critical" perspective he seeks to provide is establishing the priority of personal autonomy. Nothing reveals this more clearly than what it is that he has to say about dialogue. For unlike a figure such as Jurgen Habermas, who also displays a definite interest in the ethics of public discourse, Ackerman sees the purpose of political dialogue as being essentially restricted to the critical examination of prospective power relationships.[24] The sorts of constraints that he seeks to impose as strategies for justifying one's position affect, then, his very conception of public life. The accent is entirely on containing power and thereby promoting freedom. Anything else, especially substantive exchanges of views on other goods that might conceivably be pursued, is discouraged. And the clear implication in all that he says is that only such claims as are compatible with this purpose should have a place in public life.

Connolly has much the same objective, it would appear, but is inclined to pursue it, of course, in a rather different manner. Indeed, opposite, in a sense. For the constraints that Ackerman would like to see imposed on public discussion would appear to be—albeit in a very distinctive form—just the sort of repression of individuality in the name of a general good that Connolly thinks needs to be resisted. He maintains that *any* established institutional order or way of life is inclined to have this effect, however, so the only reliable way to insure what liberalism purports to be about is a politics of paradox that refuses to take *any* settled identity as anything more than a "contingent artifice." And one that invites, in turn, continuous, ongoing contestation against the cruelties and subjugations that are inherent in any attempt to establish a common life.

Connolly thus goes Ackerman one better, in effect, by insisting, on the basis of what he characterizes as a reverence for the inexhaustible plasticity of human existence, not only on enlarging the opportunities available to individuals to define their own identities, but also on refusing to take any particular definition (no matter how worthy on other grounds, presumably) as settled. And on making the resulting ferment and change into an integral part, in turn, of the ethos of public life. He readily concedes, to be sure, that to some extent politics must be about the adoption and pursuit of common purposes. But no less, he insists, it must also be a medium through which such purposes are exposed and unsettled. And it is precisely the allowance for such a contestation of established identities that makes a good society good, in the neo-Nietzschean sense he has in mind.

None of this, however, is self-evident. Or, more precisely, it is persuasive only if one is inclined to adopt some of the same controversial assumptions as Ackerman and Connolly make. In particular if one is not disposed to attach to the autonomy of persons quite the same priority—and meaning—that they favor, it makes little sense to embrace the type of politics they have in mind. Few arguments illustrate better Barry's observation that it takes a mind already committed to liberal values to appreciate liberal reasoning. And the really striking thing, in turn, is how little either author is given to making any sort of apologetic case for his most basic assumptions. Both chapters have a decidedly stipulative character that leaves the *reasons* for thinking in the way being commended largely unexplained.[25]

What also becomes evident, too, is how contestable are the assumptions on which both arguments rest. Not only does Ackerman rest his case, for example, on one very distinctive (and debatable) view of what "the" problem of political life is, but he clearly takes for granted a very distinctive notion of what can and cannot be accomplished through dialogue. Not only the *assertion* of partisan claims concerning the good but even their argument or defense is forbidden because of the (unspoken) assumption that no meaningful conversation about matters of this sort can possibly take place. For the good of the *intelligibility* of public discourse, he insists, such restraint must be observed, but this makes sense only if one subscribes to a very severely restricted view of the kinds of claims which are "intelligible." And it assumes, too, that one is willing to explain away the seemingly obvious empirical fact that in actuality people with differing views are sometimes able to reach, through collaboration, some degree, at least, of agreement about what sorts of behavior ought to be encouraged (and the reverse).

It takes little scrutiny of the argument Connolly advances, furthermore, to see that he, too, relies on another version of the self-same skepticism. From the bold proposition that "there is no true identity" the reader is swept quickly along to the implication that any conceivable identity that might be chosen is as good as any other, and the clear implication is that there is in fact no way, other than resort to force, to adjudicate among the arguments that might be advanced for and against other available options. The point, indeed, is precisely to preclude the possibility that any such undertaking might be taken seriously as anything other than a threat to individuality. "[A]ny set of enabling commonalities is likely to contain corollary inquiries, cruelties, subjugations, concealments, and restrictions worthy of opposition and contestation."

The other thing that can scarcely help but be noted, also, as arguments of this kind unfold, is how much of what they imply turns out, in practice, to have an unmistakably restrictive character. It is an old story, of course: one person's rights are another's constraints. But in the case(s) under discussion here, the constraints in question are nothing short of severe, and they go to the very heart of what public life is all about. The surgery that Ackerman asks us to consider performing on our "expressive repertoire" is anything but minor, and it is difficult to imagine how it could have any effect other than to eliminate much of what now constitutes the substance of political discourse as we conventionally think of it. In spite of Ackerman's apparent willingness to embrace what Rawls distrusts, namely a partisan liberalism, in the end he agrees with Rawls that liberal political discourse depends for its viability on significant exclusions. And Connolly, in like manner, would seem to have it in mind that the pursuit of the common good should be undertaken stripped of the one thing which, to date at least, has made it make practical sense—that is, the conviction that the grounds for the choice in question were more than just the contingencies of self-fabrication.

Section 4

Little wonder it is, in turn, that as the ramifications of such proposals come into focus, liberals themselves are uneasy with the results. Especially is this so when it is grasped how much of an attenuation of the terms of public discourse is at stake. For as Amy Gutmann, Dennis Thompson, and William Sullivan observe in different ways, a politics predicated on the assumption that discourse about the *res publica* can somehow be carried on without reference to people's most deeply held moral (and other) convictions can scarcely help but seem arbitrary and artificial. It would seem to be directly at variance, moreover, with one of the most pressing needs of our time. In a day and age when the trend is unmistakably toward the assumption of an ever greater collective responsibility for social outcomes, the last thing that would appear to be needed is a retreat from the possibility of achieving some sort of moral agreement on the principles and purposes operative in the making of public policy. None is oblivious, to be sure, to the possibility that such agreement might be reached at the price of oppressing discordant beliefs and values. But the danger this represents, while clearly acknowledged, does not begin to dominate their thinking in the way that it does for Ackerman and Connolly. In part this is because they have other concerns, to which they are no less attentive. But it is also due to their having manifestly different assumptions about what politics is for and the role that reason can be expected to play in it.

While not for a moment backing away from the liberal preoccupation with the freedom or respect to be accorded individuals, they also believe, at the same time, that politics has to do just as much with the creation and maintenance of a common life. And they take it for granted that the pursuit of that goal will entail, on an ongoing basis, moral deliberation about both ends and means. It is also part of the sort of liberalism they represent, too, to assume that progress can and will be made in such debate. Even if the participants disagree profoundly, it is possible for at least some degree of agreement to be reached. So the resulting policies will be adopted not just because the appropriate interests have been called into play but also because they reflect a shared sense of what *ought* to be done.

It is the establishment of the conditions necessary for this kind of public deliberation that is Gutmann's and Thompson's primary concern. They address it in the first instance by stressing the moral value of social cooperation in the governing of society. And the logic of the public philosophy to which they give expression is, then, to insist that mutual respect (not just tolerance) is the "price" that must be paid if such cooperation is to be realized. Partisanship must be disciplined, they argue, by an ethic of respectful collaboration if anything like a shared good is to be achieved. Unmistakably, this, too, implies certain restraints on the way that public discourse is to be conducted. But the restraints in question have nowhere near the sweep of those that Ackerman has in mind. And their purpose is anything but the avoidance of moral differences. Just the opposite: what they seek is a politics in which such differences are directly addressed, but through deliberation about principles rather than "bargaining among special interests."

Sullivan is inclined to press the case for cooperation even further, moreover, arguing that what is needed is a way of thinking that gets beyond, or at least significantly qualifies, the characteristic liberal preoccupation with rights—particularly "the abstract language of rights divorced from the meanings and ends in which rights are inevitably embedded in practice." It is not enough, therefore, as far as he is concerned, just to acknowledge a place for moral deliberation in public life. Every bit as important is to recognize that the right way to go about conducting such deliberation is by focusing on the *quality* of the way of life shared by the members of the society in question. This is not to suggest that an effective social policy demands a conclusive and comprehensive agreement about "the" good to be pursued by individual members or the community. The point, rather, is to enrich our public life in a way that amplifies "our social capacities to interpret and debate the common purposes on which our increasingly interdependent world depends." The common good is not so much a solution to problems as it is a shift in the perspective from which problems are interpreted and addressed. Whether the issue be race relations or homosexuality or abortion, it is the common good in this sense that he believes needs to be the primary consideration, and the drift of what he has to say is that a public orientation of this sort is what is required if much progress is to be made in addressing the problems and pursuing the opportunities which we face as a society rather than as a collection of individuals.

The renewed attention of these authors to the conditions of social cooperation is, we feel, a valuable corrective to the more atomistic and confrontational conception of human existence which is implicit, at least, in arguments such as those of Ackerman and Connolly. And the intention that is reflected in the insistence on the possibility of the efficacy of moral reasoning in public life is a step in the right direction. However, even when this is acknowledged, it is difficult to suppress the suspicion that some of the same question begging is taking place here as one finds among those who are more confident about pressing the case for liberal individuality.

Much of the success of Gutmann's and Thompson's argument, for example, is dependent upon our sharing the priority which they accord to mutual self-respect—and the interpretation they place on it, as well. But it is not at all clear why we should do so. The psychology that their construction entails requires, for example, that we value the self as a holder of conceptions of the good almost irrespective of their content or, more moderately, that we treasure "the moral value of choosing moral values" as much or more than the content of whatever is chosen. Yet it is the values to be chosen and not the choice of moral values, surely, that normally constitute the real focus of public debate, and by asking us to treat both with the same respect, they end up, we think, construing public debate in a highly formalized or rarefied manner. It is difficult not to see strong overtones of Kant in all of this and to subject it, in turn, to some of the same criticism that can be directed against Kant's highly abstract notion of freedom.

Practically speaking, moreover, the question that has to be asked is why committed partisans on any of the more deeply divisive moral issues in public life today should be expected to value cooperation so highly. And it is hard to see that much of an answer is provided. Why, for example, should a dedicated opponent of the legalization of abortion accept the attitudinal compromise that almost inescapably would be the price to be paid for granting respect to her opponents' views in the manner Gutmann and Thompson recommend? Why, more broadly, should the ongoing succession of such compromises that would almost certainly come to be the characteristic pattern of policymaking in any regime where such an outlook prevailed be looked upon as worthy of lasting respect? In a certain sense, an "objective" observer might see both *Roe vs. Wade* and *Webster vs. Reproductive Health Services* as attempted compromises between the adherents of the "pro-life" and "pro-choice" positions, yet it is probably not unfair to say that neither decision facilitated the emergence of mutual respect among the contending parties. Indeed the opposite may be true. One can understand, to be sure, why contending partisans who did indeed adopt the style of reasoning Gutmann and Thompson commend might well in fact be able to make progress in reasoning through their differences. But the question, once again, is *why* active partisans of debates currently raging within American society should see fit to submit to such a discipline. And in the absence of an answer, it is difficult to avoid the impression that here, too, the value and appeal of a certain way of life, the "way" of mutual self-respect, with its attendant virtues, are essentially being *assumed*. Thus, while the principles that Gutmann and Thompson see as regulating public discourse work to accommodate rather than exclude (as Rawls and Ackerman recommend) differences over the good, the resulting accommodation presupposes that none of the divergent visions of the good are more attractive psychologically than the attachment to mutual respect. Mutual respect in a way becomes the functional equivalent of the overlapping consensus. And as a practical matter, one could expect very little substantive difference between the institutional and policy commitments of the two perspectives.

It is difficult to see how Gutmann and Thompson can be as confident as they are about both the desirability and possibility of this priority without providing a more extensive argument in its defense. For if mutual respect is to be valued as a virtue (and it is hard to see how it can be considered anything else in the context of this particular argument), then it would seem to need to be defended as such—and a case made for it in relation to other virtues. But this would almost certainly require a more substantive conception of the person than that which is entailed by the simple psychology of mutual respect. And it could well lead to the recognition of moral values even more important than the value of choice itself. Conversely, the appeal to a more skeptical vision of the person might well diminish Gutmann's and Thompson's public moral deliberations to some form of *modus vivendi*. As it stands, then, the commitment to mutual respect seems incompletely grounded, yet its completion would seem to threaten to carry us beyond (or beneath) mutual respect.

In like manner, too, one has to wonder whether the distinction Sullivan draws between political and metaphysical conceptions of the common good can be maintained, as a practical matter, with anywhere near the consistency that would be necessary to prevent the style of public discourse he has in mind from being self-defeating. No doubt it has already been shown to be possible, to some extent at least, for people with significantly different religious and philosophical views to affirm a number of important public goods in common. But this does not mean for a moment, if the experiences in question are explored at all carefully, that such convergence is possible in the absence of *any* sort of deeper support. As students of the American experience in this regard have been inclined to emphasize, it is only because the different sectarian communities in this country have tended to be rather similar in certain of their more fundamental philosophical commitments, their *deep* visions of the good, in Henry Richardson's terms, that the accommodations that have been realized have been at all possible.[26]

But what if that agreement begins to break down (as would appear now almost certainly to be taking place)? Is it really likely that conscious attention to how we can "live decently together" in the manner Sullivan has in mind will prove to be a way of coming to terms constructively with the divisions in question? Precisely because any such focus can be expected almost inescapably to call into play the more fundamental differences that today divide the partisans on issues (abortion, education) of the sort that he means to address, it is difficult to imagine the result being anything other than the intensification of discord. It may well be, to be sure, that the preoccupation with the rights of individuals which is reflected in so much of the public discourse in societies like the United States ill serves us, and the introduction of the sorts of concerns that Sullivan means to draw to the reader's attention could serve as a helpful corrective. But it is one thing to acknowledge a place for goods beyond rights in the economy of public life today and quite another to see how their identification, much less pursuit, can be accomplished in a manner that is conducive to anything like the consensus on values he envisions.

Especially is this so, too, if the concept of the common good is invested with any of the sort of content that Sullivan himself is inclined to impute to it. His project, like those of the "social" liberals on which he draws, is clearly a revisionist one. He has in mind the adaptation of liberal premises so as to accommodate their integration with ideas drawn from other sources. And the obvious question is whether any such accommodation is really possible any more, given the other trends that are currently at work in contemporary liberalism. For the republican and religious themes that he associates with "bringing the good back in" represent just the sort of "communitarian" influence which no small number of liberals today are inclined to identify as the problem to be overcome,[27] and it is difficult to imagine, in turn, how their invocation can serve as anything other than an invitation to conflict.

Section 5

In reply, of course, Sullivan would surely maintain that, the opposition of liberal purists notwithstanding, liberal teaching needs the corrective which other sources have to offer if it is to be viable as a public philosophy. And he is surely not alone in that conviction. Many of our authors argue that thesis in one form or another, and it occupies such a prominent place in what they have to say as to constitute, arguably, the most important contribution this volume has to make. But they do not all speak with one voice and it remains to be seen what weight it is appropriate to attach to the specific claims that are advanced by each.

Much like Sullivan, Salkever clearly writes as an appreciative critic. If anything, he wants to credit liberal practice with more of an achievement than liberal theory itself does, and much of the drift of his analysis is to show that there is a great deal more to the way of life that liberal practice encourages than liberal texts would lead one to think. Indeed, he wants to commend liberal institutions, on moral grounds, for the qualities of mind and character that they promote, and the picture that he paints in this regard is one that surely ups the ante significantly in liberal apologetics. For it is *not*, he insists, just the freedom to do one's own thing (whatever it may be) that liberalism in practice is all about. Whatever its theoreticians may say, it in fact has to do with a good deal more as well. It is about the cultivation of a certain kind of character, and the virtues in question are by no means, he feels, inconsequential. Indeed, by invoking the figure of Socrates as he does, he clearly would seem to have it in mind that the way of life in question can hold its own in serious and sustained deliberation about the good.

The fault that he finds with liberal theory goes deeper, furthermore, than just neglect. In its reluctance to enter into any sort of sustained consideration of the virtues, including even those that might be characteristic of lives worthy of liberal endorsement, it undermines, he feels, the capacity that liberal institutions otherwise would have in this regard. The quest for neutrality becomes, therefore, a liability. And the more aggressively it is pursued, the harder it is to be confident that liberal practice will in fact conform to the implicit tendency toward the virtues that Salkever identifies. The remedy that he has in mind, of course, is to rethink the neglect of the question of character, and his own conviction is that what is needed, even more, is a reconsideration of the possibility of teleological thinking with reference to liberal practice. The prohibition on (explicit reference to) teleology that has been a part of liberal thinking ever since the seventeenth century is the main reason why liberals have found it so difficult to enter unequivocally into moral reflection, and most of the rationale for it is, he is convinced, misguided. It is no accident that those figures who have discussed the virtues most instructively, from Aristotle to MacIntyre, have had altogether different attitudes toward teleology[28] and there is no good reason, in turn, Salkever feels, why an appropriately nuanced version of teleological reflection could not function as just the sort of enrichment and supplement that liberal theory now so badly needs.

The point is not, he stresses, to erect some full-blown model of Liberal Man that could stand as a comprehensive direction for the design of institutions and policy, but rather simply to acknowledge and endorse, selectively, certain trends that are already apparent in practice, and to do so in a way that it is thereby made clear what precisely is the liberal stake in the goods in question. But granted this intent, one cannot help but wonder whether Salkever's portrait of the goods of liberal practices is not a highly selective one. For in point of fact the sort of irony toward the self that Salkever finds promoted by liberal practice is only one of many qualities that might come to be valued through the sort of teleological reflection that he envisions, and it is not at all apparent that it will be preeminent among them. And the obvious question would be how to proceed in the event that other desirable qualities would come to light that were not so well served by liberal institutions. Even the example of Socrates, after all, can be interpreted in a way that is not nearly so congenial to liberal practices as Salkever would have the reader think.[29]

Even more lies behind the liberal suspicion of teleology, therefore, than what he is prepared to acknowledge. In fact the most fundamental consideration of all may well be the fear that reasoning which is at all self-consciously teleological will end up yielding results that are in tension, if not outright conflict, with the way of life promoted by liberal institutions. It is hardly accidental, one has to think, that most of the figures whose names are associated with thinking in such terms (not least Plato) have not been noted for their enthusiasm for either liberal attitudes or liberal policy prescriptions, and they have often been the source, in fact, of some of the most trenchant criticism leveled against them.

Not least has this been true, of course, of Roman Catholics, and as John Langan shows in his chapter, the reasons for Catholic misgivings about the way of life to which liberal practices give rise are by no means altogether a thing of the past. A good part of Langan's exposition is given over, to be sure, to demonstrating how much the force of the traditional Catholic objections to liberalism has dissipated. And there is no mistaking the fact that this is so because, in large measure, of the respect for the historic accomplishments of liberal movements and regimes that has come to be reflected in the church's teaching. The church in dialogue with the modern world that has come into being since Vatican II manifestly is showing itself willing and able to affirm substantial parts of liberal teaching in a way that would have been unthinkable as little as three decades ago.

But at the same time, even this church cannot bring itself to embrace unequivocally the whole liberal outlook and agenda, and as Langan shows, there are good reasons why this is the case. Reading in particular what he has to say (quoting the latest papal teaching) about the trend toward "superdevelopment" that has come to be characteristic of Western societies, one cannot help but be struck by the selectivity of the picture Salkever paints of the qualities cultivated by liberal institutions. For surely the preoccupation with economic goods and continuous, ongoing expansion of the opportunities for consumption that the most recent Catholic teaching continues to stress in its criticism of "liberal capitalist" societies is at least as important as any of the features of liberal practices on which Salkever chooses to dwell. And it can scarcely help but lead, in turn, to critical questions of just the sort that expose the moral lapses to which liberal practice, every bit as much as liberal theory, is prone.

The standard liberal theoretical response to any such criticism, of course, is to deny that there is anything inherent in liberalism which is responsible for the darker features of modern life, and to insist, then, on the resourcefulness of the perspective it provides. Whether the problem be obsessive consumption, polluted air, or indifference to the fate of the wider world, all that is needed to take things constructively in hand, we are reassured, is yet one more adaptation of the liberal project. Just as earlier generations of liberal theoreticians came to grips successfully with the challenges posed by mass politics and the welfare state by reworking one or another part of the legacy they inherited from the past, so, now, the thing that is called for, it is said, is the elaboration of the late twentieth-century equivalent.

But one is entitled to doubts, especially when one considers what almost inescapably must be involved in challenging the practices in question. For they are bound to be defended—with good reason—as manifestations of the very thing in human life on which liberal teaching today, just as in the past, stakes most of its claims. It is the exercise of the right of individuals to make of their lives what they choose that is at issue, and the more aggressively the case for widening (and deepening) the range of the choices that are available, the harder it is to imagine a liberal response which does anything more than sidestep the problem of coping with the costs of questionable choices.

Section 6

The thing above all which would seem to be required, as Kenneth Schmitz and Martha Nussbaum in particular see, is a capacity to distinguish effectively between the *opportunity* to choose and the capacity for choosing *well*. And part of the appeal of teleological thinking lies in its insistence that this distinction be taken seriously—and actively pursued. That and the appreciation that it inevitably involves, as well, of the contingency of the human good, and of its avoidable reliance on factors that are beyond choice.

Nussbaum puts the matter succinctly when she says that choice is not "pure spontaneity, flourishing in spite of the accidents of nature," and then goes on to maintain that what this implies is our having to look to what human beings actually are every bit as much as what they might elect to be in order to make good *empirical* sense of what conduces to their well-being. For in point of fact it is not the mere opportunity for choice (no matter how rational, deliberate, and autonomous it may be) that makes for human flourishing. Precisely because we are beings in nature, with a nature that is already given to a large extent, and not disembodied wills, the content of the choices we make matters. There are needs of ours that must be met, and they are likely to be addressed successfully only if they are recognized and treated as such.

In her own way, to be sure, Nussbaum is every bit as concerned as the liberals with enhancing the opportunities available to people to exercise choice in the fashioning of their lives. Indeed, in a very real sense, that is what her chapter is primarily about. But what makes her an Aristotelian—and a Social Democrat—rather than a liberal is the insistence that the good of choice must be fit into a larger, more substantial concept of the human good if it is not to be counterproductive, and that the place to look for such a conception is in the activities that we know, experientially and intuitively, to be constitutive of our humanity. Indeed, what is required, she believes, is nothing short of a conception of human *excellence* (the "most choiceworthy life") derived in such manner, and the drift of her argument is to suggest, in turn, that the cultivation of the conditions that will enable people to live thus is what politics, correctly understood, is all about.

The obvious question, of course, is how far this is to be carried. And what, if any, reason there is for stepping short of conclusions that could well be much more challenging to liberal teaching. Despite the distance that Nussbaum seeks to establish between her own thinking and those of the liberal theorists she criticizes, she goes out of her way to restrict the reach of her argument to a set of considerations with which liberals can be comfortable. For all of the density that she means to incorporate into what she has to say about the human good, it is still, she insists, "vague," and perfectly compatible, therefore, with a wide degree of pluralism and choice in the actual specification of ends. And nothing is fixed. The historicity of human experience dictates that no particular determination of the meaning and content of human flourishing be taken as the last word.

Moreover, she chooses to dwell precisely on those features of the Aristotelian conception of human virtue that a liberal such as Rawls could affirm. Above all, it is the exercise of practical reason that stands out in the view she advances. Yet even in this regard it is only part of the Aristotelian teaching on which she draws. For her treatment of practical reason underscores its architectonic character while making little reference to what is, for Aristotle at least, the equally important discovery that it entails the perfection of one part of the rational soul.[30] As a perfection or completion it has a certain thick, though vague, content. Given that Aristotle characterizes *choice* as a thoughtful desire *(orexis dianoētikē)*, his conception of practical wisdom is also inextricably connected with the perfection of that part of the soul with which we desire.[31] Practical wisdom thus requires as much as it completes the moral virtues. And here, as well, there is a particular thick, though vague, content, captured perfectly in the notion that in practicing each moral virtue we should exhibit always the mean *(to meson)* for us.[32]

But hardly any of this finds expression in Nussbaum's argument. Nor, too, is there even a hint in what she has to say, here at least, that there might be other, even higher, Aristotelian excellences that are constitutive of the human good. (Perhaps in part this is because they [we suggest principally *theōria*] show clearly the limits [*perata*], the strengths as well as the boundaries, of the practically excellent life.)[33] The conception of the good that she holds out is thus almost certainly vaguer than that which Aristotle himself held because there is a point, dictated by her characteristically modern commitment to the autonomy of persons, beyond which she refuses to carry the argument. Unlike Aristotle himself, but much more resembling liberal theory, this particular Aristotelian is not given to speaking very expansively about the ways in which souls might be crafted, even though that as much as anything is *the* purpose of politics for Aristotle. "The legislators make the citizens good," as he says, "by their customs and if they do this badly they fail. This is what separates a good regime from a bad one."[34]

The case for avoiding these implications is, however, anything but compelling, and it is scarcely to be taken for granted. It is not to be settled, either, by one or another gloss on Aristotle's own argument. Arguable as it may be that the strict perfectionism which commonly is attributed to Aristotle may be less central to his teaching than we have been given to believe, the logic of teleological reasoning *per se* is quite another matter, to be argued, presumably, on its merits. A good deal more of the argument than Nussbaum may feel comfortable acknowledging, moreover, would appear destined to turn on considerations that have to do with a certain kind of metaphysics (or what Richardson sees as the *depth* of conceptions of the good).[35] There is surely a metaphysics involved in the features that she chooses to emphasize in defining what it is that gives our existence its "characteristically human shape," and this is every bit as true, too, of what she chooses to ignore or neglect.[36] But once one begins to engage in reasoning of this sort, it is perhaps more of an open question than Nussbaum admits whether that metaphysics does or does not generate conclusions that would be worrisome to liberals.

Section 7

The mere fact that thinkers who obviously have so much sympathy for what liberalism represents feel compelled to reconsider the good that it entails so critically speaks for itself. For even as they labor to make the case for the affinity of liberal practices (if not theory) to one or another alternative reading of human experience, they clearly are motivated at the same time by a sense that the resources provided by the liberal tradition itself are inadequate for addressing the problem of the good as it currently presents itself. The Socratic or Aristotelian turn which figures so prominently in so much of what is said in this volume is just one more reflection of what surely by now is appropriately characterized as a widely shared intuition that the good of liberalism (as it is understood by liberal theorists, at least) is simply not good enough.

What is no less striking, however, is that, even as the awareness of the multiplicity and importance of the deficiencies in question grows, how much of the rethinking which then takes place continues to be conducted on what is essentially liberal ground. Or on something which remains very close to it, at least. In what surely must be considered a powerful tribute to the continuing appeal which the liberal project holds, most of what is said is directed, as we have seen, at making the liberal good better. Especially with regard to what we have maintained is the core of liberal thinking about how life ought to be lived—the idea of freedom—there is little inclination to break sharply in a new and different direction. For all of the criticism to which liberal ideas are being subjected today in this respect, the faith that liberalism can accommodate, somehow, all that is worth preserving (and pursuing) in human existence obviously is still very much alive.

But if the arguments that we have examined here are at all indicative of where things are headed, this project of attempted accommodation is surely destined to be severely tested in the years ahead. For one can well imagine the "friends of Aristotle" pressing their case even more expansively than anything we have encountered here. That particular conversation, presumably, has really only begun. And just as surely, too, one can imagine those who prefer to take their cue from Nietzsche or Foucault (and other like minds) pressing their case just as ambitiously in the opposite direction. Such polarization, in fact, is almost predictable, given the currents that are at work today in the societies where the identity of liberalism is destined to be determined. For both tendencies would appear to be inherent in what liberalism is today becoming, and it is difficult to imagine either being effectively eclipsed by the other.

But just for this reason it becomes increasingly difficult, in turn, to imagine the problem being solved in anything like a coherent manner. The protean quality that all along has been characteristic of liberal thinking about the good in particular is destined to be revealed even more vividly, and in the process its coherence will almost certainly be severely challenged. For it will scarcely be possible to answer the pull in one direction without resisting the other, and the consequence, almost inescapably, will be that liberal theory will become even more varied and heterogenous than it is presently.

In the short run, what this probably means, of course, is that there will be a version of liberalism—and the liberal good—to suit practically every taste. So the family will proliferate even further, and the ends that it serves become still more diverse. The value that liberals themselves profess to place on respecting the diversity of the human good will encourage this tendency, it can be assumed, as it has in the past. But there are limits, presumably, to which this can be taken. Even among liberals, the accommodation of diversity can be carried just so far without thereby threatening the integrity of the position they claim to be upholding. As a practical matter, moreover, the issue which is posed by the availability of such widely divergent—and competing—conceptions of what the liberal project entails can scarcely avoid being joined. For they lead, inescapably, to policy differences that are every bit as pronounced, but not nearly so likely to lend themselves to accommodation. Different members of the family can be expected, for example, to endorse very different notions of the sort of education that is appropriate to a liberal regime. And in one's darker moments at least, one is entitled to doubts about whether there is any realistic possibility at all of the diverse proposals they advance being reconciled in coherent policies that could command common approval. So the play of the competing pulls can be expected to turn increasingly into a tug of war, with each side inclined to present itself as just what the family needs to meet the challenge which is posed by the emerging need for a defensible liberal conception of the good.

In the process, of course, it is always possible that the issues at stake will end up being explored with such imagination that they will be successfully resolved. Sometimes it happens that a dilemma of the sort we believe is in the making for liberals is just what it takes to produce the critical rethinking that is called for. If this were to occur, it would not be the first time in the history of liberalism that a serious impasse became the occasion for new insights to emerge that made it possible for new ground to be broken. Such is the stuff of which the moments of growth in the history of theoretical traditions with continuing vitality are made, and liberalism today certainly exhibits as much vitality in this regard as any political teaching available. But it is always possible, too, that no such resolution will be forthcoming. And no matter how probing are the reappraisals that take place, the polarization is not overcome. Indeed, it deepens. So the fissure widens, and it becomes harder and harder for the opposing points of view to accommodate one another. Such is the stuff of which the breakdown of traditions is made, and it is by no means out of the question that this is where liberals are now headed as they come to grips with the differences that are now surfacing among them over "the" good.

Section 8

We neither endorse nor expect easy solutions. However, the sort of discussion that needs to take place if any viable solution is to be found can perhaps be illustrated by a reconsideration of what is arguably the most immediate and problematic of the differences revealed in this volume.

Aristotelians such as Salkever and Nussbaum turn in the direction that they do because they clearly believe that it is necessary to do more than just affirm choice as an end in itself, and they think it is possible to do so without thereby succumbing to the danger of undermining choice by the prescription of a particular metaphysic. But any such claim is almost certain to meet with skepticism—and resistance—from those who, like Ackerman, Barry, and Connolly, believe that the challenge now confronting liberal theory is one of *expanding* the range of choice that it affirms. Ackerman, after all, suggests that almost any discussion of human flourishing is a recipe for intolerance, and the spirit of most of what he says in this vein is to suggest that the last thing which is now needed is any thickening of the good(s) with which the liberal project is identified.[37] Any hint of metaphysics in particular arouses suspicion. Even Sullivan, it needs to be remembered, is inclined to assume that the less reference is made to metaphysics, the better.

Actually dispensing with something more than a thin notion of the good (and the implied metaphysics) is, however, as we have sought to show, easier said than done. And the more one examines the various liberal defenses of freedom, the harder it is to avoid the conclusion that they, too, have definite "thicknesses" of their own. Some of them turn out, in fact, to be far less vague than the conception of the good which Nussbaum ascribes to Aristotle. In Richardson's terms, liberal visions of freedom are, more often than not, surprisingly detailed. These details, in turn, provide grounds for praise or blame that simply would not be available if one took the deceptively simple and straightforward commitment to freedom at face value. Locke's invocation of natural law, for example, becomes at once more specific and more problematic the moment it is recognized that it is being advanced on behalf of an acquisitive way of life that he chooses to characterize as "rational and industrious." And Nozick's and Mill's seemingly identical affirmations of freedom as the opportunity to pursue one's own chosen course turns out, on closer examination, to be very different once it is recognized that the activity that one envisions deriving from the exercise of choice has to do primarily with spending and getting while the other has in mind, in contrast, the pursuit of higher pleasures.

Even if it is argued, furthermore (as both Ackerman and Connolly seem to do), that liberal theory should dispense with any such specificity, it is difficult to see how such a project can succeed and still fulfill the theoretical purpose which must be served. For the question of *why* freedom ought to be valued—especially to the extent that liberals are wont to do—is unavoidable, and it is hardly to be answered convincingly without some reference to its possible (and probable) use. What makes freedom both plausible as an end and open to evaluation are the particular details of its embodiment. There is no avoiding, either, facing up to how its exercise relates to the other ends that matter to human beings. As Mill and Rawls in particular have seen, any account of freedom which stands a chance of being truly persuasive must accommodate other goods, especially those that offer the prospect of elevating its effects, and it is precisely the awareness they demonstrate in this regard, in turn, which in large measure explains the success their teaching has enjoyed.

No matter how narrowly (or thinly) the good to which liberals are committed is construed, therefore, it is difficult to imagine that it can be adequately defended without recourse to a teleology. For it entails, inescapably, the stipulation of a direction for the way in which life ought to be lived.[38] The more complete the direction, moreover, the more extensive the metaphysical ground that is occupied can be expected to be. And we find altogether convincing the suggestion that it is only in its thicker forms that the priority which liberals are inclined to attribute to the good of freedom can begin to be credible.[39]

The problem, of course, is to discover how freedom can be discussed teleologically without taking away with one hand what is given with the other. For the more its defense is tied to a specific set of purposes, the more equivocal the liberal commitment to freedom may seem to be. And the more explicitly the accompanying metaphysical commitments are elaborated, the less of an invitation to choice it may seem to provide. But this, we think, is where the arguments advanced by Salkever and Nussbaum are instructive. For if teleological reasoning is construed in the manner that they propose—that is, more as attention to certain questions than the provision of answers, then those who engage in it need not fall prey to anything like the theoretical dogmatism and practical oppression with which they are so commonly charged. It is simply not the case, as they correctly point out, that teleology has always had that character—or effect. In its original Platonic and Aristotelian form, teleology had, as they show, much more the character of an exploration than a quest for certainty, and there is no good reason why it could not recover that character again today.

What would need to occur, however, if this were to take place is that the purpose of the theoretical enterprise be reconceived. Instead of being construed as an exercise in legislation, as is our modern habit, theory would need to be viewed as an invitation to what might be called thick dialogue—a raising up of concerns for critical scrutiny that otherwise might not become the subject of sustained reflection. The point, in keeping with the original Socratic intent, would be to engage people seriously in confronting directly the more fundamental questions about the meaning and purpose of their lives. It would be to encourage a way of being that is truly aware and self-critical. And even when certain answers were held up for special consideration, this would be done more to cultivate a certain frame of mind than to bring about attachment to any one particular way of life.[40]

The thing in particular that needs to be grasped in this relation, moreover, is how much of a service to the enhancement of the quality of democratic politics itself such reflection could provide. Often teleological reasoning is assumed by its critics to be in tension, if not outright contradiction, with the freedoms and opportunities that have come to be associated with democracy in the liberal sense. But what typically is ignored in such arguments is how much is lost when the concerns that teleological thinking addresses are set aside. As Salkever notes, for all of the talk about public discourse in recent liberal theory, in point of fact it does not give all that much encouragement to serious conversation about the things that really matter in the choices that we have to make. The privatization of choice that it encourages in particular inhibits discussion of what is *worth* choosing, and when it does not actually prevent such discussion from taking place, it diminishes its value. But to the extent that the concerns which find expression in the turn back toward teleology were to regain currency, this could be expected to change. As the business of making a life for oneself came to be looked upon once again as truly serious business, calling for the best wisdom we can muster, conversation about such matters would regain its point, and public life could scarcely help but be affected.

Liberal orthodoxy inclines us almost instinctively, of course, to assume that the effects of such a development could only be negative. Going all the way back to Locke's *Letter Concerning Toleration*, there is in liberalism a presumption against any sort of joining of the differences that separate people on matters of fundamental meaning and purpose that runs very deep. History shows, we have been taught to believe, that the less engagement that takes place, the better. For the sake of both civil tranquility and the autonomy of persons, it is best, therefore, that the art of separation[41] be cultivated. But history teaches more than one lesson. The resulting "culture" of separation, too, has its costs, we are learning, one of the most important of which is a tendency toward solipsism that all too easily turns into arbitrariness.[42] When people get into the habit of conceiving of the more consequential decisions they make about the conduct of their lives as nothing but personal, it is all too easy to end up looking upon them as nothing but matters of taste. And to lose sight, in turn, of the inescapable difference that it makes, to everyone affected, not least the actors themselves, how *well* such decisions are made.

A balance has to be struck, to be sure. Democratic regimes in particular can ill afford to be populated by individuals who are so caught up in toleration that they are averse to acknowledging any sense of accountability about how they (or others) live their lives. But just as surely they are threatened, too, by individuals and groups so attuned to their own particular visions of the good that they have nothing on their minds but seeing them prevail. It would be difficult to prove, either, that private fanaticism combined with an ethos of mutual disinterest (a bare *modus vivendi*, in Richardson's terms) is particularly conducive to the health and well-being of democratic institutions.[43] What is needed, as the more thoughtful students of the subject have recognized all along, from ancient times to the present, is a *combination* of engagement with one another's lives and toleration, such that each informs and complements the other. Surely this is what citizenship in any but the most formal sense is all about, and the challenge, in turn, of liberal theory today as we see it is to explore how such balance can be effectively recovered.

These dividends notwithstanding, however, the question that remains, as we have noted all along in this discussion, is whether the ends liberals cherish—especially freedom—can in fact be discussed teleologically in a manner that ends up enriching rather than diminishing our appreciation of what they represent. Salkever and Nussbaum, each in a different way, do an imaginative job of showing why there is reason to think that such a project could in fact succeed. But what they offer is only a beginning—a series of suggestive steps down a path that will need to be explored much further before any definitive conclusions can begin to be drawn. And as long as it is not clearly established that there is a way of thinking teleologically that does not entail the inherent pull in a direction inimical to liberal values that Ackerman, Connolly, and Barry fear, the matter has to be considered unresolved.

The very fact, however, that *this* is the issue with which we are left is a clear sign of the threshold that is being crossed. From the (implied) argument between Rawls and Barry about whether liberals can endorse any single version of the good and still remain liberal, the focus of discussion now would appear to be shifting in the direction of the rather different question of whether they can embrace a vision of the good that is deeper and thicker than one that dwells on freedom alone and still be faithful to the liberal purpose. The chapters in this book do not answer this question. But separately and together they serve notice that it can no longer be avoided.

Notes

1. John Rawls, "Justice as Fairness: Political not Metaphysical," *Philosophy and Public Affairs* 14 (1985): 223–251 at 246.

2. John Rawls, "The Idea of an Overlapping Consensus," *Oxford Journal of Legal Studies* 7 (1987): 1–25.

3. Brian Barry, *The Liberal Theory of Justice* (Oxford: Clarendon Press, 1973) p. 127. In a sense, this understanding of *the* liberal good can ground the three more specific goods which Salkever identifies as endemic to liberal regimes: political autonomy, the toleration of a variety of ways of life and material productivity or comfort. (See " 'Lopp'd and Bound': How Liberal Theory Obscures the Goods of Liberal Practices," Chap. 9, this volume.) In this respect, one might wonder whether liberal theory distorts the specifically *liberal* goods of liberal practices quite to the degree that Salkever suggests.

4. Brian Barry, "How Not to Defend Liberal Institutions," Chap. 3, this volume.

5. R. M. Hare, *Freedom and Reason* (London: Oxford University Press, 1963) p. 179. This is not to say that freedom is the *only* principle from which equal concern and respect may be derived. Ronald Dworkin, for example, argues that the fundamental liberal commitment is not to neutrality (or liberty) but to equality. Neutrality and toleration thus emerge as commitments which are entailed by the prior commitment to equality. See Dworkin, "Neutrality, Equality, and Liberalism" in Douglas MacLean and Claudia Mills, eds., *Liberalism Reconsidered* (Totowa, NJ: Rowman and Allanheld, 1983), pp. 1–11. It suffices for our purposes to recognize that the principle of freedom provides adequate support for the endorsement of toleration. Furthermore, one could also make the case, not developed here, that the normative commitment to equality requires some more basic reference to that capacity wherein human beings *are* equal and that freedom is a strong candidate for that capacity within liberal theory. Rawls's first principle of justice, after all, requires an equality of basic *liberties*.

6. Barry, *The Liberal Theory of Justice*, p. 127.

7. For a brief discussion of the difficulties involved in such a problem of accommodation see also Alan Ryan, "A Law Unto Oneself," *Times Literary Supplement*, (August 4–10, 1989): 855.

8. For an excellent summary of this methodological or analytic foundation of liberal social science, see Salkever, "Freedom, Participation and Happiness," *Political Theory* 5 (1977): 391–413 at 394–395.

9. Robert Nozick, *Anarchy, State and Utopia* (New York: Basic Books, 1974) p. 333.

10. cf. *Politics* 1253 a.

11. Cf. *Leviathan*, Chap. 6; *Second Treatise*, Chap. 5, secs. 26–30.

12. As expressed, for example, in Mill's image of flourishing humanity as a many sided tree and Rawls's "Aristotelian Principle," which "does not assert that any particular kind of activity will be preferred . . . only that we prefer, other things equal, activities that depend on a larger repertoire of realized capacities that are more complex." See John Stuart Mill, *On Liberty*, Chap. 1; John Rawls, *A Theory of Justice*, (Cambridge, Mass: Harvard University Press, 1971) pp. 429–430. Within (or tempered by) this plurality, the material goods connected with commodious living continue to occupy, nonetheless, an important place. Thus, Kant's praise of a commercial as distinct from a civic republic

places him much closer to Locke than to Rousseau. And Rawls's objective or noncontroversial thin theory of the good solidifies in a way that may be far from noncontroversial our attachment to the material basis of our self-expression.

13. This course in no way mitigates the potential dangers that a commitment to utility poses for individual rights and which has prompted Rawls and Nozick, among others, to search for a Kantian alternative to utility.

14. John Rawls, "Kantian Constructivism in Moral Theory," *Journal of Philosophy* 77 (1980): 515–572 at 525–529. That Rawls's proceduralism is more minimal than necessary is underscored by Martha Nussbaum's discovery of a "thick-vague" conception of the good lying at the heart of Aristotelian ethics. See "Aristotelian Social Democracy," Chap. 10 this volume.

15. From a certain perspective, in fact, the practice of the excellences may be a constitutive source of higher pleasures. See Mill's discussion on the relation between virtue (which emerges for Mill as something like rectitude and thus as only one of the excellences) and happiness in *Utilitarianism*, Chap. 4. If the desire for virtue is explicable as a part of happiness, then one's identification of the higher pleasures affects decisively one's identification of virtue and of the excellences generally.

16. Mill, *On Liberty*, Chap. 3.

17. Rawls, *A Theory of Justice*, p. 443.

18. Rawls's partners within the original position do not, then, simply select the virtues through neutral calculative rationality. Rather, their identification of the virtues is linked intimately with their own characteristics and priorities. This leads us to extend Salkever's judgment that the early liberal theorists were implicitly teleological to include Rawls as well. For explicit reinforcement of this judgment see Victor Gourevitch, "Rawls on Justice," *Review of Metaphysics* 28 (1975): 485–519 at 495–496 and William A. Galston, "Moral Personality and Liberal Theory: John Rawls's "Dewey Lectures," *Political Theory* 10 (1982): 492–519. Much of the debate over whether Rawls's position in *A Theory of Justice* is teleological stems also from alternative views of what teleology itself involves. In speaking of teleology we share the meaning expressed by Salkever, " 'Lopp'd and Bound,' " Chap. 9, this volume, note 1. For a more elaborate distinction between teleology understood in this sense and "consequentialism" or "intentionality" see Gerald M. Mara, "Liberal Politics and Moral Excellence in Spinoza's Political Philosophy," *Journal of the History of Philosophy* 20 (1982): 129–150.

19. Rawls, *A Theory of Justice*, pp. 548–554, in which a dominant end emerges as "an end to which all other ends are subordinate . . . all lesser ends in turn being ordered as a means to one single dominant end." It can be argued that this view of dominant ends is itself extreme. There are alternative models of the structure of human motivation other than the pursuit of dominant ends, thus characterized, one the one hand, and the development of Mill's or Rawls's multidimensional sophistication, on the other. One can surely value one activity or practice over all others, for example, while still refraining from and even resisting the subordination of all other practices or activities to its requirements.

20. Rawls cannot quite categorically maintain this, of course, since he also admits (in *A Theory of Justice*, pp. 453–454 ff) that members of a society guided by the two principles will and should acquire the character needed to support just institutions through political socialization. For Rawls, though, what prevents this influence from becoming oppressively perfectionist is its restriction to the fostering of explicitly *political* virtues. See Rawls, "Priority of Right and Ideas of the Good," *Philosophy and Public Affairs* 17 (1988): 251–276. Rawls's success in avoiding inconsistency here depends, of course, on the degree to which these particular political virtues can be fostered without engendering or presupposing a more fully virtuous character of a particular sort.

21. William Galston, "Public Morality and Religion in the Liberal State," *PS* 19 (1986) 807–824 at 808. Barry's remark in "How Not to Defend Liberal Institutions," Chap. 3, this volume, that much of what a modern state does in shaping character is facilitative rather than repressive is an important exception to this general inclination. Of course, once one recognizes facilitation as an alternative to both coercion and neutrality, one can no longer see the facilitation of virtues other than strictly liberal ones as immediately coercive unless one is willing to claim that the facilitation of personal qualities is repressive *except* in the case of the fostering of freedom.

22. Mill, *On Liberty*, Chap. 1.

23. Cf. Ackerman, "Why Dialogue?" *Journal of Philosophy* 86 (1989): 5–22 at 22.

24. Habermas, on the other hand, sees the ideal dialogic situation as one wherein all moral and political issues can be examined and defended freely without artificial constraint. The only restriction is that the participants must, as members of a *discussion,* be fully committed to the goal of reaching a communicatively rational decision. What this would require in practice, however, is the participants' suspension of their attachments to "all motives except that of a cooperative readiness to arrive at an understanding" (cf. Habermas, *Theory and Practice,* John Viertel, trans., [Boston: Beacon Press, 1973], p. 18). Given that such a motivational suspension is both unlikely and (arguably) undesirable, one needs, then, an alternative to Habermas's psychologically implausible openness that does not lapse into Ackerman's artificial and restrictive closure. In part, this is what we see Gutmann and Thompson attempting to provide.

25. Ackerman, of course, develops his case for neutrality much more fully in *Social Justice and the Liberal State* (New Haven: Yale University Press, 1980). However, even there, while the justifications offered for taking the position he favors are multiple, none is explored to a degree or extent that is really satisfying. For further elaboration of why this is so, see also Henry Richardson's "The Problem of Liberalism and the Good" (See chapter 1, this volume.)

26. See R. Bruce Douglass, "Public Philosophy and Contemporary Pluralism," *Thought* 64, (December, 1989).

27. See, for example, Salkever's implicit criticism of the communitarian critique of the liberal attitude toward religion in " 'Lopp'd and Bound,' " Chap. 9, this volume, note 72.

28. This is not to say that MacIntyre's views of teleology and the virtues are in any significant way Aristotelian. For a comparison and critique see Gerald M. Mara, "Virtue and Pluralism: The Problem of the One and the Many," *Polity* 22 (1989): 25–48.

29. For a discussion of Plato's Socrates' attitudes toward questions of toleration which suggests that he qualifiedly endorses some liberal practices but not for liberal reasons, see Gerald M. Mara, "Socrates and Liberal Toleration," Political Theory 16 (1988): 468–495.

30. *Nicomachean Ethics* 1102a–1103a; 1139a.

31. Ibid., 1139b.

32. Ibid., 1106a–b.

33. In the way, say, that the portrait of the godlike human being who is himself a law shows the limitations of the (generally desirable) rule of law, politically construed (cf. *Politics,* 1287b–1288a). In *The Fragility of Goodness* (Cambridge: Cambridge University Press, pp. 373–377) Nussbaum argues that Aristotle's consummate praise of *theōria* at the end of *Ethics* is discontinuous with the substance of the work as a whole and therefore suspects that, though it was very likely composed by Aristotle, it was inserted into the *Ethics* by a later editor. This is of course possible. However, Nussbaum's hypothesis perhaps underregards the role that philosophy plays in other political or moral contexts within the Aristotelian corpus (for example, *Politics* 1267a; 1324a–1326b) and, as we suggest, it would not be at all un-Aristotelian to conclude a discussion of the practical life with a treatment of that sublime existence which goes beyond it. For these reasons, Nussbaum's hypothesis should perhaps be accepted only after less conjectural alternatives have been found inadequate. For other views of the relation between philosophy and the political life in Aristotle see Carnes Lord, "Politics and Philosophy in Aristotle's Politics," *Hermes* 106 (1978): 336–357; Gerald M. Mara, "The Role of Philosophy in Aristotle's Political Science," *Polity* 19 (1987): 375–401.

34. *Nichomachean Ethics* 1103b.

35. "Metaphysics" can mean, of course, diverse things, and it can be broadly or narrowly practiced. What we have in mind here is primarily the narrower meaning: that is, fundamental claims about the nature of human beings, which may or may not be connected to larger claims about the nature of being. Others, Nussbaum included, are free, of course, to define the concept as they choose, but we find it difficult to imagine an argument which is in the least teleological that does not also entail metaphysics in our sense. It may be implicit or explicit, acknowledged or not, but teleological reasoning of the sort recommended by several of the authors in this volume inescapably depends on one or another metaphysics of the individual. More than this, the most comprehensive explicit

rejections of teleology would appear to depend upon a certain kind of metaphysics of the person. Hobbes denies the existence of a *summum bonum* on the basis of the fundamental claim that life is but motion *(Leviathan,* Chap. 6). And Kant ultimately traces the possibility of autonomous rationality to the presupposition of pure practical reason in *Groundwork of the Metaphysics of Morals,* (Chap. III, 124–126). Once this point is grasped, moreover, it becomes more difficult to see how metaphysics can possibly be dispensed with in political or moral philosophy, or why it would ever be desirable to try to do so. There are, to be sure, difficult problems in engaging effectively in metaphysical reasoning, to which Richardson makes reference in his criticism of Kenneth Schmitz's chapter. But however serious these problems may be, they do not at all effectively remove the need for grounding practical philosophy on some kind of statement about the nature of those creatures for whom moral and political problems are of concern. And the more we observe attempts to demonstrate the contrary, the more convinced we are that the only serious question is *how* (and not whether) metaphysical judgements are to be made.

36. The necessity of proceeding on the basis of some sort of teleology or metaphysics even as we conduct cross-cultural inventories of human experiences is suggested by Aristotle's remark in Chapter 5 of the *Politics* that "it is in things whose condition is according to nature that one ought to investigate what is by nature, not in things that are defective" (1254a: Lord's translation). There is no way one can get around metaphysical (as we have used the term) judgments as one makes distinctions between things which are according to nature and things which are defective.

37. For a denial that liberal political theory can be justified by an appeal to some notions of Aristotelian flourishing see, for example, John Gray, *Liberalisms* (New York and London: Routledge, 1989) pp. 254–261.

38. We think of teleology here conventionally, as an excellence grounded in some way or other in the nature of the being in question. See note 35, above.

39. It is always conceivable, of course, to argue that the freedom to make one's own way in the world as one chooses should be treated as a privileged good regardless of the way in which it is utilized, so that no conditions are set or no expectations generated whatsoever. But it is doubtful, to say the least, that such an argument could be anywhere near persuasive enough to carry the weight it needs to carry—which is why liberal theory so rarely in fact takes this form.

40. Stripped of its concern with teleology, of course, this in a way resembles the goal toward which Gutmann, Thompson, and Sullivan direct us. But one wonders not only how theoretically defensible their various resistances to teleology, in the end, are, but also how practically salutary they might be. For a reliance upon mutual respect which contains no invitation to examine the deeper reasons for respectability would appear to be most vulnerable precisely during those controversies whose beneficial resolution required the strongest collective commitment to mutual respect. Likewise, without the opportunity for some sort of reflective commitment on why Sullivan's common good *is* good, collective pronouncements on matters of public concern may well appear to those adversely affected simply as the exercise of collective power.

41. The phrase is Michael Walzer's. See "Liberalism and the Art of Separation," *Political Theory* 12 (1984): 315–330.

42. This tendency is thoughtfully discussed in Robert Bellah et al., *Habits of the Heart* (Berkeley: University of California, 1985), esp. pp. 277–281.

43. One could argue that this scenario describes the dark side of Nozick's framework for utopia in Part Three of *Anarchy, State and Utopia,* for example.

Index

Contributors

Bruce A. Ackerman is Sterling Professor of Law and Political Science at Yale University. He has written widely on political philosophy, legal theory, constitutional law, and a variety of issues within the law. Among his most recent works are *Discovering the Constitution, Reconstructing American Law,* and *Social Justice and the Liberal State.*

Brian Barry is Professor of Political Science at the London School of Economics. Among his many works are *Political Argument, Sociologists, Economists and Democracy, The Liberal Theory of Justice,* and a forthcoming three-volume work, *Treatise on Social Justice.*

William E. Connolly is Professor of Political Science at The Johns Hopkins University. He is editor of the journal *Political Theory* and the author of a large number of books and articles in political philosophy. His more recent works include *Political Theory and Modernity, Politics and Ambiguity,* and *Appearance and Reality in Politics.*

R. Bruce Douglass is Associate Professor of Government at Georgetown University. He is the editor of *The Deeper Meaning of Economic Life.* His articles on such issues as contemporary liberalism, religion and politics, and economic justice have appeared in a variety of journals and edited collections.

Amy Gutmann is currently Mellon Professor of Politics at Princeton University, and she has held visiting appointments at the Center for Philosophy and Public Policy at the University of Maryland, the Institute for Advanced Study, and at the John F. Kennedy School of Government at Harvard University. She is the author of *Democratic Education* (1987) and *Liberal Equality* (1980), and has contributed numerous articles to current debates about liberalism, democracy, education, and their interconnections.

John Langan, S.J., is Rose Kennedy Professor of Christian Ethics at the Kennedy Institute of Ethics at Georgetown University. His interests range from Medieval philosophy to the ethics of war and peace and distributive justice. He has edited two books and published widely in collections, scholarly journals, and journals of opinions.

Gerald M. Mara is Associate Dean for Research and Professorial Lecturer in Government at Georgetown University. He has published work on classical political philosophy and on historical and contemporary liberalism in a variety of journals and edited collections.

Martha C. Nussbaum is University Professor and Professor of Philosophy, Classics, and Comparative Literature at Brown University. Her books include *Aristotle's De Motu Animalium* (1978), *The Fragility of Goodness: Luck and Ethics in Greek Tragedy and Philosophy* (1986), and *Love's Knowledge: Essays on Philosophy and Literature* (forthcoming from Oxford University Press). Her many published articles include studies in the political philosophies of Plato and Aristotle.

Henry S. Richardson is Assistant Professor of Philosophy at Georgetown University. He has published articles on Plato, Aristotle, and Hegel and is currently engaged in a study concerning the rational deliberation of ends.

Stephen G. Salkever is Professor of Political Science at Bryn Mawr College. His book on Aristotle, *Finding the Mean,* was recently published by Princeton University Press. He has also written a wide variety of articles which have appeared in scholarly journals and edited collections.

Kenneth Schmitz is Professor of Philosophy at Trinity College, The University of Toronto. He is the author of two books, *The Gift: Creation* and *What Has Clio To Do With Athena? Etienne Gilson: Historian and Philosopher* and nearly 100 articles on a broad spectrum of topics in philosophy, political theory, and the philosophy of religion.

William Sullivan is Professor of Philosophy at Lasalle University. His scholarly interests include the philosophy of social science, political theory, and public policy. He is co-author of *Habits of the Heart* and *Social Science as Moral Inquiry* and the author of *Reconstructing Public Philosophy.*

Dennis Thompson is Whitehead Professor of Political Philosophy in the Government Department and in the John F. Kennedy School of Government at Harvard University, where he directs the university-wide Program in Ethics and the

Professions. In 1987, his *Political Ethics and Public Office* was chosen the best political science publication in the field of U.S. national policy by the American Political Science Association. His previous publications include *The Democratic Citizen: Social Science and Democratic Theory in the Twentieth Century,* and *John Stuart Mill and Representative Government.*